ALSO BY BARRY STRAUSS

The War That Made the Roman Empire:
Antony, Cleopatra, and Octavian at Actium

Ten Caesars: Roman Emperors from Augustus to Constantine

The Death of Caesar: The Story of History's Most Famous Assassination

Masters of Command: Alexander, Hannibal, Caesar,
and the Genius of Leadership

The Spartacus War

The Trojan War: A New History

The Battle of Salamis: The Naval Encounter
That Saved Greece—and Western Civilization

What If ?: The World's Foremost Military
Historians Imagine What Might Have Been
(contributor)

Western Civilization: The Continuing Experiment
(with Thomas F. X. Noble and others)

War and Democracy: A Comparative Study of the
Korean War and the Peloponnesian War
(with David McCann, coeditor)

Rowing Against the Current: Learning to Scull at Forty

*Fathers and Sons in Athens: Ideology and
Society in the Era of the Peloponnesian War*

Hegemonic Rivalry: From Thucydides to the Nuclear Age
(with Richard Ned Lebow, coeditor)

*The Anatomy of Error: Ancient Military Disasters and
Their Lessons for Modern Strategists*
(with Josiah Ober)

*Athens After the Peloponnesian War:
Class, Faction and Policy, 403–386 B.C.*

JEWS VS. ROME

Two Centuries of Rebellion Against the World's Mightiest Empire

BARRY STRAUSS

SIMON & SCHUSTER

New York   Amsterdam/Antwerp   London
Toronto   Sydney/Melbourne   New Delhi

Simon & Schuster
1230 Avenue of the Americas
New York, NY 10020

For more than 100 years, Simon & Schuster has championed authors and the stories they create. By respecting the copyright of an author's intellectual property, you enable Simon & Schuster and the author to continue publishing exceptional books for years to come. We thank you for supporting the author's copyright by purchasing an authorized edition of this book.

No amount of this book may be reproduced or stored in any format, nor may it be uploaded to any website, database, language-learning model, or other repository, retrieval, or artificial intelligence system without express permission. All rights reserved. Inquiries may be directed to Simon & Schuster, 1230 Avenue of the Americas, New York, NY 10020 or permissions@simonandschuster.com.

Copyright © 2025 by Barry S. Strauss

All rights reserved, including the right to reproduce this book or portions thereof in any form whatsoever. For information, address Simon & Schuster Subsidiary Rights Department, 1230 Avenue of the Americas, New York, NY 10020.

First Simon & Schuster hardcover edition August 2025

SIMON & SCHUSTER and colophon are registered trademarks of Simon & Schuster, LLC

Simon & Schuster strongly believes in freedom of expression and stands against censorship in all its forms. For more information, visit BooksBelong.com.

For information about special discounts for bulk purchases, please contact Simon & Schuster Special Sales at 1-866-506-1949 or business@simonandschuster.com.

The Simon & Schuster Speakers Bureau can bring authors to your live event. For more information or to book an event, contact the Simon & Schuster Speakers Bureau at 1-866-248-3049 or visit our website at www.simonspeakers.com.

Interior design by Wendy Blum

Manufactured in the United States of America

10 9 8 7 6 5 4 3 2 1

Library of Congress Cataloging-in-Publication Data has been applied for.

ISBN 978-1-6680-0959-8
ISBN 978-1-6680-0961-1 (ebook)

*For our children
Michael and Sylvie*

CONTENTS

Author's Note	xi
Chronology	xiii
Cast of Characters	xv
Maps	xviii
Prologue	1
Chapter One: Pompey, Pacorus, and Herod	7
Chapter Two: The War for Herod's Legacy	35
Chapter Three: The Turncoat and the Convert	55
Chapter Four: And the War Came	83
Chapter Five: The War in the North	107
Chapter Six: Defenders of Jerusalem	133
Chapter Seven: Titus at Jerusalem	153
Chapter Eight: Survivors	177
Chapter Nine: Masada	201
Chapter Ten: Trajan, Parthia, and the Diaspora Revolt	227
Chapter Eleven: Bar Kokhba	245
Epilogue	275
Glossary of Place Names	289
Acknowledgments	293
Bibliography	297
Notes	313
Index	341

AUTHOR'S NOTE

Ancient names are, with a few exceptions, spelled following the style of the standard reference works: Ehsan Yarshater, ed., *Encyclopaedia Iranica* (New York: Columbia University, Center for Iranian Studies, 1996); Sander M. Goldberg, *Oxford Classical Dictionary*, 5th ed. (Oxford, UK: Oxford University Press, 2016); Fred Skolnik and Michael Berenbaum, eds., *Encyclopaedia Judaica*, 2nd ed. (Detroit: Macmillan Reference USA in association with Keter Publishing House, 2007).

Citations follow the guidelines of *The Chicago Manual of Style Online*, https://www-chicagomanualofstyle-org.proxy.library.cornell.edu/home.html. Rabbinic works are cited following guidelines of the Association for Jewish Studies, https://www.associationforjewishstudies.org/publications-research/ajs-review/submission-instructions.

For ancient places that are well-known modern cities I have used the modern names, e.g., Athens, Jerusalem, Rome.

"Judea," sometimes spelled "Judaea," has several different meanings. On the one hand, it refers either to a country that was first an independent kingdom and then a province in the Roman Empire. On the other hand, it refers to a region within that country, namely, the region of Jerusalem and its hinterland. To avoid confusion, I refer to the province and kingdom as Judea and to the region as Judah. Both are the same word in Hebrew, *Yehudah*, or in Latin, *Iudaea*.

CHRONOLOGY

Pompey conquers Jerusalem 63 BCE

Hezekiah raids Roman Syria 46

Pacorus invades Judea 40

Herod the Great rules Judea 37–4

Varus suppresses revolt in Judea 4 BCE

Rome annexes Judea 6 CE

Judah the Galilean and Zadok lead Tax Revolt 6

Pontius Pilate is prefect of Judea 26–36/37

Crucifixion of Jesus of Nazareth ca. 30

Caligula demands his statue in Jerusalem Temple 39/40

Agrippa is king of Judea 41–44

Tiberius Julius Alexander is procurator of Judea 46–48

Sicarii active in Judea 50s–60s

Roman defeat by Parthia at Rhandeia 62

Florus is procurator of Judea 64–67

Outbreak of Great Revolt 66

Battle of Beth Horon 66

Conquest of Jotapata and Gamala 67

Year of the Four Emperors 69

Destruction of Jerusalem and the Temple 70

Rabbi Johanan ben Zakkai founds Academy at Jabneh ca. 70

Triumph of Vespasian and Titus 71

Fall of Masada 74

Berenice in Rome 75–79

Trajan's Parthian War 115–117

Diaspora Revolt 116–117

Hadrian refounds Jerusalem as Aelia Capitolina 130

Bar Kokhba Revolt 132–136

Mishnah completed ca. 200

Gallus Revolt 351–352

Palestinian (Jerusalem) and Babylonian Talmuds completed ca. 400–ca. 500

Sasanians, Byzantines, and Muslims in turn conquer Jerusalem 614–638

CAST OF CHARACTERS

POMPEY (GNAEUS POMPEIUS MAGNUS), 106–48 BCE. A leading Roman general and statesman, Pompey conquered Judea in 63 BCE and ended its independence.

PACORUS (PAKUR), Parthian prince, who possibly ruled as Pacorus I, d. 38 BCE. He invaded the Roman Near East and put a pro-Parthian king on the throne in Judea.

HEROD THE GREAT, ca. 73–4 BCE, king of Judea 37–4 BCE. Ambitious, tyrannical, and murderous ruler, famous as a builder, Herod tried to make Judea the most loyal of Rome's client states, but faced Jewish opposition.

AUGUSTUS (EARLIER, OCTAVIAN), 63 BCE–14 CE. The brilliant Augustus ended an era of civil war and became Rome's first emperor. He treated Herod as a valuable partner in the Roman East.

AGRIPPA (also known as Herod Agrippa, whose Roman name was Marcus Julius Agrippa), 10 BCE–44 CE, r. 41–44 CE. Grandson of Herod the Great, he was educated in Rome, helped make Claudius emperor, and was rewarded with the kingship of Judea. An assertive and popular ruler, he died prematurely amid rumors of poison.

TIBERIUS JULIUS ALEXANDER, ca. 15–after 71 CE. Member of an elite family of Alexandria, he turned away from his Jewish heritage and rose high in Roman ranks. Among other offices, he served as procurator of Judea (46–48 CE) and as Titus's chief of staff in the siege of Jerusalem (70 CE).

HELENA, QUEEN OF ADIABENE, d. ca. 60 CE. Wife and mother of kings of Adiabene, a Parthian client state. Helena and her sons converted to Judaism. She lived in Jerusalem and forged ties that later led to Adiabenian participation in the Great Revolt.

CAST OF CHARACTERS

NERO (NERO CLAUDIUS CAESAR DRUSUS GERMANICUS), 37–68 CE, emperor 54–68, notorious for his decadence, but not without statesmanlike qualities. His greed and favoritism to the Greek population of Judea sparked the Great Revolt by Jews against Rome.

JOSEPHUS (JOSEPH SON OF MATTATHIAS, LATER T. FLAVIUS JOSEPHUS), ca. 37–after 100 CE. Born into the Jerusalem aristocracy, Josephus first fought for the rebels and then defected to the Romans. He spent the rest of his life in Rome with the financial support of the emperor. Josephus wrote the *Antiquities of the Jews* and *The Jewish War*, among other books.

JOHN OF GISCALA, d. after 70 CE. After leading the opposition to Rome in his home city in Galilee, John fled to Jerusalem, bringing his supporters with him. He was a major figure among the rebels until the end.

SIMON SON OF GIORA, d. 71 CE. A Jewish commander in the Great Revolt, 66–70, he engaged both in civil strife and in the defense of Jerusalem. Considered by the Romans to be the leader of the rebels.

VESPASIAN (TITUS FLAVIUS VESPASIANUS), 9–79 CE. Roman general who reconquered most of rebel Judea in 67–68, Vespasian emerged victorious in the Year of the Four Emperors (69 CE) and was the founding emperor (r. 69–79) of the Flavian dynasty.

TITUS (TITUS CAESAR VESPASIANUS), 39–81 CE, Vespasian's son, he conquered Jerusalem in 70 CE and destroyed both the city and the Temple, for which he celebrated a Triumph with his father in 71. Titus reigned as emperor 79–81.

BERENICE, b. 28 CE. Officially Julia Berenice but better known as Berenice, she was daughter of King Agrippa and queen by virtue of her marriage to the king of Chalcis. In 66, she tried to prevent the Great Revolt, without success. Afterward she supported the Romans. Berenice had a long-term love affair with Titus.

VOLOGASES I (BALSH OR WALGASH IN PARTHIAN), r. ca. 51–79 CE. One of Parthia's more successful rulers, he reasserted control of Armenia from Rome but declined to intervene in Judea against Rome during the Great Revolt.

RABBI JOHANAN BEN ZAKKAI, first century CE. Jewish tradition considers him the leading sage at the time of the destruction of the Temple. He is said to have escaped Jerusalem under siege and won permission from Vespasian to found an academy at Jabneh, where he instituted some of the practices that allowed Judaism to survive.

CAST OF CHARACTERS

TRAJAN (MARCUS ULPIUS TRAIANUS), ca. 53–117 CE, reigned as emperor 98–117. He invaded Parthian territory and tried to conquer Armenia and Mesopotamia (115–117), but failed, in part because of a revolt in the Jewish Diaspora that sprung up during his campaign.

SIMON BAR KOKHBA, d. 135 CE. He led a revolt in Judea that broke out in 132. Born Bar Koseva (sometimes Ben Koseva), he was acclaimed by some as the messiah, leading to his appellation of Bar Kokhba, literally, "Son of a Star."

HADRIAN (PUBLIUS AELIUS HADRIANUS), 76–138 CE. Emperor, r. 117–138, Hadrian decided to rebuild ruined Jerusalem as a pagan, Roman colony. That probably sparked the bloody Bar Kokhba Revolt (132–136).

RABBI JUDAH THE PRINCE (YEHUDAH HA NASI), later second–early third centuries CE. The greatest rabbi of his generation, he and his students redacted the Mishnah, which, along with the Talmud a few centuries later, is the foundation text for rabbinic Judaism.

GALLUS (FLAVIUS CONSTANTIUS GALLUS CAESAR), d. 354, suppressed a Jewish insurgency in Palestine, sometime in 351–352, that is remembered as the Gallus Revolt.

PATRICIUS, Jewish leader in the Gallus Revolt of 351–352, possibly regarded by some as the messiah.

KHOSROW II, ca. 570–628, r. 590–628, ambitious Sasanian monarch whose armies conquered much of the Eastern Roman Empire, including Palestine.

HERACLIUS, ca. 575–641, Eastern Roman (Byzantine) emperor, r. 610–641. Heraclius won back the territory conquered by Khosrow II, including Palestine, only to lose it to the rising new power of Islam.

North Sea
TEUTOBURG FOREST
ATLANTIC OCEAN
DALMATIA
ITALY
Urbs Salvia
Rome
Puteoli
ROMAN EMPIRE
Athens
Corinth
MAURETANIA
AFRICA PROCONSULARIS
Mediterranean Sea
Cyrene
CYRENAICA

ROME AND PARTHIA

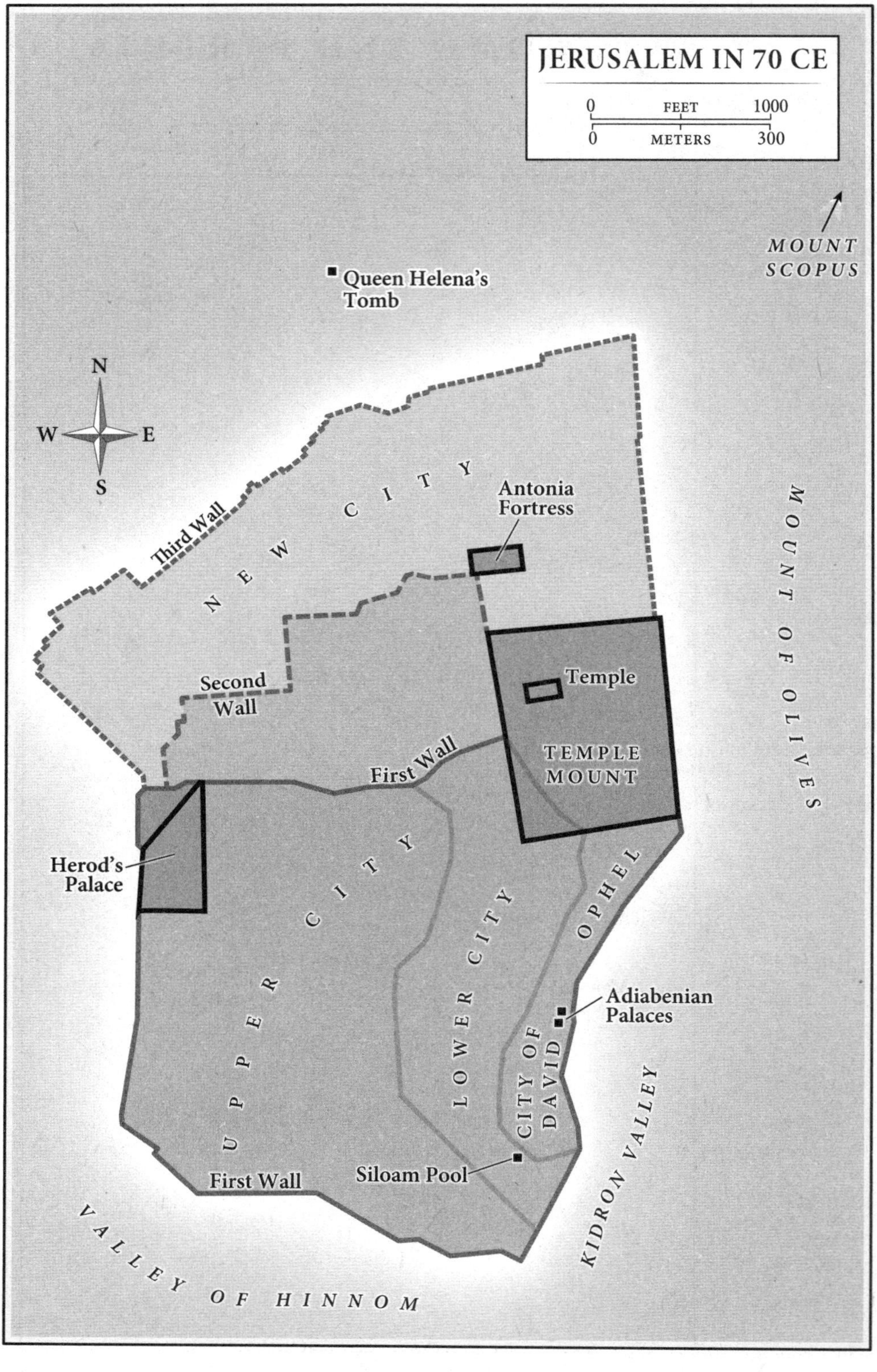
JERUSALEM IN 70 CE
0
FEET
1000
0
METERS
300
MOUNT SCOPUS
Queen Helena's Tomb
N
W
E
S
Third Wall
NEW CITY
Antonia Fortress
MOUNT OF OLIVES
Second Wall
Temple
TEMPLE MOUNT
First Wall
Herod's Palace
UPPER CITY
LOWER CITY
OPHEL
Adiabenian Palaces
CITY OF DAVID
KIDRON VALLEY
Siloam Pool
First Wall
VALLEY OF HINNOM

JUDEA
0
MILES
40
0
KM
40
N
W
E
S
Damascus
Tyre
Caesarea-Philippi
GAULANITIS (GOLAN)
Giscala
Ptolemaïs
Gamala
GALILEE
Sea of Galilee
MEDITERRANEAN SEA
Jotapata
Tiberias
Hippos
Sepphoris
Nazareth
DECAPOLIS
SAMARIA
Caesarea-by-the-Sea
Scythopolis
Pella
Sebaste
Jordan River
Joppa
PEREA
Lydda
Jabneh
Jericho
Jerusalem
Betar
Bethlehem
Qumran
Ascalon
Herodium
JUDAH
DEAD SEA
Machaerus
Gaza
En Gedi
NABATEA
Masada
IDUMEA

PROLOGUE

It was an age of unscrupulous intrigue and messianic longing, of empire and insurrection, and of geopolitical warfare that still has modern echoes.

The era from 63 BCE to 136 CE marked two centuries of violence and revolution. They witnessed the decline and fall of the Roman Republic, the rise of Rome of the Caesars and its continuing wars for dominance against the Iranian empire of Parthia, the only imperial rival to Rome left after the conquest of Carthage and the Hellenistic kingdoms. Caught in the middle, both geographically and politically, was the cauldron of tiny Judea—home of Rome's most determined insurgencies and the soil from which the seedlings of both rabbinic Judaism and Christianity would begin to grow.

Judea was fighting for its survival as a religion, a people, and a nation. It was caught between countries and empires many times its size and strength, negotiating among ever-changing allies and enemies and facing mutual hostility with its neighbors. Because Judea was not a unified state it faced ethnic conflict within its own borders. Meanwhile, the dominant group in Judea, the Jewish people, fought among themselves for power, influence, and their own conceptions of a holy life.

For today's reader, this story may seem painfully familiar. Certainly, the names of many battlefields are eerily the same in today's news as in the pages of this book. The names of our story's protagonists remain renowned, and the historical consequences of this era live on with us today. Nor were the challenges that confronted Judea two thousand years ago unique to that era. Small countries, and large countries, too, still face them in our time.

It is my hope that the history of this period, these people and these struggles, will offer context for the clash of civilizations we are witnessing today and forge a deeper understanding of the forces that propel them.

It would be hard to exaggerate the degree of excitement, anticipation, anxiety, and bloodlust that echoed in this era. What an explosion of creativity and destruction! These were two of the most dramatic and consequential centuries in history. And for the Jewish people in particular, these centuries were cataclysmic.

For the Jews, it was an era of revolution—many small uprisings during more than a century, culminating in an era of three great wars: the Great Revolt, also known as the Jewish War, 66 to 74 CE; the Diaspora Revolt, 116 to 117; and the Bar Kokhba Revolt, 132 to 136. And against whom did the Jews revolt? Only against perhaps the greatest empire in history: Rome.

From the Scottish Highlands to the Atlas Mountains, from the Atlantic Ocean to the Euphrates River, and for a moment, even to the Persian Gulf, Rome ruled a vast realm. It governed what a Roman writer called "the immeasurable majesty of the Roman peace."[1] Fifty million people lived under Roman rule in what was then, along with Han China, the largest empire on earth. Among its other achievements, Rome conquered all the people around the Mediterranean Sea and united them under one government for the first and only time in history.

And yet during the space of seventy years, the Jews, one of the many peoples under Roman rule, revolted not once but three times. No other people in the empire—and there were many other rebel nations—had such a record. Two of the rebellions took place in the Jewish homeland, Judea, the third in the Diaspora, the emigrant communities of Jews.

Today people argue over the names Israel and Palestine, but that is nothing new. They argued over the country's name in antiquity as well, with both Israel and Palestine attested long before Rome came on the scene. In the Roman era the country was commonly called Judea. The more ancient Jewish name for the country, which some patriots preferred, was Israel. It is attested as early as the thirteenth century BCE.[2]

Most rebellions occurred in recently conquered provinces. Judea was different. It was not newly conquered. In fact, Rome subdued Judea in 63 BCE, more than 120 years before the Jewish revolt of 66 CE. And Judea had first became a Roman ally even earlier, in 160 BCE. Close observers should have seen the storm coming, what with so much unrest in Judea in earlier years. But in Rome, far away and preoccupied with other, bigger provinces, it came as a surprise.

The rebels of 66 CE humiliated the Roman legions. They first threatened, and then succeeded in contributing to a Roman defeat at the hands of the only rival empire that Rome still feared. They cost the legions a huge expenditure of blood and treasure before finally the rebellions were put down. A vengeful Rome responded with a savagery not seen since the destruction of Carthage two centuries earlier.

The rebels were freedom fighters, daring and heroic, and to that extent they deserve our admiration. But they were also murderous and deluded. The revolts were magnificent, but misguided. How could the rebels hope to defeat the mighty Romans? They represented a great tide of anger and violence that sometimes turned on itself, at least in the Great Revolt, because that Jewish war against Rome was also a war of Jew against Jew: it was a Jewish civil war.

For Jewish history, the rebellions against Rome mark a major turning point. They cost hundreds of thousands of Jewish lives and sent many of the survivors into slavery and exile. They reduced the Jewish people to secondary status in their own homeland. Indeed, the revolts put the future of Jewish survival there in question, although they did not end it. It's a common misconception to think that the Romans finished the Jewish presence in the Land of Israel. They did not, but they did do an enormous amount of damage. Rome destroyed the Jewish capital, Jerusalem, and its crowning glory, the Temple. Rome ended the daily sacrifices that marked the heart of Judaism and ruined the priesthood who carried them out. Rome decimated the largest and most prestigious Jewish Diaspora community in the Roman Empire, the Jews of Egypt. As if to add insult to injury, the Romans changed the name of the country from Judea ("land of the Jews") to Syria Palaestina, or simply Palestine ("land of the Philistines"). In no other case did the Romans punish a rebellious province by changing its name. Then again, no people had rebelled as often as the Jews.

There is a holy fire, burning in the hearts of warriors, that leads to glory or oblivion. For two centuries it burned in the hearts of the nation that is the subject of this book, the Jewish people. Messiahs added to the conflagration. Even priests, resistant at first, grew dazzled by the white-hot light. Sober men saw the fire's destructiveness and tried to douse the flames. None succeeded. It was left to the Romans to drown the blaze in rivers of blood. Only then did a new generation of rabbis emerge from the ruins and turn the fire into light. At the same time, another offshoot from the Jewish experience of this turbulent era also began to grow: Christianity.

The Jewish people survived, learning how to become a religion without a state. Then, twenty centuries later, they created a sovereign state in their ancestral homeland, Israel. The survival of the Jews is one of history's great cases of resilience. Paradoxically, the same spiritual fire that drove some men unwisely if bravely into an unequal contest against an unyielding empire was the same spirituality that inspired Jewish endurance over the millennia.

Rome was not the only empire in play: there was also Parthia. The shrewd descendants of horse-riding nomads created a mighty realm, originating in what is now Iran, that stretched from today's Turkmenistan to Syria. The Parthian Empire stood astride the world's wealthiest trade routes, between China, India, and Arabia on the one hand, and the Mediterranean world on the other. Parthia was the sole empire remaining in Rome's orbit that could challenge its power. And challenge it, Parthia did: by the start of the Great Revolt, Parthia had inflicted a series of

PROLOGUE

catastrophic defeats on Rome again and again. From time to time, Rome got revenge, but the defeats stung.

Judea, located near the eastern edge of Rome's empire, looked both ways. To the west, the Jewish Diaspora stretched to Egypt, Libya, and all the way to Rome and beyond. To the north, it extended to Cyprus, Syria, and Asia Minor. The Diaspora also stretched eastward to Mesopotamia, where the Jewish population centered in the region of Babylonia. This was Parthian territory, and its inhabitants had close connections with Judea. The border between the empires was usually open, and Jews traveled back and forth as diplomats, soldiers, merchants, scholars, sages, and pilgrims. Rome fretted about Judea's loyalty, and not without reason. It was a time-honored tradition for a small state to play one large party off the other. When Rome looked at Judea, it saw the shadow of Parthia.

Many books have been written on the Jewish revolts against Rome. The scholarship is superb, and I gratefully and humbly acknowledge my debt. This book's contribution is to focus on the Jewish state's unique position between East and West, between Parthia and Rome. The narrative weaves its way through a world whose inhabitants were equally at home with apocalypse and geostrategy. And it raises the ghosts of the often-forgotten men and women of the past, whose great and marvelous deeds should not be without glory—as Herodotus, the father of history, put it long ago.

Our story begins in 63 BCE, when Rome conquered Judea. At the time, Judea was an independent country and proud of its hard-won independence from its Greco-Syrian overlords, making it the first independent Jewish state in more than four centuries. Now Rome took that away. Most Jews greatly resented that loss. The result was a constant roiling discontent that occasionally broke out into outright rebellion—and this was before the Great Revolt began in 66 CE. There was a seemingly endless cycle of dissidents, rebels, and prophets of change. Messianism grew popular. To maintain control of Judea required constant vigilance by Rome, through the measured application of carrots and sticks, and via the help of local collaborators. It all worked until it didn't.

In 63 BCE, the Great Revolt was over a century away, but all the elements were present in embryo: Roman aggression, Jewish division between acceptance and rebellion, Parthian intervention, power politics and messianic hopes, ethnic conflict between Jew and Gentile in Judea. The same themes would be sounded over and over again for the next two centuries. To understand them, we need to begin at the beginning.

Chapter One

POMPEY, PACORUS, AND HEROD

The sixty years between 63 and 4 BCE proved to be among the most dramatic in the annals of the Jewish people, a nation that had already experienced a history of revelation, exile, return, and revolution. These six decades turned life upside down in the Jewish homeland, Judea. At the start of 63 BCE, Judea was free and independent. By year's end it was a client state of the Roman Empire. Over the next twenty-five years Judea witnessed invasion first by Rome, then by Parthia, and then again by Rome. After the Romans finally established their rule, they installed a Jewish usurper as king. He governed the country with an iron fist and a taste for despotic splendor. He rebuilt the Temple in Jerusalem and restored Judea to roughly its size under Kings David and Solomon centuries earlier. But the price was tyranny and, from many Jews' point of view, excessive concessions to Rome and to the culture of the Greeks, who formed a large part of the client kingdom's urban population. Those Greeks enthusiastically supported Rome as a counterweight to their Jewish neighbors. While some Jews collaborated with Rome, others preached resistance or engaged in sedition and violence. When Rome's client king died in 4 BCE, sedition turned into outright rebellion. A dramatic period indeed, but one of its most consequential events took place quietly.

At the end of this era, perhaps in 4 BCE, the founder of one of the world's great religions was born in Bethlehem.

Judea before Rome

About six hundred years before the start of the Common Era—before the birth of Christ, for Christians—the Jews[1] marched off into exile. The Neo-Babylonian Empire sacked Jerusalem, destroyed the Temple, and deported the Jewish elite to Babylonia. Then, several decades later, a new imperial people, the Persians, conquered the Neo-Babylonians. The Persian ruler, Cyrus the Great, is one of history's great founders of empire. What he looked like, we have no idea. A carved relief in his palace of a four-winged guardian angel, tall, regal, and imposing, will have to stand in for him. That, and his tomb, a stepped pyramid in southwestern Iran, which once contained a golden coffin and a couch covered with purple-dyed hides.

Cyrus allowed the Jews to return from exile. According to the Bible, Cyrus proclaimed the freedom of the Jews to "go up to Jerusalem, which *is* in Judah, and build the house of the LORD God of Israel, (he *is* the God,) which *is* in Jerusalem."[2] Many of the exiles took Cyrus up on his offer. It was about seventy years after the destruction of Jerusalem. The returnees slowly began rebuilding the city, and they eventually rebuilt the Temple.

At first glance, Judeans looked like other people in the region. They tended to have olive skin and black hair. The men wore beards, the women covered their hair. (The kippah, or skullcap, for men only came later.) The basic articles of clothing, as elsewhere in the ancient Mediterranean, were woolen tunics, belted at the waist, covered by a mantle, which was colored for women, white for men. Sandals were the basic footwear.[3]

A closer look showed that these people were often different. Ancient women in general were expected to dress modestly, but Jewish women were expected to pay particular attention to wearing a veil in public and to keeping their hair hidden. Some Jewish men wore a mantle that had fringes (tzitzit) at each corner. Neither sex mixed wool and linen in a single garment. Some Jewish men wore tefillin, or leather phylacteries, in private and sometimes in public.[4]

These customs followed the laws of the Jews' holy book, the Torah, that is, the Five Books of Moses. They showed devotion to God, the one deity whom the Jews worshipped exclusively, setting them apart in a world of polytheism.[5] God, Torah, and the Temple were "the three pillars of ancient Judaism," as one scholar put it.[6]

The Jews were not independent. Judea (more properly in that period, Yehud) was an administrative district of the Persian Empire, answerable to the regional governor.[7] Still, many Jews felt they had all the freedom they needed. They were allowed to live in their homeland and to worship their God in His House, the Temple in Jerusalem. Political independence was not required or even desirable: better to have a good patron. Judea was a small nation, a sheep in a world of imperial wolves. Persia, which ruled with a light touch, was a good shepherd.

The chief official in Judea was the High Priest, who was in charge both of religious and political matters. He worked with a council of elders. The people had no king, and many Jews were glad of it. Monarchy was an uneasy fit for a people whose king was God. Nevertheless, the Jews had had kings in the past, both good and bad, and they would have kings again.

Judea survived for two hundred years until the Persian Empire was conquered by the Macedonian king, Alexander the Great. After Alexander's death, Judea passed from one of the successor states to another. The cities along the Mediterranean coast and to the east and south of the Sea of Galilee were largely pagan and Greek in culture. Several were settled by Alexander's veterans. Jews as well felt the impact of Greek culture. Hellenism represented the wave of progress, or so it seemed to a portion of the Jewish elite. They worked with the Greco-Macedonian king of Syria to turn Jerusalem into a pagan city and to put the Jewish religion on the road to extinction. Then a rebellion in 167 BCE led by the members of a priestly family, the Maccabees, eventually drove the Syrians out of Judea. By 140 BCE Judea was semiautonomous and by 116 BCE

Judea became an independent state. But success depended on the weakness of the Syrian state, which was, in fact, going through a long, slow-death agony.

The Maccabee brothers and their descendants ruled first as princes; eventually they took the title of king. They also obtained the support of an assembly of priests and notables to become High Priest, a hereditary office. Their dynasty was known as the Hasmoneans.[8] They emphasized Torah and Temple, but they also embraced aspects of Greek culture.

At least three groups of Jews emerged under the Hasmoneans; there were surely others, lost to the historical record.[9] The Sadducees, or "Righteous Ones," represented the hereditary priesthood who, wearing splendid robes, carried out the rituals and sacrifices at the Temple. They were an aristocracy who followed the strict letter of the Law in the Torah. The Essenes (meaning of the name is unknown) stood at the opposite end of the religious spectrum. They were a small, separatist sect who believed that they alone possessed the truth and so were the real Jews. They lived in monastic communities, such as the one at Qumran in the Judean Desert that produced the famous Dead Sea Scrolls, papyrus documents whose discovery in the mid-twentieth century revolutionized our knowledge of ancient Judaism and early Christianity. They lived ascetic lives, wearing white linen garments symbolizing purity. They observed Jewish law meticulously, but did not worship at the Temple, which, they believed, had grown corrupt.

Much of what the Essenes wrote comes under the category of apocalypse, a Greek word meaning "revelation." The Essenes were only one among several Jewish groups in this era who often thought in apocalyptic terms. Indeed, the four centuries between 200 BCE and 200 CE marked a period of apocalyptic writings in Jewish and, in turn, Christian culture. The authors of apocalyptic texts wrote as if they lived in the last generation before the end of days. As they saw it, natural disasters, such as earthquakes, signaled a greater, cosmic upheaval. History would reach its climax. The reign of wickedness would be replaced by a new and righteous world.

The third group called themselves sages—strictly speaking, the word "rabbi" was not used before the mid-first century CE—but are better known by the negative label that their opponents pinned on them: the Pharisees, or "Separatists." They were teachers and scholars who wanted to bring Judaism to ordinary people. Although some Pharisees were priests, most were not. They dressed like other Jews, except perhaps for wearing longer fringes on the corners of their mantles. The Pharisees believed in interpreting the Written Law of the Torah by means of the Oral Law, which they believed had been given to Moses at Sinai by God and passed down through the generations. They accepted the importance of the Temple, but they promoted the synagogue as a place of prayer and reading sections of the Bible. The Pharisees wanted to spread holiness among the people, and they were beloved for it. They were by far the most popular of the three groups. Like most people, they objected to foreign domination, but they preferred a hands-off foreign ruler to an impious Jewish government.

Enter the Roman Legions

The Hasmoneans expanded in all directions, making Judea a regional power. Galilee, Gaulanitis (roughly, today's Golan region of Israel), the Mediterranean coast, Idumea, Perea (roughly, today's central western part of Jordan), and areas of southern Lebanon and Syria all became part of the Hasmonean state. The central part of the country, and the Jews' original homeland, was known as Judah. It was about 1,000 square miles (2,600 km^2) in size, making it roughly the size of the territory of ancient Athens (Attica). Accurate population statistics for the country are not available, but literary and archaeological evidence suggests the following data points: Judah was almost entirely Jewish. Jerusalem was Judah's main city, and the national capital, but most of Judah's inhabitants lived in villages. Galilee, Perea, and Idumea probably had Jewish majorities. The rest of the countryside had large numbers of Jews.[10] The cities had Jewish minorities, but were largely pagan and Greek. The country was rich, vibrant, and divided.[11]

In the first century BCE, division was found even within Judea's ruling family, where two brothers fought over the throne. Eventually one of them called in help from a superpower—Rome. It seemed like the smart move. Judea had been in Rome's orbit as early as 160 BCE, with an alliance between the Maccabees and Rome. Rome supported the Jews against the Greco-Syrians, and helped win Jewish independence, but Roman support never came without a price. As far as the Romans were concerned, Judea was free—free, that is, to obey Rome. In 63 BCE, Rome's legions conquered Judea's neighbor, Syria. The Roman Empire now stretched from the Atlantic Ocean to the Euphrates River. An imperial titan now bordered the Jewish realm.

The Roman victor in Syria was Gnaeus Pompeius Magnus, that is, Pompey the Great, his country's most successful general at the time. Pompey was handsome, composed, and vain. People said that he resembled Alexander the Great, and Pompey did nothing to discourage the comparison. Pompey was a master of logistics and diplomacy. He prided himself on all the kings, consuls, and princes in his debt. He was attractive and dignified, but looks can deceive. Pompey was famously cruel. As a young commander he won the nickname "the teenage butcher."[12]

Both royal brothers as well as other Jewish leaders traveled to Damascus to make their case to Pompey, who accepted a large bribe from one of them, but kept his own counsel. He also considered a third possibility. A delegation of over two hundred eminent Jews met with him and asked that the monarchy be abolished altogether. They said that they had never accepted the legitimacy of the Hasmoneans. They preferred to be governed by the priests and the elders, as in earlier times, and they claimed strong popular support at home. Pompey chose the weaker of the two brothers, Hyrcanus, who seemed the most pliant of the three possibilities. And so, the Romans invaded Judea.

Pompey and his army, helped by Hyrcanus's supporters, marched into Jerusalem. But they still had to take the Temple Mount. They laid siege to it in summer 63 BCE and conquered the mount three months later, massacring as many as twelve thousand Jews along the way.[13] The victorious Pompey entered the Holy of Holies, to the horror of the Jewish people, but reportedly left its treasures intact. Pompey punished Judea harshly. He imposed tribute, that is, taxes, payable to Rome's agents. He took away most of Judea's territory, including its access to the sea. He freed the Greek cities of Judea from Jewish rule and granted them autonomy. The Greek elites were ecstatic, as they had hated being ruled by a Jewish king. In one city, for example, they redated the calendar from Pompey's liberation, which they called Year One.[14]

Pompey abolished the Jewish monarchy. He made Hyrcanus accept the lesser title of ethnarch, that is, provincial leader. Pompey carted off the other brother and his family to march in his Triumph in Rome. He also took thousands of Jewish prisoners to Italy. Josephus, the great historian of the Jews' troubled relationship with Rome, commented bitterly: "For this misfortune, which befell Jerusalem, . . . [the two brothers] were responsible, because of their dissension. For we lost our freedom, and became subject to the Romans. . . ."[15]

Josephus is by far the most important source for Jewish history of this period. He will be an important player later in our story, so a detailed look at the man will be deferred until then. For now, suffice it to say that he lived his life in three acts. In the first, he was the son of a minor priestly family in Jerusalem. Like most members of his class, he collaborated with the empire. He represented his country on a mission to Rome and met the emperor Nero. In the second act, he joined the rebellion in 66 CE. At the young age of thirty he got the heady responsibility of serving as governor of Galilee and organizing its defense. But he failed, which brings us to his third act: collaborator again, and on a grand scale. After personally witnessing the destruction of the city that he loved, he went to Rome and spent the rest of his life there. He became a Roman citizen and lived on a generous pension from the emperor. He devoted his last three decades to writing, and voluminously. His main subject was Jewish history, and his twin goals were to defend his people and to warn them never, ever again to revolt against the brutal and irresistible power of Rome.

In broad terms, two Jewish reactions to their loss of freedom may be imagined. For some, the story went like this: Under the Maccabees the Jews defeated a mighty empire and regained their ancestral freedom. Then the Romans came and enslaved them. Now the Jews had to fight to be free once again. And all, from start to finish, depended upon God's help. Others told a different tale: it was God's will that the Romans conquered the world, including Judea. The Jews would have to make their peace with that. Rebellion would be suicidal, even impious.

Ah, the first group might have replied, *but God has not left the Jews bereft. Remember how Cyrus the Persian, an Iranian king, freed us from captivity in Babylon and let us return to our homeland? Now large numbers of fellow Jews live and prosper in the East under the rule of another Iranian dynasty, the Parthians. The Parthians have an empire, too, and they are Rome's enemies; the Parthians will help the Jews be free, either with their own soldiers or by allowing their Jewish subjects to come to our aid.* And the second group might have replied: *That's a dream! The Parthians will not go to war with Rome for the Jews.* So the debate might have gone the day after Pompey violated the Holy of Holies and placed Judea under the thumb of Rome. And so it continued for the next two centuries. A main theme of Jewish history between 63 BCE and 136 CE was whether the Jews would learn to tolerate the hard hand of Rome or whether they would fight to death to free themselves from it.

In theory Hyrcanus ruled what was now a Roman client state, but real power lay in the hands of his strong-armed administrator, Antipater. He was an Idumean Jew who never lost an opportunity to prove himself useful to Rome. Always keeping an eye on Roman politics, Antipater changed loyalties as needed and ended up on the winning side of the civil war between Julius Caesar and Pompey and his supporters in the Senate, 49 to 45 BCE. Pompey was defeated in battle and assassinated. Antipater joined the war on Caesar's side, and Caesar rewarded him in 47 BCE by naming him the chief official in Judea. The next year, one of Antipater's four sons emerged as the terror of Jews who fought against Rome. He had been appointed by Rome to govern Galilee, Samaria, and part of what is now Lebanon. His name was Herod.

Enter the Freedom Fighters

Later, during the Great Revolt, the Roman commander Titus would be quoted by Josephus as saying angrily to the Jews, "You who from the moment

Pompey's forces crushed you have never stopped rebelling."[16] Titus might have been referring to Jewish support for Parthia, but more likely he had homegrown Judean rebels in mind. They make their first appearance in the historical record in 46 BCE. Around that time some Jews had identified the Romans as the evil invaders of Judea par excellence, a distinction previously reserved, in the time of the Maccabees, for the Syrians and other Greeks.[17]

In 46 BCE, Herod was governor of Galilee, and he took the law in his hands. At the time, a group of Jewish guerrillas was pushing back against Rome by raiding Gentile towns over the border in the Roman province of Syria. By demonstrating Rome's inability to protect villages in their province, the rebels struck a blow against the power of their hated enemy. The leader of the fighters was one Hezekiah, who came from a distinguished family of scholars, although the Romans and their supporters branded him a terrorist—actually, "chief bandit."[18] To many Jews he was a freedom fighter who raised the banner of resistance against the idolatrous and oppressive Romans.

Herod captured the guerrillas, including Hezekiah, and executed them all summarily. He received a commendation from the Roman governor of Syria, but some Jews in Galilee and Jerusalem were outraged. The mothers of the victims went day after day to the Temple to pray for justice. A reluctant Ethnarch Hyrcanus finally agreed to have Herod put on trial for murder before the Sanhedrin.

Just what the Sanhedrin was is a matter of debate. Was it a political and judicial council or a legislative body for religious matters that also occasionally functioned as a court? Was it composed of Sadducees, Pharisees, secular officials, or all of the above? Did it change over time? Was there one large Sanhedrin or several smaller ones? The sources disagree. For the trial of Herod, we know that it included Pharisees.

Defendants in murder trials often appeared in court dressed in sackcloth, pleading for mercy. Herod showed up dressed in royal purple and surrounded by armed retainers. The accusers were too terrified to push the matter. Perhaps they knew that the Roman governor of Syria had written to Hyrcanus, insisting that Herod go unpunished. And so, he did. But before the court adjourned, one of the judges stood up and protested against Hyrcanus. He predicted that one day Herod would kill them all, Hyrcanus included. Josephus calls the judge Samias; some identify him with Shemaiah, one of the leading Pharisees of the day. This Shemaiah is quoted as saying, "Love work; hate ruling; and do not become close with those in power."[19]

After the poisoning of both Antipater and his rival, Hyrcanus's brother, a new generation rose to the fore. Besides Herod, Antipater had a daughter and three other sons, but they faced a powerful rival in a new claimant to the throne, Antigonus, Hyrcanus's nephew.

The geostrategic map had changed dramatically since Pompey's invasion of Judea in 63 BCE. Antigonus could read the map, and in 40 BCE, he called in the Parthians.

Thunder in the East

Rome could not think about Judea without hearing the thunder of Parthian horsemen in the distance. For years, Parthia had loomed on Rome's horizon.

In 53 BCE, the Roman warlord Marcus Licinius Crassus marched off on what he thought would be a campaign of conquest against Parthia. It was a strong rival state that was hard to ignore—Rome had already defeated all other competing empires on its borders. Rome crushed the mighty Carthage, Macedon, the Mithradatic kingdom (stretching at its height from Asia Minor to Crimea), and Seleucid Syria, and demoted Ptolemaic Egypt to a mere client kingdom. Parthia was the only great empire left. "These two empires are the greatest: the Romans and Parthians," declared the emperor Caracalla centuries later.[20] Beginning in the third century BCE, Parthia's horsemen had ridden out of the east and carved out a powerful realm. Their empire stretched from the Euphrates River in today's Syria to the Merv Oasis in today's Turkmenistan. And it was rich, both from its own natural resources and from its control of the land route, the so-called Silk Road, as well as the maritime trade route to China, India, and Arabia.

To a predator like Crassus, Rome's wealthiest man and possibly its least scrupulous, Parthia looked like easy prey, the next victim of the mighty legions. Unfortunately for him, the Parthians thought otherwise. They had become the ancient world's best horsemen. Their ranks included both heavy and light cavalry. The heavy cavalrymen are also known as cataphracts, from the Greek for "covered." The men each wore a full suit of body armor, made of iron and tanned leather, protecting the legs and neck as well as the torso. They also wore a metal helmet. Parthian horses were covered with plate armor. The weapon of the Parthian heavy cavalryman was a long spear with an iron head, supposedly able to transfix two men at one go. The light cavalrymen each carried a bow and leather bow case, as well as a long sword and a dagger in scabbards suspended from a belt at their waist. They wore practical, Scythian-style tunics and trousers. They were expert archers, capable of shooting arrows about 50 yards (45 meters) in a frontal attack. The horse archers could also retreat at high speed, then suddenly turn and shoot the enemy, who had been lured into pursuit: the notorious "Parthian shot." It took skill and practice to carry out. The Romans were unprepared, and the Parthians mauled Crassus and his army.

The battle took place outside of Carrhae, a city on the plains east of the Euphrates River. The Euphrates was the only natural boundary in this relatively flat area, and Parthia wanted the river to mark the dividing point between the two empires, but the Romans refused. Crassus crossed the Euphrates with contempt, but Parthia's cavalrymen were waiting. On a day in May, before the plain turned dry and yellow in the summer, the Parthians crushed the Roman invaders, inflicting massive casualties on Crassus's force of about forty thousand men. The Parthians added insult to injury by capturing several legionary eagles. Crassus was murdered in a post-battle conference to negotiate surrender terms with the victors.

After 53 BCE, Parthia became a preoccupation—no, an obsession, and one that lasted for centuries. Before that year the Parthians were a challenge and an opportunity; afterward, they were a threat and a humiliation. Empires can tolerate neither.[21]

The only bright spot in Rome's tarnished honor at Carrhae belonged to

Crassus's deputy, Gaius Cassius Longinus. Best known for his later role as one of Julius Caesar's assassins, the man immortalized by Shakespeare for his "lean and hungry look," Cassius was also a skilled commander. After the battle, he saved the remnants of the Roman army by marching the men to safety in the Roman province of Syria; ten thousand Roman soldiers owed their lives to Cassius.

Parthia's friends in Judea were not so fortunate. In the years after the battle, Cassius served as virtual governor of Roman Syria. After turning back a Parthian army of invasion, in 52 BCE Cassius went after a pro-Parthian stronghold to the south, in Galilee. A small Jewish city there, on the Sea of Galilee, was a rallying point for Parthia's friends. Cassius attacked the city, captured the ringleader, and had him executed. Then Cassius enslaved the inhabitants, who amounted to thirty thousand people, according to Josephus—probably a vast exaggeration to titillate his Roman readers. But there was certainly a considerable haul of slaves. Enslavement was big business and Cassius had a reputation for avarice.[22]

Cassius's attack gave a vivid warning to the people of Judea. They were caught between two empires, Rome and Parthia. That truth would be underlined in 40 BCE, about a dozen years after Rome's massive defeat at Carrhae. It was then that the Parthians invaded Syria, Asia Minor, and Judea.

The Parthian Connection

Pacorus the Parthian rode into Jerusalem in May 40 BCE.[23] Pacorus (in Parthian, Pakur) was a royal cupbearer, a man privileged to share the name of Parthia's crown prince, also called Pacorus. He was a person of unimpeachable loyalty, as was required of the man entrusted with pouring the king's drinks in a world in which poison was a constant threat. The cupbearer was an important person at court because of his access to the king, and he could also hold a military command. To judge by an earlier Persian image, a cupbearer could balance a tall drinking cup in each of his hands. At court he would be formally attired, but this day he probably wore armor.[24]

POMPEY, PACORUS, AND HEROD

In Parthia, cupbearers came from elite families. We might speculate that Pacorus was a Jew. It would have been useful for the crown prince to choose a Jew to represent him in Jerusalem. There was precedent, as Cyrus had a Jewish cupbearer, Nehemiah, at least according to the biblical account. Babylonia, where the Parthian capital city was located, had a large Jewish population. The name Pacorus was Parthian, but it was sometimes used by Jewish Parthians, including a Jewish member of the Parthian elite.[25]

The crown prince was a three days' ride to the north, at Ptolemaïs, a port city on the Mediterranean. He was, to judge by coin portraits, a clean-shaven man with a long neck, prominent ears, and an aquiline nose.[26] He wore a ribbon of royalty—the sign of kings in the ancient world—around a head of curly hair, and a gold torque necklace, the latter a Parthian trademark.[27]

The prince had just crowned his career with the conquest of Syria, an opulent land, the jewel of the Eastern Mediterranean. There, Pacorus's men washed their spears in the sea, which extended the Parthian Empire from the mountains of Afghanistan to the Mediterranean and recalled the glory of Cyrus the Great and his dynasty. By contrast, what awaited in Jerusalem was a mere family quarrel.

The Parthians now chose to support Antigonus in his fight against his Roman-backed uncle Hyrcanus. They planned to install Antigonus in power as their client, in return for a hefty bribe: 60,000 pounds of silver (1,000 talents) and 500 women from Hyrcanus's faction, presumably for the Parthian prince's harem. Pacorus gave the mission to his cupbearer. An army of Jewish volunteers had sprung up to fight for Parthia's client, so there was no need to send in the Parthian army. The crown prince dispatched only a troop of horsemen with the cupbearer, as much to scout the country as to fight.

The Jews witnessed a popular groundswell in favor of Antigonus, or, more accurately, against Herod and his brothers, who supported Hyrcanus. Jews hated them as commoners and as foreigners: "half Jews," Antigonus called them.[28] On their father's side they were Idumeans, grandsons of a convert to Judaism. Idumeans had converted to Judaism en masse and largely voluntarily,

– 19 –

as scholars now think, when they were conquered by the Hasmoneans in the second century BCE.[29] Even so, many Jews hated Idumeans because they traced their ancestry to migrants from Edom, hereditary enemies of the Jews. The mother of Herod and his siblings was an Arab princess, but that didn't make them less Jewish. In those days, unlike later, a Jew's religion passed through the father and not the mother.

The adversaries fought with inconclusive results. Antigonus counted on Pacorus the Cupbearer, supposedly to serve as a mediator, but instead to favor him. The other side saw through his intentions, but Parthia was too strong for them to refuse.

Five hundred Parthian horsemen escorted the cupbearer as he entered Jerusalem. They surely cut an impressive figure, even in a city of tens of thousands of people, even with its numbers swollen by pilgrims come to celebrate the harvest festival of Shavuot (Weeks), because the population was packed into 165 acres (about 70 hectares)—smaller than many modern university campuses. The Parthians were the finest horsemen of the ancient world, and the cupbearer may well have recruited his five hundred cavalrymen himself. They included members of the highest-ranking families in Parthian society.[30]

The cavalrymen rode great warhorses. The men, to judge from ancient representations, had short beards, heavy mustaches, and long hair.[31] And they wore the Parthian horsemen's trademark trousers, rare in Mediterranean lands.

Pacorus's shoulders carried hundreds of years of history as the cupbearer rode into Jerusalem. For the first time in three centuries Iranians were back in the city that their ancestors had once ruled. The Parthian crown prince agreed to make Antigonus not just High Priest but king, thereby restoring the Jewish monarchy that Pompey had abolished. All that stood in the way of a new order in Judea was three men in the royal palace, Hyrcanus, Herod, and one of his brothers. Pacorus the Cupbearer offered to bring the three men to a high-ranking Parthian official in Syria to negotiate an end to the conflict. He guaranteed their safety. Hyrcanus and Herod's brother accepted the offer. Not Herod; the mother of his fiancée, a royal princess known for shrewdness, urged him to flee rather than trust a foreigner. She was right. The

Parthians imprisoned Herod's brother Phasael, who chose suicide rather than suffer torture. Hyrcanus had his ears mutilated by his nephew Antigonus, who ripped them with his own teeth, according to one version of the story. This disqualified Hyrcanus from the High Priesthood because the High Priest had to be physically perfect.[32]

Herod took his future mother-in-law's advice and left Jerusalem at night with armed loyalists and female family members. Parthian and Jewish forces went after them. After depositing his family members in safety, Herod got away, fighting and negotiating at every step. He probably cut an impressive figure. He was every inch a soldier, strong and athletic, and a good hunter, too. After a failed effort to get support from his mother's people in Petra, he turned westward.

Rome's Man in Jerusalem

Herod went first to Egypt. Queen Cleopatra received him warmly, because they had a common ally, Mark Antony. Antony was one of the triumvirs who ruled the Roman Republic. As the name suggests, triumvirs were three men, but only two of them mattered, Antony and Octavian. Both were connected to Rome's greatest general and late dictator, Julius Caesar, assassinated on the Ides of March, 44 BCE. Antony was Caesar's distant cousin and one of his chief lieutenants. Octavian was Caesar's grandnephew and designated heir. Antony ruled the eastern half of the Roman Empire and Octavian most of the West. Both men were ambitious and ruthless leaders. Antony was a better soldier, Octavian a more cunning strategist.[33]

Cleopatra, Antony, and Octavian each radiated charisma. Cleopatra was highly seductive but, to judge from coin images, more because of her charm than her looks. Her allure was magical. She had the dignity of an ancient royal family plus the wit and brilliance of a polymath. As queen she was a goddess on earth, but she was not above cracking a dirty joke or slumming at night in the poorer parts of town.[34] An audacious and cunning strategist, she won as lovers in turn the two most powerful men in the Roman world, Julius Caesar, allegedly the father of her eldest son, and Antony, who was her ally in love and war.

Herod had met Antony years earlier, when Antony fought in a Roman army sent to Judea to suppress a rebellion against the pro-Roman faction led by Herod's father. Herod impressed him enough to be named in due course "tetrarch," that is, ruler of Galilee.

Cleopatra coveted Judea. It had once been an Egyptian possession, in an earlier century, and she wanted it back. Aware of the queen's agenda, Herod accepted Cleopatra's hospitality, but left Egypt as quickly as possible. He took ship in midwinter, a dangerous season for sailing. After a rough journey, Herod reached Rome in late autumn 40 BCE.

Rome was the right place for Herod, and not just because of his family's connections there. Herod and the Romans had a culture in common, and that culture was Greek. Greek was not just the main language of the Roman East; it was the great language of ancient elite culture from Hispania to Mesopotamia. Roman nobles learned Greek the way Russian nobles in the tsarist era would learn French. Herod spoke Greek. His very name was Greek and came from the word *herōs*, "hero." Later, when he was in power, the Jew Herod surrounded himself with Greek intellectuals.

His mission in the capital was to see Antony. The ruler of the East was back in Italy to patch up differences with Octavian, with whom he had almost gone to war. Antony didn't waste time after hearing Herod's story. He decided then and there to make Herod not just tetrarch but king. On the face of it this was a nonstarter. Few Jews would accept a commoner and an Idumean on the throne. Others wanted no king at all, preferring rule by a council of priests and notables. The Roman Senate, for its part, liked to give the nod to a member of the reigning family, whenever the Senate had to approve a foreign king.[35]

Herod nevertheless served Rome's purposes. Precisely because he had so many enemies at home, he would depend on Rome; no danger of him turning to Parthia. As an old acquaintance of Herod, Antony felt that he knew the man. Octavian remembered Herod's father's support for Caesar. Both Romans found Herod's dynamism impressive. Octavian convened a meeting of the Senate, where, after various speeches, Antony sealed the deal. He put the case for Herod bluntly: he told the senators that "it was an advantage in their war against the Parthians for Herod to be king."[36] Judea was a problem; Herod was the solution. The Senate voted unanimously in favor of the motion.

Antony and Octavian walked out of the Senate House with Herod between them. The two consuls and Rome's public officials led a parade up to the Capitoline Hill nearby. There, the newly proclaimed king of the Jews took part in a sacrifice to the pagan deity, Jupiter, the chief god of Rome. A copy of the Senate's decree in favor of Herod was then deposited in the state archive.

To cap a day to be remembered, Antony gave a banquet in Herod's honor. It is doubtful that the cuisine was kosher. Never in history had a king of Israel been named in stranger circumstances.

A Throne, If You Can Keep It

Herod headed home and gathered an army to fight for his throne, but with Antigonus he faced an enemy who had the support of the Parthians and of most Jews, who considered Herod a usurper.

Fortunately for Herod, Antony and his generals launched a major effort to drive the Parthians back east beyond the Euphrates. The Roman counter-offensive inflicted defeat after defeat on the Parthians. Finally, in 38 BCE, they met the main Parthian force in northern Syria. They lured the Parthian cavalry into riding uphill. Roman heavy infantrymen and slingers drove the enemy back downhill and into confusion and disorder. Suddenly, Pacorus the Crown Prince himself fell in the thick of fighting. Some of his men tried to recover his body, but they, too, were killed. At that point, the rest of the Parthian army broke and ran. The victorious Romans sent a message to the various cities of Syria that had been playing a waiting game. That message was crude but clear: it was Prince Pacorus's severed head. The province now fell into line back behind Rome. As for Pacorus the Cupbearer, nothing more is known of him.[37]

At the same time, the Romans sent troops to help Herod, but they were poorly led and ill-motivated. Herod was made of sterner stuff: he defeated Antigonus in battle, but an insurgency quickly sprang up. For two years he fought a frustrating campaign up and down the country.

Outlaws and bandits roamed the countryside in these disordered times; at least Josephus refers to them as bandits: presumably some were insurgents and supporters of Antigonus. Herod faced a battle with the so-called bandits in Galilee. Herod subdued them. Antony gave Herod one of his most trusted generals to fight in Judea: Gaius Sosius, recently appointed governor of Syria and Cilicia.[38]

In autumn 38 BCE, Herod and Sosius set up their camp outside Jerusalem. In spring 37 BCE, they attacked the city in force. Antigonus and his troops defended the city vigorously, but they were no match for the combined forces of Herod and the Roman legions, who took the city after a siege of more than four months.

The victors went on a rampage, looting property and killing everyone in their path, whether soldier or civilian, male or female, young or old. The legionaries were eager to enter the Temple and its Holy of Holies, in imitation of Pompey's sacrilege. Herod asked Sosius to stop the slaughter, or Herod would be king of a desert. Sosius shot back, saying in effect that soldiers will be soldiers. Herod finally had to buy the Romans off, with payments to every soldier out of his own pocket. He made sure to give the officers extra and to hand over a king's ransom to Sosius, enough so that he could donate a golden crown in the Temple.

A defeated Antigonus threw himself at Sosius's feet, begging for mercy. Sosius laughed at Antigonus uproariously, called him a girl, "Antigone," put him in chains, imprisoned him, and shipped him off to Antony in Syria. Antony wanted to send Antigonus to Rome, but Herod sent a large bribe and convinced Antony to execute Antigonus.[39] Antony took the money and had Antigonus killed in a humiliating manner—the sources disagree about the details—that shocked public opinion.[40]

Herod settled another score once he had the throne. He had all the members of the Sanhedrin executed, no doubt in retaliation for the humiliation of having put him on trial for murder of the rebel Hezekiah. He spared Samias, who had criticized the trial and predicted Herod's rise to power and ultimate vengeance.

Sosius was permitted to celebrate a triumph in Rome in 34 BCE for his victory over Judea.

King of Judea

In 37 BCE, Herod had won the throne, but only by force and only with the help of his foreign patrons, especially Antony. Unfortunately for Herod, Antony would soon lose a bloody power struggle with Octavian—a civil war, in fact. The contest was decided at the Battle of Actium, a naval battle off the west coast of Greece in 31 BCE. Fortunately, Herod wasn't there. Cleopatra had sent him to fight the Nabatean Arabs, which provided a useful alibi when, in 30 BCE, Herod excused himself to the victorious Octavian. Alternating between groveling and priding himself on his value as a potential friend, Herod won Octavian's approval and kept his throne. Octavian was a realist and knew that Herod was the best man to keep Judea loyal to Rome. Shortly afterward, Antony and Cleopatra each took their own lives. Octavian was now the most powerful man in the Roman Empire. He was, in effect, Rome's first emperor, and became known as Augustus. Herod proved to be one of his most loyal supporters and was duly rewarded.

Rome gave Herod back most of the land that had been taken from Judea by Pompey. The result was a big kingdom with a complex ethnic mix. This is not surprising, because ancient states were rarely ethnically homogeneous. Judea consisted of Jews, Greeks, and Samaritans. Two Arab peoples also lived in Herod's Judea, Nabateans in the south and Itureans in the north.

There was little love lost among the various peoples under Herod's rule, especially between Greeks and Jews. Friction often prevailed between Jews and Samaritans, although the Samaritans loved the Romans no more than the Jews did. Like the Jews, the Samaritans accepted the Torah, but denied the supremacy of Jerusalem and had their own Temple. Animosities forced Herod into a balancing act that was bound to make him unpopular with some. Most of his Jewish subjects hated Herod and never accepted him as a legitimate king.[41] He was a commoner and an Idumean and was so loyal to Rome that he sent two of his sons there to be educated, eschewing a Jewish education in Jerusalem.

For the ruler of a small kingdom, Herod had a large army, an estimated 15,000 to 20,000 men. He needed it, both to suppress opposition at home and to prove his worth to Rome abroad. Most of Herod's soldiers were infantry, but there were some cavalrymen as well. Herod was first and foremost a military leader. The army's job was to hold his kingdom together, deter internal resistance, and offer the Romans a strong and reliable ally. Most of his troops were Jews, many of them Idumeans. The army also included Greeks and Syrians, as well as Nabatean mercenaries. His bodyguard consisted of foreign mercenaries: Celts, Germans, and Thracians. Some of Herod's commanders were Romans or at least Italians. They surely enabled certain Roman features in Herod's army such as Roman-style marching camps and siegecraft. Herod built a series of fortresses around the kingdom, including in Jerusalem. Their purpose, to paraphrase a Greek assessment of Macedonian garrisons in central and southern Greece, was to serve as "the shackles of Judea."[42]

The Fighting Jews of Babylon

To defend the road that led from Judea to Babylon, Herod selected a battalion of Babylonian Jewish cavalrymen. It was a good choice. In fact, the unit was so effective that it was eventually absorbed into the Roman army.[43] But it originated in the Parthian empire. Jewish communities were prominent in that empire; indeed, Jews had lived in Mesopotamia for centuries when the

Parthians conquered the region in the second century BCE. Jewish farmers, shepherds, merchants, sages, and scholars lived in Mesopotamia, especially in the southern part, known as Babylonia. Parthian Jews paid the temple tax to Jerusalem, and Parthian Jewish pilgrims visited the Holy City.[44]

Mesopotamian Jews had a reputation in antiquity for military expertise. They included men who were risk-takers and enthusiastically joined in battle.[45] Babylonian Jews knew how to fight, a skill they used both in the service of Rome and in deadly opposition to it.

The Builder

No king of Israel had ever built on a grander scale than Herod. He reshaped the architecture and economy of his country from top to bottom, and he proved to be a major funder of construction projects abroad as well. Building takes money, and Herod was rich. His wealth came from landholdings, taxes, profits on natural resources, and corruption.[46]

Herod's construction projects fit under three rubrics: Roman, Greek, and Jewish. Roman, first. In part to show that he was a faithful ally, in part for his own glory, Herod rebuilt much of his own kingdom in the Roman manner. He focused his Romanizing projects outside the majority-Jewish parts of his realm.

Rome was eager to spread the cult of Augustus around the empire. Worshipping the emperor as a god offended Jews, but pagan elites embraced it as a way of winning the empire's favor. In the East, those elites had to get in line behind Herod.

Herod built three temples to Augustus. In the hill country north of Jerusalem, he rebuilt the ancient city of Samaria as Sebaste—Greek for Augusta. A Temple of Augustus dominated the site from a hilltop. Farther north, in the foothills of Mount Hermon, close to the current Israeli-Lebanon border, Herod built another Temple of Augustus in what Josephus calls beautiful white marble. It stood on the ancient road to Damascus, which in turn led to Mesopotamia. Jewish pilgrims to Jerusalem, coming from Parthian lands, would have passed by this shrine to Augustus.[47]

Herod's third Augustus temple stood on the central coast, where he turned a small Phoenician trading post into a major port. Caesarea Maritima, or Caesarea-by-the-Sea, rivaled the harbors of Athens and Alexandria as a trading center of the Eastern Mediterranean. The earlier Phoenician city lacked a good harbor; in fact, there were no harbors facing favorable winds on the kingdom's coast. Herod solved the problem by having his engineers sink a mixture of cement and stones to build breakwaters around an enormous double harbor. A set of quays and warehouses completed the infrastructure of the port. Nearby, the Temple of Augustus overlooked the town from a high podium. The city also boasted several other pagan temples. Caesarea's urban infrastructure was Roman, from its baths to its aqueduct and theater. An amphitheater housed gladiatorial games. There was also a royal palace. The population was mostly Greek; Jews were a minority. Every four years Caesarea hosted the Actian Games, in honor of Augustus's victory at the Battle of Actium. On the coast south of Caesarea, near Gaza, Herod renamed a city after Augustus's closest adviser, Marcus Vipsanius Agrippa.[48]

Herod also endowed temples, dockyards, gymnasia, theaters, baths, fountains, and colonnades all over the Greek-speaking cities of the Eastern Mediterranean. He gave funding to the financially strapped Olympic Games in Greece. His contribution was big enough to have Herod elected permanent president of the Olympics, an honor that he was able to enjoy in person when he attended the games in 12 BCE.

Building pagan temples in the Holy Land offended pious Jewish opinion, but Herod also defended Jewish rights. In fact, he emerged as a champion of Jews in the Diaspora. He intervened with Augustus, for instance, to protect the rights of Jews in Asia Minor.

Herod didn't dare build a Temple of Augustus in Jerusalem, but he did build a theater—location unknown—as well as a hippodrome that doubled as an amphitheater, outside the city walls. As in Caesarea, so in Jerusalem Herod held quadrennial games in honor of Augustus. In addition to sporting events, musical competitions, and chariot races, the games featured lions and other wild animals brought in from abroad at great expense. The animals fought each other as well as condemned criminals. Gold and silver trophies celebrating Augustus's victories were mounted on the walls.[49]

Many Jews were outraged, especially by the throwing of men to the beasts and the trophies, which appeared to them to be graven images. The public considered gladiatorial games to be a clear violation of Jewish law and custom, as Josephus reports.[50] The Talmud states that "One who sits in a stadium is a shedder of blood," adding that it is forbidden to sell bears and lions for use in the arena.[51] The Talmud, a collection of legal opinions, stories, and traditions, is a foundational text for later Judaism. It was compiled in late antiquity.

So aroused was Jewish opinion that an assassination plot was formed. Ten Jerusalemites with daggers hidden under their cloaks planned to kill Herod while he was attending the theater. One of his spies discovered the plot, however, and the men were seized with their daggers. Defiant, they said they were ready to die to preserve the laws of the Jews. Herod had them tortured and executed. But the people found Herod's spy, seized him, killed him, tore him limb from limb, and fed the pieces to the dogs. There were many witnesses, but they refused to hand over the killers until Herod had some women tortured and they confessed. He then had the perpetrators and their entire families executed. Yet Herod still felt insecure. Knowing how much opposition he faced, he redoubled his efforts to dot the country with fortresses in case of rebellion.[52]

Herod repaired and rebuilt Jerusalem's existing walls and added a new wall that extended the city to the north. He built himself a sumptuous palace whose two wings were named after Augustus and Agrippa. The palace was surrounded by walls that made it a virtual fortress. The mansions of the wealthy stood nearby.

Herod's most notable building project was reconstructing the central shrine of the Jewish people, the Temple. He began the undertaking around 19 BCE. Josephus says that the king thought that the structure would make his name live forever.[53]

The prior sanctuary, over which the new Temple was built, was showing the signs of age. It was old, small, and humble. Herod wanted to replace it with a structure that was nothing less than magnificent. The Talmud says that "One who has not seen Herod's building has never seen a beautiful building in his life."[54] Herod was careful to put the building process in the hands of the priests. Although the Talmud considers Herod to have been generally wicked, it approves of his rebuilding the Temple.[55]

The Temple was the central part of a compound consisting of walls, gates, courts, and porticoes, all erected on a massive platform overlooking the city. The Temple stood in an enclosure. The outer court was the Court of the Gentiles. Only Jews could go beyond it to the Court of the Women, then the Court of the Israelites, and finally the Court of the Priests. Sacrifices took place on an altar in this latter court.

As for the Temple itself, Josephus says that the front of the sanctuary was gilded and "cast a fiery light" in the morning sun. He adds that from a distance, the building's white marble looked like a mountain covered with snow.[56] Enormous doors, draped by multicolored tapestries, led inward. Above them hung a golden vine with a larger-than-life-size bunch of grapes.

The Temple building consisted of three parts. The main chamber housed an altar for incense and a golden menorah, a seven-branched candlestick. There was also a table for the showbread, that is, the twelve loaves symbolizing the Twelve Tribes of Israel and the support and nourishment that God gave the Jewish people. The loaves were placed there on the Sabbath and eaten during the week by the priests. Finally, beyond a veil of embroidered Babylonian linen, another set of doors led to the inviolable Holy of Holies.

The Temple building was completed within seventeen months. Herod dedicated it with a ceremony capped by the sacrifice of three hundred oxen. But the Temple was just part—the most important part—of the vast complex that Herod had in mind. So ambitious was Herod's plan that it took eighty years to complete or, rather, to come near to completing it. It was never finished.

The Temple stood on the Temple Mount, a square-shaped hill, which Herod expanded and supported with a retaining wall, whose monumental stones are still visible. The Temple precinct was surrounded by porticoes. On the south side, the largest portico consisted of 162 columns with Corinthian capitals. Known as the Royal Portico, it served as a center for the sale of items for sacrifice.

Herod did not forget to honor his Roman patrons even in this most Jewish of sites. He had Agrippa's name engraved on the Temple gate. Herod couldn't build a shrine to Augustus on the Temple Mount, but he came up with an ingenious alternative: daily sacrifices at the Temple on behalf of the emperor. Augustus showed his approval by funding them out of his own purse.[57]

Under Herod and his successors, Jerusalem reached the peak of its prosperity. The city grew to a size that it would not attain again until the nineteenth century.[58] The Temple pulled in contributions from east and west. Jews from both the Roman and Parthian empires contributed an annual half-shekel tax to the Temple. Foreign visitors, whether Jew or Gentile, often left gifts, sometimes lavish ones.[59]

The Temple supported a large population of priests and their assistants (Levites), as well as administrators, provisioners, and builders. A large infrastructure was needed to service the pilgrims, who took part in annual festivals and saw the sights. Jews from Italy and Mesopotamia, from Alexandria and Antioch, from Libya and Assyria all poured in. Jerusalem, said the Roman writer Pliny the Elder, was "by far the most famous city of the East and not just of Judea."[60] Exaggeration, perhaps, in a region that also included Athens, Alexandria, and Antioch, but with its massive walls, its palaces, its pilgrims, and the ancient world's largest temple complex, Jerusalem was indeed famous.

An Insurrection to Avenge God's Honor

In his last years Herod suffered a putrefying illness in which parts of his body began to rot and give off a stench. The pain was so severe that he had to be stopped from taking his life. The sages said that Herod's illness was divine punishment for his misdeeds.

With the news of Herod's condition, many Jews took heart. They loathed the king, as an incident in late winter 4 BCE showed. Herod had installed a golden eagle above the Temple gate, which infuriated many Jews both as a sacrilege and as a symbol of Rome. Jewish law forbade graven images. Two Jewish sages ordered their students to tear down the hated eagle.[61] The sages were Pharisees and renowned Torah scholars. Josephus says that they attracted "an army of young men in their prime" to their daily lectures. When the sages heard that Herod was dying, they suggested to their pupils that it was the right time to "avenge God's honor and to pull down the structures that had been erected against the laws of their fathers."[62] They admitted that the deed was risky, but said that only the ignoble, those who were ignorant of the sages' teaching, would fear death.

When a rumor arose that the king was dead, the students turned to the task at hand. Presumably just a small number of youths carried out the mission. The young men climbed up to the roof of the Temple gate in broad daylight, before a large crowd. Then they rappelled down and hewed the eagle with hatchets. But Herod was not dead. He sent an officer with enough soldiers to control the crowd. Most of the onlookers fled, but forty men stayed to support the perpetrators. They were all arrested.

The arrestees were brought before Herod. They confessed their guilt. The king asked them why they had done the deed. They replied, defiantly, that they were obeying the law of their fathers. They also said that they were not afraid to die, since they were confident that they would enjoy many good things after their death. The Pharisees, it should be noted, believed in resurrection.

A furious Herod had all the offenders bound and carted off to Jericho, presumably because they would find fewer supporters there than in the feverishly religious atmosphere of Jerusalem. The king summoned the Jewish officials to a public assembly in the Jericho amphitheater. Herod wasn't well enough to stand, so he lay on a couch. After justifying himself and his record of rebuilding the Temple, Herod demanded that the officials agree that the arrestees had committed sacrilege and needed to be punished. In fear of their own lives, the officials agreed.

Herod now took his revenge. He had the men who had cut down the eagles and their two teachers burned alive as punishment. There was an eclipse of the moon that night, which allows the event to be dated precisely: it was March 13, 4 BCE. Herod handed the others over to his executioners for a less gruesome death. Finally, for good measure, Herod deposed the High Priest, on the grounds that he shared some of the blame for what happened.

The incident of the eagle demonstrated the strength of the spirit of rebellion against Rome and its enabler, Herod. It also shows how fine the line was between religion and politics in Jerusalem. It wasn't professional revolutionaries who stirred up the young rebels: it was two sages, renowned for their knowledge of Jewish law. It also demonstrates the willingness of Herod to repress rebellion brutally, at the end of his career as at the beginning. But men who were willing to die for the honor of God would not be easy to put down, nor would they lack successors.

Herod is famously accused of another atrocity. According to the Gospel of Matthew, Herod heard that the King of the Jews had been born in Bethlehem.[63] He commanded the killing of all boys two years old and younger in and around Bethlehem. Christianity refers to this as the Massacre of the Innocents. If indeed it happened, it probably took place near the very end of Herod's life. Most scholars doubt the historicity of the story because it appears in no other source. Still, its brutality and paranoia are consistent with Herod's character.

Seeing the end coming, Herod feared that the country would celebrate his death. To make sure that Judea resounded with the sound of mourning instead, he had the leading men of the country rounded up and imprisoned in the hippodrome at Jericho. He ordered that all the prisoners be immediately executed upon the news of his death. Herod died just before Passover, probably in 4 BCE. His sister gave the order, no doubt to mass relief, that the prisoners be freed. So much for Herod's diabolical plan.

Balance Sheet

Many people shaped the fate of Judea in the six decades between 63 and 4 BCE, but three men stand out: Pompey, Pacorus, and Herod. If Pompey and Pacorus each represented an extreme in the history of Judea—a stripped-down, chastened Roman client state under Pompey's iron hand; a revived Iranian vassal kingdom under Pacorus—Herod represented a new departure altogether. He would make Judea Roman and make Rome, if not quite Jewish, then at least friendlier to the Jews than ever before. He would champion Jewish, Greek, and Roman culture at home and abroad.

Herod found a way for Judea to flourish under the Roman Empire and for Jews and Gentiles alike to live in peace and prosperity in his kingdom. He would engage in a balancing act, one that was deeply unpopular with hotheads and fanatics of various stripes, but Herod kept them under control because he was, to be blunt, a tyrant. And often a murderous one as well, vicious to his own family, several of whom he ordered killed. He was one of the most creative and terrible leaders in his nation's history.

Herod made Judea an integral part of the Roman Empire. Josephus claims that Augustus considered Herod second in importance only to his loyal general Agrippa, and Agrippa considered Herod second only to Augustus.[64] As one historian puts it, "The kingdom of Herod in Judea was a jewel in the crown of Augustus's Roman revolution."[65]

Herod is often called Herod the Great, and not without reason, but it is not known if he was called the Great in his lifetime, as some other ancient kings and statesmen were. Herod made himself indispensable. He convinced Rome that he was the only man who could maintain peace in a strategic area. Judea was the hinge between the two golden doors of the Roman East, the two provinces of Syria and Egypt. Herod was the guardian of the eastern marches, Rome's local ally who could help the legions keep the Parthians out and the empire safe. And Rome did not discount the Parthian threat, even after a peace agreement in 20 BCE, which Herod helped to negotiate. The northern cities of Roman Syria lay close to the Euphrates River border, within easy striking distance of Parthia's armies.

Herod's countrymen cheered his death. Herod had struck an uneasy balance and it started to fall apart as soon as he was gone. Herod wanted the Jews to be good Romans. Providence had other plans in mind. Far from being Rome's best friend, Judea would become the empire's most rebellious province.[66]

Chapter Two

THE WAR FOR HEROD'S LEGACY

Herod had made a fatal error. He forgot the most important feature of a dynasty: succession. He killed his most talented and promising heirs because he found them threatening. Shortly before his death in 4 BCE, Herod turned on the forty-year-old son whom he had planned to name as heir after executing two older sons. Herod accused him of plotting a rebellion, which, in his bloodthirsty family, was entirely plausible. Herod had him killed only five days before Herod himself died. That left three sons, among whom Herod decided to divide his kingdom. The son who received the main part of the kingdom, consisting of Judah and Samaria, was the nineteen-year-old Archelaus. He was not merely young, but incompetent. Herod's mistake proved disastrous to the kingdom.

Succession

Herod gave Galilee and the Perea to another son, Antipas, and Gaulanitis and other nearby northern regions to a third son, Philip. Herod also left three small territories to his sister, as well as money and revenues to his other relatives.

Always alert to the power of Rome, he left a fortune to Augustus and about half that amount to Augustus's wife, Livia. Herod knew that Augustus had the final say over the succession in Judea.

Archelaus started off on the wrong foot: he broke the laws of power. If one is wise, a new ruler starts out by laying down the law and being harsh to one's enemies; concessions can come later, once authority is secure. Instead, Archelaus began by making concessions, including tax reductions and the release of prisoners. He also gave in to protesters by agreeing to replace the High Priest. They opposed the man because he was Herod's appointee and because they considered him insufficiently pure or pious.

In principle, the High Priest was supposed to be a descendant of Zadok, appointed by King Solomon when he built the First Temple. The Hasmoneans broke the rule because they served as High Priests, but were not of Zadokite descent. In the eyes of the pious, that was bad enough, but Herod had made things worse by appointing non-Hasmoneans and various men who came from outside Jerusalem and its priestly elite. Critics said they had no better qualifications than loyalty to Herod.

Archelaus's concessions demonstrated weakness, which inspired revolt. That in turn forced Archelaus to be not merely tough but cruel, a dangerous policy for a new ruler, and sure to arouse additional revolt.

Herod's army acclaimed Archelaus, but many people dissented. Some hated him because his mother was a Samaritan. Some demanded vengeance on the killers of the men who had removed the golden eagle from the Temple. Some objected to the dynasty's choice of High Priests. Some didn't want any king at all. And some despised the way Herod and his family bowed to the Romans. At Passover, when worshippers crowded into Jerusalem, they vented their anger. They rioted violently in the Temple. Archelaus sent his cavalry against them, and when it was over, three thousand people were dead. Having unleashed a massacre, Archelaus then departed for Rome to seek Augustus's approval to his kingship. But he had to oppose his brother Antipas, who followed him to Rome and made his own case to be king. If Augustus had reason to hesitate about Archelaus, it increased when he received a letter from the legate, that is, governor of Syria, Publius Quinctilius Varus. As the Roman official in charge of the province next door to quasi-independent Judea, Varus could not tolerate disorder there, especially with no king in charge.

Varus came from a patrician family. His people claimed to be one of Rome's most ancient and noblest clans, but they had fallen on hard times. Varus reversed their fortunes. He chose wisely during Rome's civil wars and supported Augustus, and afterward he rose steadily up the ladder. One indicator is his advantageous marriages to first one and then another woman in Augustus's extended family, marriages that surely required the emperor's approval. Another is Varus's public career, which began probably in 23 BCE when on a trip to the East he served as Augustus's quaestor (roughly, quartermaster).

In 13 BCE, Varus held the consulship with Tiberius, Augustus's stepson and eventual successor. In 7 to 6 BCE, Varus was made governor of Roman Africa (roughly, modern Tunisia), a wealthy province, but not a security challenge. Then came an even more responsible assignment: governing Syria, which was both wealthy and on the front lines. Syria bordered the Parthian Empire, which is why it was staffed under Augustus by three legions—that is, a little more than one-tenth of the empire's legionary manpower.

Varus's letter to Augustus announced that the rebellion had spread in Archelaus's absence. The details are unknown, but the trouble was enough to galvanize Varus into action. He marched into Judea with all three of Syria's legions, a force of 15,000 to 18,000 men. That the governor of Syria would leave his province bare of legions underscores the seriousness of the revolt in Judea. Varus put down the revolt and left one legion in Jerusalem to stop any further outbreaks. They were 5,000 to 6,000 men, with 3,000 Herodian troops to support them. They would soon have a fight on their hands. The war is referred to in a later Jewish source as the "war of Varus."[1]

The problem was the financial administrator (procurator) of Syria, one Sabinus. In theory he was Varus's subordinate, but in practice, he had his own agenda, and he was out of control. He was, frankly, eager to loot Judea. He harassed the rebels in Jerusalem, and their supporters responded with a show of strength.

Seven weeks after Passover came the third great annual pilgrimage festival, Shavuot (Weeks). Crowds came up to Jerusalem again and continued the struggle. Jews from all over the country came to fight, especially from the central region of Judah. Battles raged in both the Temple precinct and outside the royal palace. Sabinus's men burned down the Temple porticoes and killed large numbers of rebels there. They also looted the Temple treasury. In turn, the Jews regrouped and laid siege to Sabinus and his forces in the palace. Most of Herod's former troops had joined the rebels, but three thousand elite soldiers from Samaria, as well as a cavalry force, supported the Romans. Still, the Romans were unable to break out. The insurgents offered the Romans a safe conduct to leave Jerusalem, but Sabinus didn't trust them. He preferred to wait for help from Varus.

Messiahs and Crosses

The rebellion spread. Herod's former forces were divided. In general, his Jewish soldiers went over to the rebels, while his Gentile troops sustained Archelaus. The latter group included the most elite fighters.[2] In the Judean plain, two thousand royal troops, led by a cousin of Herod, supported the rebels, but Archelaus's troops forced them into the hills. Now a series of pretenders to the throne sprang up. One was Judah son of Hezekiah, the guerrilla raider who had been executed by Herod many years earlier. Judah and his followers gathered a large force and seized the royal armory in Sepphoris, the main city in Galilee. After arming all his men, he began looting the countryside. Josephus says that Judah was "eager for royal rank."[3]

A second pretender was Simon of Perea, a strong and handsome slave of Herod. He was bold enough to place the diadem on his head and to gather a band of followers who called him king. They burned and plundered in the Jordan Valley before a Roman force defeated them in battle and beheaded Simon. The third pretender was Athronges, a very tall and robust shepherd. He, too, wore the diadem and called himself king. He gathered a force that raided and plundered Judea. At one point they surrounded a Roman century (*centuria*), the basic unit of the Roman legion, and killed forty men including the centurion. At full strength, a century (despite its name) comprised eighty men.

As Josephus tells it, the would-be kings were motivated by greed and ambition. But Josephus wanted to depict Jewish rebels against Rome as mere brigands and despots who led the people astray. "Judea was filled with *lēstērion*," he writes, ". . . causing trouble to few Romans and then only to a small degree but bringing the greatest slaughter upon their own people."[4] The Greek word *lēstērion* is often translated as "brigandage" or "banditry," but Josephus usually uses it to refer to a terrorist, guerrilla, or, depending on one's point of view, a resistance fighter.[5]

How did their contemporaries see Judah son of Hezekiah, Simon of Perea, and Athronges the shepherd? Possibly each man's supporters saw him as the messiah. This may sound outlandish, and from a later Jewish or Christian perspective, it was. But "messiah" originally meant a king. "Messiah" comes from the Hebrew word *mashiach*, meaning literally, "anointed," that is, anointed with oil, the symbol of entering office for a priest or king. Later, after the death of Jesus, Christians concluded that the Messiah was divine. But Jews considered the messiah to be just a man, if an inspired one.

The idea of a messiah played a central role in much of Jewish apocalyptic thought. And the apocalypse was not far from the thinking of many Jews in this era. There were even some who considered Herod to be the messiah. One or more of the bandit kings whom Josephus described may have been greeted as messiahs, too.[6] Josephus doesn't call them that, but he had reasons not to. First, he despised them. Second, he saw it as his mission to translate Hebrew/Aramaic concepts into terms that made sense to Greek speakers living under Roman rule.[7] When referring to Jews who had claimed the kingship, Josephus uses phrases like "presumed upon the kingship" and "wearers of the diadem" as well as the pejorative "bandits" and "tyrants."[8] In Judea in 4 BCE, people might have seen things differently.

As soon as Varus got the news that his men were under siege in Jerusalem, he hurried to the rescue. He augmented Syria's two legions with cavalry and additional infantry including an allied force of Nabatean Arabs. After gathering his troops he sent some under his son and a close adviser to fight in Galilee; they captured and burned Sepphoris, which had supported Judah son of Hezekiah. The Romans enslaved the survivors. There is reason to think that Judah survived and escaped.

Varus himself went to Sebaste in Samaria, but spared the city because it hadn't joined the revolt. After Varus and his allies burned several settlements on the edge of the Judean Hills, they headed for Jerusalem. The Jewish force besieging the legion in the city fled at the sight of his troops, leaving their siegework half finished. Jewish inhabitants of Jerusalem made excuses to Varus, blaming the revolt on the influx of outsiders. Leaders of both the Roman forces and their Jewish allies came out of the city to meet with Varus. But not Sabinus; he fled to the coast; his later fate is unknown. It was said that he had looted four hundred talents of silver.

It was time to settle scores. Varus sent part of his army through the country to find those most responsible for the revolt. Although he pardoned some, he punished others with *damnatio in crucem*, "sentencing to the cross." Crucifixion was the standard Roman punishment for rebels. Roman crucifixion normally consisted of three elements: scourging, carrying of the cross by the condemned, and lifting. The victims carried only the crossbar; the upright stake had already been set in the ground. When the condemned person reached the assigned stake, the executioners hoisted him into place via a ladder and poles.

All the condemned suffered cruelly, but experiences on the cross varied. Depending on how the victim was affixed to the cross, he might have suffocated within minutes or survived in agony for days. The sources make clear that the crucified could linger: they record cases of men talking from the cross, making legal contracts from the cross, and being cut down and spared after a bribe to the officer on guard. Some victims were displayed with special grotesqueness, to mock them, and some were crucified upside down. Some of the condemned were tied to the cross by rope, while others were nailed to it.

Archaeologists have found the bones of one crucifixion victim in Israel, dated to the first century CE. Possibly named Yehohanan, his feet were nailed to the cross, but his arms seem to have been tied to the crossbar by rope. The victim was twenty-four years old and stood approximately five feet, five inches tall. Yehohanan's right anklebone still has a nail and piece of wood attached to it.[9]

All told, Varus crucified two thousand people: a significant number, if hardly the largest mass crucifixion in antiquity. In a more diplomatic vein, he allowed another delegation from Judea to sail to Rome. The mission was made up of fifty men. Augustus received them in the Temple of Apollo on the Palatine Hill, a structure that he had built at his own expense to thank his patron god for his victory over Antony at Actium. The emperor was surrounded by his advisers. The delegates from Judea had the support of eight thousand men from the Jewish community in Rome, who presumably gathered outside the temple.

The fifty men from Judea decried the crimes of Herod and of Archelaus against the people of Judea. They requested that the monarchy be abolished, and that Judea be annexed by Rome. This they called "autonomy," but it did not entail independence. They wanted government by priests and elders in Jerusalem, under the loose supervision of the Roman governor in Syria. It was a throwback to the days of Pompey, who in 63 BCE had considered a similar plea from an earlier delegation of Jewish notables. In both cases power would be returned to the priestly elite of Jerusalem, groups that Herod and Archelaus had often bypassed.

Like Pompey, Augustus turned the request down. New territory for the empire was surely tempting, but not if it meant the expense of garrisoning it with a legion—or three legions—and the risk of having Roman soldiers put down revolts. Better to give Herod's son a chance to govern Judea for Rome, so long as he was kept on a tight leash. Augustus chose Archelaus, but he denied him the title of king, making him settle for "ethnarch," or "provincial leader." The emperor held out the possibility of naming Archelaus king one day if he proved up to the job. Each of his two brothers was named tetrarch, or ruler of one-quarter of the country—a lesser title.

Femme Fatale

The explosive events of 4 BCE show that Judea was a nation whose spirit had not been crushed by Herod or by Rome. The Jews still loved liberty and they still had fighting spirit in abundance. What they lacked was the unity, the numbers, or the discipline to defeat the legions, especially when the legions were led by an able commander like Varus. His speed and brutality were a model of Roman imperialism at its most efficient.

Archelaus was brutal, too, but also tyrannical and scandalous in his private life. At issue was his wife, Glaphyra. She was one of those royal women of the Caesars and the Herodians who, even making allowances for the sexist biases and tabloid tendencies of the ancient writers, still startle with their operatic drama. She was a much-married princess from the East. She carried the genes of three nations—Greek, Armenian, and Persian—and she married into two others, Jewish and Berber (a North African people). Glaphyra means "elegant" in Greek, and that she surely was, being descended from priests, courtesans, princesses, and kings.

The family was no stranger to scandal, nor were the families that she married into. Her father was the king of a Roman client state in Asia Minor. Her grandmother, also named Glaphyra, was rumored to have had an affair with Mark Antony. Octavian himself had helped to spread the rumor by writing a dirty poem about the alleged liaison. It begins with the words: "Because Antony f—ks Glaphyra. . . ."[10] Long before ending up with Archelaus, Glaphyra had married his older brother, Alexander, a son of King Herod.

The young bride entered a hothouse in Herod's court. Alexander and Herod were at each other's throats, as were Glaphyra and Herod's sister. Things escalated, sending Glaphyra's father to Judea to talk Herod out of his murderous anger at his son. His mission succeeded and Herod sent the king home laden with gifts, including a courtesan named "All Night Long." But family peace did not last. Herod again became suspicious of Alexander and had Alexander executed. He sent Glaphyra with her dowry back to her father's house in Asia Minor. To smooth relations with Glaphyra's father, Herod even paid the dowry out of his own purse.

Glaphyra did not stay widowed for long. She married King Juba II of Mauretania, a widower himself. His first wife had been the daughter of Antony and Cleopatra. She was, it seems, a hard act to follow: Juba and Glaphyra divorced.

Glaphyra returned to her father's house in Asia Minor a second time. There, a visiting Archelaus saw her and was smitten by his former sister-in-law. He divorced his wife and married Glaphyra. She returned to the palace in Judea, where the story goes that she dreamed that her first husband, Alexander, came to her and promised to punish her insolence in marrying his brother. She is supposed to have told the dream to her female friends and, a few days later, she was dead.

Glaphyra's death did nothing to lessen public outrage at Archelaus's matrimony. According to Jewish law, marriage to a dead brother's widow was incestuous if the first marriage had produced children. Indeed, there had been three children: two sons and a daughter. In addition to being brutal and weak, Archelaus was now branded as incestuous. The men who mattered in his country had reached the limit of their patience for the ethnarch.

Soon a deputation of notables from Judah and Samaria lobbied Augustus to dismiss Archelaus. Augustus summoned him to Rome to defend himself, but the ethnarch failed to convince the emperor. Archelaus was removed from office. He had his property confiscated, and he was packed off into exile.

Archelaus lived out his days in Roman Vienna (modern Vienne, France—not Vienna, Austria) in the upper valley of the Rhodanus (Rhône) River. Vienna lay in the former territory of the Allobroges, a Gallic tribe once known for their ferocity, but now undergoing the process of Romanization. Vienna-on-the-Rhodanus no doubt had its charms, but it was a big step down from the palaces of Caesarea and Jerusalem.

The demotion of Archelaus showed that Rome had failed to find a local partner in the province that had been closest to the new, imperial regime. Augustus and Herod had been as tight as any emperor and native king could be. If Rome couldn't make the client-king system work in Judea, could it work anywhere?

Two of Herod the Great's sons continued to rule as tetrarchs: Philip over Gaulanitis and parts of southern Syria, Antipas in the Galilee and Perea. But Archelaus's former kingdom, made up of three regions—Judah, Samaria, and Idumea—was now a Roman possession. Technically, it was not a province but, rather, a region of Roman Syria, which was a province. A governor, or prefect, as he was known then, sat in Herod's former palace in Caesarea.[11] When the governor visited Jerusalem, as he did from time to time, he stayed in Herod's palace there as well. The prefect of Judea was chosen from the second-highest property class in Rome, the equestrians or knights. He was loosely subordinate to the governor of Syria, a senator—the highest class in Roman society—who had the title of legate. Syria had legions, that is, elite soldiers and Roman citizens; Judea had only auxiliaries, locally recruited troops, mostly Samaritans, who were not as effective as legionaries.

Augustus in the year 6 CE gave the fifty notables of Judah and Samaria what they had asked for ten years earlier. They were now governed by a Roman administrator. Although the prefect chose the High Priest in Jerusalem, the Romans gave the High Priest and the other priests a fair amount of freedom to run the country as they wished. In turn, the priests collaborated with the Romans and kept a keen eye out for sedition. They saw it as their job to maintain the peace.

In one sense, the new arrangements in Judea fit a standard model of Roman provincial rule. The wealthy aristocrats of the province would serve loyally under a Roman governor. From time to time, they would do the governor's dirty work for him. The unusual thing about Judea was that many of the notables were priests. Unlike the elites of many of Rome's provinces, they had little interest in funding public buildings, much less in military service. As one historian points out, that made Judea hard for Romans to understand.[12] Romans had little tolerance for other cultures and little interest in seeing things through foreign eyes. They wanted the natives to be tax-paying, orderly, and loyal. They counted on their local collaborators to help achieve those goals. And they didn't hesitate to punish those collaborators if they failed.

The Romans had no wish to interfere with the Jewish religion as long as that religion stayed clear of politics in turn. A big if. As it turned out, the response to the new system was a religiously inspired rebellion. The proximate cause was money, but the underlying cause was independence. It turned out that many Judeans, unlike the priests, found the thought of Roman rule unbearable.

The Year 6 CE: Another Rebellion

As a Roman possession, Judea was now liable to pay taxes to the emperor. The first step was doing that characteristically Roman thing: taking a census. The first prefect of Judea was one Coponius, a Roman knight who administered the province from 6 to 9 CE. But instead of Coponius, Augustus put the legate of Syria, Publius Sulpicius Quirinius, in charge of the census in both Syria and Judea.

Quirinius was a success story. First in his family to become a senator, he rose to the high office of consul. As a provincial administrator he put down insurgencies in North Africa and Asia Minor. He won the confidence of Augustus, who had enough faith in Quirinius to appoint him as supervisor of his grandson, Augustus's virtual heir apparent, when the young man went on a mission to the East in 2 BCE. Now he entrusted Quirinius with conducting the census in Judea. To do so, Quirinius visited Judea in person. He understood the sensitivity of the census, as it signaled the loss of independence to Rome. Presumably Judeans had paid taxes to Herod and Archelaus before, but paying them to a foreign ruler was different.

The Gospels place Quirinius's census and Jesus's birth during the reign of Herod. That is chronologically impossible, but chronology is not the strong suit of religious texts. Scholars place the birth of Jesus around 4 BCE, before Herod's death that year, while the census took place ten years later. Still, the conflation of the two events in the Gospels is a recognition of how important the census was in the history of Judea.

Josephus considered the census a major turning point. There was general discontent about the taxes until the High Priest convinced people to pay. Then a rebel leader appeared. He was Judah the Galilean. Josephus describes Judah as the leader of a sect. He had the support of a Pharisee named Zadok. They maintained that the census amounted to slavery. Judah said that only cowards would pay taxes to the Romans, because a Jew should recognize no master but God.[13] According to Josephus, Judah and Zadok did nothing less than start a new sect, which he calls a "Fourth Philosophy," after the three "philosophies" of the Sadducees, Pharisees, and Essenes. What he calls "philosophy" we would call a "sect."[14]

Josephus describes the new sect thus: "This school agrees in all other respects with the opinions of the Pharisees, except that they have a passion for liberty that is almost unconquerable, since they are convinced that God alone is their leader and master."[15]

Josephus calls Judah *sophistēs*, "sophist." This Greek word had a negative connotation and was often used against a thought leader one disagreed with. But the basic meaning of the word is neutral: it can refer to a wise man, a sage, or a teacher. In the first century CE Jewish context, it meant scholar.

For all Josephus's talk of novelty, the Hebrew Bible already was suspicious of kings and especially of foreign kings. Be that as it may, Josephus doesn't want to emphasize that, because his goal was to portray the Jews as good citizens of the Roman Empire, who had regrettably been led astray by a few extremists and criminals. Diaspora Jews surely were good citizens, at least until they were subjected to humiliation by Rome following the Great Revolt. In Judea things were different; there, Jews were divided. Some were content to collaborate with Rome, a great empire and a brutal one when crossed. Some just wanted to stay out of trouble. And some had a passionate, militant love of liberty.

Many scholars identify Judah the Galilean with Judah son of Hezekiah, who revolted against Archelaus in 4 BCE. If so, Judah had changed his tune. The first Judah aspired to be king, but Judah the Galilean said that God alone was king.

Many people responded to the call of Judah and Zadok, with lasting consequences. "When they had won an abundance of devotees," writes Josephus, "they filled the body politic immediately with tumult, also planting the seeds of those troubles which subsequently overtook it."[16] Judah and Zadok urged the Jews not to shrink from bloodshed, and they found followers, particularly among the youth. "People heard what they said with pleasure," writes the historian.[17] It is said that they persuaded no small number of Jews to refuse to register for the census.[18] The result was a revolt waged via an insurgency.[19] The uprising was suppressed, and Judah was killed.[20] His legacy lived on. Josephus calls his successors by the Roman name *sicarii*, Latin for "Dagger Men," an appellation referring to their habit of attacking their opponents, Jewish or Roman, with daggers concealed under their clothes. Violent men in Judea there were, but it is unlikely that the term *sicarii* appeared until the year 54.[21]

Josephus locates the roots of the Great Revolt that broke out in 66 CE in the religiously inspired tax revolt of sixty years earlier. The leaders of that earlier rebellion, says Josephus, left a legacy that eventually unleashed the horrors of a later generation: terrorism, assassination, civil war, the storming and razing of cities, and ultimately the destruction of the Temple of God itself.[22] Josephus's text can be read in a way that makes the terrorism of Jew against Jew, present in 66, start in 6 CE, but that is unconvincing. In fact, after the revolt of 6 was suppressed, the province of Judea enjoyed several decades of relative peace. There were threats of violence, actual violence, and momentary, harsh clampdowns, but the drumbeat of war and revolution began to sound loudly only in the 50s. When it reached a crescendo, Judah's son and grandson were ready, and they played leading roles in the Great Revolt that broke out in 66.

The Romans governed Judea from 6 to 66 CE, with only three thousand auxiliary troops. Another circa twenty thousand men, the personnel of four legions (raised by Tiberius from three legions), were available in the neighboring province of Syria if needed. By and large the Romans considered Judea to be a peaceful, if sometimes unruly, province. They were well aware of the existence of forces of resistance and discontent. But they were confident that they could keep them under control. They were confident because they enlisted the help of local elites to suppress potential uprisings. The Romans preferred to install a local ruler to do the job for them. Alas for them, after the death of Herod in 4 BCE, the Romans were continually frustrated in the attempt to find a suitable replacement ruler. They had to settle for the combination of a Roman prefect or procurator, and the help of the Judean aristocracy. They also had a series of Jewish client kings in the northern parts of the province. In general, those helpers did Rome's work well. But Judea always experienced an underlying resistance. It could not be otherwise. In essence, Judea was a temple state. To accept subordination to an outside force like Rome required an uneasy compromise. Hard work, maturity, and realism are necessary to make compromise succeed, and those qualities are rarely found in adequate supply.

Josephus emphasizes the religious aspect of the rebellion of 6, and it certainly had a religious aspect. But one shouldn't underestimate the political sophistication of the rebels. Josephus was loath to avoid any suggestion of Jewish betrayal. If the rebels contacted their brethren under Parthian rule, Josephus would not have been eager to share that information. After all, it would have been treason to Rome. Although we know nothing of any such contact, we can wonder whether it happened.

The Year 9 CE: Varus Meets His Nemesis

Varus achieved success against the natives in Judea, but not in his most famous assignment. In 6 or 7, Varus was appointed legate of Germania. Unlike Syria, Germania was a new province, only recently conquered. Although the Romans considered Germania to be pacified, the Germans thought differently. A local prince named Arminius at first collaborated with Rome. He fought for the empire and was rewarded with citizenship and the high rank of equestrian. Then he changed his mind, perhaps after witnessing Roman mistreatment of the people of his homeland. He decided to rebel, but hid his change of heart from the Romans.

In 9, Arminius led the unsuspecting Varus and his army into a trap. He organized an ambush in the Teutoburg Forest in northwestern Germania.

THE WAR FOR HEROD'S LEGACY

Archaeologists have identified the probable site of the battle, in a narrow pass between the foot of a high hill and a bog, near today's German village of Kalkriese. As the Romans entered the trap, Arminius excused himself on the grounds that he had to organize additional Roman allies. In fact, he took charge of the killers who were assembling nearby. Then they struck.

Shocked at first, the Romans rallied and built a camp, but their situation was bad. On either side, nimble and light-armed Germans attacked with javelins and swords. Packed together tightly, the heavy-armed legionaries were easy targets. They were hampered by wagons, beasts of burden, women and children, and slaves. As the news of the Romans' vulnerability spread, additional German warriors arrived to join in the slaughter. The weather helped them: the wind picked up and it rained. The Romans had to fight in the mud and found themselves slipping on tree roots. The Germans knew the terrain; the Romans did not.

For four days the Romans tried to fight their way out of the trap. In the end, Arminius's men slaughtered three divisions of cavalry and six cohorts of allied infantry, for a total of about twenty thousand men. Varus did what was expected of a noble Roman, and fell on his sword.

When Augustus got the news, he lost his temper. A leader famous for his cool engaged in a rare verbal outburst. Augustus is said to have cried out a memorable phrase. In Latin it is: QUINCTILI VARE, LEGIONES REDDE. "Quinctilius Varus, give me back my legions!" Augustus is supposed to have given vent to this phrase, not just once, but occasionally for months after receiving word from the frontier.

The disaster cost Rome 11 percent of its military manpower. It reduced the number of the legions from twenty-eight to twenty-five for a generation. More important in the long term, it cost Rome control of most of Germania. The new settlements were hastily abandoned, with the residents no doubt running for their lives to safety west of the Rhenus (Rhine River). Over the next few years, the Romans sent out a series of punitive expeditions to defeat Arminius and reconquer Germania east of the river. In the end, Tiberius, who replaced Augustus as emperor in 14, decided to withdraw. He recalled his leading general from Germania. In the future, the Romans would stay west of the Rhenus, except in the south, where they managed to extend their territory east of the river for a time. Most Germans remained independent.

Jewish sources often mention the death and defeat of their enemies, such as Pompey, who was murdered in 48 BCE, and consider their fate to be divine punishment. They are silent about Varus's awful end, but it seems unlikely that word of Rome's defeat in Germania never reached Judea. If Jews did hear about it, they might have wondered if Judea, too, like Germania, could have done that rarest of things: drive out the Romans.

"Under Tiberius All Was Quiet"

Augustus died in 14 CE. As he had planned, the throne passed to Tiberius, his stepson, who he eventually adopted. Tiberius was a Roman noble. A man in his fifties, Tiberius had made a career as a soldier, but now he chose to put down the sword. Although Rome had long followed a policy of expansion, Tiberius chose to keep the empire within its borders.

"Under Tiberius all was quiet." *Sub Tiberio quies.*[23] So wrote the Roman historian Tacitus (ca. 56–ca. 120) about the state of things in Judea during the reign of Tiberius. So he wrote, but it was under Tiberius in Judea that one of history's most momentous events took place. For it was there, in Jerusalem, around the year 30 CE, that Jesus of Nazareth was tried, crucified, and, as Christians believe, resurrected. Tacitus records this event as well, but he was not impressed.[24] For the Romans, the crucifixion was just a police action in response to just the latest in a long line of disturbances in an unruly province. [25]

Jesus was a Jew from Galilee. He was an itinerant teacher, prophet, wonder-worker, faith healer, and exorcist. He was manifestly nonviolent, not what would later be called a Zealot or one of the Sicarii. Still, he was perceived as a threat. Jesus stirred up a crowd at a time and a place that the Romans found menacing—not that the Romans ever were pleased to see an agitated crowd. They recognized no such thing as freedom of assembly. On the contrary: they distrusted public gatherings. What was especially problematic in the case of Jesus was that he came to Jerusalem for Passover, the season of redemption, liberation, and, not infrequently, riots against Rome. A host of supporters followed Jesus in the Holy City. Some hailed him as the King Messiah. Jesus taught that the Temple was corrupt and would be replaced by a new and pure temple. Indeed, he preached that the world as we knew it was coming to an end. The End of the Age was approaching and, with it, the Kingdom of God was at hand. To the authorities, it all sounded like trouble. Rome preferred to err on the side of caution when it came to the provinces: if someone appeared to be a troublemaker, then it was best to be rid of him. Hence, the crucifixion of Jesus.

Writing his *Annals* circa 115–120, Tacitus briefly mentioned Jesus. By that date, there was a Christian community in Rome, and Tacitus didn't like it. Christianity, he wrote, began in Judea and, like all bad things, eventually came to Rome. He considered Christianity to be a "destructive superstition" of which "Christus," as he calls him, was the founder. "Christus was put to death by the procurator Pontius Pilate when Tiberius was emperor," wrote Tacitus.[26] As far as he was concerned, that was the whole story, and Tacitus probably spoke for Roman elite opinion more generally. He had a low opinion of Jews and what he considered to be their barbarous customs, and an even lower opinion of an unorthodox Jewish offshoot, Christianity.

Tiberius is unlikely to have paid attention to Jesus. As far as the emperor was concerned, the most memorable thing to happen in Judea during his reign was probably the foundation of a new city named after him, Tiberias. It was founded circa 20 CE on the southwest shore of the Sea of Galilee. Technically, Tiberias was not in Judea. Rather, it lay in Galilee, which was ruled not by the Roman prefect but by the Jewish tetrarch. Augustus, it will be recalled, had divided Herod's kingdom after the king's death in 4 BCE among three of Herod's sons. After the emperor deposed Archelaus in 6 CE, much of the former kingdom came under Roman control. Archelaus's two brothers retained dominion over the regions they had been given. Philip ruled an area equivalent to the Golan (in Israel), Mount Hermon (straddling today's border of Israel, Lebanon, and Syria), and part of southern Syria. His brother Antipas ruled Galilee as well as Perea. It was Herod Antipas who founded Tiberias.

The city is still named Tiberias today, making it one of those memorials of long-dead rulers that survive in city names in the lands of former empires, like Alexandria, Egypt, named for Alexander the Great.

It was not Judea but Parthia, however, that was Tiberius's main concern in the East. He knew the threat of Rome's rival empire well. He himself had once served Augustus by leading an army into Armenia in 20 BCE to pressure Parthia into a negotiated agreement with Rome. Throughout his own reign Tiberius sent several emissaries to the eastern marches, often with the threat of legions to follow, to charm or bully the Parthians into maintaining an often-uneasy peace. Overall, the shrewd Tiberius succeeded. Romano-Parthian relations during his reign sometimes threatened to tip into war, but never did.

Judea was a lesser concern. Tiberius relied for most of his reign on two prefects in the region, with the governor of Syria available nearby if needed. The more memorable of the two prefects was Pontius Pilatus or, as he is better known, Pontius Pilate, the most infamous of all Roman provincial administrators, who ordered the crucifixion of Jesus.[27]

Pilate was not a man to take the threat of disorder lightly. During his administration of Judea from 26 to 36/37, he earned a reputation for harshness. Philo, an eminent Jewish philosopher in Alexandria, described Pilate as inflexible and stubborn, merciless and cruel, disrespectful and violent.[28]

It's true that Pilate was once forced to give in to a crowd protesting his decision to have his soldiers bring imperial standards with the image of Caesar into Jerusalem. But he did so only after five days of demonstrations, and only after he threatened the protesters by ordering his troops to draw their swords. On another occasion, Pilate placed some offending shields in Herod's palace in Jerusalem. Just why the shields disturbed the populace is unclear, but they might have contained an inscription declaring the emperor's divinity. Pilate agreed to remove the shields, but only under duress, after Jewish leaders wrote a letter of protest to the emperor. On another occasion, Pilate unleashed his men on a Jerusalem mob that was protesting his use of Temple funds for a new aqueduct. The soldiers clubbed some Jerusalemites to death and trampled others with their horses, which broke up the crowd.

Pilate got away with his brutality on the protest about the aqueduct, but he got his comeuppance at last after another incident, when he ordered his men to attack a group of Samaritans gathering at their holy site at Mount Gerizim, near present-day Nablus. Outraged Samaritan leaders complained to Pilate's overlord, the governor of Syria, who had Pilate recalled to Rome in late 36 or early 37. Pilate never returned to Judea; no more is known of him after his recall.

Although Pilate is today known for his role in the execution of Jesus, he might have preferred to be remembered for a different intervention in the religious life of Judea. Before his term of office was done, he made a dedication in Caesarea to the deified Augustus and Livia, the parents of his master, the emperor Tiberius. The inscription was placed within a Tiberieum, some sort of structure, perhaps a watchtower, honoring the emperor. The inscription, discovered in 1961, provides contemporary confirmation of Pilate's prefecture.[29] So do Judean coins struck under Pilate's authority.[30] Pilate could never have guessed that he had set off ripples that one day would overwhelm Rome's popular pagan cult and turn the eyes of the empire to the fractious province of Judea.

Chapter Three

THE TURNCOAT AND THE CONVERT

In the second quarter of the first century of our era, two Jews in the Middle East, as we now call it, followed opposite trajectories. One turned away from Judaism to become a loyal servant of the pagan Roman Empire—indeed, to become one of its outstanding soldiers and statesmen. His name was Tiberius Julius Alexander and he was a native of Egypt. The other abandoned paganism to adopt Judaism. She was Helena, queen of Adiabene, roughly today's Iraqi Kurdistan, and a vassal of the Parthian king. Helena and Tiberius Alexander, as we will call him, each lived for a time in Judea and exercised great influence there. Each would eventually cast a giant shadow on the great revolt that began in 66.

Tiberius Julius Alexander

Once, there was a golden family. They were wealthy, brilliant, talented, ambitious, and connected to the very highest circles of power on three continents. They were familiar figures not only in their hometown of Alexandria but in Rome and Jerusalem as well as Caesarea. Their careers took them from the

Palatine Hill to the Parthian frontier. They were at home in the synagogue, the military camp, and the academy. Their business interests ranged from Hispania to India. They were Jews but, as was usual in Alexandria, their native language was Greek rather than Aramaic or Hebrew. They read the Hebrew Bible in the Greek translation known as the Septuagint. They were bankers, businessmen, commissioners of customs, philosophers, governors, commanders, and, ultimately, a Roman senator. One generation took them from piety to near apostasy, but even in their holiest moments, they had one foot in the door that led to Greek culture and Roman power.

Their Alexandria was still glamorous, but not the queen of the Nile nor the mistress of the Mediterranean that it once had been. The Romans had looted Alexandria's treasures and decapitated its power. Alexandria was still a magnet for money, which was only logical considering the immense fertility of the Nile Valley, the grain fleets sailing for Rome, and the ports of the Red Sea teeming with the silk and spices of the East. Alexandria was still the haunt of philosophers and poets, but now also of ghosts. It housed the tomb of its eponymous founder, the ancient Greco-Roman world's most venerated conqueror, Alexander the Great. It held all that was mortal of the many Ptolemaic kings, men once denigrated by Augustus as mere corpses. And it contained the remains of that grandest and most ill-fated couple of adventurers, Antony and Cleopatra. Alexandria was still the home of hedonism and art as it always had been. But for the strivers and go-getters, it could no longer be an end in and of itself; Alexandria had become a handmaiden to Rome.

The most famous family member, the philosopher Philo (ca. 15–10 BCE–ca. 45–50 CE), sometimes known as Philo Judaeus, is still known today, his work read at least by specialists if not by the public. His nephew Tiberius Julius Alexander is even more important to our story, but his name is familiar to only a few scholars.

Tiberius Alexander was the son of Alexander, the first family member known by name, although not the first to be prominent. Josephus says that Alexander, the father, "surpassed all his fellow citizens both in ancestry and wealth."[1] Alexander held the office of alabarch, who was an important customs official, perhaps inspector-in-chief of customs. The alabarch was pious enough to donate to the Temple in Jerusalem nine massive gates overlaid with gold and silver. He was also eminent enough to marry off his younger son, Tiberius Alexander's brother, to the Jewish princess Julia Berenice, better known as Berenice, a royal descendant of Herod the Great.

Alexander the Alabarch was probably a citizen of both Alexandria and of Rome. Although Jews formed a significant minority in Alexandria and lived elsewhere in Egypt, too, few of them enjoyed Alexandrian citizenship, a privilege usually reserved for the Greek ruling class. Before the Roman conquest of Egypt in 30 BCE, many Jews served as soldiers in the armies of the Ptolemies; now the only real opening for a military career was in the Roman auxiliaries, as the legions were restricted to Roman citizens. Most Jews were craftsmen, such as textile manufacturers or sandal makers. A few rose to great wealth as bankers, bureaucrats, moneylenders, or merchants. As for Roman citizenship, a higher status than Alexandrian citizenship, that was unusual indeed for any but the most prominent Alexandrians regardless of ethnicity. Alexander the Alabarch was the rare exception. He used his wealth to establish close ties both with the descendants of Herod the Great and with the family of the Roman emperors.

Alexander was the brother of Philo, who devoted much of his work to attempting to reconcile the Torah and Greek thought. Philo made a pilgrimage to the Temple in Jerusalem, for example, but he also attended performances of Greek drama as well as Greek athletic competitions and horse races—anathema to pious Jews.

Tiberius Alexander was born perhaps around the year 15.[2] He was intelligent, ambitious, and energetic. As an adult Tiberius Alexander was not an observant Jew. Josephus says that Alexander the Alabarch "differed from his son Tiberius Alexander in his piety toward God. The latter was not faithful to his ancestral ways."[3]

Like Herod, Tiberius Alexander found the power of the Roman Empire irresistible. He chose to rise on the career ladder of the Roman army and colonial administration. Of his earliest military service, nothing is known, but by the year 42 he had reached the rank of Roman knight, and he held his first administrative position. He was *epistrategus* of the Thebaid, that is, governor of southern Egypt.

Before going on to the next stage of Tiberius Alexander's career, it's necessary to step back and survey the maelstrom that engulfed his community and his family before Tiberius Alexander ascended to power.

Race War

Caligula isn't what he used to be. Scholars have freed the reputation of the Roman emperor Gaius (ruled 37 to 41, known as Caligula, "Little Boots") from most of the slander in hostile ancient sources, but the rescue operation only goes so far. Caligula, who succeeded Tiberius, may not have been the sex maniac he was once thought to be, but he was arrogant and lacked restraint, qualities that in the end cost him his life. But first they cost many Jewish lives.

Like all imperialists, the Romans stirred up divisions among their subjects to prevent them from uniting against the empire. Under the Ptolemies, Greeks and Jews in Alexandria largely got along. Under the Romans, they were at each other's throats.

Alexandria experienced anti-Jewish riots in 38. As far as it is known these were the first such riots in the city's history. Indeed, one scholar calls them the first pogrom in Jewish history.[4] Almost all knowledge of the riots comes from two writings by Philo, who was a community representative as well as a philosopher. Although detailed, these sources are biased and incomplete; important parts of the text are missing. Certainty about the events and what caused them is not possible.

A plausible reconstruction goes as follows. Under the Ptolemies, both Greeks and Jews had privileges in Alexandria. The Greeks, as the body of citizens, enjoyed a certain right of self-government. In theory, Jews were restricted to only one part of the city, the Delta Quarter. But many Alexandrian Jews were valuable to the Ptolemaic government because they served in the army. So, Alexandrian Jews were able to live wherever they pleased. When the Romans annexed Egypt, they took away the Greek right of self-government and dissolved the Ptolemaic army. The Greeks, with some support from native Egyptians, increasingly turned against the Jews, whose prosperity they envied.

After becoming emperor, Caligula decided to side with the Greeks and Egyptians against the Jews. Because the Roman elite were traditionally philhellenes, this policy came naturally, but neither Augustus nor Tiberius had pushed the policy as Caligula did. He lacked their restraint. Caligula sneered at the Jewish custom of not eating pork and he surely had no respect for their monotheism.

In any case, Caligula decreed that Alexandria's Jews had to move back into the Delta Quarter. In the summer of 38, when the Nile was in flood and Egyptians crowded into the city, Greek and Egyptian rioters decided to take the law into their own hands against the Jews, who they outnumbered. They beat up and killed Jews and looted their property, forcing them into the Delta Quarter. Philo writes that thousands of Jews were killed, whether by stoning, beating, burning, or crucifixion. There is no way to confirm his figures, but the violence was bad enough for the Jews to send a delegation to Italy to plead with the emperor—to no avail.

The Emperor and the Statue

Marcus Julius Agrippa, grandson of Herod the Great, lived in Rome on and off from his childhood, where he enjoyed at first the protection of powerful members of the imperial family and then the ire of the emperor Tiberius. He was even thrown into jail for saying that he was eager for Tiberius to die and be replaced by his heir, Caligula, who was Agrippa's friend despite the Roman's lack of appreciation for Jewish religious customs. Maybe Caligula would have anticipated the statement of a modern anti-Semitic mayor of Vienna, Austria, who said, when queried about a Jewish friend of his: "I decide who's a Jew."[5] Six months after Agrippa's imprisonment, Tiberius died. When Agrippa got the news in jail, he exclaimed in Hebrew, in a reference to the Book of Ecclesiastes, "The lion is dead."[6] Caligula promptly freed his old friend. Not only that: the new emperor named Agrippa to be ruler of first a small part and then a larger part of Judea, eventually including Galilee, the Gaulanitis, and Perea.

Still, Caligula was not a friend to the Jews. Besides inciting a murderous riot in Alexandria, he almost started a war in Judea. Jabneh was a mixed city of Jews and Greeks located on Judea's coastal plain. Jabneh sat on the Via Maris, or "Way of the Sea," the highway linking Egypt and Syria. Jabneh was a small but significant node on an international network of communications. The inhabitants were well informed about happenings in Rome—and Rome would find out in due course what happened in Jabneh.

Greeks in Jabneh were happy to gratify Caligula and set up an altar to him, knowing this would distress the Jewish population, with whom they had an uneasy relationship. Jews indeed found this offensive, and they tore the altar down. Jews believed in only one God, of course, but the issue went deeper. As Philo writes, they thought that the altar destroyed the sanctity of the Holy Land.[7] And that sanctity meant, as one scholar puts it, that there could be only one ruler of the Holy Land: God. The Roman emperor could not accept that. In his eyes, the issue wasn't religious. Caligula saw the destruction of the altar as an act of political rebellion.[8]

In response Caligula upped the ante. Sometime between 39 and 40, he demanded that a larger-than-life-size statue of him be erected in the Temple in Jerusalem. It was a penetrating and provocative move because it forced an issue that had previously been finessed. While Rome ruled from Caesarea and, as a pious Jew might have put it, God ruled from Jerusalem, the issue of sovereignty in Judea could be put on hold. But Caligula's order required that the Jews violate the Ten Commandments, which enjoined that Jews have only one God and that prohibited statues and other graven images. Caligula demanded in effect that Jews accept that the emperor and not God ruled in Judea. Most Jews could not do that. In fact, Caligula's order was a declaration of war.

Caligula ordered the governor of Syria, Publius Petronius, to carry out his order by force. Petronius was not a man to be overly impressed by the emperor,

THE TURNCOAT AND THE CONVERT

as he had an exceptionally distinguished career to his credit and probably an equally good pedigree. A senator before his term as legate of Syria, he had been consul in Rome and then proconsul (governor) of the province of Asia. He was probably the son of a man who was a financial official in Rome and possibly proconsul in Hispania; he was probably the grandson of a prefect of Egypt; and probably the brother of another consul. Petronius, in short, came from a very prominent family.

Petronius headed toward Judea with two legions and auxiliary troops as well, perhaps a total of 15,000 to 20,000 men—a major expedition. As Philo puts it, the force represented "half the army quartered on the Euphrates to guard the passage against the kings and nations of the East."[9] Petronius marched to Ptolemaïs, where he planned to spend the winter and then make war in the spring. Large numbers of Jews—tens of thousands, in Josephus's probably exaggerated account—approached him there and begged him not to force them to fight to protect their way of life. They were unarmed, according to Philo, but there was no mistake about their willingness to take up arms if need be.

A man of Petronius's experience, and with the education of a Roman of his class, knew history and strategy, and he knew the Jews. Philo writes that it appears that Petronius "had some rudiments of Jewish philosophy and religion acquired either in early lessons in the past through his zeal for culture or after his appointment as governor in the countries where the Jews are very numerous in every city, Asia and Syria, or else because his soul was so disposed. . . ."[10] According to Philo, Petronius had no doubt but that the Jews were willing to die for their religion. And he knew that they were numerous. Philo writes of

> . . . the vast number of people comprised in the [Jewish] nation, which, unlike the other nations, needed not just the circumference of a single country allotted to itself alone, but, one might almost say, the whole habitable world. For it is spread abroad over all the continents and islands so that it seems to be not much less than the indigenous inhabitants.[11]

Philo goes on to say that Petronius knew how dangerous a Jewish war would be for Rome, what with the possibility of the Jews of the Roman Empire joining the strong, noble, freedom-loving, and high-spirited population of Judea, as Philo calls it. Above all, says Philo, Petronius feared the threat of the Jews of Parthia. Philo writes:

> He was frightened also by the forces beyond the Euphrates, since that Babylon and many other satrapies were occupied by Jews was known to him not only by report but by experience. For every year envoys were dispatched for the sacred purpose of conveying to the temple a great quantity of gold and silver amassed from the first fruits, and these envoys travel over the pathless, trackless, endless routes which seem to them good highroads because they feel that they lead them to piety. So he was naturally much alarmed lest hearing of this unprecedented dedication the Jews of those parts might suddenly take to raiding, and coming from different quarters might encircle his troops and joining hands attack them now isolated in their midst with terrible effect.[12]

Disturbed by the thought of a major war, Petronius marched to the city of Tiberias in Galilee, where he found a similar reception as in Ptolemaïs, this time with leading members of the Jewish elite present to add to the crowd's pleas. It's always wise to read the sources skeptically, but if even part of what Philo and Josephus describe is true, it is remarkable. The passion with which the Jewish population approached Petronius, their repeated profession of willingness to die for their beliefs, their courage and outspokenness all bespeak a nation in arms; only moral arms at first, but they stood ready to pick up weapons when needed.[13] The legate of Syria knew that rivers of blood would flow unless he could stop the statue.

Petronius concluded that it was not worth unleashing a war over the matter, so he wrote to Caligula and asked him to give up his plan. In one version of the story, Agrippa was in Rome, and he talked his old friend Caligula out of his plan. Then came Petronius's letter. The furious emperor wrote back to

Petronius. He doubled down on the statue and ordered Petronius's execution for insubordination, but fate or divine providence intervened. In 41, Caligula was assassinated. The matter was dropped.[14]

If Caligula had gotten what he wanted, Judea might well have risen in revolt. Instead, the province gained nearly another three decades of peace. Nonetheless, the affair of the statue underlined a point suggested by earlier events. The Temple was everything. For the Jews, it was not only the chief religious site but the chief political site as well. To govern Judea successfully, both sides had to finesse the fact that while the Jews recognized only the Kingship of God, the Romans ruled Judea. Empires embody strength; true believers burn with faith. Neither one is notable for its compromise. Knowing this, an astute observer might have worried about the future.

Agrippa Becomes King

Agrippa was in Rome at the time of Caligula's assassination. After the murder, the Praetorian Guard found Caligula's uncle Claudius in the palace—trembling behind a curtain, one source claims—and proclaimed him emperor.[15] The Senate balked, but, serving as a go-between, Agrippa fostered the negotiations that ended with Claudius being named emperor. If not for Agrippa's timely intervention, writes Josephus, an angry knot of soldiers might have massacred a party of senators en route to see Claudius.[16] Twenty-five years before the Great Jewish Revolt against Rome, a Jew played a key role in the making of the Roman emperor.

In return, a grateful Claudius expanded Agrippa's realm to include all of Herod's kingdom. King Agrippa, as he should now be thought of, also received the right to appoint the High Priest in Jerusalem. Previously, ever since the Roman takeover in 6 CE, the Romans chose the High Priest. From 41 until the outbreak of the Great Revolt in 66, Agrippa or other members of his dynasty held this power.

Claudius also conferred the rank of consul on Agrippa, a reminder that the

Jewish king had one foot in Rome. Agrippa was proud of his rendezvous with imperial destiny. He even issued a coin showing himself and his brother, who ruled a small territory in today's Lebanon, crowning Claudius as emperor.[17]

The new emperor reversed Caligula's hostility to Jews and Judea. There was no more talk of putting a statue of the emperor in the Temple in Jerusalem. Claudius also released Alexander the Alabarch from prison in Rome. Caligula had ordered his incarceration for some unknown reason, perhaps in connection with the Alexandrian Jewish embassy to Caligula in 39/40.

Agrippa was an activist king in the mold of his grandfather. He was popular with his Jewish subjects. He showed favor to the Pharisees, the most admired Jewish religious leaders. He made a point of living in Jerusalem, where he reduced taxes. He engaged in pious gestures such as standing to read the Torah, even though a king was entitled to sit.

But Agrippa also favored Greco-Roman culture, although it didn't do him much good with his pagan subjects, who would eventually cheer his death. He sponsored games in honor of the emperor at Caesarea and, in the neighboring province of Syria, endowed Berytus with a theater and amphitheater, where he sponsored massive gladiatorial contests. Christian sources remember him as a persecutor. He is said to have ordered the execution of the Apostle James, brother of the Apostle John, and imprisoned Peter, who escaped thanks to a miracle.[18]

When it came to the power of his kingdom, Agrippa thought big. He began building a new wall, north of the wall that Herod had built, to fortify Jerusalem on its vulnerable, northern side. Gaius Vibius Marsus, legate of Syria, raised the alarm about a project that could make Jerusalem unconquerable. The emperor would not ignore a man of Marsus's stature. Senator, consul, and former proconsul of Africa, Marsus had been close to Claudius's brother Germanicus. On Claudius's order, Marsus put a stop to the wall-building.

The watchful Marsus also halted a conference of kings that Agrippa hosted in 43 in Tiberias. No fewer than five client kings from Syria to Asia Minor joined Agrippa on the occasion. Marsus broke up the gathering, taking it for granted, according to Josephus, that their agreement and friendship could only hurt Roman interests.[19] With Parthia just over the horizon from several of these states, the Romans couldn't be too careful.

A year later, in 44, Agrippa suddenly died. He was about fifty-five. There were rumors of poison, as there often were when powerful people died suddenly. The Romans had reason to want to see such an ambitious ruler removed. Agrippa suffered severe abdominal pains, which stoked suspicion, but the symptoms could also point to a natural cause such as peritonitis.

Agrippa had a young son, also named Agrippa. After the king's death Claudius decided to pass over the lad, who was seventeen and lived at the imperial court in Rome, where Claudius decided to keep him for now. The emperor returned Judea to a Roman administrator, now a procurator rather than a prefect, and under the jurisdiction of the legate, the governor of Syria.

"A Certain Wizard Named Theudas"[20]

The first procurator appointed by Claudius was Cuspius Fadus. His short term of office (44–46) demonstrated just what Rome would and wouldn't do for the sake of security in Judea. The first matter was public order. Claudius demanded that Fadus punish the non-Jewish inhabitants of the cities of Caesarea and Sebaste for their raucous and disrespectful celebrations upon King Agrippa's death. Among other things, they had seized statues of the king's daughters and put them up on the roofs of brothels, then proceeded to do things that Josephus says were too indecent to report.[21] Agrippa had three daughters: Berenice, Drusilla, and Mariamme. As punishment Claudius ordered a troop of Caesarean and Sebastenian cavalrymen, either 500 or 1,000 in number, to be transferred to the Black Sea region and replaced by Syrians. But the troops sent a lobbying group to the emperor and persuaded him to back off (perhaps with a hefty bribe).

The Romans were harder on Jews, who practiced violence or engaged in provocative demonstrations, than they were on Gentiles, who disrespected authority. The issue was less anti-Semitism than Rome's insistence on holding a monopoly on force. Trouble arose when Jews living in what is now the region of Amman, Jordan, attacked and killed many of their neighbors in a border dispute. This happened without anyone consulting Fadus. He stepped in and had the three main leaders of the attack arrested; one was executed, and the two others were sent into exile. Next Fadus went after a certain Jew named Tholomaeus, described as an "arch-brigand" (*archilēstēs*)—that is, a terrorist or freedom fighter, depending on one's point of view.[22] He had attacked Idumeans and Arabs. Fadus had him executed. Afterward there was no more trouble from "brigands" in Judea during Fadus's rule. But a new threat emerged.

In 45 or 46, one Theudas persuaded many Jews to take their possessions and follow him to the Jordan River. He said that at his command the waters of the river would part, and his followers would cross easily. A pious Jew might have thought of the miraculous parting of the Jordan by the biblical leader Joshua. Theudas was a Jew who claimed to be a prophet, which Josephus disputes. Calling Theudas a *goēs*, Greek for "wizard" or "magician," sometimes with the connotation of "imposter" or "false prophet," Josephus says that he deceived his followers. The Acts of the Apostles describes Theudas as someone who "said he was somebody." Acts also says that he had four hundred followers; Josephus speaks only of "a very large crowd."[23] That Theudas's followers brought their possessions with them suggests that they were poor, otherwise they would have needed a caravan. It also suggests that they planned to move to new homes.

Fadus considered Theudas to be more than a crank. The procurator sent out a cavalry troop (500 or 1,000 men) to break up his following. It is possible that Theudas and his men were armed.[24] Even if they weren't, the Romans knew that an unarmed prophet could be dangerous. Josephus says that the cavalrymen fell on Theudas and company unexpectedly, killed many, and took many prisoners. Theudas was captured and beheaded; his head was brought to Jerusalem. Acts says that Theudas alone was killed; his followers were merely dispersed. In either case, Fadus surely closed the books on what looked to him like just another rebellion brewing in the Judean countryside. Once again, the Romans might have concluded that in Judea only a fine line separated religion and politics.

A final act of Fadus may seem like a footnote, but it was the most significant of all.[25] At issue were the vestments and ornaments that the High Priest wore when he offered sacrifice at the three annual pilgrim festivals and on the annual Day of Atonement. Jewish kings controlled the items until Judea became a Roman province in 6 CE, when Rome took custody of them. In 36, the robe and ornaments were restored to Jewish control as a goodwill gesture, but then, when Agrippa died in 44, Fadus and the legate in Syria demanded them back. The Jews petitioned to keep them. The legate of Syria thought the matter was sensitive enough to cause a revolt, and so he came to Jerusalem in person with a large force. The Jews then asked permission to send a delegation to the emperor Claudius in Rome. Permission was granted, but only on the condition that ambassadors gave their children as hostages. In Rome, Claudius agreed to restore custody of the robe and ornaments to the Jews.

If the matter seems arcane, consider the humiliating procedure when the robe and ornaments were under Roman control. The day before the festival, the Temple treasurers had to go to the Roman garrison commander in Jerusalem, show him their seal for inspection, and only then take possession of the materials. When the festival was over, they had to bring them back to the commander of the garrison, who again inspected their seal, and deposited the robe and ornaments.

Jews believed the Temple was the House of God, while the Romans believed that they were the supreme authority. The real issue in the robe and ornaments was who ruled in Judea.

The Jewish Procurator

Claudius chose Tiberius Alexander, the Jewish governor of southern Egypt, as the next procurator of Judea, where he served perhaps from 46 to 48. He was a logical choice. He had administrative experience. He was skilled and ambitious. As a Jew he was probably more acceptable to most Judeans than a Gentile would have been. By the same token he was also a reliable Roman citizen, and one whose father Claudius knew and trusted.

Few details of Tiberius Alexander's term of office have survived. Josephus writes that "by abstaining from all interference with the customs of the country [Tiberius Alexander] kept the nation at peace."[26]

The one detail of Tiberius Alexander's time in the governor's palace in Caesarea is the trial and crucifixion of two Jewish rebels. James (or Jacob) and Simon were sons of Judah the Galilean, the rebel against Quirinius and the census in the year 6 CE and the man who cofounded an anti-Roman sect. Just what his two sons did that led to their execution is not known.

In any case, although a Jew, Tiberius Alexander did not hesitate to order the crucifixion of Jews who were perceived as enemies of Rome. As his career continued, Tiberius Alexander would rise higher in the Roman service and sink lower in the eyes of Jews, who wanted freedom from the empire. After ca. 48, though, he disappears from the historical record for the next fifteen years.

He reemerges in 63 as an officer on the staff of Gnaeus Domitius Corbulo, Rome's greatest general at the time. Corbulo was involved in the fifth year of a war against Parthia, for control of Armenia. Armenia sat between Parthia and Rome, and constantly went back and forth between them. A rugged, mountainous country, Armenia offered an excellent east-west invasion route leading either to Roman territory in central Asia Minor or to Parthian realms in northern Mesopotamia. Neither empire wanted the other to control this valuable terrain.

Under Augustus, Parthia and Rome reached an agreement that Armenia would be a neutral buffer state. The deal held for about seventy-five years, until Parthian restiveness convinced Nero (r. 54–68), the emperor who succeeded Claudius, to send Corbulo and his armies to the East in 58 CE. Corbulo invaded Armenia and effected a Roman takeover. He installed a pro-Roman king, Tigranes, who was the great-grandson of Herod the Great. But Parthia struck back. It invaded Armenia and trapped the new king in a siege. Negotiations lifted the siege, but Rome decided to cut their vassal king loose. He was not heard of again.

THE TURNCOAT AND THE CONVERT

Now Parthia made its move. The Parthian king, Vologases I (Balash or Walgash in Parthian), was bold and ambitious. His coin portraits bespeak strength. One particularly fine depiction shows him wearing a diadem and a torque in rugged profile with a prominent, straight nose, a penetrating gaze, a pointed beard, and long hair. He looks like he means business.[27] While consolidating his rule domestically, Vologases also aimed to put Rome on the strategic defensive abroad. He put his brother, Tiridates, on the throne of Armenia.[28]

Rome preferred a pro-Roman Armenia or at least a buffer state, so in 62 it sent another army to Armenia. Its commander was no Corbulo. In fact, the new commander allowed himself to be cornered by a Parthian army led by Vologases in person. The site was Rhandeia, in what is today eastern Turkey. To save his men, the Roman had to agree to a humiliating surrender. The men passed under a yoke as they left their camp, that is, they walked bent down below a row of crossed spears, a sign of disgrace. The next year, Nero sent Corbulo back to Armenia with a new army. His mandate was to defeat Vologases and avenge Rhandeia.

In the spring of 63, two armies approached each other tensely, but there was hope of resolving the conflict. Enter Tiberius Alexander. The historian Tacitus describes Tiberius Alexander as "a Roman knight of the highest rank who had been sent to assist in the war."[29] The description suggests that Tiberius Alexander had garnered additional military experience since 48. In the decade following 63, Tiberius Alexander would wield enormous power as a general, including possibly command on the Roman-Armenian frontier, but ironically, his one recorded act of assistance to Corbulo was diplomatic. Tiberius Alexander served as a hostage at a high-level conference in Armenia along with Corbulo's son-in-law: into the enemy camp.

Tiberius Alexander would not have been chosen as a hostage unless he was recognized by the Parthians as a valuable person. Perhaps the Parthians felt comfortable with him because he was a Jew. Jews, as we know, were prominent in the Parthian Empire, as they were in the Roman Empire.

The meeting began with a handshake and ended with a kiss (an affectionate

– 69 –

rather than erotic gesture). A compromise was reached: Parthia had appointed Armenia's king, Tiridates, but he would do homage to the Roman emperor, first by bowing to a statue of Nero, and then by going to Rome to genuflect to the emperor in person. The hostages returned safely.

A few days later, Tiberius Alexander witnessed a spectacle to give the Romans a thrill. The historian Tacitus describes it:

> There was a grand display on both sides; on the one, cavalry ranged in squadrons with their national ensigns; on the other, stood the columns of our legions with glittering eagles and standards and images of deities, after the appearance of a temple. In the midst, on a tribunal, was a chair of state, and on the chair a statue of Nero. To this Tiridates advanced, and having slain the customary victims, he removed the crown from his head, and set it at the foot of the statue; whereupon all felt a deep thrill of emotion, rendered the more intense by the sight which yet lingered before their eyes, of the slaughter or siege of Roman armies. "But now," they thought, "the calamity is reversed; Tiridates is about to go, a spectacle to the world, little better than a prisoner."[30]

Legionary eagles shining in the sun, allied horsemen with their national flags, a foreign king practically on his knees before a symbol of the emperor: it was a vision of Rome's glory under Anatolian skies. Seven years later, in Jerusalem, Tiberius Alexander would witness a very different sight.

Helena, Queen of Adiabene

If around the year 65, on the eve of the Great Revolt, visitors to Jerusalem had gone to see the tomb where Jesus Christ was laid to rest—and where, the faithful believe, he was raised on the third day—they would not have found a major monument. Rather, they would have seen a burial cave with a rolling stone at its opening. The tomb was located on Golgotha Hill, in a quarry lying west of the city walls (nowadays the site is inside the walls of the Old City, which is larger than it was in Second Temple times). Christian pilgrims who visited, and we know that they did, chipped away, as souvenirs for the faithful, pieces of the rock of one of the several burial caves that were found in the quarry.

Had a visitor to Jerusalem around the same time continued north of the city walls, he or she would have found a tomb of an entirely different sort. It was magnificent. This tomb was so grand that Pausanias, a Greek writer of the period, ranked it with the Mausoleum of Halicarnassus as one of the burial monuments most "worthy of wonder."[31] An earlier Greek poet had rated the mausoleum as one of the Seven Wonders of the World, which puts the Jerusalem tomb in exalted company.[32]

It was the burial monument of Queen Helena of Adiabene. Adiabene was a kingdom in northern Mesopotamia, in the heartland of what was once Assyria.

Helena was a convert to Judaism who lived in Jerusalem in the 40s and 50s, and who planned her resting place in the rock-cut tomb. After her death in Adiabene, her bones were transported to Jerusalem and laid to rest in her spectacular grave monument in the early 60s. According to Josephus, they were placed in one of the three pyramids that were erected on top of the tomb at the queen's order.[33] One scholar argues that the tomb had originally been planned for King Agrippa, but he died young in 44, before the tomb could be completed. According to this theory, Helena admired the tomb as one that was fit for a queen, and so she bought it for herself and had the finishing touches put on it.[34] Queen Helena's tomb is probably to be identified with the so-called Tomb of the Kings, a magnificent if today rarely visited monument in East Jerusalem.

Both Jesus and Helena were Jews; both lived in the first century; both spoke Aramaic (although different dialects). Jesus is one of the most influential figures in history, while Helena is forgotten despite her onetime prominence, her charity, and her tomb. She deserves closer attention because her story illustrates the close connections between Judea and the Parthian world. Those connections did not end in 37 BCE, when Herod became king. Far from it. They run like an underground stream through the history of the Land of Israel as long as the Parthian state existed. They continued after it was replaced by a new dynasty in the third century, the Sasanians. The connections extend all the way to the Islamic Conquest in 638.

Viewed from Rome, Jerusalem lay at the eastern edge of the empire. But if your reference point was Jerusalem, you stood between two empires. The city of Rome, which lay to the west, could be reached on a fast trip by land and sea in about three weeks. Closer to Judea lay two great Greek-speaking cities of the Roman Empire, each with large Jewish populations: Alexandria, in Egypt, and Antioch, in Syria, each about seven days away from Jerusalem.

It might seem as if Jerusalem's world was purely Roman, but not if you looked eastward. The caravan route from Jerusalem to Babylonia, old and time-worn, the haunt of soldiers and merchants, pilgrims and thieves; crowded with donkey-driven carts, horses for the wealthy, and weary feet for the poor, typically took about three weeks. Babylon lay in southern Mesopotamia, which contained not only the Parthian capital of Ctesiphon but a centuries-old Jewish community. No wonder the connection between Parthia and Judea was strong. And, because of the work of Queen Helena and her family, it would grow stronger.

Riding to Jerusalem

Helena took her first trip from Adiabene to Jerusalem around the year 45.[35] Imagine her seated in a well-appointed horse-drawn wagon, attended by servants. She was probably wearing a diadem, the ribbon that symbolized royalty in antiquity. She was the mother of the king of Adiabene, Izates. The Queen Mother could be important and influential in the Parthian world. We can envision Helena having carefully coiffed hair and wearing a beaded necklet, luxurious robes, and leather sandals.[36]

A military escort would have accompanied the queen; supplies, carried by camels, would have followed. They would have traveled westward from her capital city of Arbela. They could have crossed the lazy waters of the Tigris near the ruins of Nineveh, the former Assyrian capital, then headed in a northwesterly direction to the city of Nisibis, on the edge of Armenian

THE TURNCOAT AND THE CONVERT

highlands to the north. From there the caravan would have continued westward to Edessa, on the border of Roman Syria, near which they would have crossed the swiftly flowing Euphrates. From there they would have headed southward through Syria to Judea and finally to Jerusalem.

The trip would have taken a little more than a month. It could not have been comfortable bouncing in a wagon along an ancient road, not even in relative luxury. The Queen Mother of Adiabene would not have made the journey without a good reason. In fact, she had three reasons: religion, politics, and trade. She was a Jew through conversion, and a player at the game of power by birth. Queens need money and there was a lot of it to be made in trade with luxury items from Arabia, China, and India. Although the evidence is slim, there is some reason to think that Jewish merchants played an active role in this trade, as they did several centuries later.[37] Certainly, Adiabene and Judea both participated in the commerce. The Silk Road passed through Adiabene on its way to the Mediterranean coast. The cities of Judea and Phoenicia have been described as "the chief silk-processing centers of the Roman Empire."[38] The weavers of Galilee, Gaulanitis, and Beth Shean (Scythopolis) were known for making half-silk products. All in all, a connection to Judea could prove lucrative to Helena. A trip to Jerusalem could help her advance in various ways. Josephus describes her religious motivation:

> Now she had conceived a desire to go to the city of Jerusalem and to worship at the temple of God, which was famous throughout the world, and to make thank-offerings there.[39]

Let's imagine the queen timing her visit for one of the three great pilgrimage festivals that marked the Jewish year: Sukkot (Feast of Booths or Tabernacles), that is, the fall harvest festival; Pesach (Passover), the spring festival commemorating the Exodus from Egypt and the origin of the Jewish nation; and Shavuot (Weeks), marking the wheat harvest and the giving of the Ten Commandments at Sinai. The pilgrimage to Jerusalem was a great event. Think of the Muslim pilgrimage to Mecca—the hajj—or the medieval

Christian pilgrimage to Canterbury, England, described in Chaucer's *Canterbury Tales*, or the various sites of Buddhist and Hindu pilgrimages.

Adiabene

Northern Mesopotamia is at the geographic center of the Middle East. First-century Adiabene lay beside the Iranian highlands to the east. Northward stretched the foothills of Armenia, the prize over which Rome and Parthia fought a series of wars. To the west stretched the great plains of the Tigris and Euphrates Rivers. Nothing but those waters stood in the way of an invading army from Roman Syria.

Lying on the main trade route of northern Mesopotamia, Adiabene was a wealthy place that had once been the cradle of empire. The former Assyria, in its heyday centuries earlier, had been the bloodthirsty conqueror of the ancient world. Long since more peaceful, first-century Abiadene was a crossroad of cultures. The main language was Syriac, a variant of Aramaic, the language spoken by most of the Jews of Judea. The name Adiabene is a Greek adaptation of the Aramaic name Hadyab.

With its central location, its position on the trade route, its proximity to the disputed Armenia, and its wealth, Abiadene was a geostrategic player. In principle, it was a client state of the Parthian king, who valued Adiabene as the military link to Armenia. In practice, Abiadene had a certain amount of freedom to chart its own course. Parthian power was relatively loose, with both vassal states and obstreperous Parthian nobles often able to rein in ambitious Parthian kings.

The World of Queen Helena

Helena was born a royal princess and became queen by marrying her brother, Monobazos I, the king, who was passionately in love with her. Zoroastrianism, the main Parthian religion, did not forbid brother-sister marriages. In fact, it considered such marriages, as well as any marriage between close kin, to be the height of piety.

Helena and Monobazos I had two sons, Izates and Monobazos II. We don't know if they had daughters. The boys were not the king's only sons. He had many sons by various wives, as polygamy was the rule in Parthian dynasties.

The king's favorite was his younger son by Helena, Izates. Knowing that the other brothers were jealous of the boy, King Monobazos I sent him to live with another Parthian vassal king down the Tigris, near the mouth of the river. This other king had his capital at Spasines' Fort (Spasinou Charax), a port city at the head of the Persian Gulf.

Spasines' Fort was a prosperous and cosmopolitan harbor town. And one of its traders was a Jewish merchant named Ananias. He introduced Izates to Judaism after first introducing it to the king's wives: they persuaded Izates to become a Jew. Or, rather, they persuaded him to follow some Jewish customs. It appears that Izates became what in other contexts is called a "God-fearer." He showed sympathy to Judaism without embracing it entirely. In Josephus's telling, a fairy-tale-like coincidence followed. Back in Adiabene, Helena also was attracted to Judaism. A Jewish community existed across the Tigris from Adiabene, in the city of Nisibis, with a prominent rabbi, and perhaps he taught her. Perhaps Helena had heard of her son's change in his way of life and wanted to join him, either as a gesture of support or as a means of keeping her influence over him, or perhaps out of genuine religious interest.

When King Monobazos I grew old, he called his son back home and gave him a district of the kingdom to rule. On the king's death it was Queen Helena who called the notables of Adiabene together. She persuaded them to honor her husband's wish to give the throne to Izates. (Monobazos II succeeded to the throne later.) They bowed low before the queen and accepted Izates as king. Izates decided to complete his conversion process to Judaism by being circumcised. The ancient world barely knew the separation of faith and nationality that is common today. By undergoing circumcision, Izates would become a member of the Jewish nation. It was a change not just in religion but in nationality, dangerous for a king. But some of Izates's brothers and relatives, including Monobazos II, followed him into Judaism.

The nobility of Adiabene was not pleased. When a new king took the Parthian throne, the nobles asked him to name a new ruler of Adiabene who would follow a traditional religion. The Parthian king agreed and prepared to invade Adiabene. Knowing that he couldn't resist the Parthian army, Izates prayed, fasted, and dirtied his head with ashes—and his prayers were answered. A sudden invasion of Parthia by nomads forced the Parthian king to back off.

However sincere the conversion of the Adiabenian ruling family to Judaism, it surely also had a strategic element. By becoming a presence in Jerusalem, the Adiabenians achieved two complementary goals. On the one hand, they offered Parthia a kind of diplomatic and intelligence beachhead in enemy territory—on the quiet, of course, for they could hardly oppose Rome publicly in a city that Rome governed. On the other hand, they opened a potential channel of communication with Rome, one that they could use as needed to place stumbling blocks in the way of Parthian projects that didn't suit them. Information is power, as the experienced heirs of an ancient empire knew well.

Helena in Jerusalem

Izates was long settled on the throne when Queen Helena let him know of her wish to go to Jerusalem, to worship at the Temple, and to make thank offerings. The new king not only supported his mother's goal but funded her and accompanied her part of the way.

When Helena arrived in Jerusalem, she found a cosmopolitan city teeming with visitors. According to the New Testament, she would have encountered

> Parthians, and Medes, and Elamites, and the dwellers in Mesopotamia, and in Judaea, and Cappadocia, in Pontus, and Asia [the Roman province of that name, roughly central-western Turkey], Phrygia, and

Pamphylia, in Egypt, and in the parts of Libya about Cyrene, and strangers of Rome, Jews and proselytes, Cretes and Arabians. . . .[40]

Helena lived in Jerusalem for quite some time, although we don't have a clear picture of the chronology. The Temple was surely the focus of her life. Imagine her purifying herself at the Pool of Siloam, located in the City of David, that is, the lower, older part of Jerusalem. From there she would join other pilgrims on the Pilgrim's Road that stretched about 700 yards to the Temple Mount. It was a steep trek, since the Temple stood about 350 feet higher than the Pool.

Female Jewish worshippers at the Temple would have stood in the middle court, the Court of the Women, between the outer court, the Court of the Gentiles, and the inner court, the Court of the Israelites, i.e., the Court of the Men. Both sexes might have enjoyed a memorable ceremony in the Court of the Women, for men were allowed to be there (but women weren't permitted in the Court of the Israelites). It was the annual "Rejoicing of the Water-Drawing House," performed every morning during the fall festival of Sukkot to ask God for the blessing of rain. The water was drawn from the Pool of Siloam and carried uphill on the Pilgrim Road to the Temple.

The ceremony was spectacular. At the end of the first night, for example, the priests and their assistants, the Levites, would light a candelabra in the Court of the Women. It was so bright, says the Talmud, that "there was not a courtyard in Jerusalem that was not illuminated from the light."[41] The account in the Talmud continues:

> The pious and the men of action would dance before the people who attended the celebration, with flaming torches that they would juggle in their hands, and they would say before them passages of song and praise to God. And the Levites would play on lyres, harps, cymbals, and trumpets, and countless other musical instruments. The musicians would stand on the fifteen stairs that descend from the Israelites' courtyard to the Women's Courtyard, corresponding to the fifteen Songs

of the Ascents in Psalms, i.e., chapters 120–134, and upon which the Levites stand with musical instruments and recite their song.[42]

In the morning, when the rooster crowed, two trumpeters stood in the Upper Gate between the Court of the Israelites and the Court of the Women and emitted blasts at intervals to mark the progress of the water from the Pool to the Temple. The Talmud sums up the festival by saying:

> The Sages taught: One who did not see the Celebration of the Place of the Drawing of the Water, never saw celebration in his life.[43]

We might imagine Queen Helena watching the festival for the first time, caught up in a pious spirit of rejoicing.

In addition to worshipping at the Temple, the queen dedicated golden objects.[44] She made Jerusalem her second home by building a palace near the Temple.

Jerusalem in the first century really consisted of two cities. It sprawled along the side of a hill and the summit. The newer part, consisting of both the Upper City and the New City, looked like a Greco-Roman city. It had streets laid out on a grid plan, covered porticoes, palaces, towers, a theater, and even a hippodrome. The only difference between Jerusalem and a Greek or Roman city was that there was only one temple, to one God, rather than the variety of temples to be found in a city that worshipped many different deities. The Lower City, better known today as the City of David, looked more like a Near Eastern city, with its closely packed, low-lying houses and narrow streets. Jewish aristocrats lived in the Upper City, but Helena built her palace in the Lower City, as Josephus states.[45]

Excavators had found a large mansion in the northernmost part of the City of David, close to the foot of the Temple Mount.[46] It was a spacious and monumental building, unlike any other in this part of Jerusalem, at least two stories high, with long halls decorated by colorful frescoes and well-appointed ritual baths. The place may have been Queen Helena's palace, although for

THE TURNCOAT AND THE CONVERT

now that is just a hypothesis. Archaeologists have said that the architecture of the palace had a Parthian look to it. If that turns out to be the case, then it would add to the Near Eastern feel that its location in the City of David provided. Helena's royal family erected two other large buildings in the City of David, for a total of three such structures, all standouts in an area consisting mostly of modest houses.[47]

A famine struck Judea around the time of Queen Helena's arrival and she responded with vigor. She sent her servants to Alexandria to buy grain and to Cyprus to buy dried figs, which she distributed to the suffering population of Jerusalem. It was presumably Helena who alerted her son, King Izates, to the city's plight. He sent funds to Jerusalem's leaders, which were distributed to the poor. "She has left behind a very great memory of her good deeds for all our people," wrote Josephus of the queen.[48]

When Izates died young, Helena returned to Adiabene. She was heartbroken according to Josephus, but consoled by the thought that her elder son, Monobazos II, was the new king.[49] Perhaps one reason for her trip home was to help Monobazos II manage the often-obstreperous nobility.

She didn't outlive Izates long. Helena had made careful plans for her burial. King Monobazos II ordered that both her bones and those of Izates be transported to Jerusalem. Josephus says that the remains were to be placed in the three pyramids erected by Helena atop the tomb.[50] And so it happened. Since there were three pyramids, most probably Monobazos II's bones later ended up there as well. The three members of the dynasty rested side by side: two ruling brothers and an indomitable mother, the daughter, wife, and mother of kings.

It was a burial in a place of honor just outside the walls of Jerusalem. But was it a Jewish burial? Jewish law mandated that bones be placed below the ground, but Josephus states that the queen and her son were buried in the pyramids *above* the ground. Burial in a tower wasn't the Jewish way, but it was a widespread practice in the Near East. Perhaps Helena decided to maintain one last vestige of her pagan ancestry.[51]

To a passerby, the Corinthian columns and carved frieze of the queen's tomb bespoke Greece and Rome. But the three pyramids evoked Egypt and southwestern Asia. They were among the first things one saw on the road northward from Jerusalem, the road that led either to Rome or to Parthia.

Legacy

Helena and Izates had arranged to continue their dynasty's connection with Judea. Izates sent five young sons to Jerusalem to learn Hebrew and Jewish culture. Just as the Herodian dynasty sent their sons to be educated at Rome, so the Adiabenians sent their sons to Jerusalem. Izates had many other sons, and he might have sent them, too, but he didn't. Perhaps it seemed safer to keep the sons at home, where he could keep watch on them, especially if they were older and potential sources of rebellion. There was another security factor as well. In Jerusalem, the members of Izates's family were at the mercy of Rome, should trouble break out. In fact, when on one occasion the Parthian king asked Izates to join him in a war against Rome, one reason why Izates refused was fear for his five sons.[52]

As mentioned, Jerusalem gave the dynasty of Adiabene a base away from home. It was a place to engage in diplomacy with Rome, a place to gather intelligence to share with their Parthian overlord, a place to strike up friendships with powerful Romans, which might prove handy in the face of renewed hostility from a Parthian ruler. It was also a place to cement contacts in the luxury trade that passed through Adiabene. Jerusalem could serve as a refuge, should it ever be necessary to go into exile from an unstable situation at home. Since Jews traveled back and forth between Mesopotamia and Judea on pilgrimages and trade, they offered an information network to co-religionists. With large Jewish Diaspora communities in the Roman Empire, Jerusalem also served as a conduit of information about other parts of Roman territory, information that might increase the value of the Adiabenians in Parthian eyes.

While in Judea, Queen Helena is likely to have met with both Jewish and Roman officials. Her sojourn overlapped with the terms of several Roman procurators, including Tiberius Alexander. Among other high-ranking Jews, she surely came to know King Agrippa II. Claudius had allowed him to return to the East in 48. Herod Agripa II didn't rule Jerusalem—his territories lay to the north—but he had business in the city, for he was supervisor (tetrarch) of the Temple, and he also had the right to appoint the High Priest.

An eavesdropper on Helena's conversations in Jerusalem might have heard questions from her interlocutors about points east. For example: How Jewish was the royal dynasty of Adiabene? How much opposition did they face from their largely pagan homeland? How fared the Jews elsewhere in Mesopotamia? What was Parthian foreign policy? Did the Parthian king retain an interest in Judea, as in the days of Pacorus? Would peace prevail between Rome and Parthia? Would there be another war? A strategist, as Helena seems to have been, would have carefully revealed only what benefited her country, while gathering intelligence in return. Any clues that she picked up to Rome's plans in the East could be passed on to King Izates.

Between her charity and her building projects, Queen Helena left a striking impression in Jerusalem. So did the presence of her five grandsons. Jews could only be flattered by the attention given to the Holy City by a convert. One might wonder if they even have believed that the Adiabenians were long-lost descendants of the Ten Tribes conquered and deported by the Assyrians from the Land of Israel in the eighth century BCE.

If the kings of Adiabene dreamed big, then they might have imagined one of their descendants becoming king of Judea one day. They were converts, but Herod had come from a family of converts. Judea belonged to Rome, but it had belonged to Parthia not long before, and the wheel might turn again.[53]

If the Jews of Jerusalem thought that the royal converts of Adiabene sympathized with their cause, they were right. But it was perilous to think that the Adiabenians could deliver a significant amount of aid from the Jews of Mesopotamia or the king of Parthia, whom they served. It was an illusion to imagine that a friendly army from the East could appear as easily as the Adiabenian royal palaces had arisen in the City of David. Even so, the rebels indulged the illusion. Queen Helena, the convert, and Tiberius Alexander, the turncoat, were each destined to leave a mark on the Great Revolt that broke out in Judea in 66. Helena was no longer alive then, but her descendants, Jews themselves, fought for the rebels. The rebel leaders sent embassies eastward in the hope of getting more aid from their Jewish brethren in Adiabene and elsewhere in the Parthian realm. But Rome was adamant, and one of the leaders of its army in the campaign to crush the revolt was none other than Tiberius Alexander.

Chapter Four

AND THE WAR CAME

On an October day in 66, the Roman army was marching to Jerusalem. They were a large force with a core of Roman legionaries, all citizens. They numbered thirty thousand men at the start of the campaign in August, but were smaller now, with garrisons left behind in various places along the way.[1] The legionaries wore heavy metal armor, from their helmets to their breastplates to their shin guards. Each man had his weapons, a sword and dagger, hanging from his belt, and he carried a long body shield. Onward the legions tramped, in their heavy-soled hobnailed boots, marching together with their ranks exact, in the orderly cadence for which they were famous. Onward and onward toward Jerusalem.

Besides the legionaries the force consisted of auxiliaries, that is, local, non-citizen troops who served in the Roman army, and allied cavalry and archers. A long baggage train of pack animals carrying supplies and artillery—battering rams and arrow-launching catapults—followed behind.

The Jerusalem-bound legionaries were drawn from four separate legions, and the main one—the only full legion there—was the Twelfth Legion, the Fulminata or "Thunderbolt." Legionaries were supposed to be Rome's best soldiers, and the men of the Fulminata once were. Julius Caesar himself had created the unit, and it fought at his victorious side during the civil war in the previous century. But in 62, just four years earlier, the Twelfth suffered humiliation in a war against Rome's main rival, the Parthian Empire. Soon afterward, Rome managed to find a tolerable settlement with Parthia, but the Twelfth Legion was sidelined as a mark of disgrace. The men were hungry for victory now.

Early in the campaign, the army marched south from Syria. Once in Judea, they mixed diplomacy with terror. After ravaging part of Galilee, they headed to the Mediterranean coast and marched south to Caesarea. Then they continued to Joppa. They destroyed the town and massacred its inhabitants, killing, we are told, 8,400 people.[2] Next, the Romans sent a detachment back to Galilee. At Sepphoris, the capital city of Galilee, the detachment renewed the good relations that they had with the leadership, but to be on the safe side, they took hostages and sent them to a city on the coast. Elsewhere in Galilee they confirmed friendships where they existed, but looted, burned, and murdered where they found resistance. After rejoining the main army at Caesarea, they all marched up-country toward Jerusalem.

At their head rode the governor of Syria, the province of which Judea was a part. Like his father before him, Cestius Gallus was a Roman senator and had served as consul, which put him in the stratosphere of the elite, but he was past his prime. At the age of at least sixty-six, Cestius had reached the point at which a Roman male often suffered from illnesses such as hypertension, arthritis, or gout. But the governor had a job to do, and so he persevered.[3]

When he left the city of Antioch in Syria in August, Cestius might have seen his job in classic Roman terms. As the poet Virgil wrote, the Romans were the rulers of nations, destined

To impose the laws of peace,
To spare the defeated and to subdue the proud.[4]

Pride had reared its ugly head in a part of his province: Judea. In the year 66, Jerusalem, the Holy City, was in turmoil. Riots erupted. Militant factions threatened Rome's friends, the upper classes who normally dominated the city. The militants laid siege to the Roman auxiliary garrison. But their boldest coup came on the Temple Mount, and with help from high places. No less a figure than the son of the former High Priest was the prime mover of an act of rebellion. He was Eleazar son of Ananias, the assistant (*sagan*) to the current High Priest. Eleazar's father, Ananias son of Nebedeus, had served an unusually long, twelve-year term as High Priest, from 47 to 59. Ananias was a wealthy man whose influence lasted even after his term of office. He knew how to be tough and on one occasion hired mercenaries who took part in Jerusalem's urban violence. He was no revolutionary, though; in fact, Ananias was one of the most pro-Roman Jews in Judea. Not his son, Eleazar, who rebelled not only against Rome but against his father. Eleazar persuaded the priests who carried out the daily sacrifices to close the Temple to foreigners and foreign donations.[5] It was an unprecedented act with a political consequence, because it effectively stopped the daily sacrifices for the sake of the emperor. Jewish priests carried out the sacrifices, but the emperor paid for them. "Denying the Romans access to their God was a declaration of theological and political separation and independence from Rome," as one scholar put it.[6]

Everyone knew that this was a grave action. The chief priests and the most prominent men in the city tried to stop it, but it had popular support. Eleazar played the key role. He was a member of the Establishment and a figure of a new generation: he was, according to the Jewish historian Josephus, "a very bold young man." Josephus highlights the significance of the decision that he helped put into place: "This was the beginning of the war against the Romans."[7]

As often happens in revolts, the young showed especial enthusiasm for war. In other provinces besides Judea, a common pattern was found. The older generation learned to live with the foreign rule. The young bristled at collaboration, and youth likes to court risk.[8]

Why Now?

We are so used to the idea of the Jewish War, as Josephus's book is called, and of the destruction of Jerusalem and the Temple, that the Great Jewish Revolt against Rome seems inevitable. Likewise, the continuation of the conflict in two later rebellions makes it seem as if the war could never have been avoided. Nonetheless, there was another way.[9]

Ever since Pompey conquered Jerusalem in 63 BCE, the Jews of Judea trod two different paths. Those on the first path resisted Rome violently, at times even turning on their co-religionists. Some were moved by holy fire. They had visions of apocalypse, of redemption, and of driving out idol worshippers from the Holy Land. Some blamed Rome for the problems of debt and poverty that were endemic in Judea. Those problems existed throughout the Roman Empire, but the twin forces of religion and nationalism, along with the obvious support of Rome by the local elite, made it easy to blame the outsider. Some opponents of Rome sought the help of Parthia or of Jews from the Parthian Empire, and at times they obtained it. More often, they had to settle for promises of future aid.

Judeans on the second path accepted the reality of Roman rule, whether they did so grudgingly or via enthusiastic collaboration. They included the high and mighty, whether royalty, priests, or aristocrats. They included those who profited from the Roman peace, whether through trade or through service in the royal administration in Galilee and elsewhere. If later sources can be trusted, they comprised some sages as well, who rejected the apocalyptic vision that fueled many of the rebels. They probably also included the followers of Jesus of Nazareth. Jesus's rebellion against Rome was strictly spiritual, but it created enough of a disturbance to arouse Rome's ire.

Until a few years before the outbreak of revolt in 66, most Judean Jews accepted Roman rule, albeit grudgingly. Despite periodic spurts of violence, Judea remained largely at peace between Varus's repression in 4 BCE and the outbreak of the Great Revolt in 66 CE. Other Roman provinces, too, experienced violence from time to time. Judea looms larger because of Josephus and the New Testament. If the Romans governed with prudence and restraint, and if they found willing local allies, they managed to maintain order. For all the longing of some for freedom, for all the wishing that the Holy Land be ruled from the House of God rather than from the House of Caesar, very few Jews took up arms against Rome.[10]

Ethnic conflict complicated matters, but when it came to the Pax Romana ethnicity was not a deal-breaker.[11] True, the various peoples of Judea engaged in turf wars, insults, and occasional violence. Intercommunal conflict occurred more generally in the broader region of which Judea was a part. A special factor in Judea was resentment of the former hegemony of the Hasmonean kings over Gentiles. All troubling, but nothing that sound imperial management couldn't handle. But sound imperial management wasn't always on offer. Roman government, like all government, was rarely more than moderately competent at best. It was often corrupt, lazy, or too occupied with other matters to pay attention to a provincial backwater like Judea. When the Caesars let things slide, minor irritations began turning into major problems and then, suddenly, war loomed.

When it did, several streams in Judean society converged to raise the banner of rebellion. Zealots and Sicarii who believed that Jews should have no king but God. Debtors who wanted relief from aristocrats and creditors. Messianists who believed that the Redemption was in the offing. Strategists who thought that help from beyond the Euphrates was available. Bandits who just wanted to cause trouble. All of these had long been suppressed by the alliance between Roman power and Judea's elite. Suddenly, the elite lost its faith in the Romans. Many if not most of the priests, formerly pillars of the collaborationist establishment, decided to rebel. They had wide support.

Josephus is at pains to make the Jewish revolt seem like the work of a few radicals and terrorists: it's one of the central themes of his book. The historical record suggests otherwise.[12] There were no opinion polls in antiquity, and the extent of support for the revolt cannot be measured. What can be said is that, throughout Judea, there were many thousands of enthusiastic rebels who preferred to flee to Jerusalem and continue the struggle there rather than to submit to the Roman army that slowly reconquered the countryside. There were, of course, also supporters of Rome and defectors who rebelled at first and then gave up. But the rebels remained in control of Jerusalem and they were fighters.

And so, we come to the events that led to the closing of the Temple to foreigners and to all the havoc of war that followed.

In July 67, a half year after closing the Temple, the militants in Jerusalem went for blood. They massacred the Roman garrison, even though it was the Sabbath, and even though they had promised the men safe passage. These soldiers were non-Jewish auxiliaries recruited from Samaria, hence their murder not merely attacked Rome; it also enflamed ethnic rivalry. Many of Rome's Jewish allies fled the city, afraid that their radical countrymen had all but declared war on Rome. In short order, the rebels turned on other Jews.

The Romans themselves had provoked these actions. Not Cestius; he knew that his job was to maintain good relations with the urban elites of his province, who were Rome's partners in empire. Rome preferred governing everywhere through local leaders rather than by taking on the burden itself. The problem wasn't the governor Cestius, but the procurator or administrator of Judea, Gessius Florus.[13] Unlike the Italian Cestius, Florus was born in a Greek city in Asia Minor. He had a heavy dose of the hostility to the other group that often marked Greek-Jewish relations in this period. Florus was wealthy, but no senator; rather, he belonged to the next highest class on Rome's social ladder, the equestrians, or Roman knights. As far as the emperor was concerned, that was a plus, since equestrians were hungrier for advancement and more pliable than the supercilious senators. A senator might have treated the subjects in his province with a certain sense of noblesse oblige. An equestrian was a better bet for getting to the heart of the matter: money. And Rome's current emperor needed plenty of that.

That emperor was Nero, the most notorious of Augustus's descendants and, as it turned out, the last of them to rule Rome (r. 54–68). Nero was childless and had had all his cousins murdered, so his death marked the end of a dynasty. Handsome as a young man, Nero had deteriorated physically after a life of luxury. He had a thick neck, protruding belly, and thin legs, unsightly effects accentuated by his average height. He liked to spend money and he needed more of it. Nero's chief expenses were lavish games and free grain, which he offered in Rome, as well as wars in Armenia and Britannia.

Above all, there was the cost of rebuilding Rome after the Great Fire of 64, which burned down a large part of the city. Nero appropriated the center of town for a new palace, thereby feeding the rumor that he had ordered the fire as a vicious sort of urban renewal.

Because Nero needed money, he ordered his procurators to squeeze the provincials. This was nothing new. In fact, the last procurators of Judea before the Great Revolt, beginning with Cumanus in 48, treated the province as a bank account and paid little attention to the feelings of the locals. Incident followed incident. In one case, a Roman auxiliary soldier "mooned" worshippers in the Temple during Passover, leading to a riot in which large numbers of Jews were trampled to death. On another occasion, Jewish "bandits" robbed a Roman official, leading the procurator to have certain Jewish villages attacked. A Roman auxiliary soldier got carried away and burned a Torah scroll. The procurator had to order the soldier's execution to calm things down. The auxiliary soldiers in question were Samaritans, the Jews' rivals.[14]

As things got worse Rome's enemies got stronger. One of them was the rebel Eleazar son of Dinai, a veteran of twenty years of guerrilla activity against Rome. His hideout was in the hills. After the procurator refused to punish a Samaritan who had murdered a pilgrim from Galilee, Eleazar came down to the lowlands and organized vigilante justice. He and his followers attacked Samaritan villages and killed the inhabitants. Eleazar escaped Roman punishment on this occasion, but he was later captured and sent to Rome, where he was probably executed. The rabbinic tradition remembers him as a murderer, but also as someone who tried to hasten the coming of the messiah before he came to a bad end. His fate did not discourage the ranks of the Jewish rebels; far from it.[15]

This was the situation that greeted Florus, who was appointed procurator in 64. Florus was happy to comply with Nero's wish to steal from the locals. Making this easier, Nero "despised the [Jewish] nation," as Josephus put it bluntly.[16] The Romans tried not to let likes and dislikes get in the way of empire, but they couldn't hide how difficult they found the Jews. Nero preferred the Greeks. Compared to the Jews, Greeks were culturally more like the Romans and politically more submissive. Nor was Nero alone in this preference. "When push came to shove," as one scholar put it, "the Romans in the East would always favor the Greeks over all others."[17] As a result, when it came to fleecing Judea, Florus turned on the Jews. Besides, they made a prime target.

Judea contained one of the glories of the ancient world, the Temple of Jerusalem, a magnificent structure and an engineering marvel. The Temple's coffers had been filled by visits from pilgrims, by gifts from foreign rulers, and by the payment of the annual half-shekel tax owed by all Jews from Hispania to Mesopotamia. For a greedy administrator, the opportunities were overflowing.

In principle, Florus reported to Cestius, the governor of Syria. In practice, Florus was independent because he had direct access to Nero. Florus intended to satisfy his emperor.

Florus's avarice was bound to upset Judeans, but that was only the start of the problem. The procurator sat in Caesarea, the seaport on the central coast. But the heart and soul of the Jewish people was in Jerusalem.

Jerusalem was a royal city, bedecked with palaces as a spring garden is with flowers. Centrally located, the city was called by some the navel of the country.[18] It was a fortress city surrounded by massive walls with seventy-four towers, sited above ravines on three sides with only the level ground to the north giving a glimmer of hope to the invader. Above all, it was a holy city, crowned by the Temple of God, whose sacrifices would have imbued everything with the sizzling smell of flesh if not for the mountain of incense that was burned to cover up the odor.

Jerusalem lies only thirty miles from the Mediterranean, but it felt like another world. It is a hill town, surrounded by pines. From the hills above the city, a person could see the Judean Desert and the Dead Sea. The mind turns more naturally to the east, to the caravan routes to Mesopotamia and Persia, than it does to the sea and ships that sail westward to Italy. That is, if the mind turns at all. If you are in Jerusalem, why think of anywhere else? But to govern Judea, one had to do just that.

Governing Judea, indeed, governing any part of the Roman Empire, was a balancing act. Rome and the conquered populations had an implicit agreement. Rome ruled through local elites, who were concentrated in cities. The Romans would respect their customs and traditions, so long as the elites kept a lid on hotheads and troublemakers. The locals would pay taxes and show respect to the emperor and his representatives. Rome, in turn, would keep the peace among various factions and groups within each province. In Judea, that meant maintaining at least basic harmony and cooperation between the Jewish majority and the two main minorities, Greeks and Samaritans; Arabs were also present. The Greeks were pagans. The Samaritans worshipped the same God as the Jews, but they had a separate ethnic identity and a separate temple in their own territory. Their origin was, and is, much disputed. Another group were the Idumeans, who inhabited the region south of Jerusalem. They had converted to Judaism in an earlier generation. They were loyal to Jerusalem, but maintained their own ethnic identity.

Florus upset Judea's delicate balance. He favored Greeks and Samaritans over Jews.

In May 66, violence broke out in Caesarea between Greeks and Jews. The incident was trivial, but Josephus underlined its consequences, calling it the pretext for the war.[19] At issue was access to a synagogue, which a Greek tried to restrict by building workshops right next to it. Young Jewish hotheads tried to stop the construction; Florus suppressed them; prominent members of the Jewish community offered him a bribe to prohibit the building project. Florus took the money, promised protection, but then reneged and left town. The situation escalated one Sabbath when the Gentiles sent a man to make a mock sacrifice of birds outside the synagogue, an insulting gesture meant to suggest that the Jews were lepers. A fight ensued, led by youths. The local cavalry commander tried to restore order, but the Gentiles overcame him. A delegation of Jews traveled about seven miles to see Florus and ask for his assistance, but he had them arrested.

The news provoked anger in Jerusalem, but it would have died down had Florus not made things worse by helping himself to seventeen silver talents from the Temple, a substantial sum. Jerusalem responded with a demonstration in which some made fun of Florus by going around with a basket and soliciting charity as if he were "poor and miserable."[20]

Florus responded violently. Rather than restoring order in Caesarea, which was still in turmoil, he turned on the Jerusalemites. No legions were stationed in Judea, but the procurator had an auxiliary force, made up mostly of Samaritans. They belonged to the units that had raucously celebrated the death of King Agrippa I in 44. During the decade of the 50s they brutally suppressed Jewish rioters in Caesarea and plundered their homes.[21] In 66, they were only too happy to carry out Florus's order to massacre civilians in Jerusalem. The rampaging soldiers killed men, women, children, and even infants: there were, it is said, 3,600 victims.[22] Florus also punished Jewish men who were Roman citizens and, like Florus, equestrians, by having them whipped and crucified. This marked an unprecedented violation of Roman law, both because equestrians were supposed to be treated carefully and because Roman citizens had a right to a trial. Florus followed up these atrocities by ordering the massacre of a peaceful crowd that had gathered outside the Jerusalem city gates to welcome a detachment of Roman troops.

Roman administrators were not known to treat provincials gently, but Florus's violence was something else. It shocked Jewish public opinion. Judea had experienced bad procurators before. The moderates had always won the day by arguing for gritting one's teeth and waiting for the next procurator. But by butchering civilians in the holy city, Florus wrecked the argument for restraint and sounded the starting bell for interethnic pandemonium.

Judea erupted. In Caesarea, Greeks massacred twenty thousand Jews and expelled the rest, wiping out the Jewish minority from the city.[23] The figure is probably exaggerated, like most of Josephus's figures, but the massacre was real enough. According to Josephus, the carnage took place on the very same day as the slaughter of the Roman garrison in Jerusalem. In its aftermath, ethnic violence erupted elsewhere in Judea and Syria. Jews attacked Greco-Syrian villages and cities. In Syria, Gentiles went after not just Jews, including converts, but also so-called God-fearers, Gentiles who followed some Jewish customs without converting. Josephus claims that there was killing and destruction of property on both sides, from Gaza to Tyre and from the Mediterranean to the other side of the Jordan River.[24] But the most consequential violence took place in Jerusalem. Rome's Jewish friends tried to stop it, none with more effort than King Agrippa II and his sister, Queen Berenice.

In an ideal world, the Romans managed hard-to-govern regions through a local king. In the past they did so with great success in Judea, most notably with Herod the Great. But Rome judged most of Herod's heirs as not up to the job. For most of the seventy years since Herod's death in 4 BCE, prefects and procurators governed Judea. The most famous (and infamous) was Pontius Pilate, prefect circa 26 to 36. At least, the prefects and procurators governed the heart of the country. Rome allowed Herod's descendants to continue to rule in Galilee, the Gaulanitis, and other parts of the north. Only King Marcus Julius Agrippa I, better known as Agrippa, was permitted to rule the whole country, but he died young after a successful but brief reign (41–44).

In 66, his son, King Marcus Julius Agrippa II, better known as Agrippa II, ruled in the Gaulanitis, parts of Galilee, and parts of today's southern Syria and western Jordan. Agrippa II was also supervisor of the Temple and had the right to appoint the High Priest. Agrippa II did not rule either Jerusalem or central Judea, both of which were under Florus's administration.

The king was Herod's great-grandson. He was a Jew, but his name was Latin. Having a first, last, and middle name was a Roman custom; Jewish men were known by their own name and their father's name, e.g., Bava son of Buta. The king's triple names indicate that he was a Roman citizen, and not just any citizen. Julius honors the ruling dynasty of Rome, all of whom belonged to the Julian clan. Marcus and Agrippa both commemorate the second-in-command to the emperor Augustus, Marcus Vipsanius Agrippa, himself a friend of Herod's dynasty. The king was also known as Herod Agrippa II; Herod wasn't a Jewish name, either, but a Greek one, derived from the word "hero." Agrippa II had been educated in Rome at the imperial court. He lived and breathed loyalty to the empire.

Agrippa II was a bachelor; his sister Queen Julia Berenice served as his de facto first lady. She, too, was a Jew and a Roman citizen. She had one Latin name, Julia, and one Greek, Berenice. She was three times married and three times widowed, once to a prominent and pro-Roman Jewish Alexandrian, and twice to Eastern kings. Agrippa II gave his sister a magnificent diamond, which spurred attention and fed malicious—and false—rumors of incest.

Berenice was beautiful and charming as well as pious. She was also ambitious, politically savvy, and courageous. In the spring of 66, she witnessed Florus's atrocities in Jerusalem firsthand and tried to stop them at great personal risk. She was in Jerusalem to fulfill a Nazirite vow made when she was ill, that is, an act of self-sacrifice as an offering to God: thirty days of abstention from wine, with her head shaved, before sacrificing at the Temple. Alarmed by events, Berenice sprang into action. She sent her military officers to plead with Florus, but his soldiers not only tortured and killed them in her presence but threatened to kill her, too. These soldiers were the same units, although probably not the same men, who had abused the statues of Berenice and her sisters after the death of their father, King Agrippa I, twenty-two years earlier. Berenice next followed her surviving soldiers to Florus's headquarters. Barefoot, she begged Florus in front of his tribunal to call his soldiers off, but to no avail. Berenice now fled to the royal palace (which was available for her family's use in Jerusalem) and spent an uneasy night there guarded by her troops. Agrippa II was in Alexandria, Egypt, at the time, but he hurried to Jerusalem to join Berenice.

Despite the massacre unleashed by Florus, the two royal siblings were dead set against revolt from invincible Rome. First Agrippa sent a cavalry force to try, in vain, to restore order to the city. Then Agrippa came himself. He and Berenice tried to talk the Jewish public out of rebellion—Agrippa II with a speech, the two of them with tears—but in vain. They fled Jerusalem. Then the insurgents burned the palaces that the two had there and helped themselves to a (small) part of the royal treasure. They also burned the palace of Ananias, the former High Priest.

Jerusalem was gripped by violence. Insurgents torched the public archives, which contained debt records. A series of assassinations of leading pro-Romans took place, followed by revenge killings of leading rebels.

"Jewish patience lasted until Florus became procurator; under him, war broke out," wrote Tacitus.[25] Florus acted "as if he had contracted to fan the war into flame," was the verdict of Josephus.[26]

Cestius, too, blamed the war on Florus, but even so, Cestius marched to Jerusalem.[27] He took the main road from the coast, which rose from the plain to the Judean Hills through the Beth Horon pass. About six miles beyond the pass was the hill of Gabaon (biblical Gibeon), where Cestius planned to camp. The rear of Cestius's column was probably still just exiting the Beth Horon pass when the van reached its campsite at Gabaon. Jerusalem lay another six miles to the southeast. Before the Romans could reach there, Jewish rebels struck.

By now the news of the massacre at Joppa and the attacks in Galilee had surely reached Jerusalem. Before the violence unleashed by Florus and Cestius, cooperation with Rome seemed the most sensible policy to most Judeans. To some, it still did, but that argument was harder to justify. The hour had come, it seemed, for those militants who preached armed resistance.

Unlike the Roman troops, the militants were lightly armed. A few, with professional military experience, might have looked dashing, but most were likely dressed in simple tunics. Most probably fought on foot, using spears and arrows as their weapons.

The fighters represented at least three different groups of Jews opposed to Rome, the "kingdom of arrogance," as they called it.[28] Jewish society, then as now, was famously diverse in its opinions. One set of militants had been fighting Rome for generations. They were a dynasty of rebels from Gaulanitis. As noted earlier, their followers were called by the Romans Sicarii, literally, "dagger men," because of their habit of attacking their opponents, Jewish or Roman, with daggers concealed under their clothes. They probably got the name in the decade or so before the outbreak of the Great Revolt, because it was then that they came to prominence as assassins both in Jerusalem and in Judean villages. Josephus describes one incident circa 60 when one of the Sicarii tried to set himself up as a messiah figure in the countryside, only to have the procurator send out troops to kill him and his followers.[29]

Josephus condemned the Sicarii bitterly. He denounced their methods, especially their murders, and above all, the murders that they committed in the Temple. Josephus wrote that, in his opinion, the impiety of the Sicarii turned God Himself away from the Jewish people. He concluded that the Temple was unclean and so he inflicted the Romans on Jerusalem with all the evils that came with them: purification by fire and enslavement of women and children as well as adult men. A believer despite it all, Josephus concluded that the divine purpose was just: God wished to correct His people by these disasters.[30]

It was the Sicarii who, during the violence in Jerusalem in the summer of 66, killed the former High Priest Ananias and his brother, who were pro-Roman. In revenge, Eleazar, the leading priestly rebel at this point, had the Sicarii leader Menahem son of Judah and some of his followers killed. The remaining Sicarii fled to Masada, where they spent the rest of the war. Masada offered several advantages, besides its remove from Jerusalem. It lay on a north-south highway to Arabia, it was well-fortified and defensible, and it contained a large cache of weapons.[31]

A second group was drawn from the Jerusalem priesthood and focused on the Temple. Eleazar was one of their leaders. Josephus calls them Zealots, explaining that "so they called themselves, as though they were zealous in the cause of virtue and not for vice in its basest and most extravagant form."[32] More likely they described themselves by the Hebrew word *Kanna'im*, which is associated with the biblical priest Phinehas, who became famous for the "zeal" with which he battled paganism.[33] In an earlier period, they might not have opposed Rome at all, but in the Florus era, they decided to fight. A third group consisted of men from other outlying regions. They included converts, some of them immigrants from far away, and some, it is likely, Roman citizens. They included proponents of transferring wealth from the rich to the poor and of liberating slaves. This group was popular in the countryside.

Even so, a part of the Jewish population preferred not to fight. They called for bowing to the reality of Rome's overwhelming force and preserving what they thought really mattered, the Temple in Jerusalem and the Torah. They represented an opinion that went back to the days of the Babylonian Captivity

(586–539 BCE), when the prophet Jeremiah preached acceptance of the divine judgment. God would redeem Israel in His own good time, the argument went; in the meantime, it was best to cooperate with the ruling power.

The militants stood in a different tradition. They could point to the lesson of the Maccabean Revolt, a ragtag uprising in the 160s BCE that built an army and eventually liberated Judea from the Greco-Syrian overlord who had tried to turn the Temple into a pagan shrine and to abolish some of the basic laws of the Torah. If the Maccabees had won freedom, with God's help, their descendants could win it again. Or so some said, but they were appealing to a "Maccabean myth," as one historian put it.[34] Syria was a state in decline that eventually collapsed from within, while Rome was the mightiest empire that the Mediterranean world had ever known. And that empire was on the march.

As Cestius and his men headed toward Gabaon, the Jewish militants went on the attack. It was both the autumn harvest festival of Sukkot and the Sabbath, the day of rest, but that did not deter them. "The passion that shook them out of their piety gave them an advantage in the battle as well," writes Josephus. "They fell upon the Romans with such an impetus that they broke their ranks, drove through the middle, and destroyed them."[35] He writes that they killed 515 Romans, 400 infantry, and 115 cavalry, while losing only 22 Jews.[36] The Roman cavalry and certain infantry units circled back to help, which prevented even greater Roman losses.

Josephus claims that this was a frontal attack on the Romans, although that hardly seems like the tactic that irregulars would use—or that they would succeed with. He says that they then made another attack on the rear, which is more plausible. Perhaps they launched both attacks at the same time, in a coordinated manner. The second attack succeeded in capturing large numbers of the Romans' mules and baggage.

Several Jewish heroes emerged from the fighting, according to Josephus.[37] Niger of Perea came from what is now western Jordan. Niger is a Latin name, which may indicate that he was a Roman citizen. Silas the Babylonian was a deserter from Agrippa II's cavalry. His name is Aramaic, but might be a transliteration of the Latin Silva or Silanus, raising the possibility that he had served as a Roman auxiliary soldier. It's likely that he belonged to the Babylonian Jewish community established east of Galilee by King Herod. There were two princes from a family of foreign converts: Monobazos and Cenedaeus of the kingdom of Adiabene, both relatives of King Monobazos II, and probably the grandsons of that famous Adiabenian convert to Judaism, Queen Helena.

The Adiabenians played an outsize role, at least in the rebels' minds. Adiabene was by far the most important kingdom to be ruled by a Jewish dynasty, but it was not Babylonia, the main area of Jewish settlement in the Parthian Empire, in which Adiabene was a vassal kingdom. The rebels, it seems, hoped for help from their Jewish brethren all over the Parthian Empire.

From the outset, according to Josephus, the rebels looked east. He states that the Jews "hoped that the whole of their race beyond the Euphrates would join in their venture."[38] Josephus has Agrippa II deride this in his speech in Jerusalem in 66. The rebels had high hopes for help from Adiabene, said Agrippa II, but their king would never take the risk. Besides, even if he wanted to, his overlord, the Parthian king, had too much invested in his treaties with Rome to allow his vassal to drag Parthia into war by violating that treaty.[39] Several years later, according to Josephus, the Roman commander Titus berated the rebels for sending embassies "beyond the Euphrates" in a vain attempt to "stir up revolt."[40] But vain as the expectation of such aid turned out to be, both rebels and Romans might have considered it in their plans. There was always the possibility, as one scholar puts it, that Jews from east of the Euphrates might come "flooding Jewish ranks and overwhelming Roman troops with their size and strength."[41]

The sources record another Jew from Parthian lands who fought for the rebellion, another Adiabenian.[42] There were probably others who went unrecorded. After all, Josephus, our main source, had reason to downplay their presence. As a Jew in Rome he was constantly on guard against the charge that Jews in the Roman Empire cooperated with their brethren in Parthia and therefore were a threat to Rome.

The Adiabenians attracted attention, but the man of the hour was Simon son of Giora. He led the attack on the Roman rearguard and inflicted a beating. He was young, a man of physical strength and courage. The charismatic Simon was well on his way to being idolized by his followers, who would be tied to him by iron bonds. A descendant of converts, he may have come from a Jewish city in what is now Jordan, which had a substantial Jewish population at the time. He would eventually emerge as the chief leader of the revolt.

Cestius licked his wounds at Gabaon for three days. Before he could attack Jerusalem, King Agrippa sent two representatives to parley with the rebels. The two men were authorized to issue full pardons, but they never entered the city. The rebels attacked the king's men outside the walls, killing one and sending the other, wounded, back to the Roman camp.

Cestius finally advanced toward Jerusalem, stopping first at Mount Scopus, a little over a mile away. Scopus means "scout" or "lookout" in Greek, and is aptly named, since the hill offers a bird's-eye view of the city below, with the Temple directly ahead. Cestius then attacked. Josephus says that Cestius burned the northern suburbs and laid siege to the city. He hoped that Rome's friends would open the gates, but the militants were in control and they held fast. Cestius tried to storm the walls, but their defenses proved too stout. Or so Cestius thought. Josephus argues that he could easily have fought his way in, restored peace, and stopped the war before it had really begun. The historian attributes Cestius's failure to bad advice from his commanders, who, he says, had been bribed by Florus.[43] Another week of attempts to storm the walls failed in the face of determined opposition, and the legionaries had to defend themselves with the famous shields-locked-overhead or "tortoise" (*testudo*) maneuver. Nothing worked, and a frustrated Cestius decided to retreat.

Just what happened at Jerusalem is unclear, as the details of Josephus's account don't add up.[44] For example, a veteran commander like Cestius would not have planned to begin a siege in October, at the start of the rainy season, yet he brought siege equipment with him. Perhaps he got bad advice; perhaps his commanders were corrupt; perhaps he lost his nerve. Perhaps the Twelfth Legion was still a broken reed. More likely, Cestius never planned a real fight at Jerusalem; he expected to overawe the troublemakers and restore order easily with the help of Rome's friends. That would have been a failure of intelligence on his part. Cestius assessed the militants too lightly.

His troubles were only beginning. Any victory against the mighty emboldens the weak. Cestius should have expected rebel raiders on his march home, especially after their strikes on his advancing column, but he failed to prepare. First the militants attacked the Romans on the march back from Jerusalem to Mount Scopus, and then on the march from Mount Scopus to Gabaon. The light-armed Jewish rebels raided the slow-moving, heavily armed Roman infantrymen with impunity, in each case aiming at the rearguard. Not only did they kill a legionary commander; they forced the Romans to dump most of their equipment, which ended up in rebel hands.

For the next two days the Romans marched from their camp at Gabaon back to the Beth Horon Pass. Cestius ordered them to kill all the beasts of burden and abandon their loads, "that therefore he might fly the faster."[45] It didn't help, and the insurgents attacked them in the pass.

The pass extends for about two miles, so narrow in its easternmost part that there wasn't enough room for two camels to go up or down at the same time.[46] That is probably where the insurgents concentrated their attack, hurling javelins and shooting arrows at the Romans. They made the enemy bleed. The Romans took refuge in a town at the lower end of the pass, but Cestius was worried about their ability to continue, so he resorted to a night march and a ruse. He chose four hundred men to stay in the town overnight. He ordered them to go up on the roofs and give the watchword over and over, as if the entire army were still camped there. In the meantime, he and the bulk of the troops escaped.

Cestius and his soldiers covered a considerable distance overnight. At first light he had the men speed on, leading them to panic and abandon their remaining battering rams and arrow-launching catapults. In the meantime, the insurgents discovered Cestius's trick and massacred the men left behind. The Jews pursued the Romans nearly all the way to the coast, but couldn't catch up. The rebels gave up the chase at Antipatris, where a narrow pass forms a natural boundary between the hill country to the east and the Mediterranean plain to the west. They turned back and carried off the artillery left behind by the Romans. They also stripped arms and armor from the dead and marched back triumphantly to Jerusalem. According to Josephus, the Jewish insurgents had killed 5,300 Roman infantrymen and 480 cavalrymen, while suffering few casualties themselves.[47]

One of the leaders of the victory over the retreating Romans was Eleazar son of Simon. Unlike the heroes of the rebel raid on the Romans on their way to Jerusalem, Eleazer was a member of the priestly elite and a Zealot. In the ancient world it was often outsiders—immigrants, peasants, hill-country residents, slaves—who raised the banner of rebellion. With Eleazar we have a full-fledged member of the Establishment leading the fight against Rome. And he was not alone. Seeing that the rebels had won the day, many of the moderates joined them. The Jerusalem Establishment let themselves be swept up by the unexpected success of the young, moved either by enthusiasm or fear. In short order, a government was set up and generals were appointed to command various districts.

Cestius's failure set off shock waves. It was less disastrous than the ambush at the Teutoburg Forest six decades earlier, when Rome lost three legions, but it was grave nonetheless. Cestius lost the equivalent of about one legion. But the politics were not the same. Germania was a freshly conquered Roman province, its colonies still in the process of being laid out. Judea was different. In 66, Judea had been a Roman province ever since the year 6, with a brief period of independence from 41 to 44. Before that, Judea had been a client state. Earlier still, in 160 BCE, Judea had become Rome's ally. Altogether, Judea had been in Rome's orbit for 225 years when it rebelled in 66. Rome couldn't tolerate humiliation in an established part of the empire like Judea.[48]

Cestius was disgraced, but Rome demanded honor. The emperor made the next move.

Nero

Nero's name is synonymous today with decadence and depravity, and for good reason. It's not just his luxurious lifestyle, his murder of his mother, his vicious mistreatment of his wives, his execution of senators and philosophers, his persecution of Christians, and the suspicion of guilt for the great fire that ravaged Rome. Nero's excesses provoked deep discontent in the Roman elite. In 65, he uncovered a conspiracy involving many senators and officers of the Praetorian Guard. Nero ordered the execution or exile of several dozen high-profile people, including his former tutor and chief aide, Seneca the Younger.

Elite discontent at Nero continued, fueled also by his blunders in foreign policy. His encouragement of misbehavior leading to a revolt in Judea was not his only failure. There was also a major setback on the Parthian front.

In May 66, Nero endured a foreign-policy humiliation in Armenia that was cleverly disguised as a triumph. As mentioned previously, Rome had tried to put its man, one Tigranes, on the throne of Armenia, but was forced to back down and accept a Parthian king, Tiridates. In 63, Rome and Parthia had agreed that Tiridates would go to Rome and accept his crown from Nero, as if Tiridates ruled at Rome's sufferance. In principle, Armenia would be neutral but, in practice, its king was part of the same family that reigned over Parthia, meaning that Armenia would lean toward Rome's enemy.

In May 66, three years after an agreement over Armenia had been struck, the new king finally came to Rome. Nero put on a wondrous spectacle, as if celebrating a triumph, but Tiridates spoiled the party. An ancient writer described his trip to Rome from the East, accompanied by a royal retinue and three thousand Parthian cavalrymen as a triumphal procession. Although he agreed to bow down in public before Nero, he bowed Parthian style, in a deep salaam. He refused an order to put down his dagger, but kept it in its scabbard. Later, at a gladiatorial game put on in his honor, Tiridates is supposed to have pulled off a feat of skill: he got up in his seat and shot an arrow at two bulls, killing them both with a single shot. The Parthians were famous archers. Although it is difficult to kill two bulls with one arrow, it is possible with a sufficiently powerful bow, the animals standing side by side, and a broadside shot aimed just right. The message was that Tiridates may have bestirred himself to travel to Italy and bowed down to the emperor, but the Parthian remained very much in charge. All in all, it was a bad showing for Nero. But it was just the start of the year's embarrassments.[49]

The family of Herod was at the heart of Nero's failed plan, most notably in the choice of Tigranes, who was Herod the Great's great-grandson. The collapse of Nero's scheme made the Herodians as well as Rome look weak. At home, Nero faced the simmering hatred of the Roman elite. One can understand why a Jew who was discontented with Roman misrule in Judea might have concluded in 66 that the hour had come to rebel.

In October 66, when Cestius met disaster outside Jerusalem, Nero was in Greece. He was on his only foreign tour as emperor. The tour served no military or diplomatic purpose but, rather, furthered Nero's ambition of winning prizes in Greece's famous games. Nero took part in four different types of contests: he sang and accompanied himself on the lyre; he acted in tragedies, wearing a mask and costume; he raced chariots; and he joined in the contest of heralds. To no one's surprise he was declared the winner of every event in which he competed.

The winter of 67 found Nero in Corinth, the capital of Roman Greece. Famous for its wealth and excess, Corinth made an appropriate base for the luxury-loving ruler. Corinth also offered a reminder of how the Romans did business. Corinth had led a rebellion in 146 BCE and the Romans laid siege to it. When the town fell, they sacked Corinth, killed all the men, sold the women and children into slavery, and left the city in ruins. A century later, they refounded Corinth as a Roman city. In 67, it had a mixed population of Greeks, Romans, and Jews.

Nero may have been a decadent, but he was also a Caesar. He had no intention of letting the defeat of a Roman army go unpunished. By now, the Romans were used to provincial rebellions and to the need to suppress them with force. Rome accepted the inevitability of rebellion; it was the price of doing business, so to speak: How not, with so many recently conquered peoples, and with an army of only three hundred thousand men to police an empire that stretched from Britannia to Syria?[50] Beginning with Augustus, rebellions broke out in Illyricum (6–9 CE), Germania (9–16), Gaul (21),

Numidia (ca. 17–24), and Britannia (60). Rome always sent in the legions. Now it was Judea, but its situation was unusual.

From the Roman point of view, Jewish rebellion expressed ingratitude and arrogance. It was, as one scholar suggests, a "great Jewish betrayal."[51] Judea was no freshly conquered territory, but a province of the Romans for over a century, even if Rome had tolerated rule by Jewish client kings there for a time before simply annexing most of the country. A Roman might have looked at the violence in and around Jerusalem and asked: Who were the bandit elements of a minor people of barbarous habits to challenge the legions? Why, the Jews had the effrontery to deny the existence of the gods of Rome! And the same Jews flirted with the enemy, Parthia.

One of the reasons for Romans' success as an empire was that they saw the big picture. Nero, wrote Josephus, was concerned not only about revolt in Judea but also in its neighbors, who were "catching the disease." It was a matter not just of one country but of a region: the East.[52] By destroying Cestius's legion Judea moved in Roman eyes from the category of rebel province to foreign enemy. Consequently, Rome had to respond forcefully. So concludes a comparative study of Imperial Rome's response to provincial rebellions.[53]

Nero needed a general to punish the Jews. The obvious choice was Corbulo, the wily veteran of war on the Parthian front, but he was unavailable because the ever-suspicious emperor felt threatened by Corbulo's success and forced him to take his own life. Nero chose instead a competent but less glamorous general to lead an expeditionary force to suppress the rebellion in Judea and pacify the region. He was a fifty-seven-year-old veteran, Titus Flavius Vespasianus, one of the men who had conquered Britannia for Rome. Vespasian, as we know him today, was every inch a soldier, riding on horseback among the cavalry in the army's marching column, mixing with the men, and paying attention to their safety and well-being while driving them forward.

Vespasian was slow, steady, and unflappable. He was, says one writer, the equal of the great generals of old in everything but his greed, but that criticism might just have been an aristocrat's sneer.[54] Vespasian knew his way around the court and was no innocent in Roman politics. But he was no threat to

Nero. A man of rough manners from a family with a business background, Vespasian came from the Sabine hill country north of Rome. Blunt and earthy, Vespasian was rooted in the common sense of rural Italy. According to one anecdote, when the commander of a cavalry unit came to see him drenched with perfume, Vespasian said that he would rather that the officer smelled of garlic. In other words, he preferred his officers manly and uncouth to soft and cultured. The most famous anecdote concerns a tax on public urinals, which offended his highfalutin younger son, Domitian. "Money has no smell," is Vespasian's famous reply.[55]

Vespasian had no connection to the Roman nobility. No one could suspect him of harboring ambitions of replacing Nero as emperor. Most important of all, Vespasian, unlike Cestius, could get the job done. And so, the war was on, beginning with a Jewish victory at Beth Horon.

A Failure of Statesmanship

Just as the unanticipated assassination of the heir to the throne of Austria-Hungary at Sarajevo sparked the First World War, it was the rebels' surprising victory at Beth Horon that ignited the flames of the Great Revolt. Their success, writes one historian, was "a windfall of unimaginable proportions to those advocating rebellion."[56] Rome could tolerate an incident in which the locals killed a legionary or two, but Rome could not tolerate the destruction of a legion. Beth Horon ensured that Judea would be plunged into a major conflict, in fact bigger than anyone could foresee. The Great Revolt, also known as the Jewish War, lasted from 66 to 70, with the destruction of the final rebel outpost at Masada in 74. As a result of Rome's victory, tens of thousands of Jews would be killed or enslaved. Large parts of the land would be confiscated and handed over to Romans. Three cities would be destroyed, among them, Jerusalem, the capital, the Holy City. The Temple, whose rebuilt splendor had been completed only a few years before, would be left in ruins. The centerpiece of Jewish religious practice, the daily sacrifices to God at the

Temple, would be no more. The priestly aristocracy would be swept away. A Roman legion would be permanently encamped outside the ruined city. The annual half-shekel tax that all Jews were expected to pay to the Temple would now be paid to Jupiter Optimus Maximus, the chief deity of Rome.

Nor were the problems that led to war in 66 solved by 74. They would simmer below the surface and then explode again, not once, but twice in the next seventy years.

All wars are avoidable until they are not. A combination of responsible leadership, careful management, the will to compromise, and just plain fear: these can make peace prevail. No matter how seemingly irrepressible, every conflict can be repressed. But youth, passion, and arrogance can win the day and cause a war. That was the fate of Judea in the year 66. Strong underlying causes fanned the flames of conflict. Still, without a Nero or Florus on the Roman side and without an Eleazar son of Ananias or Simon son of Giora on the Jewish side, peace might have prevailed. Herod and Augustus would have managed matters with ease, but they were long gone. Even after them, it was still possible to put the brakes on. "For the most part," wrote one historian, "wise legates in Syria with the aid of Judaean royals and an emperor such as Claudius kept things in check."[57] Then came Nero. Accident played a role as well. If Cestius had displayed more caution in the Beth Horon Pass, then the major incident that drove Rome into all-out war might never have happened. So it is with most wars: no matter how flammable the tinder, careful management can avoid a conflagration. Luck helps, too.

The outbreak of war in 66, disastrous for Judea and destabilizing for Rome, demonstrates the absence on both sides of what is essential for peace: statesmanship. Hope, fear, and wishful thinking all replaced realism. The result was the destruction of Jerusalem and the Temple in Judea—and civil war in Rome.

Chapter Five

THE WAR IN THE NORTH

In the year 64, when he was twenty-six, Josephus went on a mission to Rome. Or, rather, the man who later became Josephus; at the time, his name was Joseph son of Mattathias. He was not a Roman citizen nor a companion of generals and emperors. He was not yet T. Flavius Josephus. He was a Jew and a native of Jerusalem.

The authorities chose Josephus—as we will call him, for simplicity's sake—not just because he was young and vigorous but also because he was an aristocrat and a priest and renowned for his intelligence. He surely knew Greek, the language needed to speak to the Roman procurator in Caesarea. It was in Greek and not Latin that Rome's administrators communicated with the empire's subjects in the East. Every educated Roman needed to know at least some Greek. That Josephus was picked for the mission shows that he was an up-and-coming person in Jerusalem.

A member of the city's nobility, Josephus belonged to the most eminent clan of the priesthood, and, on his mother's side, he was of royal blood, descended from the Hasmoneans. That gave him a better pedigree than Herod the Great had.

Josephus's job was to try to rescue Jewish prisoners in Rome. The procurator had arrested certain priests who Josephus knew personally, "noble gentlemen," as he calls them, and sent them to the capital in chains, to face Nero, on what Josephus calls a "slight and trifling charge."[1] He provides no details. A sign of their nobility, according to Josephus: as prisoners they survived on figs and nuts to avoid eating nonkosher food.

Josephus sailed on a large vessel with six hundred people aboard. The voyage from Caesarea to Ostia, the port of Rome, took three weeks or more. In the middle of the Adriatic Sea the ship foundered. Josephus and his fellow passengers had to swim all night. About daybreak they saw a ship of Cyrene. The eighty fastest swimmers, including Josephus, outstripped the others and were taken on board. Approximately a week later, Josephus landed in Puteoli, the port of Naples.[2]

The spareness of Josephus's description of this disaster is notable. He doesn't mention the fate of the 520 passengers who didn't swim fast. He doesn't state the cause of the shipwreck, nor does he dwell on the ordeal of having to swim through the night. Did he have trouble staying above water? Did he hear the cries of those who couldn't swim as they began to go under? Josephus attributes his salvation to divine providence. The terseness of his narrative underlines the miracle of his survival.[3]

Although he was a blue blood, in Italy Josephus stooped to get help from an actor—a lowly profession in priestly eyes. The actor was a Jew and a favorite of Nero. Through this actor Josephus met Nero's wife, Poppaea Sabina. She was a famous beauty who took a daily bath in the milk of five hundred donkeys to preserve her skin and inspired a line of cosmetics named after her. Josephus describes her as a "God-fearer," that is, someone who took an interest in Judaism without becoming a Jew. Limited as that interest probably was, Poppaea nonetheless helped Josephus to get the priests released. He claims that she also gave him "great gifts."[4] Then Josephus returned to Judea, his mission accomplished.

Two years later, Josephus was back home in Jerusalem when the war against Rome broke out. He was an eyewitness to events. More, he was a major player in some of them. Consider the outlook of the rebels who took power in Jerusalem. Josephus, they concluded, could be useful.

The Spirit of 66

The rebels of 66 believed that they were building a government and they thought it would last. The coins they struck testify to their hopes and beliefs. During the five years of the rebellion (66–70), they issued both silver and bronze coins. The coins were notably precise, professional, and pure, with an impressive silver content of 98 percent, making them more pure than Nero's silver coins. More important, they were the first, and perhaps the only, true rebel coinage ever issued in the Roman Empire. From Augustus on, only the emperor had the right to mint silver (or gold) coins. The Jewish silver coins marked a real break. They were a clear declaration of independence.[5]

Both the legends and symbols of the Jewish rebel coins are striking. The legends are in Paleo-Hebrew, already an archaic form of the Hebrew alphabet in 66 and one that looked to the ancient past. Aramaic was the common language of the Jews of Judea. Why did the rebels use Hebrew? As one scholar concludes, Hebrew was the language of Jewish nationalism and independence.[6]

The rebels named their state not "Judah" or "Yahud" or "Judea" but "Israel." The choice of Israel was deliberate. "Israel" had an emotional and religious resonance that "Judea" lacked. "Israel" was an ancient name for the Jewish people attested both in the Torah and in secular inscriptions going back over a thousand years earlier. In the Bible, "Israel" refers to the whole people, while "Judea" (more accurately in this case, Judah, a variant of the same word) refers only to a part. Only in later centuries, under first Persian and then Greek and Roman rule, did Judea come into use as the name of the country. "Israel" rebranded Judea and reached beyond Judea. It referred to all Jews, whether they lived in Judea, Egypt, Syria, Babylonia, or anywhere else in the ancient world. The choice of Israel may signal the rebels' hope that they would get support from Jews abroad, especially in the Parthian Empire.

Each coin was inscribed on the obverse with a chalice and the legend "Shekel of Israel." The new name marked a break with Roman nomenclature and Roman imagery: gone was the head of the emperor in profile, as was found on Roman coins. The chalice may represent an omer measurement recalling the offering made after Passover, or perhaps it depicts a cup used in the Temple. The image on the reverse of the coin is thought to be either a pomegranate, symbol of the fertility of the Land of Israel, or a priest's staff. The legend reads "Jerusalem is Holy" in the coins of the first year and "Jerusalem the Holy" in the coins of years two through five. (Each coin was marked by a number, signified by a Hebrew letter, testifying to the year of the revolt.)[7]

The silver coins represent an ideology that was surely not invented overnight. The very striking of silver coins, the use of Paleo-Hebrew, the name of Israel, and the invocation of Jerusalem's holiness also suggest a program on the part of people who knew what they were about. The bronze coins suggest an even more radical program, one that reflects the Fourth Philosophy, as Josephus called the sect that began in 6 CE and that preached violent opposition to Rome in pursuit of freedom for Jews in their homeland.

The bronze coins date from years two through four and depict a wine jar and a vine leaf. Other symbols associated with the Feast of Tabernacles (Sukkot) appear as well: date palms, a yellow citrus fruit (*etrog*), and a palm branch (*lulav*). The coins of year three bear the legend "For the Freedom of Zion," and those of year four, "For the Redemption of Zion." "Zion" is a term that appears frequently in the Bible. It can refer to a hill in Jerusalem, to the city itself, or to God's presence in the Temple.

The coins have occasioned many scholarly debates about who produced them, where, and what their legends and symbolism mean. Arguably, the silver coins were minted by the priesthood, who controlled the Temple and its treasure. Likewise, the bronze coins were arguably minted by more radical groups who dominated Jerusalem beginning in 68.

Whoever produced them, all the coins avow independence from Rome. They also proclaim Jewish nationhood: They are coins of Israel. They are not secular. Few, if any, coins of ancient states were secular. Greek and Roman coins refer to their various pagan deities. Jews do not depict God, of course, since that was prohibited by the Ten Commandments. But the various symbols used on these coins and the references to Zion and to the holiness of Jerusalem make the religious character of the rebels' program unmistakable. It was a program to appeal to Zealots, who wanted their country to be a Jewish state, ruled from the House of God in Jerusalem, rather than a pagan state ruled from the House of Augustus in Caesarea. The reference to freedom surely also appealed to the Sicarii, who had long emphasized freedom, although they were driven out of Jerusalem early in the revolt. In fact, the famous Sicarii remained largely offstage until the final act of the drama at Masada, eight years later.

The rebels were freedom fighters. The coins offer the most eloquent but not the only testimony of this. Josephus, for example, states repeatedly that freedom was their primary goal. He wrote in Greek and uses the Greek word for freedom (*eleutheria*), but the coins, inscribed in Hebrew, use the Hebrew term: *herut*.

Freedom (*herut*) had a specific meaning in the ancient Jewish context. It meant liberation from slavery, debt, and exile as well as repatriation to one's homeland, where a person could worship God in His Temple. It had both positive (freedom to) and negative (freedom from) connotations, but it differed from the Athenian notion of freedom as participating in politics—literally, the affairs of the polis, or city-state—and "living as you please." Jewish freedom meant subordination to God's law. The new Jewish state would be a temple state, not a civic state. And it would govern itself. Redemption (*geulah*) connotes the nation's hope that God would deliver Israel from its tribulations and restore it so that Jews could live in the land safely, in obedience to the divine law and protected by an eternal covenant. Redemption surely had a messianic connotation to many Jews.[8]

It wasn't only the minters of rebel coins who cited "freedom" and "redemption." People doing ordinary business used the terms as well. The words "freedom" and "redemption" appear on six papyrus documents from the era of the Great Revolt. They were found in caves in the Judean Desert, where they were probably brought by refugees from Jerusalem or Masada. They are legal documents having to do with buying and selling, land access, or divorce. They all use the dating of the new state of Israel. Three of the documents are in Aramaic, but the other three are in Hebrew, a clear statement of support for the revolt because Hebrew was not otherwise used in legal texts.[9]

The ideals of "freedom" and "redemption" referred specifically to the Jewish people, but they did not require going it alone. On the contrary, they allowed for subordination to a foreign patron, if that patron permitted the Jews to worship God's law in His land. To many Jews, Rome seemed a bad patron. Some looked hopefully to Parthia instead.

The rebels were motivated by ideals, but they were not dreamers. Driving the Romans out of Judea was beyond their reach, but getting the Romans to agree to let them govern a kind of ministate in and around Jerusalem might have been possible, as one historian argues.[10] After all, the Romans had conceded most of Germania to Arminius and his fellow rebels, while maintaining the Rhineland under Roman rule.

The Jewish rebels might have looked back to the success of the Maccabees in winning independence from the Seleucid Kingdom and thought that they, too, might break free from the Roman Empire. Rome was bigger and stronger than the Seleucids, but its capital was far away rather than in nearby Antioch. Nero was decadent and tarnished by rebellion at home and defeat abroad.

General in Galilee

Jerusalem in 66 was immersed in blood and turmoil. A relatively moderate group, however, managed to take control of the revolutionary government. One of the leaders was a former High Priest, which indicates support for the revolt by the Establishment. Later, the radicals accused these moderates of insufficient commitment to the cause. The moderates, they charged, were always looking over their shoulders for a way out, always searching for a deal with the Romans. The charge has some substance to it. The moderates might have reasoned that honor and safety required an uprising against Florus, but prudence dictated a compromise before Roman vengeance came down hard. For the time being, the moderates displayed commitment to the war. The

THE WAR IN THE NORTH

mere fact that they had stayed in Jerusalem when others left shows that "these men were committed to fight on behalf of the independent Jewish state," as one historian puts it.[11]

They appointed two generals to raise the walls of Jerusalem and six other generals of the regions that had once belonged to Herod the Great's kingdom. This represented an ambitious stretch of territory from Gaulanitis and Galilee in the north to Be'er Sheva in the south and extending across the Jordan River into Perea. Most of those regions were part of Roman Judea, but others were governed by King Agrippa II. As far as is known, almost none of the new leaders had military experience. In 66, there were Jewish soldiers, some of them even legionaries who had fought for Rome. Unfortunately for the rebels, as it turned out, most of those experienced men would fight against the revolt rather than for it.

A leader who was left out of a position of power was Eleazar son of Simon, one of the heroes of the defeat of Cestius in 66. A Zealot, he was probably considered too extreme to be part of the governing council. But he remained in the city and bided his time.

Jerusalem was defended by two strong walls. The First Wall, which protected the southern parts of the city, had sixty towers, while the shorter Second Wall, to the north, had fourteen towers. These two, along with the steepness of the topography, rendered the city all but impregnable on three sides: the south, east, and west. But the north side of the city faced level ground, which left Jerusalem vulnerable. Then, too, the city had expanded to the north, and much of it lay outside the two walls. Recognizing this, King Agrippa I had tried to build a new third wall farther to the north in 41 to 44, but the ever-watchful Romans forced him to stop after laying the foundations. Now the rebels resumed construction. By the year 69, the Third Wall had ninety towers. Josephus says that Agrippa I's wall would have rendered Jerusalem impregnable had it been continued as it began. The rebels had no choice but to build their Third Wall in haste. It was not as strong as Agrippa's wall would have been.[12]

But the rebels were not content with defense. Josephus blamed them for letting their unexpected success against Cestius go to their heads, "as if they had been set on fire by fortune."[13] In their enthusiasm they turned on an old enemy of the Jews, Ascalon (Ashkelon, Israel), an independent city, largely Syrian-Greek in population. It was located on the Mediterranean coast, about sixty miles from Jerusalem. The rebels sent an army against Ascalon under the command of three experienced men: Niger of Perea and Silas the Babylonian, both heroes of the fight against Cestius, and John the Essene, who had been appointed general for northwest Judah.

It may seem odd that an Essene was a general. After all, the men of the Qumran community, who were probably Essenes, are known for their monasticism and retirement to the desert. But the Essenes despised the Romans. The Romans eventually reciprocated by destroying Qumran and subjecting the monks there to extreme torture. Josephus proudly reports that they refused to give in to the Romans' demands, regardless of the agony inflicted. So an Essene commander in the revolt makes sense.[14]

The rebel forces outnumbered the defenders of Ascalon, who had only two small units, one infantry and one cavalry. But their commander, a Roman, to judge by his name—Antonius—knew what he was doing and had veteran troops, unlike the rebels' largely untested forces. He took advantage of the level terrain around Ascalon to crush the attackers with his cavalry and kill two of the three rebel generals, John and Silas. The Jews fell back, but they rallied and made a second attack. Antonius was prepared and ambushed them in the passes. They suffered massive losses and retreated. Although Niger demonstrated great courage on the retreat, the Ascalon campaign was a disaster. It did nothing to encourage an aggressive policy elsewhere, for instance, in Galilee, where Josephus would serve.

After the attack on Ascalon the rebels engaged in no further offensives. They did not take advantage of their knowledge of the country's hilly terrain and narrow passes to lay traps for the enemy or to cut their supplies. Their strategy in Galilee, to the extent that a half-hearted leadership had one, was to hole up in fortresses and wear the Romans out. They fought hard to defend those fortresses, but otherwise their policy appears cautious.

THE WAR IN THE NORTH

The reason may lie in the nature of the rebel military. The rebel forces, as one scholar argues, were less a national army than a cluster of gangs—the "bandits" that Josephus complains about incessantly. They had limited loyalty to the priests who ran the government in Jerusalem. None of the individual gang leaders was eager to risk losing his forces in a renewed offensive, especially not after the fiasco at Ascalon.[15]

The Establishment knew Josephus: as a priest, he was one of their own. More committed revolutionaries probably distrusted him, given his ties to Rome. And well they might have, as events would make clear. Nevertheless, the revolutionary government appointed Josephus to a position of authority in Galilee. They knew how important the region was. It was wealthy and parts of it lay under the nominal control of Rome's Jewish ally, King Agrippa II. He strongly opposed the rebellion and supported Rome. Galilee adjoined the Roman province of Syria, an imperial stronghold. Rome's counterattack would probably begin in Galilee, so the region mattered a great deal.

Josephus fortified several sites in Galilee and personally led the resistance to Rome in the first siege of the war. Whether on his own initiative or on orders from the revolutionary government in Jerusalem, he followed a defensive strategy. He did not engage in irregular attacks on the enemy or in attempts to cut off their supply lines. Either he hoped to exhaust the legions before stiff and well-defended fortifications or he hoped to use the walled towns as bargaining chips to negotiate some kind of agreement with the enemy. Josephus was nothing if not a negotiator.

That much is clear, but much else is not. Aside from a few references in Roman writers, Josephus is our only source for his life, and he is more than usually deceptive. Archaeology confirms some of Josephus's story, but it doesn't shed light on his measures or his motives.

Josephus wrote two different, diametrically opposed narratives of the Galilean War, both while in exile in Rome. One version, in *The Jewish War*, was written a few years after the events and published between 75 and 79. It depicts Josephus as an energetic general committed to the fight against Rome. The other, published about twenty years later in a short biography known as

The Life, states that Josephus was something of a double agent. In this version, he was not a general but a member of a board of three priests. Their mission was to cool tempers in Galilee and to negotiate peace with Rome. Fortunately, there is a certain amount of common ground in the two accounts, but the reader still must ask: Which version is the truth?

Neither version is straightforward. Both accounts reflect Josephus's uneasy status among Romans as a Jew and a former rebel and among Jews as a turncoat. In *The Jewish War* Josephus had good reason to exaggerate when it came to his military record. He was writing military history, a genre that demands war. Besides, his most dangerous readers were a group of hardened Roman soldiers. By then the general Vespasian had fought his way to becoming emperor by winning a civil war. He and his supporters climbed to the palace over piles of bloodstained corpses, not by way of speeches in the Senate or dinner parties on the Palatine. They were Rome's commanders in Judea. The harder Josephus appeared to fight against them, the more they admired him. But there was a catch: he also had to charm them with his speech and wow them with his prophecy. Soldiers are famously superstitious.

Around the year 95, Josephus found himself in a different position. The emperor at that time, Vespasian's younger son, Domitian, was no soldier. Unlike his father, or his older brother Titus, Domitian had not fought in the Jewish revolt. Domitian was less interested in Josephus's military prowess, but he would not have overlooked Josephus's treachery, which is exactly the charge that Josephus faced. His rival historian, a Jew named Justus, from Tiberias, published a work around this time that claimed that Josephus stirred up the revolt against Rome and King Agrippa. Justus served as the king's secretary. Josephus wrote his *Life* in part to refute these charges. *The Life* is a short work, perhaps originally an appendix to his magnum opus, *Antiquities of the Jews*.

Which version is true? Did Josephus try to galvanize the Jews of the north into fighting Rome, or did he try to defeat the hotheads there and negotiate surrender? Knowing Josephus, one concludes that he hedged his bets and might have kept lines of communication open to King Agrippa II. At the same time, Josephus certainly played a major role in organizing the cities of the region into building or strengthening their walls. To the extent that he had a military strategy it was purely a defensive one. Apparently, he gave no thought to fighting a guerrilla war or launching a series of raids to cut Rome's supply lines.

If he raised an army, he did not do a good job. In *The Jewish War*, Josephus claims that he tried to turn 100,000 men in Galilee into a Roman-style army, of whom 60,000 survived his training, the rest presumably having deserted. But his narrative offers no sign that this army ever existed. Besides, the numbers, like many in Josephus, are wildly inflated. No reliable population figures for Judea in this period survive. Modern scholarly estimates are ingenious, speculative, and varied, but none of them imagines enough young men in Galilee to provide an army of 60,000.[16]

Then there is the embarrassing fact, which Josephus cannot hide, that he was fired. The authorities in Jerusalem decided to recall him. Josephus blames this on his personal enemies, especially his archenemy, John of Giscala, that is, John son of Levi, a strongman from a town in Upper Galilee with a small army of his own. John wanted to replace Josephus, in part because John was ambitious and in part because John was committed to the anti-Roman cause. He suspected that Josephus was not—and it turned out, of course, that John was right.

It wasn't only John: the leaders in Jerusalem passed a decree in the assembly to ratify the decision to fire Josephus, so it must have had widespread support. They even sent out a military force to bring him back dead or alive. Somehow, Josephus managed to get the decision overturned. He doesn't offer a convincing explanation of how.

There is probably some accuracy in the picture that Josephus paints of Galilee in turmoil. It was a region divided among loyalists to King Agrippa II and Rome, on the one hand, and revolutionaries of various stripes and factions on the other, with many people caught in between.

Galilee at the start of the revolt, as Josephus describes it, was humming with danger: disorder, violence, mobs, rebellion, brigandage, infighting, and near–civil war. His account in *The Life* reads like a picaresque novel, with himself as a hero. Every sort of transportation was employed: horses, camels, litters, boats. Various soldiers are mentioned: infantrymen, cavalrymen, sentries, deserters, bodyguards, escorts, officers, mercenaries, Josephus's men, John of Giscala's men, and Romans. There were many crowds: approving crowds who greeted Josephus with acclamations; violent crowds stirred up by demagogues; crowds including women and children shouting abuse; a furious crowd that filled a hippodrome and howled for blood; noisy crowds beaten with cudgels by the angry soldiers they confronted; olive branch–waving crowds afraid for their lives; crowds of the men, women, and children of Tiberias begging Josephus to spare the city; cowering crowds of the leading citizens of Tiberias forced to name names by Josephus and his victorious soldiers. There were prisoners and men in chains; men flogged until their flesh had been torn to ribbons; misbehaving soldiers who were whipped. There were skirmishes, ambushes, sneak attacks by night, battles, the seizure of one city by storm and another by a ruse. There were narrow escapes from mobs or assassins. Couriers delivered messages and counter-messages back and forth, almost none of them straightforward.

The Jews seemed exhausted by infighting and near–civil war before ever coming into hostile contact with a Roman soldier. In fact, Jews plundered the Jewish cities of Sepphoris and Tiberias. Josephus and two of his bodyguards entered a synagogue, Josephus wearing a breastplate and carrying a sword, the bodyguards with daggers concealed under their clothes. And a good thing, too, because, after the prayer service, Josephus's enemies attacked him and his bodyguards had to draw their knives to save him, while his supporters picked up stones and threw them at his enemies. Later, Josephus's enemies at Tiberias mocked him by laying out a bier, standing around it, and mourning him with jests and laughter. The Jewish royal palace of Tiberias was looted and burned down, amid Josephus's feuds with Justus of Tiberias and John of Giscala.[17]

Whatever happened among the Jews of Galilee, they still had to face the overwhelming force of the Roman army. That army, led by Vespasian, gathered in the spring of 67 at Ptolemaïs. The fifty-seven-year-old Roman commander was joined by his son, Titus, age twenty-seven, who was one of Vespasian's subordinates. The Romans had a large force. At its core were three Roman legions plus additional legionary cohorts. These men, all Roman citizens, were mostly infantrymen. They amounted to a total of about 25,000 to 28,000 soldiers (depending on the real vs. nominal strength of the legions). In addition, there were 3,000 to 6,000 cavalrymen, all auxiliaries, that is, non-Roman-citizen troops. Vespasian also called on the services of allies: client kings and their troops, who amounted to 15,000 men (11,000 foot soldiers and 4,000 horsemen). Antiochus IV of Commagene, Agrippa II, and Sohaemus of Emesa each provided 2,000 infantry archers and 1,000 cavalry. Malchus II of Nabataea sent 1,000 cavalry and 5,000 infantry, primarily archers. These figures add up to a force of circa 50,000 to 60,000 men; according to Josephus, the grand total of Vespasian's army was 60,000 men. In any case, this was a huge force, larger than Cestius's circa 30,000 men in 66 or the force of 40,000 men with which Rome had invaded Britannia in 43 CE.[18]

Vespasian's allies were a varied lot. Emesa and Nabataea were both Arab kingdoms. The kings of Commagene were of mixed Iranian and Greco-Macedonian descent. Agrippa II, as discussed, was Jewish. His cavalry included descendants of the Babylonian Jewish horsemen that Herod had settled in the northeastern marches of his kingdom. In fact, Agrippa II's chief general was the grandson of their original leader.[19] In short, several thousand pro-Roman Jews took part in the Roman army aimed at suppressing the Jewish revolt.

The Siege of Jotapata[20]

For a moment, in the summer of 67, the fate of the war depended on Josephus. He led the defense of a small city in Galilee that faced the fury of the Roman legions and the deft hand of their best general.

There were only two real cities in Galilee, Sepphoris and Tiberias. Both had either been founded (Tiberias) or refounded (Sepphoris) by Herod Antipas, son of Herod the Great. The elite in these two cities generally sided with Rome.

The leadership of smaller cities also was pro-Roman. As property owners they did not want to take risks.

The propertyless were more favorable to the rebellion. These consisted of urban poor such as fishermen or day laborers, and refugees—Jews who had fled for their lives from the anti-Jewish violence of Greek and Syrian cities in the region. They had less reason to support the status quo.

Sepphoris was the most important city in Galilee. It surrendered to Vespasian as soon as he arrived on the coast. Sepphoris's central location made it an excellent site for Rome to pacify the rest of Galilee. Rome's first move was to station a garrison of seven thousand troops there including one thousand cavalrymen. These forces roamed the countryside with the goal of "pacification," which meant the usual tactics of roughing people up or killing them, looting, and rewarding Rome's friends. Then came the main Roman army, led by Vespasian and Titus.

Galilee had a large population of free, landholding farmers. These farmers of Galilee, like such farmers more generally in the ancient world, were independent, suspicious of outsiders, and ready to fight when they considered themselves threatened. Rural refugees poured into the cities of Galilee in 67, and those refugees forced some of the cities into fighting.

The central Galilean hill town of Jotapata saw its population swollen with such refugees. Jotapata was not an important place. Although Israel has made it a national park, the site is a lonely hill. Jotapata could have surrendered like much of the rest of Galilee, but it did not. Vespasian might have ignored it, but it was bad strategy and bad politics to leave an armed fortification in his rear. Besides, the enemy commander, Josephus, was in Jotapata, and he was a prize worth capturing—or so Josephus, who tells the story, states.[21] It's not clear why Josephus left the relative safety of Tiberias, where he had been, but he went to Jotapata and led its defense. It's been suggested that he hoped to negotiate a surrender. When he realized that wasn't possible, he tried to leave Jotapata, but the townspeople begged him to stay—a plea, he suspected, that would have been enforced with iron if he had tried to leave.[22]

At Jotapata the first major siege of the Great Revolt occurred. It was a hot, summer battle, taking place from late May through early July, when the average midday weather is sunny and around 90 degrees Fahrenheit (32°C).[23]

Josephus wrote an eyewitness account of the siege of Jotapata, a rare first-hand narrative of the experience of an ancient city under siege. As the losing commander, as an apologist of his own career, and as a historian who was not shy about taking license with the facts, Josephus is not entirely reliable. Still, most of his story rings true with what is known of ancient sieges from other ancient texts. Jotapata was excavated by archaeologists over six seasons beginning in 1992. Archaeology confirms evidence of a heavy battle along the lines described by Josephus, with the consequent murder and ruin.[24]

Jotapata's name is Persian, perhaps dating back to the days when the land was part of the Persian Empire. Jotapata consisted of about 12.5 acres of livable space. The excavators estimated a peacetime population of 1,500 to 2,000 people and a refugee-swollen wartime population of about 7,000. Jotapata's economy depended on agricultural pursuits such as olive oil production, spinning and weaving, and pottery production. Although there was a wealthy class who lived in luxury, most of the Jotapatans were poor, simple, rural people.

Jotapata was defensible, but only just. Although the site of the town was not particularly high, it was protected by a precipitous drop on the eastern side and gradual slopes elsewhere. Earlier fortifications protected the town's summit. Now defenders threw together a new wall on its lower slopes, with special attention to the northwestern side, which offered the easiest access to an enemy attacker.

At first Vespasian tried to take Jotapata by storm. He had his men construct an assault ramp, defended by protective screens, and fortified by palisades. Modern excavators found evidence of the ramp, on the town's northwestern side, with its several layers of soil, stones, and mortar. They also found signs of the Romans' attack: arrowheads, part of a catapult, ballista stones, and hobnails from soldiers' boots.

When the defenders sallied out and destroyed the Romans' protections on the ramp, Vespasian decided to try a blockade instead. But the Jews did not surrender, so he went back on the offensive.

Josephus is a marvelous storyteller, if not a precise or always trustworthy one. His eye for detail stands out in his narrative of the siege. As Josephus tells it, the Romans were steadfast and well equipped with deadly technology, while the Jews were courageous and inventive. Among the weapons in the Romans' arsenal were bolt-shooting catapults, ballistas that could shoot sixty-pound stones for more than 550 yards, slings and arrows wielded by expert allied soldiers, and a powerful battering ram. Roman military engineers were able to throw up an assault ramp complete with protective palisades and gangplanks to ease their soldiers' way over rough ground to the town. The defenders in turn made use of various stratagems, such as pouring boiling oil on the attackers, followed by pouring boiling fenugreek (a clover-like herb) on the gangways that the Romans had erected to reach the town, making the boards so slick that the soldiers slipped and skidded.

The Romans evidently knew that Jotapata had no spring, but depended on rainwater in cisterns, whose supply would surely run out in the summer heat. When Vespasian thought that the defenders were about to suffer from dehydration, Josephus had the Jews hang wet clothing from the ramparts, in a sign of sublime contempt for the enemy. There are more such details, and the whole narrative is worth reading if not entirely trustworthy, especially not the parts that make Josephus look good. Yet it is undeniable that Josephus won the rare distinction of holding off the mighty Roman legions for more than a month.[25]

Josephus tells the story of a long and dramatic day about four weeks into the siege.[26] The Romans first softened up the enemy by an attack with their catapults, archers, and slingers. Then the Romans brought up an enormous battering ram, reinforced at its end by an iron lump in the shape of a ram's head. It was suspended by ropes hanging from a beam attached to poles driven into the ground. A large number of men pulled the ram backward and then heaved it forward to smash into the town's wall. It sounds like a Hollywood touch, but it was deadly effective. Josephus states that he responded with aplomb by having his men hang sacks of chaff from ropes that they lowered from the ramparts, thereby softening the impact of the ram's blows. But the Romans parried his move by attaching scythes to long poles and cutting the ropes. The desperate defenders grabbed whatever dry wood they could find, rushed out of the gates, and started setting fire to the Roman siegeworks.

Josephus highlights heroism on both sides of his story. Tales of Jewish valor made Rome's achievement of victory seem all the greater for Roman readers and they flattered the Jewish audience. Josephus, therefore, zeroes in on a Jewish soldier named Eleazar son of Sameas from the village of Saba in Galilee. Eleazar hurled an enormous rock from the ramparts that broke off the head of the battering ram. Then he supposedly jumped down from the wall and carried back the ram's head, like a trophy, to the foot of the ramparts. There, despite taking five arrow wounds from the enemy, Eleazar started climbing the wall and finally fell to his death with the ram's head still clutched in his hands. Josephus also mentions two courageous Jewish brothers, Netiras and Philip, from the village of Ruma in Galilee, who rushed the soldiers of the Tenth Legion (presumably of a subunit) with such force that they broke its ranks and forced the men to flee. Or so Josephus claims.

The fighting continued back and forth all day, like scenes out of Homer's *Iliad*, until evening. Then a lucky Jewish archer struck Vespasian with an arrow in the sole of his foot. The Romans feared the worst at the sight of their commander's blood, especially when Titus rushed to his father's side, but Vespasian calmed them down. It was just a flesh wound, and the fifty-seven-year-old general got up to show the men that he was fine, which spurred them to fight harder. "Mastering his pain, he hastened to show himself to all who trembled for his life, and so roused them to fight the Jews more fiercely than ever," writes Josephus.[27]

Fierce fighting continued at night, with both sides launching arrows and stones. Roman artillery proved devastating to the Jews, who made easy targets in the glare of their own lamplights. Josephus provides a few gruesome examples: one defender on the ramparts standing beside Josephus had his head shot off by a blow so forceful that it carried the head for three stades, that is, about 600 yards (640 meters). A pregnant woman leaving home at daybreak was struck by a blow that ripped out her fetus and flung it for half a stade, about 100 yards (90 meters). These are probably tall tales, but the whistling sound of Roman missiles in flight, the shrieks of the women and children, the moans of the dying, and the echoes from the surrounding hills are plausible specific details.

Near the hour of the morning watch the ram finally made a breach in the wall. The defenders rallied and kept the enemy out. The battle continued for more than another week. Finally, fear, exhaustion, thirst, and the overwhelming advantages of a hardened, well-supplied professional army against a ragtag, outnumbered, and increasingly dehydrated defense force came into play. The Romans at last got their assault ramp over the top of Jotapata's walls. They then found a traitor, as the winning side often did. He pointed out that the exhausted Jewish sentries tended to fall asleep in the predawn hours. In fact, this was probably not news to the Romans, since ancient sieges often ended at this time of day. Led by Titus himself, according to Josephus, the Romans broke into Jotapata and overwhelmed the defense. They moved so silently that it wasn't until broad daylight that most of the townspeople realized that the enemy was among them.

The siege was over. It probably took about five weeks for the Romans to capture Jotapata.[28] The victors ranged through the town and engaged in slaughter. Josephus says that 40,000 Jews died at Jotapata. The archaeologists, more plausibly, reckoned the death toll among the 7,000 people under siege as about 2,000; they accept Josephus's statistic of 1,200 taken captive. Vespasian ordered the city to be destroyed.

The excavators found grisly evidence of Jotapata's fate: the bones of twenty men, women, and children in a cistern as well as the bones of a man on the floor of a room luxuriously decorated with frescoes, clearly a wealthy person's residence. The most unusual and eloquent discovery was an etched stone. It contains two crude drawings. On one side, there is a mausoleum. On the other side there is a crab—*cancer*, in Latin—which suggests the zodiac symbol for, roughly, the month of July. Jotapata fell in summer. The archaeologists believe that the etchings are either a townsman's grim recognition that he was about to die or perhaps a humble memorial to the dead left on someone's return to the ruins after the war was over.

"If This Be Treason..."

For Josephus, time stopped, in a way, on a summer day in a broad valley in Lower Galilee. After Jotapata fell, Josephus took refuge in a cave with forty other Jewish survivors. It was there that he participated in an event that branded him for life. Josephus wrote that the other men in the cave wanted mass suicide. He opposed that and tried to talk them into surrendering instead, but they insisted on death. In his history he said that he proposed a method that avoided trusting each man to kill himself, which might allow a shirker to escape. Instead, they would draw lots—presumably numbered 1 through 41—after which the man who drew 2 would kill the man who drew 1, then 3 would kill 2, and so on. In the end only Josephus and one other man were left. He convinced the other man to save both their lives, and so, Josephus survived.

That was good fortune or divine providence, Josephus maintained. Others say it was trickery. Perhaps Josephus rigged the lottery somehow to make sure that he drew number 41. Or perhaps he gamed the system in a more sophisticated way by using some other rule to convert the lottery numbers 1 through 41 into the sequence of killers and killings—a rule to which he knew the "solution," the not-so-obvious winning number that he should contrive to draw for himself. (Modern mathematicians have studied a collection of such rules and how to solve them, calling it the Josephus problem.)

A medieval translation of *The Jewish War* in old Russian says that Josephus "counted the numbers cunningly and so managed to deceive all the others."[29] The old Russian translation may have been based on an earlier draft of Josephus's book, but it is possible that this is simply prejudice. The Jew as traitor is an old slander, going back in Christian tradition to the figure of Judas

Iscariot, who betrays Jesus in the Gospels. Before condemning Josephus as a traitor, a historian needs to be sure to account for any implicit bias.

Josephus explains why he preferred surrender to death. Josephus considered himself a skilled interpreter of dreams and what they indicated of the deity's will. He was, after all, he says, a priest and descendant of priests and he knew the prophecies in the holy books. He had experienced a series of dreams night after night in which God foretold the fates of the Jews and the Roman emperors. He offered a silent prayer to the Almighty: "Since You have decided to break the Jewish people whom You created, and since all good fortune has passed to the Romans, and since You chose my spirit to state what will happen in the future, I willingly give myself into the hands of the Romans and so live. I call You to witness that I go not as a traitor but as Your servant."[30]

Not long after the lottery that saved Josephus's life there came a date that casts Josephus in infamy, the rendezvous with destiny in the form of the commander of the Roman legions in Judea: Vespasian.

It took place in the Roman camp outside Jotapata, the city that they had just destroyed. Brought in chains before the man who, only recently, he had been trying to kill, the Judean fought for his life by thinking on his feet. Josephus knew that Vespasian would probably send him to Nero in Rome, where he would face execution after being tortured. To prevent that, Josephus needed to make himself useful to Vespasian. He did that by prophesying a great future: Vespasian, he said, would become emperor. It worked. Vespasian retained Josephus instead of sending him to Nero. He kept Josephus in chains, to be sure, but that beat by far the fate waiting him in Rome.

In brief, Josephus saved his skin by kissing up to the enemy. He would in short order prove himself to be a loyal supporter of Rome, one who tried to talk the proud rebels of Jerusalem into surrender. For this, he has suffered damnation as a traitor. But he saw it differently, as others in ancient times might have.

Josephus belongs to a select group of turncoats. Although they changed sides and came under heavy criticism, they felt justified. They were not traitors, they argued, because they were loyal to a higher principle. Alcibiades of Athens (ca. 450–404 BCE) is one prominent example from ancient Greece. During the Peloponnesian War he defected to Sparta rather than face a hostile court at home. There he proceeded to give away Athenian state secrets. Alcibiades defended himself in a public speech at Sparta by saying:

> And it is not, as I conceive, against a country still my own that I am now going, but for rather one no longer mine that I am seeking to recover. And the true patriot is not the man who, having unjustly lost his fatherland, refrains from attacking it, but he who in his yearning for it tries in every way to get it back.[31]

Alcibiades's checkered career eventually took him into Persia's service as well, but at one point he returned to Athens and did his country an outstanding service by preventing a civil war.[32]

A closer case in chronology to Josephus, and which comes from the Roman Empire, is that of Segestes, a leader of the Cherusci, a German tribe, and rival of his fellow tribal leader, Arminius. Arminius was Rome's greatest enemy, but Segestes was a staunch supporter of Rome; both men were Roman citizens. Before the ambush at the Teutoburg Forest in 9 CE, Segestes warned Varus, but to no avail. Afterward, Segestes was forced by the public opinion of his tribe into changing course and joining the fight against Rome. But the winds of fortune blew in various directions over the next years and Segestes returned to Rome's side. In 17, he appeared, as an honored guest, at the triumph in Rome of the imperial general Germanicus.

No doubt Josephus, too, was a mix of principle and pragmatism. As commander of Galilee, he was a failure. He neither defeated the Romans nor negotiated a surrender that spared the region violence. Nor did he stop the outbreak of civil war. His defense of Jotapata displayed heroism and ingenuity, only to fail and be followed by his surrender in less-than-happy circumstances. No wonder that he spent some of the following twenty-five years trying to justify the decisions that he took during six months in Galilee.

Josephus was an intellectual and an exile whose writings attempt to rationalize a series of actions made on the fly in response to trends and circumstances that lay beyond his control. But he was also a believer who constantly tried to find his footing on the bedrock of his faith.

But life rarely exposes bedrock. More often, we are at sea, just as Josephus was on that long and unforgettable night when he swam for his life after being shipwrecked. Whatever his flaws Josephus figured out how to survive. He was a pro-Roman who joined the Jewish rebellion in order to subvert it, or so he later said; he was a stern governor who forced one opponent to cut off his own hand, but invited another opponent to dinner. He was a crypto-anti-rebel who nonetheless led a heroic defense against the onslaught of the legions; a quick thinker who talked his way out of one suicide pact at Jotapata, and later wrote a book that immortalized another suicide pact, at Masada; and ultimately he was a prisoner of war in a dusty marching camp whose golden tongue melted away his chains and exchanged them for a villa in Rome.

In short, Josephus was pragmatic and principled, admirable and appalling, brutal and benevolent. He became a Roman citizen, but retained the faith of his fathers. Against the common tendency to see things in terms of black or white, Josephus appears in shades of gray. He was one of the most human, all-too-human people in the ancient world.

Before leaving the subject, one more question must be asked. Aside from the unpleasant circumstances of his defection, is it possible that Josephus was right? Would it have been better to make a deal with the Romans than to have continued the war? This question will come up again.

Vespasian Continues the War

After conquering Jotapata, Vespasian dispersed his troops to rest in the vicinity of cities on the Mediterranean coast or in the Jordan river valley. He enjoyed a respite in the cool shade of one of Agrippa II's palaces, at Caesarea Philippi. Not to be confused with Caesarea-by-the-Sea, Caesarea Philippi was a second city named after Caesar Augustus by a member of Herod's dynasty. Today the imposing ruins of Agrippa's palace can be found in Banias in northern Israel at the foot of Mount Hermon and near today's Lebanese and Syrian borders.

In September 67, Vespasian took his troops back onto a military campaign, with Agrippa II and his forces beside him. Arguably, the rebels saw Agrippa II and not Rome as their primary target, but since Agrippa II was "Our Man in Galilee" from the Roman point of view, the difference had little practical significance. Allied kings like Agrippa II played a key role in Rome's management of the Near East. Each king knew his territory, unlike some neophyte governor shipped out from Rome. It was cheaper to have the locals maintain order than to turn an allied kingdom into a Roman province and pay to install Roman troops there. So, Vespasian was no doubt glad to help Agrippa II.

Before long, Tiberias surrendered. Refugees fled into nearby Tarichaeae (Magdala or Migdal) on the Sea of Galilee. The "sea" is in fact a lake. At first, the refugees sallied out and attacked the Romans, who were building a wall for their camp, but the Romans drove them back. After that, the Romans held the initiative. They assaulted the rebels with infantry, cavalry, archers, and ships. Titus made short and bloody work of the enemy both on land and in the lake. Josephus writes that the lake was stained with blood and filled with corpses. The shore was covered with wrecked ships and corpses decaying in the summer heat and giving off a terrible stench. Josephus claims that 6,700 defenders were killed, another 1,200 of the elderly and "useless" were marched to Tiberias and executed in its stadium, and a third group of 6,000 sent to Greece to work on the canal near Corinth that Nero was having dug.[33] All told, 30,000 people were sold into slavery. As usual, Josephus's numbers are probably exaggerated, but he is surely right that a massacre took place. Even by Roman standards, the slaughter in the stadium was grotesque, especially because Vespasian had given the survivors permission to leave Tarichaeae, although he had left their fate unclear. As for Nero and his canal, the emperor never finished the project. Despite various later efforts over the years, the Corinth canal was only completed in 1893, eighteen centuries later.

In October, the Romans turned on Gamala (Gamla, Israel), a fortress city in Gaulanitis. Gamala, whose name means "camel" in Aramaic, was situated on a precipitous, ridgeback hill resembling a camel's hump, in a valley surrounded by rugged cliffs. Today it is an archaeological site, first excavated in 1976. Among archaeological excavations in Israel today, Gamala is second only to Masada in the drama of its location.

Gamala's rugged position and strong fortification walls made it difficult to capture. Josephus claims that he put up the walls, but more likely, walls already existed and he simply improved them. The town had already withstood a siege of several months from the forces of Agrippa II, and now they faced both the Jewish king and the Romans. Vespasian brought 60,000 troops to attack 9,000 defenders, according to Josephus.

The rebels in Gamala issued bronze coins. Historians have sought clues to their motives in the coins, but they are hard to interpret. Like the rebel coins of Jerusalem, they are written in Paleo-Hebrew and display a chalice or at least what appears to be a chalice, a symbol of freedom or redemption. The legends say "Of the Redemption" on the obverse and "Holy Jerusalem" on the reverse. Or do they? Some scholars argue that the legend on the obverse says "In Gamala." If the first interpretation is correct, the rebels of Gamala tied their resistance to that of Jerusalem, but if the second reading is right, then the Gamala rebels had the much-more-limited goal of independence from Agrippa II. In either case, Josephus makes it clear that the rebels believed in God and divine providence, so whatever their motive was, it included a religious dimension.[34]

Before the assault began, Agrippa II approached the walls and tried to parley with the defenders about surrender. They responded by hitting the king on the right elbow with a stone shot by one of Gamala's slingers. This was the ancient equivalent of the American general's response to the German demand for surrender when they had surrounded the Americans in Bastogne, Belgium, in December 1944: "NUTS!"

The inhabitants of Gamala put up a dogged defense and held out for over three weeks. Two men, Joseph and Chares, led the defenders. The Romans had to use their artillery, including catapults, ballistas, and battering rams. The site was abandoned for two millennia after the battle and yielded rich finds to archaeologists. The excavators found the walls, houses, a synagogue or meeting hall, ritual baths, and coins. They also discovered artifacts of Rome's artillery barrage on the town, including over 1,500 arrowheads and almost 2,000 ballista balls.

Eventually, the Romans broke through the walls, but hard fighting still lay ahead. At one point, Vespasian found himself under assault inside the walls of Gamala, in a maze of tottering houses and treacherous terrain. As the general in command, Vespasian fought in the thick of things. Ordering his men to link shields in a protective formation, he and they withdrew calmly and did not turn their backs until they were safely outside the walls. He then went on to regroup and, on a later day, conquer the town.

As at Jotapata, Titus led the final assault on Gamala, according to Josephus. One rebel leader, Joseph, fell in the fighting while the other, Chares, died in his sickbed, apparently of a heart attack. The defenders fought furiously, but eventually realized the hopelessness of their position. Josephus claims that 4,000 fell to the Romans, while another 5,000 died by jumping into the deep ravine below the town. In both groups, the dead included women and children. The only survivors were two women who hid themselves at the time of the capture and who happened to be the nieces of one of Agrippa II's commanders. As at Jotapata so at Gamala Vespasian ordered the town to be abandoned permanently.

While the fighting continued at Gamala, Vespasian sent a unit to capture the fortifications on Itaburion (Mount Tabor), located near Nazareth. Josephus had fortified the heights. The Romans lured the defenders down from the summit. They were planning to attack the Romans on the plain, but the Romans tricked them and killed or captured most of the defenders. The survivors fled to Jerusalem.

That left only one rebel holdout in Galilee, the town known in Greek as Giscala. Giscala was an agricultural settlement in the fertile hills of Upper Galilee, near today's Israel-Lebanon border. In 67, it was the hometown of John of Giscala, a wealthy Jewish patriot who turned on Rome at the start of the revolt. He was bold, aggressive, cunning, and charismatic. He was not a priest, a Zealot, or a messiah figure. John would later emerge as one of the leaders of the rebellion in Jerusalem. He comes across as tough, ruthless, and flexible in his principles.

Vespasian sent a small force under Titus to take Giscala. John negotiated a surrender, asking only for a delay for the Sabbath. Titus agreed. On Sabbath Eve (Friday night) John fled the town with his armed followers and a large civilian contingent, including women and children. Titus discovered the deception the next morning and sent a cavalry squadron after the escapees. They failed to capture John, but killed 6,000 adult males and brought 3,000 women and children back to Giscala, according to Josephus.[35] Titus had part of the town's walls torn down, but otherwise treated it gently, no doubt thinking he could do business with the pro-Romans in town. To be on the safe side, he left a garrison in Giscala. As for John, he reached Jerusalem where, according to Josephus, he received a rapturous reception.

Josephus's mission in Galilee was a failure. He neither held off the Romans nor negotiated peace with them. He had saved his life after fighting bravely, but at the cost of his honor, at least in the eyes of his countrymen if not his own.

Vespasian had pacified Galilee, but at the price of convincing a portion of the population that he was a brute. John and his followers were not the only ones to flee to Jerusalem, and others followed from additional parts of the country that Vespasian ravaged. They were angry, frightened, and bristling to avenge their lost honor. The unintended consequence was to harden Jewish opposition. It also concentrated that opposition in only one place, but Jerusalem was a powerful fortress.[36]

By the end of 67, Rome and its ally Agrippa II controlled the north of the Land of Israel. The battle of Galilee was over. The battle of Jerusalem lay ahead. Upon its outcome would depend the future of Jewish civilization and, as it turned out, the direction that the followers of Jesus would take.

Chapter Six

DEFENDERS OF JERUSALEM

Two heads are better than one, but not in war, which needs a single, unified command. Unfortunately for the rebels in Jerusalem, they had not two but three heads vying for the leadership. The situation reached a crisis in 68, when the revolution could hardly afford it. In that year the rebels faced a serious challenge and then a historic opportunity.

After conquering much of the rest of Judea, Vespasian encamped outside Jerusalem with his army. He was poised to attack, and then suddenly he withdrew. On June 8, 68, Nero committed suicide, and the news reached Vespasian a few weeks later. With Roman politics in turmoil, Vespasian beat a prudent retreat to Caesarea-by-the-Sea, where he would await orders from the new regime. It was nearly a year later, in May 69, when he resumed activity and conquered most of the rest of the province of Judea. Only Masada and two other fortresses remained out of the Romans' hands—those and Jerusalem itself.

For the Jews, the period of Vespasian's inactivity was a time to pull together, to prepare resources, and to harass the enemy via raids and ambushes. The rebels went on the attack, but the target wasn't the Romans: it was each other. The revolution devolved into civil war. This was not surprising. Societies without a strong central government often split up into factions led by charismatic leaders. One example was Germania in the era of Arminius. No sooner had the tribes joined together to defeat Rome at the Teutoburg Forest in 9 CE than they divided and fought each other. Within Arminius's own tribe, his relatives grew suspicious of his ambition. In 21 CE, twelve years after Arminius saved Germania at the Teutoburg Forest, they killed him.

Although the Jewish rebels would later reconcile and unite in 70, the period of years of violent infighting from late 67 to early 70 left scars that could not be healed. The sources speak of three main factions within Jerusalem, shaped by a flood of refugees and by an intervention from the south. They barely mention a fourth group, volunteers from the Parthian Empire, in particular, from Adiabene. They, too, were present in Jerusalem, but whether they were watching and waiting, some from royal palaces, or whether they were actively taking part in the domestic conflict, we do not know.

The ancient sources, from Josephus to Tacitus to the Talmud, which largely disapproves of the revolt, are hostile to the defenders of Jerusalem. Manifestly they failed, with disastrous results for their country. Much of what follows criticizes the rebels in Jerusalem. Let their good qualities be noted as well: courage, cunning, determination, patriotism, and self-sacrifice.

John of Giscala

The story of civil strife in Jerusalem starts with John of Giscala.[1] John was a wealthy man, a member of the elite, and originally pro-Roman. When news of the revolt in Jerusalem in 66 reached Giscala in the hills of Upper Galilee, some of the townspeople wanted to raise the banner of rebellion. John restrained them, only to see the Romans stand by and do nothing while non-Jews sacked and burned Giscala. John sprang into action: he armed his followers, marched on the people who had destroyed Giscala, and defeated them in battle. He then led the effort to rebuild Giscala and gave it fortification walls. Josephus says that John organized four hundred followers, all "good, strapping fellows, with stout hearts and military experience."[2]

Later, also according to Josephus, John took an unspecified number of his followers with him to Jerusalem.[3] They were refugees who had been radicalized by their experience of the hard hand of Rome. More refugees would come in the following year or so, fugitives from the Roman army's brutality or from infighting among the Jewish population. One of the few numbers in the sources is Josephus's claim that two thousand fugitives from Tiberias were in Jerusalem at the time of the Roman siege in 70.[4] Their presence made Jerusalem ever more adamant in its resistance to Rome. Tacitus refers to this, writing,

> The population [of Jerusalem] was increased by a great influx of rabble from the defeat of other cities. For, whoever was most obstinate fled for refuge there and they behaved even more seditiously.[5]

The possibility of a negotiated settlement receded in the distance.

Josephus portrays John as an unscrupulous, cunning, greedy liar, but Josephus considered John his archenemy. If we judge a man by the company he keeps, then we must have a higher opinion of John. For he was an ally of Rabban ("Rabban" is an honorific title) Simon son of Gamaliel, a Jerusalemite whom Josephus describes as a Pharisee of a very illustrious family with an unsurpassed knowledge of Jewish law; a person of intellectual gifts and excellent judgment. Simon was as supple as he was prudent. *The Wisdom of the Fathers* (*Pirkei Avot*), a rabbinic collection of sayings by wise men, quotes Simon as praising silence, reticence in speech, and wise deeds—which sounds like a prescription for surviving in a time of war and revolution. In happier times, during a joyous festival, Simon displayed his elation by his ability to juggle eight burning torches at a time and his devotion by the depth and flexibility of his bowing.[6] Surely a man like Simon would have steered clear of John if the latter were all bad.

John received a hero's welcome in Jerusalem. Unlike Josephus, who had covered himself with shame, John had fought the Romans and survived. True, he had lost many followers to the enemy, but John could persuade people to think positively. He went from group to group to arouse their courage for war. He represented the Romans as weak after having worn out their siege equipment against the walls of Galilee. "Even if they had wings," he said, "the Romans would never climb over the walls of Jerusalem."[7] Later on, at the height of the siege, John added that he would never fear that the Romans would take Jerusalem "because the city belonged to God."[8]

John's words may call to mind Psalm 91, the so-called "Soldier's Psalm" because of its popularity among soldiers in the world wars.[9] The psalmist calls God his refuge and his fortress, who will keep him safe from war and plague. A verse of the Psalm reads:

> A thousand shall fall at thy side, and ten thousand at thy right hand; but it shall not come nigh thee.[10]

John's audience might have had similar thoughts. But there were also Jews fighting for Rome, and they, too, surely prayed. Only one side could win.

Regime Change

Many a revolution begins in moderation and then turns increasingly radical. In the process, as each group comes to power it turns violently on its predecessors. As a disillusioned observer of the French Revolution commented, "the revolution devours its children."[11] So did the Great Revolt.

In the winter of 67, violence broke out in the still-unoccupied parts of the countryside between those Jews who supported the revolt and those who wanted to make peace with Rome. Many of the rebels made their way to Jerusalem. They added weight to the party of the Zealots, priestly radicals who were dissatisfied with the inaction of the revolutionary government. Their leader was the priest Eleazar son of Simon. He had been overlooked for power before. Now, he felt it was his turn. It was probably Eleazar and the Zealots who were responsible for the militant steps that followed.

The radicals turned first on several members of the Herodian royal family who were still in the city. They accused the royals of negotiating with the Romans; they had them arrested and executed. Next the radicals abolished the system of choosing the High Priest from the aristocracy and replaced it with a lottery. Josephus fulminated against the man who was chosen, but the new system was probably less corrupt than the old and was certainly more democratic.

The moderates called an assembly and attacked the Zealots. At this point in his narrative Josephus sneers at the name "zealot," writing, "so they called themselves, as if they were engaging in good practices and not outdoing themselves in the zealous pursuit of the evilest deeds."[12]

At that assembly the Zealots' opponents rallied the people of Jerusalem against them. The Zealots then took refuge in the Temple, which they fortified. High on a hill above the city, the Temple made an excellent fort. The moderates and their supporters besieged them; the Zealots were hard-pressed, but help was on the way. They had called in support from the southern part of the country, from Idumea, a region known for its soldiers. Thousands of Idumean troops reached Jerusalem and turned the tide in favor of the Zealots. There followed a bloodbath of the moderates. It was winter 67/68.

The leading figure in the moderate government had been Ananus son of Ananus, a former High Priest. Now his corpse was left unburied along with those of his comrades. Josephus mourned his death. He eulogized Ananus as a patriot, a lover of freedom and democracy, and a realist. Ananus, he wrote, understood the terrible power of Rome. Had Ananus lived, wrote Josephus, he would have negotiated peace or, at the least, delayed Rome's victory. "I would not be mistaken," Josephus summed it up, "if I said that the capture of the city began with the death of Ananus."[13]

As soon as the war had begun, some people decided to leave Jerusalem, either out of political or safety concerns, but the numbers were small. After the coup d'état against the moderates, the number of deserters increased.

Thereafter, with every new turn of the wheel, whether domestic disturbances or Roman progress in the siege, more people fled.[14]

Josephus portrays John of Giscala as a snake in all this turmoil. According to the historian, John started out on the side of the moderates, then portrayed himself as an honest broker between the two sides only to encourage the Zealots to call in the Idumeans and to betray the moderates. Since John had more troops than the Zealots, he became the leader of the revolution in Jerusalem in 68. But not for long.

Simon Son of Giora

In 66, Simon son of Giora was the hero of the rout of Cestius and his legion. Then Simon was passed over for command by the new, moderate government in Jerusalem, which was dominated by aristocrats and priests. With his military success, his devoted following, his humble origins, and his populist politics, it is no wonder that Simon appeared threatening to the new regime. Simon struck out on his own, first in a base in northern Judah and then at Masada, where the Sicarii warily cooperated with him. They didn't fully trust any leader outside the dynasty of Judah the Galilean. In 67 and 68, Simon proceeded to take over much of the region of Judah as well as the region of Idumea in a seesaw series of campaigns in which he now lost and now won. The leadership in Jerusalem tried but failed to defeat him.

Simon probably came from a city in Perea.[15] There was a considerable Jewish population east of the Jordan River. Simon was descended from converts, but lacked nothing in his devotion to the Jewish people.

Simon owed his success in part to the force and magnetism of his personality, in part to his success in war, and in part to his social program. He championed the poor and looked down on the rich. Simon was powerful and courageous. Josephus writes that among the commanders in Jerusalem, Simon was held by his men in special "reverence and awe, and they each heeded his orders to such an extent that if he commanded them to kill themselves, they would have been absolutely ready to do it."[16] Some treated him like a king, which may suggest that they saw him as a messiah. Another possible messianic note: only when Simon was at the peak of his power in Jerusalem were coins struck whose legend read "For the Redemption of Zion." The "redemption" suggests the hope of a better world at the end of days.

Simon was not an aristocrat himself and he often targeted the rich on behalf of the poor, whom he championed. Eventually he proclaimed freedom for all slaves. He won widespread support among humble people in various parts of the country.

In their conflict with Simon, the Zealots in Jerusalem kidnapped his wife and held her as hostage, only to be forced to release her when Simon ordered his troops to ravage the suburbs of Jerusalem and threaten the population within the walls. Finally, in the spring of 69, Simon was invited inside the city, apparently by the Idumeans and the High Priests. When he entered the city, Simon turned on the people who had invited him in. A period of fighting went on for months.

The Roman historian Tacitus describes the violence thus:

> John and Simon were strong in numbers and equipment, Eleazar had the advantage of position: between these three there was constant fighting, treachery, and arson, and a great store of grain was burned.[17]

Casualties were heavy. Parts of the city were destroyed. Some Jerusalemites deserted to the enemy. As bad as all this was, the loss of grain was even worse. The authorities had stored enough food to feed the city for a very long time. Burning each other's grain supply allowed each faction to punish the other, and perhaps it steeled the population to do or die, but it was also an invitation to a famine, which is precisely what the vandals suffered.

After two years of fighting each other, the rebels had turned the Holy City into an armed camp with three separate and competing headquarters. Think of the urban landscape as follows. In rough terms, Jerusalem consisted of three parts: the Lower City, the Upper City, and the Temple Mount. Simon controlled the Upper City and part of the Lower City. The Zealots under Eleazar controlled the Temple. John of Giscala and his supporters held the outer part of the Temple Mount and that part of the Lower City just below the south wall of the Temple Mount.[18]

Josephus says that Jerusalem was defended by 23,400 men, of whom Simon led the lion's share—15,000 troops. These were composed of Simon's own 10,000 fighters and a separate force of 5,000 Idumean soldiers who also followed Simon. John of Giscala commanded 6,000 men. Eleazar son of Simon led 2,400 Zealots.[19] Josephus's numbers are less than reliable, but they may approximate the power equation in Jerusalem. The Roman authorities considered Simon the leader of the rebels, and the Roman historian Tacitus listed Simon first among the Jewish commanders.[20] As one modern historian points out, it is remarkable that of all the men in Jerusalem—including Zealot priests, elite leaders like John of Giscala, and Adiabenian royalty—of all of them, it was the lowborn son of a convert who became the chief of the rebellion.[21]

The new leaders in Jerusalem were a remarkable generation, men capable of the best and worst in their national character. They were patriotic, brave, swift, mobile, and deadly in battle. They were also factionalized and guilty of "causeless hatred" (*sinat hinam*), as the Talmud calls it.[22] If they had devoted as much energy to uniting as they did to dividing, they might have saved their city or at least have made the Romans pay a higher price for it. There were troops to be trained and weapons to be readied. There was plenty of work to do to strengthen the Third Wall, the new construction on Jerusalem's vulnerable, northern side. Rather than passively waiting for the Romans, the rebels could have sallied out and ambushed the enemy. The hill country that runs along the central spine of the Land of Israel was perfect for ambushes, and the abundant caves made excellent hideouts for raiders. Instead, the rebels wasted their time and energy on civil war. It was military and political malpractice.

The only saving grace was that Rome, too, had given up imperial management for the dubious pleasures of civil war. But Rome had a lot more room for error. Rome ruled a 2-million-square-mile empire that spanned three continents. By late 69, the rebels were largely confined to a city that was about 425 acres (175 hectares), that is, less than a square mile in size.[23]

Waiting for Vespasian

It was shrewd of Vespasian to wait after Nero's suicide in June 68 and to call off most major military activity in the rebel province of Judea. Civil war broke out in the Roman capital in 69, with three men succeeding to the throne in rapid succession: Galba, Otho, and Vitellius. Then Vespasian concluded that he deserved the throne himself. The strife among these men was the first civil war in the century since Augustus had established his rule. The year 69 has gone down in history as the Year of the Four Emperors, a bloody twelve months of killing. The fighting included revolts in Gaul, Germania, and Hispania; heavy street fighting in Rome that led to the destruction of the Temple of Jupiter, the city's chief shrine; two bloody battles in northern Italy and the four-day sack of an Italian city; and the death of three of the four emperors, two by murder and one by taking his own life.

Vespasian had the allies and armies to make good on his claim to the purple. The governor of Syria and the commander of the legions on the Danube supported him, as did the Jewish King Agrippa II and his sister, Berenice. Vespasian's most important backer was the governor of Egypt, none other than Tiberius Julius Alexander. When last seen, he was serving on the Parthian frontier with Corbulo in 63; since then, he continued to rise on the career ladder. In 66, Nero appointed Tiberius Alexander as prefect, that is, governor of Egypt. Egypt was Rome's wealthiest province and its breadbasket, but its population was often turbulent, especially in the capital city of Alexandria. So, the prefect was one of the most important governors in the empire. His support was a prize and he awarded it to Vespasian. On July 1, 69, Tiberius Alexander had the legions of Egypt swear an oath of loyalty to the would-be emperor. This made Tiberius Alexander the first governor to declare support for Vespasian.

It was the first open sign of rebellion against Vitellius, who controlled Rome, but it was also a revolution in the traditional system. Vespasian was the son of a tax collector from the Sabine hills of central Italy, and now he was hailed as the ruler of the world. The heir of the Caesars lacked even an ounce of noble blood. This successor of Augustus's line was proclaimed far from the Forum, in the city of Antony and Cleopatra. The shouts of the soldiers in their red woolen cloaks in Alexandria replaced the orderly deliberation of the senators in their purple-bordered togas in Rome; and a Jew had played kingmaker of the Roman Empire. A few days later the legions of Judea and Syria followed their brothers in Egypt. It took another five months until December for the Senate to recognize Vespasian, and sticklers were annoyed in later years when he marked July 1 as the anniversary of his reign.

One man who felt unalloyed joy at Vespasian's acclamation was Josephus. His prediction of the Roman's ascent to the purple had come true. The emperor-designate remembered the Jewish prisoner and his prophecy made after the fall of Jotapata. According to Josephus, Vespasian consulted his top commanders and, upon their consent, ordered that he be freed after two years as a Roman prisoner. Josephus claims that Titus even requested that the prisoner's chains not just be loosened but cut off, the usual acknowledgment of false imprisonment.[24] Since we know that Josephus presented a copy of his *Jewish War* to Titus, the story is probably true.

It might have been in 68, while Vespasian was waiting outside Jerusalem, that a celebrated incident took place. Jewish tradition reports it in four different versions.[25] A leading Jewish sage, Johanan ben Zakkai,[26] left the city and defected to the Romans. Johanan was no Zealot; arguably, he hoped to negotiate an agreement between the rebels and the Romans. When he realized the situation was hopeless, he decided to flee Jerusalem, but the rebels wouldn't let anyone out. Supposedly Johanan had his students pretend he was dead and carry him out in a coffin for burial. He reached Vespasian and won his favor by declaring that Vespasian was destined to be emperor. This sounds suspiciously like the story of Josephus, and some scholars doubt the historicity of Johanan's escape, but perhaps both stories are true.[27] After all, it wasn't a secret that commanders were open to flattery. Johanan supposedly asked for and received permission from Vespasian to set up a school.

One other event might have happened during this period, if not even earlier. Jerusalem was the mother city of the followers of Jesus Christ. According to a fourth-century Christian writer, at the outset of the revolt in 66 they fled the city for the safety of Pella.[28] Pella was one of the Greek cities of Palestine, located in the foothills east of the Jordan River, about twenty miles south of the Sea of Galilee. Some scholars think a date of 68 is more likely.

The historicity of the two events—the early community of Christ followers escaping to Pella and Rabbi Johanan ben Zakkai's mission to Vespasian—has been questioned. But surely the underlying point that the two stories make is correct, which is, despite the ring of steel that was about to be drawn around Jerusalem, the representatives of two great religions managed to escape. Unfortunately, no such good fortune lay in store for most of the inhabitants of the beautiful but doomed Holy City.

Anatomy of Resistance

Even a glancing familiarity with Roman history would show that the Romans did not leave enemies unpunished, however long it might take. For example, in 215 BCE King Philip V of Macedon made a treaty with Hannibal, the Carthaginian general who had invaded Italy, crushed a series of Roman armies, and brought the young empire closer to defeat than it had ever come. Little came of the treaty, and Rome bounced back. The Romans devoted their energies to defeating Hannibal; Carthage surrendered in 201. But Rome did not forget Philip, on whom it declared war the next year. Three years later, the legions inflicted a devastating defeat on the Macedonian phalanx in the hills of northern Greece. The lesson: the long arm of Roman vengeance did not always strike quickly, but it almost always came down hard in the end.

Another lesson of history was Rome's excellence at taking walled cities, either by assault or siege or, on occasion, by intimidation at the mere sight of the Roman army outside the walls. Carthage and Corinth are just two of the many fortified cities that Rome conquered—and two that they left in ruins (both in 146 BCE). Experience, money, and technology all contributed to Rome's advantages in the art of mastering such cities. So did the discipline and solidity of Roman institutions, especially the political system and the army. Cultural factors played a big role as well. The Roman military prized aggression, while the emperors rewarded victorious generals (as long as they didn't threaten to outshine the emperor). Small-unit cohesion was the backbone of the legions. Both teamwork and individual prowess were held in the highest esteem. Soldiers knew that competitiveness, risk-taking, and putting oneself in harm's way for the sake of one's comrades could all lead to promotion. Many an ambitious young warrior staked his life on being first over the wall in an assault on a hostile city to make a name for himself. Morale qualities such as these gave Romans an edge over most of the enemies whose cities they attacked.[29]

If Rome was so good at taking cities, why did the rebels of Jerusalem think they had a chance to win? Was it just religious fanaticism? In retrospect the rebels had no hope, but retrospection, like a fun-house mirror, distorts our view. From the perspective of the year 70, the rebels had rational grounds for thinking they might prevail in a Roman siege of Jerusalem.[30] However good the Romans were at sieges, they didn't have a perfect record. In the years since Pompey took Jerusalem in 63 BCE, the Romans had failed in several sieges: Gergovia (in central France) 52 BCE, against Gauls; Phraaspa (in northwestern Iran) 36 BCE, against Parthia; and Dyrrhachium (on the Adriatic) 49 to 48 BCE, a civil war battle against fellow Romans. These failures don't necessarily reflect poorly on the Romans because taking a city by siege was not easy. Defense is usually the strongest form of warfare. Given the sizable Jewish population under Parthian rule, the rebels may well have heard about Phraaspa, if not the other two Roman failures.[31]

The defenders of Jerusalem were outclassed in terms of technology. They had captured some artillery from the Romans in 66, but it took time to learn to use the weapons properly. But when it came to hand-to-hand combat, the defenders were excellent fighters. They excelled at raids, ambushes, feints, and the other tricks of the trade of irregular warfare. They were highly motivated. Of course, in one form of technology, Jerusalem was first-class. It was one of the most highly fortified cities in the ancient world. Jerusalem was not Jotapata, with its makeshift walls, or Gamala, whose walls were not built to withstand the blast of Rome's multiple artillery weapons. Jerusalem's walls were stout enough that they might have given Vespasian pause.

Numbers may have factored in as well. Scholarly estimates of the size of the population of Jerusalem in 70 vary radically. "We don't know" is the safest conclusion, but an educated guess of 50,000 is not impossible.[32] Josephus's statement of 23,400 soldiers defending is surely also an educated guess. That doesn't mean it is right, because there was no official recordkeeping for Josephus to check and because Josephus is rarely reliable about numbers, which he often inflates to flatter Roman achievements. Nor do his numbers include civilians, particularly women, who are known to have taken part in the city's defense. They may not take account of Roman defectors, who added to the ranks of Jerusalem's defenders. These included both soldiers of Agrippa II and Roman auxiliaries and perhaps even legionaries, exhausted by the terrible struggle of the siege.

Still, the numbers make sense when compared to the number of Roman attackers. For the Roman side, Josephus had access to accurate records, not to mention his own personal observations on the campaign, in which he took part. A recent scholarly calculation concludes that Titus's siege army, with its four legions and various auxiliary and allied contingents, consisted of between 48,200 and 67,000 combatants. (The ancient sources relate the various units in Titus's army, but not the number of men in each unit, so we must estimate.) A rule of thumb in military affairs states that a successful attacker needs a three-to-one superiority in numbers to break through a well-defended enemy. If Jerusalem's defenders had significantly fewer than Josephus's estimate of 23,400 soldiers, then the Romans should have been able to break through quickly, which they could not.

Another number: Titus had four legions, that is, approximately 19,000 to

24,000 men, or less than half his army. The legions were Rome's elite troops. The rest of Titus's army was made up of auxiliaries, that is, allied units in the Roman army, and of forces sent by Agrippa II and other Roman allies in the East. Of those four legions, one was the Twelfth Legion, a proven failure both against Parthia in 62 and against the rebels at Beth Horon in 66. Furthermore, the other three legions faced questions about their experience and cohesion, since a substantial amount of their manpower—between 25 and 33 percent—consisted of substitutes, replacing units that had been sent to Italy to fight in the civil war to put Vespasian on the throne. Titus's manpower numbers, therefore, look less impressive on closer examination.[33]

And then there was the state of Rome itself. After nearly two years of revolution and civil war, was the Roman state sufficiently united and resolute to fight the war against the Judean rebels to the finish? Would the house of Flavius Vespasianus be able to command the loyalty that the house of Augustus—the Julio-Claudian dynasty—had inspired? In short, was Rome still Rome?

In addition to civil war, Rome faced a revolt in the West. A native chief in what is today the region of the Dutch-German border led a rebellion in 69 to 70 that forced the surrender of several legionary garrisons. The Romans put down the Batavian Revolt, as it is often called, but not before the end of 70. If news of the rebellion reached Judea, it could only have encouraged the rebels there.

Roman soldiers were known to be tough, experienced, and motivated. Their training emphasized honor and achievement in combat. The prizes of looting a rich city like Jerusalem could be enormous. Yet everything depended on leadership. Vespasian was a seasoned commander, but he was now in Rome. In his place was his son Titus. He was thirty years old, an age that the conservative Romans considered still adolescent. Titus had seen war, but nowhere near to the degree that his father had. Would Titus have the tactical experience, the political savvy, the good judgment, and above all the iron will that he would need to drive his army to victory, despite casualties and setbacks, against a very well dug-in and determined enemy?

Then there was the lure of the East. Judean rebels hoped to get aid from "beyond the Euphrates," as Josephus calls it.[34] Romans feared that they would succeed.[35] Vespasian didn't trust Parthia: not in Judea, and not anywhere in the Roman Near East. When Vespasian declared for the throne in the civil war of 69, he sent ambassadors to Parthia and Armenia to ensure that they would not take advantage of a border stripped of the legions who were marching on Rome.[36] Around the same time the rebels in Jerusalem sent ambassadors across the Euphrates in hope of finding help.[37]

The King of Parthia

Rome had used its influence in the past to stir up trouble domestically for Parthia. It was in the interests of Adiabene and Parthia to return the favor in Judea, as long, that is, as their fingerprints were not visible. Arguably Adiabene wanted more from the revolt than just to cause trouble for Rome. After all the investment they had made in Jerusalem and elsewhere in Judea, the rulers of Adiabene did not want to show themselves as weaklings who were unable to help their co-religionists. They may even have imagined a prince of their dynasty becoming king of Judea one day. So, they intervened, visibly, if not formally.[38]

No official support for the rebels came from Parthian lands. There were, however, volunteers—or should one say "volunteers"? It was well-established policy in the ancient world to smile on unofficial forces to carry out a state's bidding without committing that state to open support or, worse, treaty violation.[39]

Individual men from Adiabene fought for the rebels in Jerusalem. Some of them were members of the royal family and so represented the highest level of elite, but they were still individuals. As far as we know, the king of Adiabene did not send any official aid to Judea, let alone an army to intervene on behalf of the rebels. Nor would he have done so without the approval of the king of Parthia, Vologases I. And this, the Parthian was unwilling to give.[40] According to Josephus, Titus accused the rebels of sending embassies across the Euphrates to stir up revolt.[41] It's not clear to whom the embassies were directed: to Jewish communities, to the king of Adiabene, to the king of Parthia, or to all three. In any case, Vologases did not help the rebels. Why not?

Vologases was an astute and accomplished statesman who sat on the throne for twenty-seven years, from 51 to 78. He consolidated control of his kingdom, defeated internal rebellion, extended his family's control as far as Armenia to the west and, in the south, to the head of the Persian Gulf. There he built new cities to assert control of the lucrative commerce with Arabia and India. Vologases also put a new emphasis in Parthian life on Iranian culture in place of Greek culture. In short, he made Parthia a stronger and more formidable state than it had been.

Vologases might have been confident of his army's ability to cross the Euphrates, invade Syria and Judea, and defeat the Roman legions. But he had to reckon that, if he did so, the Romans would return in force, handing Vologases a long war. That would not serve his interests, because the king had more valuable tasks in other parts of his empire. Like Germany in the era of the world wars, Parthia faced armed rival powers on two fronts, and then some. The Romans lay to the west. On the east, Parthia faced the threat of a new state, the Kushan Empire, that expanded into Bactria and drove the Parthians out. In response, Parthia strengthened its military presence in central Asia. Around the same time, to the northeast of Parthia there loomed the Alans, a fierce nomadic people. Around 72, they in fact invaded Parthian territory.

Vologases had reason to opt for stability in the west, having scored a coup in Armenia. By placing his brother on the Armenian throne, Vologases blunted Rome's ability to threaten Parthian territory. The two powers swore a treaty in 63; there was good reason to keep it in place and not help the rebels in Judea.

Finally, Vologases might have asked himself if an independent Judea served the interests of Parthia, even if Judea became a vassal state. Parthia had a large Jewish population, a population that included enough soldiers to have run a state within a state in Babylonia within living memory. Independent Judea would certainly attempt to build close relations with its Jewish brethren in Parthia, thereby empowering a countervailing domestic force to royal power.

All things considered, Vologases chose neutrality during the Great Revolt, even if that hastened a Roman victory. If Adiabenian volunteers, even royal volunteers, wanted to help the rebels as private citizens, so be it. If nothing else, they could send intelligence reports back east.

Meanwhile, Vologases engaged in what was probably a diplomatic ploy. He reached out to Vespasian late in 69. The Roman was in Egypt then. With the news that Vitellius was dead and the throne was his for the taking, Vespasian prepared to depart for Italy. Vologases sent an embassy offering forty thousand horsemen to help Vespasian conquer Judea. It was a trap, and Vespasian knew it, because to accept would have branded him a weakling and a Parthian vassal. He might also have understood it as a threat. If Parthia could field forty thousand cavalrymen to help Rome, it could field the same number to hurt Rome. He thanked the ambassadors and told them to bring their offer to the Senate in Rome. Nothing more came of it, but Vespasian surely added it to his understanding of Parthia as a dangerous foe.[42]

The irony is that for all their disagreements, the Parthians and the Romans could agree on one thing: neither empire wanted to see an independent Jewish state.[43]

Adiabene

Even so, some number of soldiers from beyond the Euphrates did arrive in Jerusalem. Individuals contributed to the rebel cause in person. Josephus mentions only three names, all Adiabenians, two of them from the royal dynasty, who had converted to Judaism. He also speaks of others, the "son and brothers of King Izates." Royalty does not travel alone. Surely the Adiabenians would have brought servants and bodyguards with them. A staff was needed to man the three Adiabenian palaces in Jerusalem and to defend them, and surely some of the staff would have been trusted people from home.

Cassius Dio (ca. 164–after 229), a Greek senator and author, wrote a massive, multivolume history of Rome based on earlier sources. All that survives of the material after 46 CE are excerpts and later summaries. In one of them, he writes of a larger contingent of outside supporters of the rebels:

> The Jews also were assisted by many of their countrymen from the region round about and by many who professed the same religion, not only from the Roman empire but also from beyond the Euphrates.[44]

Add their retinues to the Adiabenian royals in Jerusalem, and then add others "from beyond the Euphrates" who might have joined them, and Cassius Dio's "many" becomes plausible. Consider also that Josephus was at pains to downplay Judean connections to Parthian lands because those connections expressed disloyalty to Rome. That may explain why he mentions so few Adiabenian and other Eastern Jews who fought in Jerusalem for the rebellion.

That any Jews from abroad, especially from the Parthian Empire, put their lives on the line is itself impressive. But there were practical limits on the number of Jews "from beyond the Euphrates" who could help. To reach rebel territory, those Jews would have had to pass through the Roman province of Syria and then through King Agrippa's realm. If they came on war-horses or with arms and armor brandished, Roman soldiers would have stopped them. They probably had to pretend that they were merchants or pilgrims. One wonders how many soldiers "many" really was. One hundred? Several hundred? Perhaps, but probably not more.

If the Adiabenians had a large force behind them, one of them could have emerged as a faction leader. But none did, presumably because they lacked the manpower. They could not match the 2,400 Zealots who supported Eleazar son of Simon, let alone the 15,000 men fighting for Simon son of Giora.

Whether many or few Adiabenians were in Jerusalem, they were highly visible. The royal dynasty had built three palaces in the city. They served as a vivid, physical sign of help from abroad: a symbol of hope. Alas, hope alone does not win wars.

A reasonable person in rebel Jerusalem might have concluded, nevertheless, that there was a chance of fighting Rome to a standstill. Or at least one might have talked oneself into believing it. Not that everyone in the beleaguered city was reasonable. Passion motivated some, faith fortified others. Tacitus, no friend of the Jews, was unimpressed by the material resources that the rebels could deploy in a siege. What did strike him was Jerusalem's mountainous topography and what he calls the "stubborn superstition" of the Jews. A less tendentious way to put it would be: a religion-fueled nationalism, buttressed by vengeance and the dictates of honor, moved the city's defenders.[45]

In truth, much of Jerusalem's strength had been squandered in civil war. Now a diminished city stood, sharpening its swords, praying and sacrificing, and holding its breath, waiting for Titus.

Chapter Seven

TITUS AT JERUSALEM

On a spring day in the year 70, the Roman army marched again to Jerusalem. At this time of year, the land bloomed with wildflowers, among them anemones, buttercups, poppies, cyclamen, and daisies. It was the season of mild temperatures before the heat of the summer. More cautious than Cestius when he attacked the Holy City in 66, the Romans this time divided their forces. They had four legions, as well as twenty cohorts of auxiliary infantry, and eight of auxiliary cavalry. Agrippa II and the kings of Commagene and Emesa as well as the Nabateans provided allied forces. The total number of men, as previously mentioned, was between about 48,000 and 67,000. It was roughly equivalent to Vespasian's force of 50,000 to 60,000 men in 67 and perhaps twice as large as Cestius's force of roughly 30,000 men. As one scholar notes, it was a very substantial force, roughly 15 percent of the Roman Empire's armies.[1] And the commander, Titus Caesar Vespasianus, son of the new emperor, had full access to the center of power in Rome.[2]

His intelligence service, fed by deserters from Jerusalem, told Titus about the civil war of Jew against Jew. As striking as were the signs of Jewish division inside the walls of the city, even greater signs of division appeared outside. Agrippa II, the Jewish king of Galilee and Perea, was there fighting for Rome along with perhaps 3,000 of his soldiers. The sources don't report the size of his contingent, but Agrippa II had provided 2,000 infantrymen and 1,000 cavalrymen to Vespasian in 67, and one might expect a similar contribution in 70.

As incongruous as the presence of Agrippa II may seem, even stranger was Titus's relationship with Agrippa's sister, Berenice, the former queen of Chalcis (a territory in south Lebanon, annexed by Rome in 53). Titus and Berenice were lovers. The affair arguably began in 67, when Titus visited Agrippa's capital of Caesarea Philippi, which was by then home to Berenice as well. As he headed to make war on the Holy City of the Jews, Titus had a prominent Jewish mistress.

Agrippa II was a valuable ally, but another Jew represented the most important military support for Titus. The Roman commander's chief of staff was none other than Tiberius Julius Alexander.[3] His position represented a reward for Tiberius Alexander's early and fervent support of Vespasian as emperor, but it was not simply a patronage job. Titus needed Tiberius Alexander. Titus was young, only thirty, handsome, and strong. He had been raised on the Palatine in Rome and was lucky to escape with his life from the poison that killed his close friend Britannicus, the son of the emperor Claudius. He was an all-rounder: a good soldier, a good horseman, a good speaker in Greek as well as Latin, and a passable singer and player of the lyre. He served first in Britannia and Germania and then went through the fire of war in Vespasian's campaign in Galilee. But that was a far cry from laying siege to one of the most well-fortified cities in the world. Siegecraft was a job for an experienced professional. Enter Tiberius Alexander. In his mid-fifties, he was more than twenty years Titus's senior. Tiberius Alexander had learned the art of war on the Parthian front from the greatest Roman commander of the era, Corbulo. Josephus wasn't just currying favor when he praised Tiberius Alexander for his sagacity and experience in the business of war. When Josephus was writing in the 70s, to be sure, Tiberius Alexander was a VIP in Rome, worth flattering. But what Josephus wrote was probably also true.[4]

In addition, Tiberius Alexander knew the province of Judea and Jerusalem intimately, having served as procurator. And perhaps it was thought that as a Jew he might be able to negotiate a settlement with the rebels. He left no doubt about his willingness to use harsh methods against fellow Jews. He had demonstrated that in his most recent position in the Roman administration.

In 66, Nero had appointed Tiberius Alexander as prefect, that is, governor, of Egypt, one of the highest and most sensitive positions in the administration of the Roman Empire. His was not an easy tenure. The year that the Great Revolt broke out was a period of violent conflict between Greeks and Jews in the Eastern Mediterranean, Egypt included. According to Josephus, a riot erupted in Alexandria when some Jews attended an assembly that the Greeks of the city had called. The Greeks attacked the Jews and the Jews responded in force and got the better of things. Tiberius Alexander tried to calm the situation by meeting with the leaders of the Jewish community, but he failed and the violence continued. At this point he called in the army. To suppress the Jewish rioters he sent in the two Roman legions that were assigned to Egypt, roughly 10,000 men, as well as 5,000 men from neighboring Libya. They stormed the Jewish Quarter and attacked everyone they found, whether insurgents or civilians, young or old. Josephus says that before order was restored no less than 50,000 Jews were killed. Surely that is another exaggeration, but the death toll was no doubt significant.[5]

That had been an easy if bloody victory, but something different lay ahead. Tiberius Alexander knew that it was one thing to send the legions against the unarmed Jewish civilians and ragtag defenders of Alexandria's Jewish Quarter and quite another to hurl them against heavily fortified Jerusalem, with now experienced and quite possibly fanatical champions on the walls, many of them ready to fight to the death rather than surrender. He, and no doubt Titus as well, surely hoped to settle the battle of Jerusalem by negotiation rather than fighting to the finish.[6]

Agrippa II and Tiberius Alexander were reminders of Rome's unsuccessful tactics in Judea. Rome had tried to find local rulers who could govern the area for them. King Herod succeeded, but he neglected to provide for a competent successor. His grandson, Agrippa I, restored the dynasty, but his life was cut short. That left only Herod's great-grandson Agrippa II. Tiberius Alexander was his former relation by marriage, because Agrippa's sister, Berenice, was the widow of Tiberius Alexander's brother. Agrippa II and Tiberius Alexander represented the tattered remnants of the failed policy of Jewish collaboration with Rome. As they rode beside Titus, they might have been heading toward that policy's funeral.

The two Jews and the Roman commander were reminders of something else as well, of the cyclical nature of history. A little over a century earlier, in 37 BCE, another Roman general, Sosius, and another Jewish royal, Herod, laid siege to the Holy City with their armies.

One other Jew in Titus's entourage deserves mention. As previously noted, Josephus was there, an eyewitness to the siege of his native city, from the Roman side, and an occasional participant in diplomatic efforts to reach a peace agreement.

Josephus is also our main source for the siege. As usual he can be trusted only up to a point. He wasn't privy to the commanders' conversations and his knowledge of Latin was limited. The speeches that he reports are at best rough approximations of what was said, if not outright fiction. He was at pains, on the one hand, to showcase Titus's generalship and his humanity. On the other hand, Josephus emphasized both Jewish heroism and Jewish fanaticism. Above all, he aimed to demonstrate the role of divine providence.

Several other literary sources exist. The surviving part of Tacitus's *Histories* sketches a few details of the siege. So does Cassius Dio's *Roman History*, which was written about 150 years later, but that draws on earlier sources. A few other literary works also provide details. The archaeology of Jerusalem has also yielded information.[7]

Titus at Jerusalem: First Blood

From the beginning of the Roman siege until nearly the end, the defenders of Jerusalem fought fiercely and well. This should have been no surprise to the attackers, not after Beth Horon, Jotapata, and Gamala. But Titus underestimated the enemy at first. As usual in Roman sieges, he began with the hope of intimidating the foe into surrender. His informants, presumably including Josephus, assured him that most of the population of Jerusalem was eager to negotiate. This was, of course, not true. Morale remained high among the defenders for most of the siege. The combatants could not have done their job without widespread support in the population. Many if not most of them believed that Jerusalem was impregnable.

Titus and his forces arrived in Jerusalem in April.[8] When the Roman forces arrived at the city and rode up close to the walls, a Jewish raiding party poured out and cut them off. Titus was lucky to escape with his life. Next the defenders turned on one of his legions. The Tenth Legion was in the process of digging a camp on the Mount of Olives. They paid little attention to security, thinking themselves protected by the ravine-like Valley of Kidron that separated them from the walls of the city. Once again, the Jews surprised the Romans by sallying out. As so often in the past, the legionaries were at a loss in irregular warfare. Their forte was lining up in heavy armor and crushing the enemy, not in wheeling round and round and parrying the blows of a light-armed, agile, fast-moving foe.

The Jews drove the legionaries from their camp. According to Josephus, they would have been routed had not Titus arrived and rallied them. Josephus, of course, had a vested interest in flattering Titus, so skepticism about Titus's role is called for. The Romans drove the enemy back toward the walls of the city. Then a watchman on the walls waved a cloak, a signal for fresh Jewish troops to leave the walls and join the fight. The Romans panicked and fled. Once again, if Josephus can be believed, Titus turned the tide by leading a counterattack. The Jews put up a fierce fight but, in the end, they retreated behind the walls. The Tenth Legion finished building its camp.

The assault on the Mount of Olives captures the difference between the two sides and their respective ways of war. The Jews were light-armed fighters. Their weapons were swords, daggers, and stones either thrown by hand or by sling. They had few archers or javelin men. They had shields, but they lacked body armor. They had no cavalry to speak of, and attacked on foot. Raids, stratagems, ambushes, and the other tools of irregular warfare were their specialty. They were fast and mobile. The Romans were heavy-armed infantrymen. Their weapon par excellence was the gladius, the short sword that was the legionary's trademark. They wore heavy armor and carried long oval shields. Their allies provided cavalrymen and archers. The Romans excelled at conventional battle. Unfortunately for the rebels, the Romans also excelled at sieges.

After their success, the Jews turned to another round of infighting. It was now Passover. The Zealots on the Temple Mount, under Eleazar son of Simon, allowed the people to ascend and worship at the Temple. It was a mistake that John of Giscala was quick to take advantage of. He armed some of his men with hidden daggers. Once on the Mount they attacked the Zealots and drove them out. In effect, there were only two parties now in Jerusalem, John's and Simon son of Giora's. The Zealots were much reduced as a factor. A victory for John, but it was essentially a defeat of the unity needed to prevail against the Romans.[9]

Titus used Josephus as a go-between to invite the rebels to a parley, but they refused to answer. The next day the rebels sent out a group of men, who pretended to be expelled from the city. When the Romans approached, the supposed exiles turned on them and surrounded the Romans. Defenders on the battlements joined in and pelted the Romans with stones and various other projectiles. The Romans took casualties, but finally broke out of the circle and retreated. The Jews followed them all the way to Helena's tomb, assaulting them as they went. The victorious rebels made fun of the Romans with a victory dance in shouting and raising their shields.

Titus chewed his men out and threatened a collective punishment, probably decimation, that is, killing every tenth man in the unit. He allowed the soldiers to plea for mercy and he pardoned them. But he now realized that the defenders were tougher and more dangerous than he had thought. He had to make changes. What he decided to do was to move camp closer to the walls. First, he had the ground leveled near the walls, where the terrain allowed, and then he provided airtight security for the movement of his baggage train and support troops. He protected them by deploying his infantry and cavalry as well as archers in a thick formation seven lines deep. The maneuver was effective and allowed two camps to be set up about four hundred yards from the walls. It sent the defenders an encouraging message nonetheless: the Romans feared them. For Titus, the opening phase of the siege was an education. The real work was about to begin.

John and Simon at Jerusalem

After shedding gallons of their own countrymen's blood in Jerusalem, John of Giscala and Simon son of Giora called a truce and turned on the Romans. "When the Romans drew near," wrote Tacitus, "foreign war produced unity."[10] In the defense of their city, their men demonstrated courage, daring, cunning, and high morale. So did the women of Jerusalem, wrote Tacitus: they were as committed and as fearless as the men.[11] Despite their professionalism and technology, the Romans found themselves frustrated and even despondent.

The Roman army was good at sieges, but it didn't like them. Sieges were more dangerous and frustrating than open battle, which was often decided in a day; a siege could last months. In offering to negotiate, Titus was probably trying to drive a wedge in the enemy's morale. Nothing short of surrender would do, but the Jews had no reason to surrender to an army that kept losing. Titus would have to get down to the dirty business of assaulting the walls.

Ancient sieges tended to go through a regular series of stages. They began with intimidation. In Titus's case, that failed. They progressed to light assault, with ladders and grappling hooks. If that failed, then came the heavy assault. In this stage the Romans would typically build a ramp and then attack with battering rams and siege towers. Often the attacker built a circumvallation wall around the besieged city, a ring of structures that cut the defenders off from resupply or escape. The attacking army would man the circumvallation wall, but its personnel were typically encamped just outside. If the attacker succeeded in capturing the city, there followed the bloodiest stage of all—the sack.[12]

Titus now proceeded to a heavy assault. As was logical, he targeted the Third Wall, the weakest part of the city's defense. As one historian points out, the Romans should have been able to take the Third Wall via a light assault with ladders and grappling hooks. But they had to make a heavy effort and build a siege ramp: testimony to the high morale and excellent fighting skill of the defenders.[13]

At first it was Simon's men alone who counterattacked; John was too afraid of his rival to have his men leave the Temple Mount. Simon's men posted artillery on the ramparts, but made only limited use of them. They had captured the weapons in 66 and, despite tutoring from Roman deserters, they found it hard to operate these complicated machines. So, the defenders counterattacked mainly by throwing stones, shooting arrows, and sallying out from the walls in daring and dangerous raids. The Romans, by contrast, had experts to man their artillery, and they inflicted barrage after barrage of heavy stones on the defenders, who had watchmen in turn to warn their comrades about incoming missiles. The Romans also had allied archers to help drive the counterattacking defenders back.

Slowly the Romans finished building siege ramps to approach the wall. When the ramps were ready, the Romans brought up battering rams that were suspended from wheeled towers. When they struck, the crashing sound was deafening. Fear seized the rebels throughout the city. They probably knew the rule of ancient siege warfare: once the ram touched the wall, no further negotiation was possible.[14]

John and Simon decided to unite against the enemy. They "became one body," wrote Josephus, and joined together on the ramparts to throw firebrands and try to defeat the assault.[15] There followed two Jewish sallies outside the walls to try to burn the ram towers. Josephus praises "Jewish daring," although he says it was born of desperation. The Jews almost set the towers on fire, but Titus led a cavalry unit that defeated the first sally and an elite unit of Alexandrian soldiers defeated the second one.[16] After ordering a Jewish captive to be crucified, as a warning to the defenders, Titus had three large towers approach the walls, towers containing artillery as well as rams. When one of the towers made a breach in the wall, the defenders fell back. The Romans finally captured the Third Wall in early May, after an effort that took fifteen days. They entered the northern part of the city, which the rebels abandoned for the safety of the other, stronger walls beyond.

When the Romans broke through the wall, deserters fled. Desertion made most sense for the rich. Titus enslaved the poor but, in typical Roman fashion, he tended to preserve the wealthy on the grounds that they might prove useful after the war. But desertion went both ways. As the siege wore on and it seemed that the city would never fall, some Roman soldiers defected to the Jews. Although the Jews were short of food, they fed the deserters well, since their presence boosted Jewish morale and had the opposite effect on the enemy.[17]

Action now moved to the Second Wall. At first the two sides skirmished. The Jews dashed out and engaged the Romans in hand-to-hand combat. Although the legionaries prevailed, the rebels impressed Josephus with their reckless courage and their tenacity amid setbacks.[18] Then the Romans brought up their rams. Within five days, they took down a tower and rushed into the narrow breach in the Second Wall that they had opened. But the defenders were ready. They ambushed the Romans in the narrow streets and forced them out again. The defenders' morale soared. For three days they fought resolutely and held back the Romans. Finally, on the fourth day, the Romans retook the Second Wall, which they proceeded to demolish. It was mid-May.

Titus decided to suspend the attack. His men needed a break, and there was always the hope that the rebels might surrender. To boost his soldiers' morale and to frighten the enemy, he ordered his men to parade outside the walls in full armor and with professional discipline. If that wasn't enough of a display, it was payday, and Titus had the officers count out each man's earnings in full view of the enemy. Josephus writes of the defenders that, at the sight, "terrible consternation fell upon even the boldest."[19] If so, it doesn't seem to have made them give up an inch. After four days of paying his troops, Titus had to renew the siege. His twin goals now were the Upper City, that is, the wealthy quarter on the western hill of the city, and the Temple Mount, the most sacred part of the Holy City. The walls facing the Romans here were the stoutest and most daunting of all. Titus ordered the building of four embankments, that is, ramps of soil, rock, and wood. Two of the embankments rose opposite the Tomb of John, which lay beside the First Wall, and two opposite the Antonia Fortress, which guarded the Temple Mount at its northwest. It took seventeen days to complete these works.

All the while, the defenders kept up a counterattack. Simon's men and the Idumeans sallied out in raids. John's men and the Zealots bombarded the Romans from the ramparts with the artillery that they had become more adept at using.

Titus sent out Josephus to speak to the defenders to try to convince them to surrender. He addressed them in Aramaic. *The Jewish War* claims that Josephus first made a combined appeal to pragmatism and religion: the Romans were winning because God was on their side. This was met with catcalls and stones. At this point, he supposedly switched to a long historical disquisition, which, if indeed delivered, might well have bored the listeners. What rings most true in his remarks is Josephus's concern for his family inside the city.

The defenders were presumably well-fed, but food was becoming ever scarcer for most Jerusalemites. Large numbers of people, some fighters but most just poor civilians, began scavenging for scraps in the valleys outside the walls. Titus sent out the cavalry to capture them. They were subjected to torture and crucified, supposedly no less than five hundred a day. The frustrated Romans hanged the condemned in various grotesque poses. Either Titus allowed this, to let his men blow off steam and intimidate the people in the city, or Titus was forced to tolerate it, as a breach of discipline that hid a deeper dissatisfaction.

Worse was to come for the Romans. No sooner had they completed the ramps to the Antonia Fortress than the defenders destroyed them. John had tunneled under the ground and attacked the Roman works with bundles of sticks coated with pitch and bitumen and set on fire. The Roman works came crashing down. Two days later, Simon's men destroyed the two other embankments, the ones facing the First Wall. These operations were the high-water mark of the rebels' success. It left the Romans "deeply demoralized," writes Josephus, after the loss of seventeen days' worth of work: "many despaired of ever carrying the town with conventional siege engines."[20]

Many Jews poured out from behind the walls and risked their lives to burn down the Roman siege engines. Josephus singles out three of Simon's men for their bravery in rushing out with firebrands and plunging through the massed ranks of the enemy, despite arrows and sword thrusts, until they set fire to the Roman engines. "Neither bolder nor more fearsome men than these sallied forth from the city during the war," writes Josephus.[21] It is interesting that none of the three men was a Jerusalemite. One was a Galilean, a second was a deserter from Agrippa II's army, and the third one was Adiabenian. He was the son of a certain Nabataeus, but better known by the nickname Ceagira, from the Aramaic for "Lame Man."[22] Jerusalem had attracted rebels from all over the country and beyond.

If the Jews were short of food, they had plenty of water because Jerusalem is fed by a natural spring. The Romans had a tougher time finding water, which had to be brought in from a distance. Knowing this, the defenders came up with a way of harassing the enemy. Cassius Dio writes:

> The Jews found in their underground passages a source of strength; for they had these tunnels dug from inside the city and extending out under the walls to distant points in the country, and going out through them, they would attack the Romans' watercarriers and harass any scattered detachments.[23]

Eventually Titus closed the passages. Still, some Jewish captives and deserters attacked the Romans' water supply and killed isolated Roman soldiers. Titus was forced to stop receiving Jewish deserters for the time being. Later, he began accepting them again.

Titus called a council of war in early June. As he explained, he didn't want to wait the enemy out and starve him into surrender. The soldiers considered that beneath their dignity, and Titus agreed.[24] A rapid victory, he said, was the only way to win glory.[25] It was also a way of halting the decline in Roman morale. Both domestic and foreign politics also argued in favor of action. Titus represented a new dynasty whose hold on the public's affection was untested. The bigger his victory at Jerusalem, the more solid his family's power in Rome. In addition, he knew that the Parthians were watching, and he wanted to give them a message of Roman power not passivity.

Choosing to be bold but not foolhardy, Titus rejected a direct assault on the walls, as some suggested. He decided instead to surround the city with walls of circumvallation. This would cut off any food smuggling to the defenders and weaken the city further before the Romans brought up their siege engines again. It would also give his dispirited men a positive task. They set eagerly to work and supposedly cut the city off completely within three days.

The rebels had already destroyed most of each other's food supplies. Now, as a result of Titus's circumvallation walls, the famine in the city got even worse. A Roman writer once described what he called "the worst evil that can befall men even during a siege—the lack of provisions."[26] By now, the lack of food forced Jerusalem's defenders to give up their sallies outside the walls. The city was well on its way to starving to death, and Josephus paints a gruesome picture of the suffering within the walls. But Titus had no intention of waiting for the city to die.

Relentless, the Romans built four new embankments opposite the Antonia Fortress. They believed that victory depended on the success of these constructions. Should they be destroyed, there was little wood or other necessary material left to replace them. Roman soldiers were weakening in both their stamina and psyches. To their dismay, the defenders remained resilient. The Jews "possessed a fortitude of soul that could surmount faction, famine, war and such a host of calamities," writes Josephus.[27]

Or so the Romans thought. In fact, the defenders were beginning to flag. John launched an attack on the Roman ramps that was hesitant and disorganized. It lacked, according to Josephus, "the characteristics of the nation—daring, impetuosity, the simultaneous charge, the refusal to retreat even when worsted."[28] The attack failed and the Roman ramps held. It was late July and hard fighting still lay ahead.

Roman attacks brought down part of the Antonia's stone wall, only to find an improvised defensive wall behind it that John's men had built. Titus called for volunteers to attack that defensive wall on foot. Only a dozen men answered the call, and they failed. But a second attack the next night surprised the defenders and the Romans broke through. After a bloody battle, the Romans took the Antonia. As one historian notes, it wasn't Rome's mighty siege engines that made the final push; it was a small group of legionaries. The morale of the army might have been shaky, but Rome still had a few soldiers who, whether through esprit de corps or a response to powerful rhetoric by their leaders or hope of the big payments provided to men who made a difference, were willing to put everything on the line.

It is easier to understand why Jewish morale was weakening, what with the sight of the circumvallation works, the worsening of the famine, and renewed desertion. At this point for the first time in the siege, the daily sacrifice of two lambs in the Temple had to stop. Jews found the news devastating. At Titus's command, Josephus gave a speech to try to persuade John to surrender and spare the Temple. John refused, but the leading priests and other members of the Jerusalem elite now deserted, discouraged no doubt by failure of the sacrifice.

The capture of the Antonia Fortress was the turning point in the whole campaign. The greatest prize of all now lay within Rome's reach: the Temple.[29]

The Destruction of the Temple

Titus launched another small-unit night attack to try to take the Temple, but a hard-fought Jewish defense stopped it. Instead, the Romans had to build ramps again, four of them, taking another seven days. The Romans now sensed victory. Titus called another council of war to decide how to treat the Temple once it was in their hands.

To this day, Jews mourn the destruction of the Temple. The traditional date is the 9th of Av, that is, August 70. Ever since, a debate has taken place as to whether the destruction was deliberate or accidental. Cassius Dio, writing around the year 200, hedges, stating that the soldiers hesitated to enter the Temple out of superstitious fear, but then Titus ordered them inside.[30] Another ancient writer, a Christian, writing in the fifth century, states flatly that Titus ordered the destruction of the Temple.[31] He possibly based his assertion on a statement in a now-missing part of the *Histories* by Tacitus. If so, that would be significant, because Tacitus was a great historian who took care with his facts. But Josephus insists that Titus opposed the destruction of the Temple and, in fact, tried to save it. Then again, because Josephus wanted to flatter Titus, his account is questionable.

Josephus wrote that some of Titus's key commanders and provincial administrators called for the destruction of the Temple on the grounds that it was the center and symbol of Jewish resistance. They advocated enforcing the "law of war," that is, the rule that cities that refused to surrender should be sacked. Others said that the Temple ought to be spared if the Jews abandoned it. Titus argued that under no circumstances should the Temple be destroyed; rather, it should be saved as an ornament to the empire. Only three of those present supported him, but Titus was supreme commander and his word was final.[32]

It's possible that Titus really did call a council and ordered that the Temple be spared. But if he did so, one suspects that it was just to give himself plausible deniability. Surely Titus knew that, after the long ordeal of the siege, the troops would run wild and sack the city. They were, after all, both ferocious and greedy for booty.[33]

The Temple complex stood on a platform that covered 36 acres (14.4 hectares), thereby making it the largest single temple complex in the Roman Empire. All things being equal, it would not have enhanced Titus's reputation to destroy it. But there was that "law of war" and the lure of booty. The Temple's golden external decorations gleamed in the sun, and the imagination expected even greater treasures inside. Of course, the soldiers wanted to pillage it. And they did. Josephus says that in disobedience to Titus's order, a rogue soldier threw a firebrand into the Temple. As soon as he got the news, Titus rushed to the scene and tried to have the blaze put out, but it was too late. The legions had their blood up and they pretended not to hear him. The Temple Mount went up in a sea of flames. The blood of the defenders—men, women, and children—who were slaughtered there made a ghastly sight, as Josephus reports.[34]

The Romans celebrated their success with a ceremony of blunt paganism. They brought into the Temple area their military standards. These were poles decorated with each unit's symbols. The Romans then sacrificed to the standards, a bluntly pagan way of worshipping their weapons. The message was clear: the gods of the legion had defeated the God of the Jews. Then the soldiers hailed Titus as a victorious commander—an imperator. This was surely sweet music to his ears. Josephus states that the soldiers took so much loot from the Temple Mount that the value of gold in Syria went down by half.[35]

In later years, Vespasian and his two sons, Titus and Domitian, had no qualms about trumpeting the destruction of the Temple as a success. The joint Triumph of Vespasian and Titus in Rome in 71 featured golden treasures from the Temple as well as a scroll of the Torah. About ten years later, circa 81, Titus's brother Domitian included a sculpted relief of the Temple treasures being carried in the Triumph on the arch that he had erected in memory of Titus, who was deceased by then. The Arch of Titus still stands on the edge of the Roman Forum.

It's been said that history is tragedy. What role did Tiberius Julius Alexander play? It is a fact that Titus's chief military adviser at the siege of Jerusalem, the architect of the victory that destroyed the city, was a Jew. He, along with two legionary commanders, argued in favor of Titus's position that the Temple should be spared. That, at least, is what Josephus claimed. If that report is true, a seasoned commander like Tiberius Alexander surely knew that once Rome's armies broke through, the House of the Lord faced mortal danger. The man whose father spent a fortune adorning the Temple with gold and silver did as much as anyone to seal its doom.

Destruction

The defenders of Jerusalem still held the Upper City. Titus expressed a willingness to accept their surrender, but they set an unacceptable condition: they wanted safe passage to flee into the desert. Titus angrily refused. He gave his men permission to sack and burn the rest of the city once they captured it. Not that he had a choice. Once an army took a city after a siege, the "law of war" allowed the men to go on a rampage. He ordered his men to build additional siege ramps. It took eighteen days to do so, in part because there were no more trees within eleven miles and wood had to be hauled from a distance.[36] In the meantime, Titus's men destroyed first the Ophel, as the area due south of the Temple Mount was known, and then the Lower City (also known as the City of David), whose structures ran down the slope below the Ophel. Finally, the Romans assaulted the Upper City and took it with success: an easier task now that the defenders had all but given up hope. In the final fighting, Titus claimed to have killed twelve defenders with twelve arrows.[37]

When the Romans took this last of the city's walls, the soldiers erected their standards on the towers. They began chanting and singing to celebrate their victory. Then they went on a rampage of slaughter and destruction in the Upper City. The next day the sun rose over Jerusalem in flames.[38] The city was dead, but its wealth lived on, now plunder in Roman hands. It was early September. The siege was over.

The decision to destroy Jerusalem was both difficult and easy for Titus. On the one hand, it was the jewel of the East, a famous city, an adornment to the empire, and a fortress of potential use to Rome. All that argued for sparing the city, after executing the leaders of the rebellion. On the other hand, Jerusalem was the head of the snake, the perennial center of insurrection. The Romans did not need the city to govern Judea, a province that they ruled from Caesarea. They might have seen Jerusalem, to paraphrase what an Athenian once said about its neighbor and archrival Aegina, as "the eyesore of Caesarea."[39] The rebels had done Rome a favor. By concentrating in Jerusalem, they gave Rome the excuse to clean house. Just as Vespasian had brutalized much of the rest of the country so Titus was ready to brutalize Jerusalem. If, as one scholar argues, the Romans now considered Judea to be the equivalent of a foreign foe rather than a rebel province, then demolishing the capital city becomes more understandable.[40] Still, even in the bloody annals of Roman violence, such devastation was the exception and not the rule.

Destroying Jerusalem was a revolutionary solution, to be sure, but the Flavians, as Vespasian and his family are known, were revolutionaries. They were bourgeois who had stormed the Roman nobility and taken it over. In a way they were analogous to men like John and Simon, who had stormed the citadel of the Jerusalem aristocracy. Nero might have hesitated before allowing Vespasian to destroy Jerusalem. He would surely have preferred a negotiated surrender. Nero was jealous of his generals, and he wouldn't have wanted Vespasian getting the credit for such a stupendous deed. With Titus in charge of the attack on Jerusalem, Vespasian didn't have to worry: his own son was not about to turn on him.

Perhaps Nero had even shared his old tutor Seneca's admiration for defenders who withstood a siege. Seneca called them great-souled men who preferred to "breathe their last in the arms of liberty" rather than surrender.[41] The Flavians were cut from coarser cloth.

Adiabene

Titus's conquest was a famous victory for him and for the new dynasty that ruled in Rome. Yet for the makers of Roman imperial strategy, it was a means to an end. In their mind Jerusalem wasn't the Holy City but just another piece on the imperial chessboard. For them, the war had little to do with the inhabitants of a small provincial city in a tiny province. Rome had put down many other rebellions and destroyed other capital cities. Judea was a small concern in the Roman East. Rome wasn't fighting a war against the Jews, but a war against the latest rebel who dared challenge the *imperium sine fine*, the empire without end.

Besides, for Rome, Judea played a minor role in the imperial drama. The antagonist in that story was Parthia, and the destruction of Jerusalem was a message to the Parthian king that Rome would not tolerate an armed base near its eastern frontier, a base that might one day be used by Parthia. Rome might have endured a setback in Armenia, but it would not tolerate a second failure in Judea. The suffering of Titus's troops in the battle for Jerusalem told the Parthians that Rome was willing to pay a heavy price in blood for its empire.

Nothing symbolized the real stakes for Rome better than one small detail: the Adiabenian prisoners. Among the smoldering ruins of Jerusalem in 70 were no fewer than three palaces built by the royal family of Adiabene: one by Queen Helena, another by her son Monobazos II, and a third by another royal woman named Grapte.[42] These palaces represent a major investment in the city on the part of the Adiabene dynasty, but they pale in terms of the personal commitment by its sons, who were in Jerusalem fighting for the rebellion. With the battle lost, they decided to surrender. It was early September, on the same day that Titus's troops set fire to various parts of the city including the Ophel, where the Adiabenian royal palaces were located. Presumably the Adiabenians were holed up there until they realized that all was lost. The Adiabenians joined a crowd of eminent Jerusalemites who went to Titus and begged for his protection. Josephus doesn't identify the Adibenians by name, calling them only "the sons and brothers of [the former Adiabenian] King Izates."[43] Perhaps they included Monobazos and Cenedaeus, kinsmen of the current Adiadenian ruler, King Monobazos II, men who distinguished themselves in the defeat of Cestius four years earlier in 66.[44] Josephus says that Titus was angry but merciful, but perhaps he was also gleeful: he surely noticed the value of his prisoners. He eventually sent the Adiabenians to Rome in chains, where they served as hostages. Presumably they were among the prisoners paraded in the Triumph for the conquest of Judea held in Rome in 71. To the Romans, the Adiabenians were a sign of victory; to the king in Adiabene, a worry, a setback, and a disgrace.

As they left Jerusalem, the prisoners from Adiabene may have passed the tomb where the remains of Helena and Izates lay, reminders of the faith that their dynasty had put in the now-ruined city. It was the end of a dream. Arbela, the capital of Adiabene, still stood, but no longer could it be yoked to that other capital, Jerusalem, the holy city of the people that Helena's sons and grandsons had joined.

Surrender

Many of Jerusalem's defenders died fighting, but not John of Giscala or Simon son of Giora. Like quite a few other rebels, John fled to an underground tunnel beneath the city. Starving, he finally surrendered to the enemy. Titus ordered that John be transported to Italy.

Titus had already left the ruins of Jerusalem for Caesarea when he got word of the capture of that other leading rebel, Simon. Like John, Simon went underground when the city fell. He and his party included stonecutters in the hope that they could extend one of the tunnels and mine their way out of the city and into freedom. They ran out of food before they got very far, though, and they decided to surrender. According to Josephus, Simon made one last roll of the dice. He tried to scare the Romans into backing off by emerging from the ground in royal robes. Dressed in a white tunic and a purple mantle, he rose on the very spot where the Temple had stood. At first the ploy worked and the terrified Romans kept their distance, but then they approached. Simon refused to identify himself to anyone other than the Roman commanding officer.

Titus treated John and Simon as the propaganda coups that they were. He wanted to ship them back to Rome alive and well enough to march in his triumphal parade through the streets of a cheering city. Afterward, John would face life in prison, but Simon was being fattened like a lamb for the slaughter. Roman Triumphs always culminated in the execution of the enemy chief. Since he had most of Jerusalem's soldiers under his command, Simon was destined for execution.

Balance Sheet of the Siege

It took the Romans three long years of siege, from 149 to 146 BCE, to conquer the heavily fortified city of Carthage (in modern Tunisia). By contrast, Corinth (in Greece), also in 146 BCE, collapsed three days after losing a battle outside the city walls to the Roman forces. Jerusalem lasted five months, a respectable showing, if not comparable to Carthage. The Jewish rebels might have lasted longer if they hadn't destroyed their own food supplies and thereby brought about a famine. As one scholar wrote, "Perhaps it is not entirely vain to wonder how much longer Jerusalem could've held out had the defenders actually spared and rationed food and planned strategy, making more effective use of their considerable resources."[45]

Besides, the two cases are not comparable since Carthage was more powerful. Jerusalem was a rebel city with only the thinnest of institutional structures to hold its feuding factions together. Carthage was an independent state of very long standing, with an established government, a field army, and a navy. It was presumably much more populous than Jerusalem. The walls of Carthage had a circumference of about 20 miles, while those of Jerusalem were only about 3.5 miles.[46] The main approach to Carthage by land was defended by three lines of defense. Carthage was a port city and could be resupplied by sea. In short, it is understandable that Carthage held out far longer than Jerusalem. Then again, Jerusalem in 70 did not last much longer than Jerusalem in 63 BCE. At that earlier date, Pompey was let into the Upper City by Jewish collaborators. It took him three months to capture the Temple Mount, although in 63 BCE Jerusalem's fortifications weren't nearly as strong as they were in 70. In 37 BCE, Jerusalem had faced another siege, this time from outside the city walls, a siege led by Herod and his Roman ally, Sosius. On that occasion, the city held out for over four months.

Jerusalem in 70 should have been able to survive much longer than five months had it not erupted in civil war. Josephus makes his opinion clear. "I say," he wrote, "that it was civil strife that subdued the city, and the Romans the civil strife, and civil strife was a foe far mightier than the city's walls."[47] As the Talmud states, "causeless hatred" (*sinat hinam*) destroyed Jerusalem.[48]

But one other factor came into play. The enemy gets a vote, as they say in the military. For one thing, the Romans brought a huge force against Jerusalem, roughly 15 percent of their total armed forces, as noted above. For another thing, the Romans "voted" to make a blood sacrifice on a barbaric scale—a sacrifice of their own men. As far as their commander was concerned, no burden seemed too great to bear. Titus threw his men against the walls of Jerusalem the way the Great Powers threw their citizens against the machine guns and barbed wire of the Western Front in World War I. No wonder some Romans deserted to the enemy.[49]

No ancient source provides casualty figures for the Romans, not for the dead or the wounded. Nor do they provide such figures for the other sieges during the war. Perhaps that suggests that the number of Roman casualties was too high for public consumption. Josephus names several of those who fell on each side. Titus was struck on his left shoulder with a stone, leaving a permanent weakness in his left arm. Josephus took a direct hit on his head from a well-aimed stone during one of his speeches to the rebels and was knocked unconscious. He wrote that he would have been dragged off by the rebels, who felt a special hatred for him, had not Titus sent a rescue party for his high-profile turncoat.[50]

As for the people of Jerusalem, Josephus wrote that 1.1 million were killed in the siege. The figure is wildly implausible, since even the largest city in the empire, Rome, had a total population of at most 1 million, and Jerusalem was much smaller than Rome. An estimate of tens of thousands killed in Jerusalem is plausible, if not provable.[51]

It is impossible to read Josephus on the siege of Jerusalem without admiration for Jewish courage combined with horror at Jewish disunity. Nor can one contemplate the failure of the Great Revolt without asking whether it was a good idea poorly executed or a bad idea from the start. On the one hand, the Romans refused to tolerate a rebellion by a long-standing part of the empire—Rome had controlled Judea for over a century—and one with a history of looking favorably on Rome's archenemy, Parthia. On the other hand, Rome had negotiated solutions to its eastern problems before, one as recently as the year 63 with Parthia. Had the moderates stayed in control in Jerusalem, they might have negotiated a restoration of peace with Rome on the understanding that the emperor appoint more reasonable procurators than Florus and his predecessors. It becomes harder to imagine a happy outcome for the rebels once the radicals took control of Jerusalem, but even then, a better resolution might have been possible than the disaster of 70.

If the rebels had done everything right—made unity their lodestar, left Jerusalem's food supply untouched, attacked Roman supply lines—then maybe they could have made a strong-enough showing to bring Rome to the negotiating table. Unfortunately, the rebels did everything wrong, everything that is, except fight hard. But the defenders fought magnificently in a situation made nearly hopeless by their own misdeeds. Shouldn't they have surrendered to Titus at some point before it was too late?

While the city still stood, the Jews fought with a passion and a vigor that bespeaks deep hatred of the Romans. Perhaps some of those feelings only arose in response to the brutal tactics imposed first by Cestius in 66 and then, much more methodically, by Vespasian in 67 to 69. But after 120 years of Roman rule, after two prior conquests of Jerusalem and after an endless number of humiliations, police actions, and battles, after taxation and robbery of the Temple, it is impossible to believe that the warrior fury that drove the defenders of Jerusalem only sprang up overnight. Some of it surely had been brooding in angry breasts for many years.

For the House of Vespasian and his new dynasty the bloody destruction of Jerusalem was a triumph, usable as the justification for his violent accession to the throne. For the Jewish people, it was a tragedy, yet one that they survived. For the young Christian community, it was a historic turning point. Christ followers in Jerusalem were Jews who insisted that Gentiles convert to Judaism. The loss of Jerusalem did not end their movement, but it gave more weight to those followers of Christ, like Saint Paul, who took a different approach. They wished to bring Gentiles to the worship of the God of Israel through

Jesus without also converting them to Judaism. That would prove to be a historic change, but not one that much interested the Roman elite at the time.

For the Jews, the destruction of Jerusalem and the Temple was a disaster, but it seemed to be less an end than a reset. Both the city and the shrine had been destroyed before and rebuilt. Jews had faith that both would be accomplished this time as well. And they had more than faith. Hard men were already planning revenge against Rome. They streamed out of Judea and headed to safer harbors, there to design new strategies for winning back their homeland and its holy city.

Josephus is unrelenting in his conviction that a small minority of bad men, the "bandits" and their "folly of revolutionaries," were responsible for the destruction of the once magnificent city of Jerusalem.[52] By the same token he goes out of his way again and again to emphasize their warrior prowess, their courage, daring, high spirits, and resilience. Perhaps he meant only to flatter the Romans by making it seem as if they had defeated a formidable opponent. Or perhaps he knew the nature of his own people. They were bloody, but unbowed.

The task facing Rome in 70 was to defeat the Jewish revolt. In that, Rome succeeded decisively, even if it would require a few more years to douse the last smoldering embers of rebellion in fortresses like Masada. The harder job was to translate military success into strategic advantage and a lasting peace. Rome failed at that task, with disastrous results both for itself and for the Jewish people. Within sixty years, Rome faced not one but two more Jewish revolts, each of which required a major expenditure of blood and treasure to put down.

Chapter Eight

SURVIVORS

The conquest of Jerusalem settled everything and it settled nothing. It did not put out the holy fire that stirred the rebels. It did not douse the ambition of the House of Herod. It did not establish an enduring peace on the Roman-Parthian frontier. And it certainly did not dissuade the Jews from their covenant with God. On the contrary, it inspired flexibility and resilience. Perhaps the destruction of Jerusalem had a bigger impact on the community of Christ followers, in which the center of gravity switched from the Holy City to the Diaspora, with an enormous long-term impact on the movement that would become Christianity.

In Rome, Vespasian was a busy man whose responsibilities stretched from the Irish Sea to the Euphrates River. In the East, he had two pressing tasks. He had to settle Judea and he had to reestablish Roman authority on the border with Parthia after having withdrawn legions from there to fight in Judea. He took on both tasks with the energetic help of Titus. As it turned out, Vespasian's arrangements in Judea also served another important goal, which was to establish his dynasty.

Settling Judea

The Great Revolt was over, but the sentiments that moved the rebels still survived. It no longer made sense, therefore, to police Judea with only a small auxiliary force. Instead, Vespasian installed the Tenth Legion in what was left of Jerusalem in late 70. It was not standard practice to set up a military camp in a city, but Jerusalem wasn't quite a city anymore. Besides, the presence of the legion served as a vivid statement that Rome would not tolerate the revival of Jewish nationalism in its hallowed capital. Judea also housed some additional cavalry units and infantry cohorts, for a total of about ten thousand troops. They were an army of occupation, as one historian has called it. Judea was the only small interior province in the empire to have so many troops.[1]

Vespasian changed Judea from its previous status as a region administered by a procurator of equestrian rank, who worked under the supervision of the governor of Syria. Judea now became an independent province with a higher-ranking governor, a legate of senatorial rank and ex-praetor. The new governor sat in Caesarea-by-the-Sea, as had the procurators, with a detachment of the Tenth Legion for protection. Caesarea had supported Rome during the Great Revolt, and it was now rewarded with the status of *colonia*. Its official name was Colonia Prima Flavia Augusta Caesarensis. It was named after the Flavians, the family of Vespasian, and after Augustus Caesar. A *colonia*, usually translated as "colony," was a Roman city whose privileged inhabitants (those who were not enslaved) were Roman citizens and exempt from taxes. Usually those privileged few were imported settlers or military veterans. In Caesarea, they were probably auxiliary soldiers who had served in putting down the Great Revolt.

The province of Judea was divided into two districts. The first consisted of cities, both Jewish and non-Jewish, and their hinterlands. They had largely been loyal to Rome in the Great Revolt and were administered by the governor and his officers. The second consisted of the region of Judah as well as Idumea. It was a military zone administered by the Tenth Legion.

Jews were permitted to visit Jerusalem, and some did, but to others it was too painful a site. All that was left of the Temple was the western portion of the supporting wall of the massive platform on which the shrine and its associated buildings had stood. Today, known as the Western Wall, it is considered the holiest spot in Judaism because of its closeness to the western wall of the Holy of Holies, which stood on the Temple Mount above it. A site of hope and prayer, it was long a center of mourning, which gave rise in European languages to the name "Wailing Wall."[2]

Josephus considered the fields he owned outside of Jerusalem to be unprofitable because of the Roman garrison, which commandeered them. He imagined the surviving rebels decrying a Jerusalem that consisted only of old men sitting beside the ashes of the Temple and a few women kept by the enemy for the most shameful violation.[3]

The Talmud tells a different story. A group of rabbis visited the ruined city. When they saw the remains of the Temple from a distance, they tore their clothes in a gesture of mourning. When they reached the Temple Mount, they saw a fox emerging from what had been the Holy of Holies. They all began to weep except for one: Rabbi Akiva laughed. When challenged on this, he explained. Previously, he had not known whether to trust the biblical prophecy that elderly men and women would yet sit in peace in the streets of Jerusalem. But now he was confident of its truth. The Bible, it seems, connected this happy vision to an earlier prophecy of the destruction of Jerusalem and the Temple. That earlier prophecy imagined the Temple Mount becoming wild, desolate, and overgrown with grass and shrubs, the sort of place where a fox might roam. Now that he had seen a fox, Rabbi Akiva was confident that the prophecy of destruction had come true, and therefore, so would another prophecy, one of reconstruction. And so, he laughed for joy.[4]

Even so, the Jewish survivors of Judea after the war had much to weep over. Several cities such as Jotapata, Gamala, Tarichaeae, and, above all, Jerusalem lay in ruins. Jews had lost land and, in many cases, their lives in ethnically mixed cities such as Caesarea and Scythopolis (the Greek name of the city whose Hebrew name was Beth Shean). Vespasian confiscated land belonging to rebels. It was sold or given to the emperor's friends. How much of the province's land this amounted to is unknown, but the number of rebels was not insignificant. Although some Jews continued to own land, others were now rent-paying tenants. A small veterans' colony of eight hundred men was set up at Emmaus. On the whole, Judea was poorer than it had been before the Great Revolt.[5]

According to Josephus, 97,000 Jews were enslaved after the revolt.[6] For once, his figure might be accurate, since slavery was big business and Romans kept count of the human capital involved. If the calculation is even roughly correct, it would have represented a devastating loss. The population of Judea in antiquity cannot be determined, but conservative estimates put the Jewish share of it at between 500,000 to 1 million.[7] Those estimates would mean that approximately 10 to 20 percent of the Jewish population was enslaved. Total population losses would have been even higher if one adds deaths in battle and civil war or by disease or famine. Some scholars estimate a loss of up to one-third of the Jewish population of Judea.

Still, the situation wasn't entirely bleak. The province of Judea still retained two-thirds or more of its Jewish population. While the Romans probably destroyed rebellious villages, they also probably spared those that didn't fight. Even in the Jewish heartland, the region of Judah, Jewish life in the countryside recovered after the Great Revolt, a fact hinted at in the Talmud and demonstrated both by archaeological evidence and papyrus documents.[8] Vespasian did not build roads to facilitate troop movement around the country. Some Jews moved to Galilee and Gaulanitis, and some fled abroad. The latter added to the communities of the Jewish Diaspora in the Roman and Parthian Empires, some of which were already centuries old. Still, Jewish life continued to thrive in the province of Judea. Although Jerusalem was dominated by the legion and its support personnel, and although veterans were granted lands nearby, a few Jewish villages continued to remain in close vicinity to the city. Vespasian limited the number of foreign settlers into Judea.[9]

Countries do recover from devastating defeats in war, as did Germany and Japan after World War II. Rome had every reason to expect Judea to rise again, which might have been a cause of anxiety. It made sense for the ruling power to show its authority, and a new tax was a manifestation of that.

Rome imposed the *fiscus Judaicus*, the "Jewish fund," a head tax of two drachmas a year on every Jew in the empire. No questions were asked about whether the Jew lived in Judea, Rome, or Hispania or whether a person had supported the rebellion or not: everyone had to pay. To the poor it may have been a burden, but even to the wealthy it was a humiliation. Vespasian imposed the tax as a replacement of the previous annual contribution that Jews had paid to the Temple in Jerusalem. It was as if the new tax was meant to say that Jupiter had triumphed over the God of the Jews. In 69, the Temple of Capitoline Jupiter in Rome was destroyed in the civil war fighting. It was rebuilt and rededicated in 75, only to be destroyed by a fire in 80, after which it was rebuilt in 82. The tax was a reminder that there would be no dispensation for the House of the Lord in Jerusalem, which would remain in ruins at Rome's insistence. As one scholar argues, one of the points of the tax was to force Jews to direct their loyalty to Rome. Jerusalem was dead. The treasures of its Temple were booty, relocated to Rome, where they were put on display as a symbol of a pacified people.[10]

The *fiscus Judaicus* was an unusual punishment, but the Great Revolt was an atypical rebellion. One scholar compares the tax to a war indemnity on the grounds that once the rebels had destroyed a Roman legion, they were no better than a foreign enemy. That Judea had been a loyal ally for so long before rebelling only added to the injury.[11]

One other thing is striking: Gentiles in Judea were not required to pay the tax. The Romans targeted the people, not the province. On the one hand, that might have strengthened support for the empire among Greeks, Syrians, Samaritans, and Arabs in Judea. On the other hand, it stigmatized Jews. The tax is a reminder that, after 70, Rome perceived Jews as a greater security threat than was Judea. But the tax may have backfired. One scholar speculates that it had the unintended effect of producing Jewish solidarity in response.[12] Rome might also have remained concerned about Jewish connections in Parthia.[13]

Triumph

In the spring of 71, Titus took ship in Alexandria and returned to Rome. He brought with him Josephus and, one might guess, Tiberius Alexander. Also on the journey were the two captive leaders of the rebellion, Simon son of Giora and John of Giscala, together with seven hundred Jewish prisoners chosen for size and appearance. They would be shown off in the triumphal parade in Rome. Vespasian, his other son, Domitian, and a large crowd of citizens were present to greet the returning hero. Gossip said that Titus had to mend fences with his father for having accepted royal-like honors in the East, but of course gossip would say that.[14]

Shortly after Titus's return, Rome celebrated victory in Judea. The Senate had voted Vespasian and Titus each the right to hold a separate Triumph, the state's highest honor for a victorious general. But a Triumph for what? Vespasian had won the throne through a bloody civil war. The Senate would not vote a Triumph for a victory in a civil war, in which the victims were fellow Romans. Not to worry: there was a precedent, established by Augustus and others, of using a foreign victory as a fig leaf. Judea was technically already part of the Roman Empire when it rebelled, but the senators were in no position to quibble with Vespasian and his legions. Besides which, they wanted to distract the Romans from the civil war. So, 69, the Year of the Four Emperors, was forgotten: Rome would celebrate a triumph over the Jews.

In a Triumph, the victor and his soldiers would march through the city, showing off loot and prisoners; conduct sacrifices to the gods; and sponsor public feasts, all to the cheers of the crowds. Vespasian and Titus decided to hold a joint Triumph. Josephus, who was probably there, provides a detailed account, although he leaves out some of the particulars. He claims that the whole city turned out for the event. It's plausible that a large part of the citizenry really did show up, perhaps one hundred thousand people or more. Spectacles like this offered rare entertainment, followed by free food at public banquets, and the chance of seeing Rome's new rulers was not to be missed.

Tiberius Alexander was, one imagines, one of the many unnamed VIPs present at the Triumph. He may have stood with the other equestrians who, with the senators or magistrates, were at the Portico of Octavia in central Rome, awaiting the arrival of Vespasian and Titus. Or perhaps he accompanied the troops who had assembled for the triumphal procession in the Field of Mars the night before.

After preliminary sacrifices, the procession got under way. One would expect that the senators and magistrates took part in the march. Certainly, the troops did, row after row of them, wreathed in laurel and probably singing bawdy songs about their commander. The seven hundred prisoners Titus had brought from Jerusalem marched as well. Josephus mentions only Simon son of Giora, but presumably John of Giscala was there. It's likely that the Adiabenian hostages who had surrendered to Titus in Jerusalem, "the sons and brothers of [the former Adiabenian] King Izates,"[15] marched, too. Romans set great store by hostages as a sign of victory. They were proof of a general's right to a triumph. Hostages marched in Republican-era Triumphs, and in Vespasian's day as well a general still boasted of taking hostages on campaign. Adiabenian hostages would have been symbolic stand-ins for victory over Parthia, always an important card for a Roman to play. Hostages and prisoners of war typically marched in front of the victorious general's triumphal chariot. A coin image can be interpreted as showing Simon marching in front of Vespasian's chariot. That brings us to the most important figures in the procession, Vespasian and Titus, mounted on chariots.[16]

There was an assortment of silver, gold, and ivory; gems, tapestries, and purple-dyed fabrics. Even the animals, present in an abundant variety of species, and the prisoners all wore expensive garments. The exhibition of treasures that day, wrote Josephus, "displayed the greatness of the Roman Empire."[17] The crowd-pleasers were the floats with their moving panoramas. They showed scenes of war including slaughter, siege engines smashing walls, the defeated begging for mercy, temples set on fire, and rivers of blood. Josephus says that on each float there was the defeated general of the conquered city. Whether these were statues, reenactors, or, at least in some cases, the actual person is an open question. Josephus was surely spared the humiliation of having to portray himself. He was probably safely watching the parade.

Several ships on wheels followed the floats, symbols of the naval battle on the Sea of Galilee. Then came various spoils, carried in heaps on portable stretchers. Three items from the Temple in Jerusalem stood out: the golden Showbread Table, on which the priests would display twelve loaves of bread, symbolizing the Twelve Tribes of Israel; the golden menorah; and the "Jewish Law," presumably one or more Torah scrolls. After them came a large group carrying gold and ivory statues of Nike, goddess of victory. Finally, Vespasian passed by on his chariot, followed by Titus on his. Each was dressed in a purple robe and crowned with a laurel wreath. Behind them came Domitian on a very fine horse. In some Triumphs, and perhaps in this one as well, a slave held a golden wreath over the triumphator's head—in this case, over two heads—and whispered into his ear from time to time, "Remember, you are mortal."

The procession stopped at the city's most sacred shrine, the Temple of Capitoline Jupiter. There they waited for news from the state prison nearby. Simon had been removed from the procession. He was dragged by a hangman's noose and whipped en route to the nearby jail, where he was strangled to death. Executing the chief enemy prisoner was a traditional part of the ceremony of the Triumph.

They were a paradoxical people, the Romans. They had strong institutions: the Senate, the imperial bureaucracies, the courts, and, above all, the army. In spite of that, they took everything personally. The legions might have won the war, but the victory wasn't sealed until Vespasian and Titus rode in triumph, with the enemy chieftain, Simon, led off to be slaughtered.

When the crowd got the news of Simon's death, they burst into applause. Vespasian and his son continued with prayers and sacrifices at the temple. They then hosted a banquet. Feasting took place all over the city. All over, that is, except in the city's Jewish community. They no doubt took a different view of the event, and perhaps they mourned quietly. John was made a prisoner for life, which was probably not long. The rest of the seven hundred prisoners were, one expects, enslaved.

Only the emperor and the men of his family were permitted to celebrate a Triumph. But victorious generals were granted triumphal honors, which entailed the right to wear triumphal garments in public. These included a golden laurel wreath, an ivory baton, and a purple tunic embroidered with gold thread. Triumphal honors also entailed the right to have a bronze statue erected in the Forum of Augustus as well as a statue in one's own house. Tiberius Alexander seems to have been one of those awarded triumphal honors, at least to judge from a sneering reference by a contemporary Roman poet.[18] Statues were strictly forbidden by Jewish law, but Tiberius Alexander seems to have been past caring.

The Triumph over Judea was the only Triumph in Roman imperial history for reconquering rebel territory. Normally Rome downplayed the significance of suppressing rebellions. Victory over rebels offered little glory because it merely preserved the empire of the Roman people without expanding it—and the Romans always wanted more. Besides, it was in Rome's interest to reintegrate a wayward province into the empire as quickly and quietly as possible, so it was wise not to make a fuss. The famous Triumph over the Judean Revolt was different.[19]

Historians have advanced various theories to explain this anomaly: they are not mutually exclusive. Judea had been a potential ally of the Parthians. The presence of the Adiabenian captives in the triumphal parade, if they were there, would only have underlined the point. Judea had been in the Roman Empire for 120 years when it revolted. Such a betrayal, from the Roman point of view, required exceptional recognition, which the Triumph offered.[20]

To turn to domestic political factors, Vespasian was no ordinary emperor. He was a usurper. Augustus had begun his dynasty by celebrating a Triumph. Vespasian was founding a new dynasty, and one that desperately needed a legitimating principle, since he was not a member of the Roman nobility. He, too, had to celebrate a Triumph, whether it was justified or not. Vespasian needed to work hard to demonstrate his legitimacy. By treating Judea as a new conquest, he gave an implicit message that he had increased the empire.

In the wake of the Great Revolt, Romans did not give up their willingness to do business with Jews or to have friendly relations. But there was an undeniable element of fear and loathing. Members of the elite mocked Jewish customs such as circumcision and not eating pork, but they derided German, Thracian, and Egyptian customs as well. Jews were not popular in Rome, but rebels never were. The Romans' main concern with the Jews was security. Jewish rebellion had forced Rome into a long and expensive war. Now the empire was constrained to garrison Judea with a legion. The rebellion raised the specter of intervention in Roman territory by forces from the Parthian Empire. Nor was Judea the only part of the Roman Empire where Jews represented a security threat. Trouble had already taken place in Alexandria and Antioch. A shrewd and cynical Vespasian might have reasoned that wars put armies in the hands of ambitious men like himself. Another Jewish war might lead to a future usurper seizing power in Rome, as he had. All the more reason to parade Roman power in a triumph over a still-dangerous enemy.

But there was another issue, and that was the Jewish claim of Jerusalem to be the center of the world, and of the Jewish God to be superior to the Roman gods. Vespasian believed that he had belied that claim, but he wanted to underline it with his victory and to amplify it with additional measures. To Romans, it was a matter of pride, but to Jews it was, as one scholar argues, a "devastating challenge." She wrote of "Roman policies that led to the lasting erasure of the Jerusalem Temple and the city itself, which could be interpreted as a desire to substitute Rome for Israel as the elected people and its city, long before Rome became Christian."[21]

In any case, the Triumph wasn't enough. Its message needed to be amplified to convey the greatness of Rome and of Vespasian and his sons. It was customary to erect a structure in Rome to commemorate a Triumph, but Vespasian and his family went overboard and practically rebranded the heart of Rome as a monument to their victory over Judea.

The dynasty erected two triumphal arches in Rome in memory of Titus, conqueror of Jerusalem. Only one of them still stands: the Arch of Titus on the Sacred Way (Via Sacra) on the edge of the Roman Forum. It displays a vivid relief of looted items from the Jerusalem Temple, notably a seven-branched candelabra (menorah), being carried in the triumphal parade. The other arch carried an inscription that announced that Titus was the first man ever to have conquered Jerusalem. Like the notion that Judea was newly added territory to the empire, that was a lie. Rome had conquered Jerusalem twice (in 63 and 37 BCE) before Titus, and there were other, earlier conquerors.[22]

Not far away, the emperor Vespasian erected the so-called Templum Pacis, or Temple of Peace, a project completed in 75. The Temple was a complex that contained looted objects from Jerusalem along with a cornucopia of statuary from around the empire, especially from Greece, many of the works the fruit of earlier wars of conquest. A statue of the goddess of peace, Pax, stood in a central hall. This was one of the truly great collections of sculpture in the Roman world. A marble plan of the city of Rome was also put on view. In addition, the building complex included gardens with plants from all over the empire. It was as if the whole world was on display in Rome.

"Peace" sounds like an Orwellian name for a monument filled largely with war booty, but peace meant something different in Rome from what it means today. Romans believed that conflict was natural. Peace required hard work to establish, either by diplomacy or war. Think of the Templum as the "Temple of Pacification," and one gets a clearer notion of its original meaning. "The war is over," was the building's message. "We have peace because a new dynasty fought for it." It was the peace of Vespasian and his sons.

Treasures from the Jerusalem Temple had a notable place in the structure. And rightly so, in Vespasian's eyes, since he expected Jews to recognize Rome and not Jerusalem as the object of their veneration. But there was another, more sinister meaning. Visitors to the Temple of Peace received the message that the Roman Peace required the defeat of the Jews. Not a happy message for Jews in the empire, but their reputation was collateral damage in the making of a new imperial dynasty and the restoration of the Pax Romana. Vespasian and Titus had conquered the Jews and thereby brought peace to the Roman world. That was the overarching theme.

The Temple of Peace was a vast, ambitious, marble structure whose dimensions were circa 360 feet (110 meters) × circa 445 feet (135 meters), making it about two and a half times the size of the White House.[23] Little of the Temple survives today. Visitors to Rome can see an outline of the complex, with part of its foundations and a few restored columns visible. It's hard to imagine the grandeur that it once represented. Not so with the pièce de résistance of the Flavian building program, which is also the most famous monument of Roman antiquity, the Colosseum. It was also known as the New Amphitheater or the Flavian Amphitheater. Everyone the world over knows that the Colosseum was a spectacle on a grand scale. The amphitheater was likely financed in part by spoils from Judea.[24] Originally the entrance was topped by a victory monument of Emperor Vespasian in his chariot. Today, the Colosseum is the symbol of the city of Rome. In antiquity, it represented the ability of the Flavians to deliver bread and circuses to the Roman people, thanks in part to a wealth transfer from Judea. The Colosseum, like the Temple of Peace, was a victory monument.

Roman coins also prominently featured the victory over Judea. Various designs were struck, but a typical coin displays a male and female captive next to a palm tree, a symbol of Judea, with the legend IUDAEA CAPTA, "Judea has been conquered." The coins, like the Triumph, give the impression that Judea was a newly conquered territory and not a rebellious province. No other Roman victory was commemorated by so many coins.[25]

One IUDAEA CAPTA coin was struck in the year 80/81, the tenth anniversary of the destruction of the Temple of Jerusalem, as well as the year in which the Colosseum was dedicated. The obverse of the coin shows the Colosseum; on the reverse is depicted Emperor Titus, surrounded by war booty. Visible inside the arches of the Colosseum is a four-horse chariot, symbolic of a Triumph. Directly above it is a palm tree, a symbol of Judea. On each side of the tree stands a figure, one of whom may be the emperor or a winged victory and the other possibly a Jewish man or woman.[26]

Dealing with Parthia

Vespasian mistrusted Parthia. He knew all about rebel attempts to gain support from "beyond the Euphrates," in Josephus's words.[27] When reaching for the throne in the civil war of 69, Vespasian had sent ambassadors to Parthia and Armenia to keep the peace on the border.[28]

After achieving victory against the Jewish rebels, Vespasian made it a priority to beef up border security on the Euphrates frontier. Before celebrating the joint Triumph in Rome, Vespasian sent Titus with an army to the border in late 70, just months after conquering Jerusalem. In 71/72, the client kingdom of Armenia Minor (in north-central Turkey, west of the Euphrates River) was annexed. So was the client kingdom of Commagene (south of Armenia Minor) a year later. In both cases, the Romans put forward pretexts: barbarian invasions in the former case, alleged collusion with Parthia in the latter. Two legions were stationed in these regions. By the late 70s, all central Asia Minor was one great military province. Assiduous roadbuilding in the area eased the transport of men and supplies. Farther to the north and east, two adjacent kingdoms in the mountains of the Caucasus became, in effect, Roman clients.

The strategic purpose of all this was to surround Armenia. Vespasian knew that Parthia had expanded its power into Armenia at Rome's expense under Nero. Now he was trying to shift the balance of power back into Rome's favor. Parthia noticed.

At some point in Vespasian's reign, perhaps in 72, the Alans, a nomadic people, invaded Armenia and Media (northwestern Iran), two kingdoms ruled by brothers of the Parthian king Vologases. The Alans did serious damage. When Vologases asked Vespasian for help, the Roman deadpanned a response that he wouldn't dream of interfering in another country's business.[29] Somewhat later, perhaps in 76, Vologases threatened war, but Rome's newfound strength in the East forced him to back down.[30]

From Pompey on, the Romans tended to rely on client kings to rule the eastern frontier of the empire. But in the middle decades of the first century, they began to lose their patience with such middlemen; they started to annex their kingdoms and put them under direct Roman rule. The process accelerated under the Flavians. There were few client kingdoms left in the Roman East after Vespasian and his sons got through with them. From Judea to the Euphrates River the region was now largely under direct Roman control.

Herod's descendants were the immediate losers, but some managed to find their way. Agrippa II's younger cousin, Gaius Julius Alexander, was married to the daughter of Gaius Julius Antiochus, king of Commagene. The king sent troops to fight alongside Vespasian and then Titus in Judea, but nevertheless lost his kingdom when Vespasian decided to take over the frontier. The deposed king of Commagene lived in retirement in Sparta and Rome. His daughter and son-in-law fared better. They received a consolation prize, a small kingdom in southern Asia Minor that Vespasian created for them. That son-in-law, Gaius Julius Alexander, was a great-great-grandson of Herod the Great. When the emperor Domitian (r. 81–96) took that kingdom, too, away, he allowed Julius Alexander to retain the title of king, while also making him a Roman senator. Julius Alexander's sons in turn held important positions in the Roman administration of Asia Minor in the second century. His grandson was a wealthy and important public official who went on embassies to Rome. In his hometown he erected statues of Greek gods and heroes. Herod, too, had shown a love for things Greek but, unlike Herod, his great-great-great-great-grandson, also named Julius Alexander, gave no signs of Judaism.

Titus and Berenice

In September 70, before the following year's Triumph in Rome, Titus began the mission that would take him to the Euphrates frontier. After conquering Jerusalem, Titus went to Caesarea-on-the-Sea. Then, continuing northward, he stopped at Caesarea Philippi, the capital of his ally, the Jewish ruler, Agrippa II. He wasn't there just to see Agrippa II, but also his sister, Queen Berenice. As mentioned earlier she and Titus were lovers, arguably since meeting at Caesarea Philippi in the year 67. At that time, Titus was twenty-eight and

Berenice thirty-nine. He was the son of the most powerful Roman in Judea; she was the sister of an important client king. A liaison under such circumstances is not surprising, despite the age difference. What is surprising is that the affair continued for a dozen years. That might suggest, as one scholar argues, that the two were in love.[31]

But the connection was not merely amorous. Each partner had something to gain from the affair. Like earlier members of the House of Herod, Berenice had a talent for making friends with important Romans. To Berenice and Agrippa II, the Roman legions were the only thing that stood between them and the pitchforks and firebrands of the rebels. In 67, sharing a bed with Titus had been a small price to pay for sealing a friendship with the commander of those legions, Titus's father, Vespasian. Berenice knew how to deepen the bond. In 69, she and Agrippa II had thrown their support behind Vespasian's bid for the throne. In doing so, they joined Berenice's former brother-in-law Tiberius Alexander, who was then the governor of Egypt. When Vespasian became emperor, all three stood ready to reap the rewards that usually await early adopters.

For Titus, Agrippa II and Berenice held the keys to Jewish backing. That support still mattered. Syria had a large Jewish population. The Jews now stood at the mercy of their Greek neighbors. However much they hated Rome for the destruction of Jerusalem, they still needed Rome's protection, so they still represented a potentially loyalist faction. And the status of Jews in the eastern Roman Empire was not unrelated to the elephant in the room: Parthia, which of course had a large Jewish population of its own. Berenice, who had support in Syria, could prove quite helpful to Titus with Syrian Jews. It is not unlikely that she accompanied Titus, as some have suggested, throughout his travels in Roman Syria in the autumn of 70 and the spring of 71. Titus wasn't on a tourist's jaunt. His main goal was to strengthen the border with Parthia. Tiberius Alexander, a deft hand when it came to dealing with the Parthians, probably traveled with Titus as well.

Titus engaged in victory celebrations at Caesarea Philippi. He celebrated his brother Domitian's birthday there on October 24, 70. According to Josephus, more than 2,500 Jewish prisoners were slaughtered in spectacles such as mass gladiatorial combats—a special event, since usually gladiators fought one-on-one. The prisoners were thrown to the beasts, or burned on pyres. Titus then continued to Berytus, where he engaged in similar spectacles and massacred many more captives in celebration of Vespasian's birthday on November 17. Although Josephus makes no mention of Agrippa II and Berenice, scholars have argued that they not only attended the spectacles, and in both cities, but approved of them. After all, the rebels had burned down their palaces and forced them to flee Jerusalem. There may be a hint that Agrippa II and Berenice convinced Titus to moderate the slaughter as reflected in Josephus's comment that the Romans complained that too few prisoners were killed.[32]

Titus next traveled from place to place in Syria, everywhere with his Jewish captives in a blunt display of the fate of rebels against Rome. He then proceeded to Antioch, the capital of Syria and the greatest city of the Roman East after Alexandria. There he turned down a local petition, made on two separate occasions, to expel the Jews of the city, confirming their civil rights instead. He thereby demonstrated that even the conqueror of Jerusalem could still prove to be a friend of Jews who were loyal to Rome. One imagines that Agrippa II then returned to his kingdom, but perhaps Berenice accompanied Titus to the city of Zeugma-on-the-Euphrates, in northern Syria. Zeugma, literally "bridge" in Greek, was the most important crossing of the Euphrates River in antiquity. It marked the boundary between Rome and Parthia.

Titus went to Zeugma to accept an embassy from Vologases, the Parthian king. The emissaries brought him a golden crown to commemorate the Roman's victory over Judea. After accepting the gift Titus reciprocated their hospitality with a banquet. The presence of Berenice would have sent a message to Vologases not to play the Jewish card against Rome. It offered a reminder that Rome still had powerful Jewish friends in the region who would help look after its interests.

Titus headed back south, beginning the long trek to Rome. At Jerusalem, he contemplated the ruins. Romans were busy digging through the wreckage in search of gold, silver, and other precious items that Jerusalemites had stored underground. Presumably, any informants received freedom, or maybe just their lives, in exchange for what they knew about buried treasure. After visiting Egypt and sacrificing to the local gods, Titus hurried home to Italy. With him were Josephus and probably Tiberius Alexander.

After spring 71, Titus and Berenice did not see each other for another four years. Berenice probably returned to Caesarea Philippi and lived in her brother's court, where she served as the official hostess for the bachelor king. Titus served in Rome as praetorian prefect, effectively the minister of security for the capital of the empire. The evidence indicates that he shared that office with his old comrade Tiberius Alexander, making the latter one of the most powerful and influential people in the Roman Empire. But he might not have been done: Tiberius Alexander capped his career, evidence suggests, by being admitted to the Senate.[33]

In 75, Berenice came to Rome, accompanying Agrippa II, who was being awarded high honors by the emperor. Agrippa II was appointed to a praetorship, while his sister moved into the palace with Titus. Berenice now stood near the summit of power. On one occasion Vespasian invited her to sit on the imperial council in a case involving her own interests, perhaps some matter involving the Jewish community of the city of Rome, with no less than the great Quintilian as her lawyer. A prominent orator, he held a chair in Latin rhetoric established by Vespasian. Quintilian wrote a book on oratory that has continued to influence people until modern times.

People said that Berenice expected to marry Titus—or even that he promised it—and that she behaved as if she were his wife. That seems unlikely. Aside from such a marriage violating Jewish law, Berenice was past childbearing age. To some in Rome, she was another Cleopatra, an Eastern queen who bewitched a powerful Roman man, while to others she represented the Jewish enemy, whose revolt cost Rome so much blood and treasure. When two philosophers denounced Titus and Berenice in the theater, Titus had one flogged and the other beheaded.[34]

Berenice would have been less than human if she hadn't gazed at the palace and dreamed of sharing it with Titus as his spouse one day. Had that happened, and if Berenice had become the wife of the Roman emperor, she would have become the most influential member of the House of Herod since Herod the Great himself. Nonetheless, the end was never in doubt. When in 79 Titus became emperor after Vespasian's death, he sent Berenice away. It was a case, wrote the biographer Suetonius (ca. 70–ca. 130), of *invitus invitam*: "against his will and her own."[35]

Presumably, she went back to Caesarea Philippi, but Berenice's fate is unknown after 79. Berenice was the last *Jewish* member of Herod's dynasty to have a place in the halls of power in Rome. The Herodians had enjoyed a remarkable run in the imperial capital since Herod the Great's first visit there in 37 BCE, when Antony and Octavian were his hosts. Other descendants of Herod numbered kings, an ambassador, Roman senators, magistrates, and even a consul or two among them, but they had become pagans.[36]

Claudia Aster

Another Jewish woman from Judea lived in Italy after the Great Revolt, Claudia Aster. Her name is known from her tombstone, which has survived by chance. The relatively simple stone was first found in the eighteenth century and then recently rediscovered in Naples's archaeological museum. It apparently comes from a tomb located near the road between Naples and Puteoli, closer to Puteoli. The inscription reads:

> Claudia Aster, prisoner from Jerusalem. Tiberius Claudius Proculus, imperial freedman, took care (of the epitaph). I ask you, make sure through the law that you take care that no one casts down my inscription. She lived 25 years.[37]

The gravestone tells a survivor's story. Claudia Aster took her first name from Tiberius Claudius Proculus, who put up the stone. "Aster" means "star" in Latin, a word borrowed from Greek, but it could be a Latinization of a Jewish name. If so, Claudia Aster was born Esther. Assuming that the then-Esther was made a prisoner, and therefore enslaved, on the fall of Jerusalem in 70, the inscription dates to sometime between 70 and 95. It is the earliest known epitaph of a Jewish woman in Italy. Claudia Aster and Proculus were almost certainly husband and wife. Several clues point to this. This inscription fits the pattern of others that a spouse put up for his or her departed partner. The deceased's two-part name, Claudia Aster, tells us that she died free and was either a Roman citizen or the holder of another, less privileged, but nonetheless free status. As a freedwoman, Claudia Aster would have taken her former master's name, as she does here (Claudius/Claudia). She died at the age of twenty-five. Roman law did not normally permit slaves to be manumitted before the age of thirty, but marriage was an exception.

It is likely that Proculus purchased Claudia Aster as a slave and then freed her from bondage and married her. It was not unusual in the Roman world to manumit and then marry a slave. Puteoli was a busy port and shiploads of enslaved Jews were likely unloaded and sold there in 70 and shortly thereafter. As an imperial freedman, Proculus had a higher status than almost everyone in Italy except the Roman nobility, who disparaged freedmen as vulgar inferiors who didn't know their place. A noble wouldn't have been caught dead marrying a slave and probably not a Jew, either, but a freedman was more flexible.

All the more interesting, then, that Proculus named Claudia Aster in her tombstone as a prisoner and a Jerusalemite, neither of which would have passed a senator's smell test. Proculus was under no obligation to supply these details; he chose to provide them. Perhaps he was proud of Claudia Aster's story. It is not known if Proculus himself was a Jew, but if he was, then he might have considered Claudia Aster's survival to be a sign of divine providence, and he might have wanted to advertise the fact. But the form of the epitaph is entirely Roman; in Jerusalem, a simple name would have sufficed. That might suggest that Proculus was not Jewish or that he was assimilated enough to adopt a Roman custom. It is not known if there were separate Jewish burial areas in Italy at this point. In any case, there were Jews in Puteoli, and perhaps Proculus had them in mind as an audience.

Strikingly, he calls Claudia Aster a Jerusalemite (*Hierosolymitana*) rather than a Jew (*Iudaea*). Perhaps "Jewish prisoner" (*Iudaea captiva*) would have been too close to the "Conquered Judea" (*Iudaea capta*) of the imperial coins. Perhaps being from Jerusalem, despite everything, still conferred a certain status. Perhaps it even conveyed a proud affirmation that the city would be rebuilt, just as Claudia Aster had survived.

Proculus tells anyone reading the epitaph not to knock down the gravestone. It is unclear whether the "law" to which he refers is Roman law or the Torah or both. The emotions he might have felt on burying a young wife, age only twenty-five, speak for themselves.

Josephus and Johanan ben Zakkai

After 70, some Jews gave up their Jewish identity, for practical purposes if not in formal terms. Tiberius Alexander is the prime example. But most Jews probably did not give up. They responded to the defeat of 70 in different ways. The failure of the Great Revolt might have discouraged Jewish apocalyptic thinking, as it certainly did among some early representatives of the rabbinic movement. In spite of that, many Jews doubled down on the apocalyptic vision.

Several Jewish literary works of the generation or two after 70 sound all the notes of the apocalypse, from the messiah to the breaking of the heathens to the restoration of Israel. For example, *The Apocalypse of Ezra*, written circa 100, imagines a lion, symbolizing the messiah, destroying an eagle, representing the wicked Roman Empire. The author envisions a woman, mourning her exiled sons. She becomes a heavenly city, which stands for the redemption of Jerusalem. Another text, *The Apocalypse of Baruch*, dating somewhere between 70 and 132, speaks of dark, nefarious waters flooding the world after the destruction of the Second Temple and then, with a flash of lightning, the replacement of corruption by the new, messianic age. Apocalyptic thinkers predicted, with passion and enthusiasm, the ultimate triumph of the Jewish people over Rome.[38]

Jewish apocalypse writers were convinced that the messiah would come in due course, however long that might take. The followers of Jesus, many if not most of whom still thought of themselves as Jews, believed that the Messiah had already come: Jesus. The oldest Gospel, the Gospel of Mark, was written shortly after the destruction of the Temple. In Mark, Jesus warns of the danger of false messiahs and prophets arising in the future.[39] A Christian apocalypse, the Book of Revelation, is generally dated to sometime around 96. It writes of the conflict of Rome and looks toward the ultimate triumph of a new Jerusalem.

Other Jews responded to the defeat of 70 in non-apocalyptic terms, but in diverse ways. Consider two examples, the historian Josephus and the rabbi Johanan ben Zakkai. Both believed deeply in the God of Israel. Both cared passionately about the survival of the Jewish people. Both depended for their survival on the kindness of the Roman emperor. Otherwise, they could not have been more different. One lived in Judea and the other in Italy, but that only scratches the surface of their dissimilarity.

After personally witnessing the destruction in 70 of Jerusalem, the Holy City, and his hometown, Josephus went to Rome and spent the rest of his life there. Vespasian rewarded Josephus with Roman citizenship, housing, a stipend, and an estate in Judea, tax free. These were nice gifts, propelling Josephus into the elite, but they were small change compared to the rewards given Vespasian's most treasured comrades.

If you lived in Rome around 75 CE, you might have seen Josephus at one of the emperor Vespasian's morning audiences. There, amid the marble and the bronzes, the mosaics and the Egyptian glass, the frescoes and the gilded furniture, in a space filled by senators, oligarchs, secretaries, pagan priests, military officers, foreign emissaries, slaves, praetorian guards, and the occasional ordinary citizen, stood a Jew. Josephus had come to present his book to the commander of nearly thirty legions. At least, that is a plausible account of how the text was delivered to the emperor.

This Jew probably traveled to the emperor's residence in a litter; he could have afforded it. What he looked like, we don't know. His face might have borne the marks of his victories and defeats. He had lost everything and seen his country ruined, but then he built a new life abroad. His home life was a seesaw if the gossip can be believed. It was said that he had four wives: one killed in the siege of Jerusalem, two divorced, and a fourth who would apparently outlive him. He had three sons who survived to adulthood. He was a man of means, and he had powerful friends. They included members of the Jewish royal family in exile, Roman officers who had served in Judea during the war, and, finally, the emperor himself. In later years he enjoyed the patronage of a wealthy, Greek-speaking freedman, who supported his writing.

Josephus might also have been observed in the narrow streets of the Transtiberim region of the city, the modern Trastevere, across the Tiber River from the core of Imperial Rome. Transtiberim was the ancient Jewish quarter. There perhaps the man worshipped in one of the neighborhood's several synagogues. Or perhaps not, as some Jews in Rome despised him as a traitor. Others might have simply shrugged. It was a common pattern on the empire's frontiers. Armies came and went, and so did people's loyalties. A man did what he had to do to survive—although this man's treachery was anything but ordinary.

He was born Yosef ben Mattityahu. As a Roman citizen, he became Flavius Josephus, possibly Titus Flavius Josephus, although his first name is not recorded.

Josephus cared deeply for the Jewish people. He worried about their future, of course, as any Jew would who lived through the horror of the war with Rome. He cared about the Jewish soul, convinced, as he was, that God had brought ruin upon His people for their sins, which therefore required repentance. Finally, he cared for the Jews' honor. Again and again in his writings Josephus went out of his way to defend Jewish honor, even to underline it. It was risky business writing such words in Rome, a city less than friendly to the rebel people that had cost the empire so much. Risky, too, to write them when his connections in the imperial family were sure to employ men who looked over his shoulder. It took courage.

Around the same time, in Judea, Johanan ben Zakkai laid the groundwork for rabbinic Judaism. As already noted, Jewish tradition states that Johanan ben Zakkai escaped from Jerusalem and presented himself to Vespasian, who was then the commanding general under the emperor Nero. Like Josephus, he predicted that Vespasian would replace Nero as emperor. When that came true, Vespasian is supposed to have asked Johanan what he wanted as a reward. The answer was the small city of Jabneh, located on the coastal plain near the Via Maris, the "Sea Road," the great north-south highway in this part of the ancient Near East. There, Johanan would gather wise men and study the Torah. Scholars debate the truth of the tale, but there is no doubt that Jabneh was the seedbed of rabbinic Judaism, the movement that saved Judaism from the disaster of 70.

The word "rabbi," literally, "my teacher" or "my master," was not used as a title for the sages before the mid-first century. The rabbinic movement grew out of the work of two groups that existed while the Temple stood, the Pharisees and the scribes. While priests continued to exist (indeed, priestly descent exists to this day among Jews), they no longer had a temple to serve. It was the rabbis who became the religious leaders of Judaism. The new movement sought ways to bring into everyday life the holiness that had been in the Temple. Tradition says that Johanan ben Zakkai promulgated a series of ordinances that allowed Jews to follow their laws without the Temple. Scholars disagree as to the extent that these ordinances were indeed his or whether they were the work of his successors.

The importance of the work of the religious leaders at Jabneh is certainly clear, though. Nor can one escape the irony that they worked under the patronage of the family that had destroyed the Temple and Jerusalem. Vespasian gave his permission to Johanan ben Zakkai to set up his school at Jabneh. The emperor probably owned the land directly. Some Jews did not forgive the rabbi for surrendering to Vespasian, just as they didn't forgive Josephus.

The rabbinic movement was dedicated to preserving the Torah as the law and the love of the Jewish people. One historian gives an assessment of the significance of their efforts:

> The Torah may well have been all that remained to the Jews after the destruction of Jerusalem and the Temple, but it was the single most

important thing in Judaism, its essence and its real strength, which ultimately even proved to be stronger than Rome.[40]

In the long run, the Torah indeed overcame Rome. In the short run, however, the Jewish people were still engaged in an armed struggle. That, alas for them, played to Rome's strengths.

Chapter Nine

MASADA

In winter 74, the Romans were on the march again in Judea.[1] It was that rare time of year when green shoots are visible in the usually parched desert. The veterans of the Tenth Legion marched south from their camp in the ruins of Jerusalem, the city they had helped to destroy. Joining them were soldiers from auxiliary units, probably Samaritans and Syrians, along with army slaves and Jewish forced laborers, for a total of about thirteen thousand men.[2] At their head rode the commander of the legion. He was also the emperor's legate, the procurator of the province of Judea, Lucius Flavius Silva Nonius Bassus, better known as Silva. Their destination was Masada.[3] There they would face a small group of Jews, the last in Judea to remain independent of Rome. The Sicarii, or Dagger Men, the most determined of Rome's opponents, formed the dominant group among them. Their leader was a third- or fourth-generation rebel against Rome, Eleazar son of Yair.

Masada may be the most famous postscript in military history. The Romans assaulted Masada more than three years after the end of the war in Judea. We know about it today because Josephus wanted us to, and he strove to make Masada memorable. Despite that, from the Roman point of view, Masada was a standard mopping-up operation, if one with logistical challenges. Another such operation had taken place nearly a century and a half earlier, in 60 BCE, when the legions destroyed the southern Italian mountain refuge of the last survivors of Spartacus's slave revolt, an uprising that had ended eleven years earlier in 71 BCE. But with no Josephus to record it, the mopping up after Spartacus's men is all but forgotten. "He put an end to them" is all the sources say about the fate of Spartacus's remaining followers at the hands of the Roman commander.[4] By comparison, Josephus devotes about four thousand words of Greek to Masada (twenty-one pages in the Loeb Classical Library edition of the Greek text).

The location of Masada is so overloaded with symbolism that no novelist would dare invent it. Masada is a steep-sided plateau, crowned by two palaces and a set of fortifications, that rises dramatically in the wilderness. Masada lies in the desolate and forbidding landscape of the Judean Desert. To the west rise scarred and craggy hills. To the east, the Dead Sea. Beyond the Dead Sea rise the rugged mountains of Moab. The Dead Sea is the lowest place on the surface of the earth. The Bible says that this is the valley of the cities of the plain, Sodom and Gomorrah, destroyed in a hail of fire and brimstone. Various attempts have been made to find the site of the destroyed cities. At its northern end, the Dead Sea receives the Jordan River, flowing southward from its source in Galilee; there is no outlet. In a place about six miles north of the mouth of the Jordan River is the traditional location where John the Baptist baptized Jesus. In the hills west of that place is the traditional location of Jesus's forty-day sojourn in the wilderness. And farther north in the valley of the Jordan lies one of the oldest cities on the planet, Jericho. All of this sets the scene for Masada and its stirring story.

Masada is a steep rock formation that rises about 1,300 feet (400 meters) above the Dead Sea. The summit is diamond-shaped and relatively flat, a mesa or "tabletop" mountain. It is about 1,900 feet (850 meters) long from north to south by about 650 feet (200 meters) wide from east to west at its widest point. The name, Masada, is a Greek version of *Metzada*, meaning "fortress" in Hebrew or Aramaic, and fortress it was. Masada's natural defenses were considerable, but Herod added to them. He fortified the summit with a casemate wall of about 4,250 feet (1,300 meters) and twenty-seven (not thirty-seven) towers. A casemate wall is a double wall with space between the walls divided into separate rooms.

Herod turned Masada into a deluxe refuge. He built not one but two palaces there (Josephus mentions only one), each sumptuously decorated with mosaics, frescoes, carpets, tapestries, and other signs of opulence. There were heated baths and even a swimming pool. The northern palace has an impressive setting on terraces that spill over the cliffside. Inscriptions on several jars refer to gourmet food and wine imported from Greece, Italy, and Spain. Excavators have found many cisterns and other signs of Herod's elaborate and efficient water-supply system. It is estimated that four days of winter rain would be enough to supply Masada with water for a year.

Details of the Roman operation against Masada exist only because Josephus recounts them. No other ancient literary source survives. Archaeology contributes an enormous amount to our understanding of the event, although the interpretation of the archaeological evidence is controversial. Still, the material evidence makes clear what one might already expect of Josephus: his account is not straightforward. Josephus makes Masada into a parable. He pits Jewish love of freedom—romantic, foolish, doomed, but noble—against Roman power—brutal, relentless, irresistible, and yet ungrudging in its admiration of courage, even on the part of its enemies.

To add to the complexity, Zionism, too, made Masada into a myth. Masada came to stand for Zionist resolve, a principle summed up in a line from a celebrated poem of 1927: "Masada shall never fall again."[5] The mountain became a central symbol of Israeli identity, but also of critics of that identity, especially critics within Israel itself.

Masada is now a major tourist destination. Since 2001 it has been a UNESCO World Heritage Site. The scientific reasons for that are simple. Thanks to its isolation and the preservative effect of the desert atmosphere, Masada probably contains the best surviving example of Roman siegeworks. It also offers remarkable specimens of first century BCE architecture and engineering. And then there is the stark beauty of its location.[6]

Masada, therefore, is a war story, and in more ways than one. But Masada is also one of the great detective stories in the annals of history, literature, and archaeology. It is exciting to try to unravel the mystery and ponder the secrets that remain to be revealed if they ever can be.

The following pages recount the story first as Josephus told it and then as archaeology and literary study revise it. Finally, we focus on the drama between the two leaders at Masada, one Roman and one Jewish.

Josephus

Josephus[7] prefaces his account of Masada with the details of two previous Roman operations to clean out rebel-held fortresses, Herodium, located near Bethlehem, and Machaerus, near the northern end of the Dead Sea. Sextus Lucilius Bassus, governor of Judea beginning in 71 or 72, carried out these actions. Herodium seems to have surrendered without fighting. Machaerus took more effort.

Josephus says that it was necessary to wipe out the rebels at Machaerus, because they occupied a stronghold that might encourage many others to revolt.[8] Clearly, the spirit of rebellion was not dead in Judea. Machaerus sat on a steep hill crowned by a fortress built by Herod. Bassus attacked with the Tenth Legion and other forces, presumably auxiliaries. He set the soldiers to work on an embankment to reach the hilltop, but the defenders came down to attack them. In one skirmish the Romans captured the most daring of the defenders and proceeded to whip and threaten to crucify him before the horrified eyes of his people. He was a young man of a prominent and very large family, and they had enough influence to convince the defenders to negotiate a surrender. The defenders left the fort under safe conduct and the Romans returned the young man. The non-Jews who lived in the lower town of Machaerus were less fortunate: the Romans massacred or enslaved them. Whether or not the victims took part in the rebellion, they serve as a reminder that, in wartime, guilt by association is often enough to convict people.

Bassus learned that many rebels were living in a grove near the Jordan River. They were escapees from Jerusalem and Machaerus. When the Romans surrounded them, the rebels decided to fight rather than surrender. An unequal battle: in the end, wrote Josephus, the Romans lost only twelve dead and several wounded, while the Jews died to a man, all three thousand of them. Among them was a Zealot named Judah son of Ari, who had fought with distinction in the siege of Jerusalem and escaped the city through an underground passage.[9]

Bassus died in office. The new governor of Judea, Silva, decided to attack Masada because it was the only rebel fortress left in a country that was otherwise entirely in Rome's hands. Masada, wrote Josephus, was the Romans' "final deed in their war against the Jews."[10] Silva marched on Masada with all the forces in the province. Josephus does not give the year of the operation, but he does supply clues for the season in other parts of his narrative. Josephus states that the fortress fell on the fifteenth day of Xanthikos, reckoning by the Macedonian calendar, which was widely used in the Greek-speaking world: that is, roughly, April.

At the siege of Jerusalem, Josephus was an eyewitness, indeed a participant, on the Roman side. He had personal contacts within the walls to report on the siege from the point of view of the defenders. Masada was different. Josephus was in Rome when it happened, and he had to get his information secondhand. He might have had access to Silva's reports or spoke to Silva himself. Earlier in his life, Josephus spent a considerable amount of time in the Judean Desert, and so he probably had seen Masada at least from a distance. It is unlikely that he ever visited the top of the mountain, as it was a Roman garrison before 66. With those limitations in mind, consider what Josephus reports.

Silva marched on Masada and took control of the whole area around it. He set up garrisons at appropriate points and built a circumvallation wall that, well guarded as it was, cut off the fortress from the outside world. He established his own camp between Masada and the nearby mountains, which was convenient for a siege, but not for supplies. It was necessary to bring in food and water from a distance. That meant arduous work for the Jewish laborers forced into service for the campaign. Silva next worked out a plan of attack, which required considerable technical skill and effort because of the strength of Masada as a fortress.

A high rocky plateau of considerable circumference, with sheer precipices and steep ravines, Masada has only two points of access: a relatively easy path on the west and a twisting, dangerous trail on the east called in antiquity the Snake Path. A Hasmonean king first fortified the spot, but Herod was the true developer of Masada. He turned it into a palace-fortress complex to serve as a redoubt both against an uprising by his Jewish subjects and an attack by Queen Cleopatra of Egypt. She coveted her ancestors' control of Judea and constantly tried to push her lover and political partner, Mark Antony, into agreeing to kill Herod and making her queen of the Jews. She failed.

Herod enclosed the top of Masada with a stout stone wall measuring seven furlongs, about three-quarters of a mile (1.2 kilometers) in circumference, about 18 feet (6 meters) high, and about 12 feet (4 meters) broad.[11] Josephus says the wall contained thirty-seven towers: each about 75 feet (25 meters) high. To bar access from the easier, western way up the mountain, Herod erected a great tower at the path's narrowest point. On the flat summit Herod built a palace, itself also fortified, and sumptuously decorated. He had cisterns cut into the rock to hold an ample supply of rainwater. As for provisions, he laid in so much food, and highest-quality food at that, that it was still available about a century later when Eleazar and company arrived. Thanks to the aridity of the desert, the stored provisions were in perfect condition. In addition, Herod took advantage of the rich soil on top of Masada to have it farmed, thereby providing even more food.

Silva's reconnaissance showed that the only way to besiege Masada was to attack it from the west. Below the tower that Herod had erected was a broad rock projection about 450 feet (150 meters) below the summit of Masada. Silva's men occupied that rock projection, which was called Leuke ("White"). He had his men throw up an approximately 300-foot (100-meter) mound upon it, and on top of that a stone platform that was about 75 feet (25 meters) wide and high. Upon that sat an approximately 90-foot (30-meter) high tower, encased in iron. The Romans shot bolts and ballistae at defenders from this tower. At the same time, they assaulted the wall with a battering ram that opened a breach. But the defenders were prepared. They had built another wall inside, constructed of an earth mound and wooden beams, which cushioned the blows of the ram. Creative thinking—but Silva responded with equal creativity and sent his men with burning torches to set fire to the wood-and-soil wall. At first, a north wind blew the flames into the Romans, which made them fear for their siege engines, but then the wind shifted direction and destroyed the defenders' wall. It could only have been divine providence, Josephus concluded. The happy Romans retreated to their camp. They would keep careful watch that night and attack the enemy the next day.

Eleazar realized that there was no hope of either defeating the Romans or escaping from them. The future promised enslavement or death. Josephus doesn't mention it, but the rebels knew that the lucky ones would die in battle: the rest would face crucifixion. Instead, Eleazar tried to convince his followers to choose a nobler end. They should first kill their wives and children, and then each other. According to Josephus, it took two speeches and all his persuasive power, but in the end, Eleazar succeeded. The men said goodbye to their wives and children with tears and kisses and then killed them. Next, they quickly piled together all their possessions and set them on fire. Finally, they chose by lot ten of their number to kill all the rest. Each one lay down beside his wife and children and bared his throat for the slaughter. When only ten men were left, they drew lots again. The one who drew the lot killed the other nine. After checking to make sure that no one was left alive, he set the palace on fire and fell on his sword. In fact, two women, one a relative of Eleazar, had survived, along with five children, by hiding in a cistern or aqueduct. The total number of victims was 960, including women and children.

At daybreak, the Romans armed and prepared to attack. When they entered the area on top of Masada, they found only silence. After they shouted, the two women emerged from their hiding place and informed the Romans of what had happened. One of them, Eleazar's relative, gave the Romans a clear description of Eleazer's speeches. The Romans then proceeded to find the rows of dead bodies. The amazed Romans expressed admiration for their brave enemies. Josephus does not state the fate of the seven survivors.

Silva left a garrison at Masada and departed with his troops for Caesarea. The war was over at last. Josephus wrote:

> There was not an enemy left in the land. The whole country had already been subdued by the long war which had been felt by many, even by those living farthest away, and which had subjected them to the risk of upheaval.[12]

Archaeology and Literary Criticism

Josephus meant for Masada to demonstrate the folly of fighting Rome. Archaeology tends to back him up. Look at the ring of Roman camps at the foot of the mountain, eight in all, or the still-surviving ruins of the Roman wall surrounding Masada and cutting it off from the outside, or the Roman ramp leading up to the mountain. It's enough to show the disparity of force between the two powers.

The German archaeologist and historian Adolf Schulten explored Masada in 1932. In 1963 to 1965, Israeli archaeologist Yigael Yadin led two seasons of excavation at the site. There have been important additional excavations since then, notably of the Roman camps, which Yadin did not focus on, as well as reassessments of Yadin's work. A major effort, Yadin's excavation received worldwide publicity and put Masada on the map. His spadework has stood the test of time, but many have criticized his interpretation of the evidence. In addition to being an archaeologist, Yadin was a general in the Israel Defense Forces. He gave a Zionist interpretation to Masada. For instance, he and his team turned the Sicarii into Zealots and made the latter into freedom fighters.

Nationalism has played a role in archaeology in all countries, often with an anti-nationalist pushback. Nowhere has the connection between archaeology and national identity been keener than in Israel, and nowhere has the debate been more fervent. The truth, in fact, is complicated; both sides have added pieces to the puzzle of what really happened at Masada, even if much remains missing. Literary scholars have helped to unriddle Masada as well. Here is an outline of what is now known:

Excavation has unveiled the world of the rebels. Based on various indicators such as the number of rooms occupied by the defenders and the number of stoves and cooking ovens, excavators estimate that hundreds of people were living at Masada at the time of the siege. It appears that the occupants polished off Herod's leftover food supplies and had to make do with what they could find or steal. Conditions were not easy: some of the food remains were infested with insects. A comb for removing lice was found, with lice eggs still detectable.

The rebels paid attention to defense. They seem to have used weapons left in Herod's armory, but they also built workshops and manufactured arrows. Josephus makes no mention of the defenders fighting Romans. They were badly outmatched. Assuming that half the people at Masada were women and children, there were less than five hundred men to fight eight thousand Roman soldiers. Sorties outside the walls could have achieved little. Nor did the defenders have artillery to shoot at the attackers. Slings and arrows might have picked off a few Romans, but could not have done significant damage.[13]

The defenders took the worship of Judaism seriously. For example, they used unfired clay vessels, which the ancients considered to be resistant to impurity. They constructed ritual baths (*mikvot*) and converted a room in the casement wall into a synagogue.

Women played an important role among the rebels. The presence of spindle whorls and loom weights demonstrates that weaving was done at Masada, and weaving was usually the preserve of women in ancient times. Hairnets, jewelry, and cosmetics also were found. Inscribed ostraca (broken pieces of pottery) at the site refer to such women as "the wife of [Ze]beida," "the wife of Jacob," "the daughter of Domli," and "Shalom (or Salome) the Galilean."[14]

A bill of divorce was found in a cave not far from Masada, dated to "Year Six at Masada." The divorced couple were Joseph and Miriam. The find site of the document suggests that they had left Masada while people still could.[15]

So far most of the evidence has a scholarly consensus. The controversy concerns the effort made by the Romans and the reaction of the defenders, especially the mass suicide (or, to be more accurate, voluntary slaughter) described by Josephus.

Josephus does not state how long the Masada military operation took. Some historians have estimated three or six months, but time was at a premium for the Romans because of the difficulty and expense of transporting food and water to the site. On a persuasive reconstruction, it took between four and nine weeks, with seven weeks being probable.[16] The Roman force was large, but not massive. A plausible estimate is 13,000 men: 8,000 soldiers, both legionaries and auxiliaries; 2,000 military slaves, and 3,000 Jewish conscripted laborers.[17] Still, that represents virtually the entire military force of the province. The Roman wall of circumvallation stretched over 2.5 miles (4 kilometers) and included fifteen towers. Presumably, the wall served a psychological as well as military purpose. Standard practice in Roman sieges was to give the defender an opportunity to surrender, and that probably happened at Masada, although Josephus doesn't mention it.[18] If so, the Jews on the mountaintop refused. Perhaps they figured that a lack of supplies would convince the Romans to go home; perhaps they put their faith in God. In either case, they stubbornly held their ground (again, assuming the Romans gave them the chance to surrender). The Romans had to assault the rebels to defeat them.

The excavators found a breach in the wall opposite the top of the site of the Roman ramp and siege tower. They also found iron arrowheads and light-caliber ballista balls. A first suggestion was that the ballista balls came from the defenders, but it is likely that they came from the Romans. The light caliber suggests that they were aimed at human targets rather than the wall. No catapult bolts have been found, but the Romans surely used them, so they may have picked them up after the siege and recycled them. Some of these weapons might have killed defenders. If their bodies lay unburied because of time constraints, then Josephus might have counted them among those who accepted voluntary slaughter.

The Roman siege ramp is much debated. The ramp is nearly 750 feet (225 meters) long and about 650 feet (200 meters) wide at its base. It becomes narrower as it climbs 240 feet (75 meters), measuring only about 150 feet (45 meters) wide at the top. Josephus's account seems to suggest that a major feat of engineering was required. Modern investigation shows that the ramp was mostly bedrock and only 90 feet (27 meters) of additional material, stone and earth, was needed—a manageable job. The ramp was 42 feet (13 meters) short of the summit. A stone platform once crowned the ramp and served as a base for an ironclad siege tower, which Josephus says was 100 feet (30 meters) tall. A 2016 study by geologists argued that the ramp was never completed, but a rebuttal by archaeologists shortly afterward demonstrates that the material remains of the ramp are consistent with the Romans having completed it. Besides, the Romans breached the defenders' wall precisely above the top of the ramp today, and the distribution of the ballista balls suggests that they were fired from the siege tower, so the ramp surely was completed.[19]

Another question concerns whether a group of the defenders made a last stand in the northern palace rather than engage in mass killing/suicide. Some interpret a heap of rubble piled up outside the palace wall as a makeshift Roman siege ramp to attack those last holdouts.[20] Perhaps.

The greatest controversy concerns the deaths of the defenders. In one place, Yadin's excavation found eleven inscribed potsherds, one of which contained the name "Son of Yair." Yadin's team believed that these were the very lots drawn by the ten defenders who killed the women and children and then killed each other. Josephus wrote of ten and not eleven men who did the killing, but he may simply have opted for a round number. But the excavators also found many other inscribed potsherds, so not much can be made of the eleven. Yadin's team also found a cave outside, below the southern wall, with twenty-five skeletons, and some argued that they were the remains of some of Masada's defenders. A later study argued that they were in fact the bones of Roman soldiers.

The biggest question is not archaeological but literary: Can Josephus be believed? The reader knows that Josephus is often unreliable on numbers. He embellishes and perhaps invents speeches. And he wants to depict the rebels as bandits who ruined their country but were also somehow brave and noble. In his account of Masada, Josephus presents the Sicarii as just that: brave and noble bandits.

Although Jewish law today prohibits suicide, and it probably did in Josephus's day as well, it allows exceptions in extreme circumstances such as to avoid severe torture. The people at Masada may well have interpreted Jewish law as justifying suicide rather than accepting crucifixion or slavery and subjection to the heathen.[21]

Greeks and Romans went further: they had great respect for those who chose death before enslavement or execution by foes. In fact, the ancient sources contain other accounts of suicide on a massive scale in the face of defeat. One study found sixteen cases in the Greek and Roman sources. Only one of the ancient authors expressed qualms about killing women and children.[22] There are reasons, however, to consider the ancient reports exaggerated. In at least three of the cases, later evidence shows that there were survivors. This is not surprising, since historians in ancient times had a weakness for sensational tales; in fact, their readers expected them. All of this is to say that Josephus had both motive and method to exaggerate the fate of the defenders at Masada. Perhaps many did commit suicide, while others fought or meekly surrendered. A medieval retelling of Josephus in Hebrew has it both ways: the defenders first kill their wives and children and then die in battle, fighting the Romans.[23]

The New Man and the Rebel Royalty

The Roman general who took Masada and the Jewish commander who faced him are a study in contrasts. Silva was, the evidence suggests, a "new man," as the Romans called the first in his family to enter the Senate.[24] Eleazar son of Yair was descended from rebel royalty. Let us consider the Roman first.

MASADA

Silva was an Italian success story. It was Nero who first elevated Silva to the Senate, but it was Vespasian who would find Silva to be a man after his own heart. They were both hard men, ambitious, proud, and violent. Both Silva and Vespasian rose from the provincial elite rather than the Roman nobility. Vespasian came from the Sabine country north of Rome, while Silva came from Picenum in central Italy. Both men were upwardly mobile, and both, it seems, had the help of connections. Vespasian's uncle (his mother's brother) was a senator, while Silva may have been married to a woman whose brother was substitute, or suffect, consul in 71.[25] Silva's family name, "Flavius," suggests that he and Vespasian might have been related, but that is uncertain.

Silva was born in 43, making him four years younger than Titus. Silva's hometown was Urbs Salvia, a regional city located at a crossroads in the foothills of the Apennine Mountains. He made his way in Rome, beginning as a low-level magistrate in the judicial system in 62. He then proceeded to a military career. He served first as a battalion commander (military tribune) of the Legio IV Scythica and may have served on the Parthian front under Corbulo. After returning to Rome, Silva served as quaestor, probably in 67 or 68, which qualified him for the Senate; then, around 69, he became tribune of the plebs, an important step in a senator's career and one carrying prestige, although no longer a powerful political office, as it had been during the Republic. Not long afterward he was appointed commander of Legio XXI Rapax ("Beast of Prey") in Germania. Silva probably backed Vespasian in 69, the Year of the Four Emperors, because Vespasian would have entrusted command only to a reliable supporter. In 73, Silva received more honors from the Flavians, inclusion in the high-ranking patricians and praetorians. It was probably also in 73 that Silva was appointed governor (*legatus Augusti pro praetore*) in Judea, an office that he held until circa 80. He was about forty-one years old when, the next year, Silva marched on Masada, in 74.

Conditions for the attackers at Masada were difficult. Food and water had to be brought in from a distance. Silva and his fellow officers fared better than the common soldier. The latter used mess kits, but the officers had fine ceramics and glassware, as shown by the excavation of Silva's living quarters in one of the eight camps built by the Romans at the base of the mountain. The stone platform on which Silva addressed the men has also been discovered.

After his victorious term in Judea, Silva came back to Rome. In 81, he reaped his reward: he was appointed *consul ordinarius*, a prestigious position, although not one with real power, which made him one of the two men who gave his name to the year. It was an honor that the Flavian emperors (r. 69–96) shared with very few men outside the imperial family, and so a sign of the esteem in which Silva was held. At one point he was also one of the pontiffs, or priests, a visible status in Rome, where religion was part of the state's responsibilities. But Silva stood out back in his hometown as well.

In Urbs Salvia, Silva was named patron of the city and twice held an important honorary office. The city had reason indeed to thank him. Silva built an amphitheater there at his own expense and on his own property.[26] Three inscriptions (one very fragmentary) erected over the entrances to the structure provide the historian with the details of Silva's career. Otherwise, nothing would be known of him other than what little survives in Josephus. The arena was 320 by 245 feet (98 by 75 meters) and the seating is estimated to have held 7,000 spectators. There was an external porch as well. The structure was small compared to the Colosseum in Rome, which is about twice the footprint as well as much taller, and seated approximately 50,000 spectators, but the Urbs Salvia amphitheater was big for a small city. At the inaugural games, Silva paid for forty pairs of gladiators to fight—this in an era when games usually featured ten to twenty pairs of gladiators. One wonders how Silva paid for all this. Did he bring back slave labor from Judea to serve as low-cost construction workers? Did he compel Jewish prisoners of war to fight as gladiators, just as Titus had done? Did he sell war booty looted from Judea to raise funds?

Another detail stands out: Silva built the amphitheater not only in his own name but in that of his mother and his wife. His mother's name has been tentatively restored as Annia; his wife's name is unclear. To modern sensibilities there is something disturbing about their mention. Not only does Silva take pride in sponsoring men who fight each other to the death, but he brings his wife and mother into the picture. Perhaps they each contributed to the cost of the enterprise. With Masada in mind, the family inscription seems macabre.

A small provincial city in a corner of Italy would never have had so grand an amphitheater had not one of its favorite sons conquered Masada. There would have been no blood on the sand of the arena in Urbs Salvia without the blood on the stones of Judea. Contemplating this, one is tempted to say of the ruins of Urbs Salvia, in a paraphrase of Rupert Brooke's poem: "There is some corner of a foreign field that is forever Israel."[27]

Silva trumpeted his women's sponsorship of a blood sport. Eleazar son of Yair slit his women's throats before taking his own life or letting a comrade kill him.

Josephus is the only ancient source of information about Eleazar, aside from what can be gleaned from archaeology. Josephus introduces Eleazar as the tyrant of Masada.[28] But Josephus, remember, despised men like Eleazar, who belonged to the faction that he called Sicarii, the Dagger Men. The reality was more complex than the "tyrant" label.

In Josephus's account, Eleazar appears in Jerusalem in 66, at the start of the Great Revolt. Josephus states that Eleazar was the descendant of Judah the Galilean, founder of a movement, the so-called "Fourth Philosophy."[29] In the year 6, Judah raised the banner of revolt against the Romans. Several decades later, his followers became the Sicarii. Two of Judah's sons, James (or Jacob) and Simon, were crucified by Tiberius Alexander when he was procurator of Judea in 46 to 48. Eleazar came from a dynasty of rebels. Judah may have been the son of an earlier rebel, making Eleazar the heir of either 70 or 120 years of revolt against Rome.

Another son of Judah the Galilean (the rebel of the year 6) was Menahem. At the start of the war in 66, Menahem captured Masada with some of his friends, broke into the well-stocked armory left there by Herod, and armed both his fellow townsmen (from Galilee?) and other "bandits," as Josephus calls them. They returned to Jerusalem, where Menahem behaved first like a king and then a tyrant, complained Josephus.[30] Menahem and his men besieged the royal palace and killed all the Roman soldiers they could get their hands on. Then they killed the former High Priest and his brother.

At this point the Zealot priests turned on the Sicarii and raised a mob to fight back. After rebelling from the Romans out of a longing for liberty, wrote Josephus, they weren't about to accept a public executioner from their own people or a master.[31] They massacred as many of Menahem's followers as they could capture. They tortured and killed Menahem and his lieutenants. A few managed to escape, including Menahem's relative (nephew? cousin?), Eleazar. They sneaked off to Masada, which they took through some kind of treachery; Josephus provides no details.[32] And there they stayed.

From 66 to 74, Eleazar and his followers held Masada. Along with their wives, children, and relatives, in 74 the Sicarii forces numbered 967 people, according to Josephus.[33] As noted, they found some food in the stocks that Herod had left at Masada about a century earlier, supposedly still fresh because of the arid desert climate. But they needed additional supplies. The Sicarii marauded nearby territories. When they heard in 68 that the Jews in Jerusalem were too busy fighting each other to bother with the bandits at Masada, they went on a big raid. They attacked the oasis of En Gedi about ten miles north of Masada. Those inhabitants who could, fled, but the rest were trapped. Josephus claims that the Sicarii killed more than seven hundred women and children, and then carried off their spoils.[34] Again, Josephus's numbers are often exaggerations.

En Gedi was a Jewish settlement. Josephus emphasizes the depraved behavior of the Sicarii by pointing out that they attacked during Passover, which, he notes, Jews celebrate in memory of their release from slavery in Egypt. So much for the Sicarii claim of being freedom fighters. He also notes that the Sicarii attacked En Gedi at night. As Josephus doesn't need to point out to Jewish readers, night was the time of the Exodus. Next, the Sicarii graduated to attacking the whole district as far as Idumea, with new recruits coming every day to join in the plundering. They justified their attacks on fellow Jews by claiming that their victims had slavishly submitted to Rome, thereby becoming enemies. The Sicarii declared that they had a perfect right to take their goods and cattle and to burn down their homes.[35]

To sum up, if Josephus is right, from 66 on, the Sicarii made war only on Jews and perhaps Gentile neighbors: they no longer fought the Romans. This, of course, is a far cry from both the love of liberty that Eleazar cites in the speeches that Josephus gives him and from the honor as freedom fighters in which the defenders of Masada are held today. But Josephus has an axe to grind. In general, he wishes to portray the Sicarii as depraved individuals who led the people of Judea to ruin. Although the Sicarii did not contribute directly to the struggle against Rome, they participated indirectly. Not only did they occupy the former Roman military base of Masada, but Masada served as a transit point for people who wanted to continue the fight against Rome elsewhere.

Masada was a station on an ancient version of an Underground Railroad. It was a place where Sicarii and other freedom seekers might stop before continuing to Egypt, Libya, Arabia, the Parthian Empire, or Galilee.[36] One could say Masada functioned like an ancient Maroon community of the 1700s and 1800s, refuges that sheltered enslaved Africans who had escaped bondage and their descendants. Both Josephus and archaeology demonstrate that not only Sicarii made up the population of Masada; furthermore, they show that people came and went.

Josephus reports that Simon son of Giora sought refuge at Masada for himself and the women of his family in winter 66/67. Simon was not one of the Sicarii, and the people at Masada distrusted him at first. Eventually, they warmed to Simon and invited him to join in their raids, which he did until hearing of revolution in Jerusalem in 67. He was ambitious to do more than merely steal from the locals, so he left Masada and went into the hill country nearby, where he proclaimed freedom for slaves and rewards for the free and gathered many followers.[37]

More than 2,300 rebel coins, silver and bronze, have been found at Masada, representing all five years that they were issued (66 to 70), especially 67 to 69. The coins must have been brought from Jerusalem. The coins had various purposes, from purchasing supplies to serving as dowries. In some cases, they represented most or all of a family's wealth.

Fragments of texts that are also found at Qumran have been found at

Masada. The community at Qumran is generally thought to have been the sect known as Essenes. The Romans destroyed Qumran in 68. Some, but not all, scholars believe that refugees from Qumran brought the texts to Masada.[38] Qumran texts evince strongly anti-Roman sentiment. Although life at Qumran was monastic, not all its members need have been pacifists. After all, one of the Jewish generals at the start of the revolt was John the Essene, who fell fighting at Ascalon. Perhaps other fighting Essenes made their way to Masada.

Josephus states that some Sicarii fled Judea for Egypt and Libya, where they continued the armed struggle against Rome.[39] They might well have stopped at Masada on their way south. Masada served as a safe house for the armed wing of the Jewish resistance that planned to continue the struggle in North Africa. In that way, the Sicarii at Masada contributed to the continued revolt against Rome. Their actions would bear immediate fruit in Egypt and Libya, but the harvest would be small. Only two generations later would the real yield of their contribution come forth.

For all his harsh criticism of Eleazar and the Sicarii, Josephus attributes two speeches to Eleazar that are moving encomiums of freedom. Indeed, they are among the classic statements on freedom written in ancient Greek. (Josephus wrote in Greek, but Eleazar would no doubt have spoken in Aramaic or possibly Hebrew.) As we saw, when Eleazar realized that there was no longer any hope of resisting the Romans or of escaping them, he concluded that mass suicide was the honorable choice, and tried to persuade his followers of that. In the first speech he addressed what Josephus calls only the bravest of his comrades, all males. Josephus's Eleazar reminded them of the creed that inspired the founder of his sect generations earlier: to serve neither the Romans nor anyone else other than God, the only true and righteous Master of humanity. Eleazar stated his pride in being descended from the first Jews to rebel against Rome, and now being the last to bear arms against them (at least the last in Judea). Josephus has Eleazar admit that he and his followers deserved to die for their crimes—something that Eleazar surely did not say, no matter how much Josephus wanted to believe it. Eleazar urged his men to slaughter their families and each other, and so to choose to die nobly rather than to live on in slavery or be killed by the Romans. He summed up his advice with this exhortation:

> Let our wives die unravaged and our children innocent of slavery, and after them let us do each other a generous favor, preserving our freedom as a noble winding sheet.[40]

But many of his followers were unconvinced, so Eleazar gave a second speech, in which he supposedly went on a rhetorical flight of fancy about the immortality of the soul. Once again, he foregrounded freedom. He stated that death is the ultimate liberator of the soul, sounding as much like a Greek philosopher as a believing Jew. He maintained that there was no shame in being defeated by the Romans, especially since the Romans could not even take credit for the many defeats inflicted on the Jews in recent years by Egyptians in Alexandria, and by Greeks and Syrians in and around Judea. With Jerusalem in ruins, he argued, it seemed hard to continue living. He summed up his advice with an appeal to family and freedom:

> Unenslaved by the enemy let us die, and as free men let us leave life together with our children and our wives.[41]

Modern historians have questioned whether Eleazar ever gave these speeches. Josephus says when the Romans saw the wind change and the fire destroying the defenders' wall on the summit of Masada, the Romans retired to their camp at night and kept a strict guard to prevent escapees. At dawn the next day they entered the mountaintop and attacked, only to find everyone dead. Some say that Romans prized aggressive action too much to have given the enemy the night to regroup.[42] Certainly, the Romans did value bold action, but sending an army through a wind-driven blazing wall was not sensible procedure.[43] Nor was it wise to confront a well-dug-in enemy in a built-up area at night. Silva followed sound doctrine by waiting until the next morning. Besides, Josephus would not have included this information had it reflected poorly on a favorite of the emperors like Silva. It is safe to say that the Romans, therefore, waited overnight before making their final attack. The defenders did have time to hear speeches and engage in mass killing/suicide.

Even so, it is unlikely that Eleazar ever uttered the beautiful words that Josephus gave him, although some of those words might have been true to Eleazar's thinking. Josephus claims that one of the two women who survived in hiding gave the Romans a clear description of the speeches: presumably she was Eleazar's relative, whose intelligence and education Josephus noted.[44] Be that as it may, it is unlikely that the women heard either speech, especially the first one aimed at a few males. If they did hear the speeches, they probably remembered only bits and snatches, and who knows what was lost in the telling to their Roman captors. But more to the point, historians in Greece and Rome considered it their responsibility to compose beautiful speeches based on what they believed the occasion called for. Accurate knowledge of what was said was optional. The two speeches by Eleazar, therefore, are probably largely Josephus's creations. And that makes them even more striking.

Josephus chose to give noble words to a man he despised. Furthermore, he graced Eleazar and his followers with what the ancients called "a beautiful death." When the Romans discovered the dead, as previously described, they were amazed at the nobility of their plan, their unhesitating behavior, and their contempt for death.[45]

Josephus's speeches convey, at best, the gist of what Eleazar really said. But Josephus's narrative of Masada is largely persuasive. As the excavations have shown, Roman engineering in reaching the mountaintop was impressive, but not as impressive as Josephus makes it. There is no good reason to doubt that Eleazar addressed the defenders. There is no good reason to doubt that a mass slaughter/suicide took place, even if archaeology does not confirm it, and even if some of those who were slaughtered perhaps did not go willingly. Josephus may exaggerate the number who died, and he may leave out those who fell fighting or who were captured and enslaved. Such hyperbole is common among ancient historians and is especially characteristic of Josephus. Yet the basic facts of the account hold true.

Josephus adds a detail that clarifies his intention in the Masada story: the date (the month and day, but not the year). He states that the defenders of Masada carried out their mass killing on the fifteenth of Xanthikos. Xanthikos is the month on the Macedonian calendar corresponding to the Hebrew month of Nisan.[46] The fifteenth of Nisan is the first day of Passover. Josephus doesn't always record dates, so whether the end of Masada really did fall on this date or whether he "improved" it by changing a nearby date, he meant to convey a message. Passover was (and is) the festival of freedom. To Josephus, Masada was the last word on the tragedy of the misplaced Jewish love of freedom in the face of Roman power. The last word, that is, in Judea, but not in the Roman world altogether.

Egypt

After stating that Silva left a garrison at Masada and departed for Caesarea, and after proclaiming Rome's complete pacification of Judea, Josephus turned in the very next sentence to Egypt. Many Jews died in its capital city, Alexandria, he wrote, because Sicarii fled there from Judea and exported revolution. Having escaped from the ruins, they preached freedom to Alexandrian Jews. The Alexandrians, they said, ought not suppose the Romans to be better than them in any way: they should think that God alone was their master.

But certain prominent Alexandrian Jews pushed back. The Sicarii responded by murdering them and pressing the other Jews of the city to revolt. As usual, wealthy and influential Jews had a stake in the Roman order and would not support revolution if there was a choice. The elders of the Alexandrian community responded vigorously. They called an assembly and warned the people that the Sicarii refugees threatened to ruin them. The only way out was to turn over the Sicarii to the authorities.

The warning worked. Members of the Jewish community rounded up six hundred Sicarii and handed them over to the Romans. Some Sicarii managed to escape as far away as Upper Egypt, 600 miles (965 kilometers) by ancient routes south of Alexandria, but it was not far enough.[47] They were arrested and brought back to Alexandria. It was a struggle not just of Jew against Roman, but of Jew versus Jew. In short, the conflict followed a sad, familiar pattern.

All of this sounds like what one might expect from Josephus. Still, what follows is surprising. Instead of disparaging the Sicarii, Josephus marveled at their endurance. Everyone who encountered them, he wrote, was struck by what was either desperation or strength of conviction; he was uncertain which. No form of torture or outrage to the body could get the Sicarii to acknowledge Caesar (the emperor) as their master. Josephus wrote:

> No one gave in or was about to speak. They all proved superior to the force of necessity and maintained their convictions. They accepted tortures and fires as if they felt them only in their bodies while their souls rejoiced in them.[48]

The most impressive thing of all was the behavior of the children. Not one of them could be forced into swearing that Caesar was the master. "The power of their daring," wrote Josephus, "conquered the weakness of their bodies."[49] When Josephus penned these words he lived in Rome. He had thrown in his lot with the Caesars; he survived at least in part on handouts from the emperor. Even so, he depicts the Jews, including the Sicarii, as a race of heroes. He knew that the Romans admired courage, and perhaps he thought that his readers would respect not only the Sicarii for remaining resolute but himself as well for recording it.

The governor of Egypt immediately reported the troubles with the Sicarii to Vespasian. The emperor, wrote Josephus, "was suspicious of the Jews' incessant revolutionary spirit" and he ordered preventive action.[50] He told the governor to close the Temple of Onias. This remarkable structure, located near modern Cairo, had stood for more than two hundred years. It was also known as the Temple of Leontopolis, or "Lion City," after a previous temple to the Egyptian lion goddess that once occupied the site. Onias IV (probable identification), a legitimate claimant to the High Priesthood in Jerusalem who lost out in factional struggles, sought refuge in Egypt around 170 BCE. Egypt's Ptolemaic rulers were happy to welcome him, as his opponent was a client of Seleucid Syria, Egypt's archrival. Onias probably brought with him Jewish soldiers, who formed a military colony. Two centuries later, there were still Jews in the area who worshipped at the Temple of Onias.

The governor began carrying out Vespasian's order. When that governor died mid-task his successor finished the job. Between them they stripped the temple of its treasures, threatening to punish the priests if they held anything back. Then they turned away worshippers and closed the gates. That was the end of the temple. Between Jerusalem and Leontopolis, Vespasian and his son destroyed the two temples where Jewish sacrifice took place because they associated them with rebellion.

Cyrenaica (Eastern Libya)

The Sicarii and their message of revolt spread to Cyrenaica, a district of northeastern Libya consisting of Cyrene and four other cities. They were originally Greek colonies, now in the Roman Empire. All had well-established Jewish communities. Josephus wrote about events there with a poison pen, since they ended up affecting him personally and negatively.

The "desperation" of the Sicarii struck Cyrenaica "like a disease," Josephus wrote. A weaver named Jonathan, "the most wicked of people," and a refugee in Cyrene, attracted many followers among the poor. Jonathan must have been a man of charisma, because he persuaded his adherents to follow him into the desert. There he promised signs from heaven, which sounds like a vision of the Kingdom of God, familiar from Jewish apocalyptic writings.[51] In Cyrene, the highest-ranking Jews reported this exodus to the Roman governor, Catullus. Once again, Jews turned on each other. Governor Catullus sent a force of infantry and cavalry after Jonathan and his followers, who were unarmed and easily defeated. The soldiers killed most of the unfortunates and brought the rest back as prisoners. The affair is reminiscent of the fate of Theudas and his followers in the Judean Desert, who the Romans suppressed decades earlier in 46. The only difference is that the Romans beheaded Theudas and brought his head back to Jerusalem as a trophy. Jonathan escaped the Romans at first, only to be caught after an extensive search and hauled off to Catullus—but with his head still attached.

Jonathan, too, set on his Jewish enemies. He pointed a finger at wealthy Jews, who he said were the real brains behind his movement. Catullus purposely exaggerated the whole business and got Jonathan to accuse one of Catullus's personal enemies and his wife. Then Catullus attacked and executed all the prosperous Jews of the region, three thousand in all in Josephus's telling. To square it with Rome, Catullus confiscated their property and handed it over to the imperial treasury. The next step was to suborn perjury from Jonathan and a few other arrestees. They accused the most reputable Jews in Alexandria and Rome of plotting revolution. One of the people he denounced was Josephus.

Catullus came to Rome, bringing Jonathan and the others in chains. Vespasian himself heard the case. No less a person than Titus intervened on behalf of the defendants, who had been denounced. They were all acquitted. Jonathan was tortured and burned alive. Catullus got away with a censure, but not long afterward he died of a miserable disease that attacked his mind as well as his body: proof, wrote Josephus, that God punishes the wicked.

Several points stand out from Josephus's account. Sicarii escaped from Judea and spread their message of revolution far and wide. The distance from Jerusalem to Cyrene in ancient times was an estimated two and a half weeks by sea or nearly seven weeks by land.[52] Class consciousness and intra-Jewish conflict are part of the story. Jewish unity was as desirable as it was rare. The message of the Sicarii fell easily on the ears of the poor of Cyrenaica. Their lives were hard and they took readily to a message of redemption delivered by a charismatic figure. Wealthy and prominent Jews, by contrast, seem to have made their peace with the Roman order and wanted no part of revolution. Nevertheless, Jews were such figures of suspicion after the Great Revolt, even in far-off Cyrenaica, that an unscrupulous governor was able to slaughter them. No less a man than Josephus, who had the patronage of the emperor and his heir, was a target. So troubled was the lot of Jews in the Roman Empire in the wake of revolution and defeat.

Josephus ended his long book on the *Jewish War* with the story of Catullus's tortured end. It proved, he wrote, that divine providence imposes judgment on the wicked. Perhaps that stands as the moral of his work. Josephus, the former priest, never doubted that God is just: the Jews had only themselves to blame for their terrible fate. No one could serve as a harsher rod of divine vengeance than the Romans in all their awful brutality. No doubt Josephus hoped that his Jewish readers would learn the lesson never to repeat their mistake of rebelling against the empire to which God Himself had transferred His favor. But they did rebel, and twice more.

Vespasian died in 79. Titus succeeded him, but reigned for only a short time, less than three years (r. 79–81). He died at the age of forty-two. The most memorable event of Titus's reign was probably the eruption of Mount Vesuvius in southern Italy, which destroyed the cities of Pompeii and Herculaneum, among others, and claimed thousands of victims. One of the few victims who is known by name is Marcus Antonius Agrippa. He was the son of Drusilla, Berenice's sister, and her husband, Antonius Felix, the onetime procurator of Judea. Agrippa was Herod's great-great-grandson.[53]

Titus was followed on the throne by his brother, Domitian (r. 81–96). Domitian's tyrannical ways earned him many enemies, and he was eventually assassinated. His successor, the elderly senator Nerva (r. 96–98), was forced by the army to adopt a leading general as his heir. That man was Marcus Ulpius Traianus, better known as Trajan, who took the throne upon Nerva's death (r. 98–118). Nerva relaxed the tax on Jews, but Trajan brought it right back. Trajan's father had commanded the Tenth Legion under Vespasian during the Great Revolt. Trajan was not likely to go easy on the empire's Jews.

Meanwhile, those Jews watched and waited. The spirit of rebellion continued to burn among some of them. This time, it burst into flames not in Judea but in the diaspora.

Chapter Ten

TRAJAN, PARTHIA, AND THE DIASPORA REVOLT

On the night of December 13, 115 CE, an earthquake struck Antioch in Roman Syria. Located on several fault lines, the city has been devastated by quakes repeatedly over the centuries, most recently on February 8, 2023, when a violent convulsion destroyed Antakya, Turkey, built on Antioch's ancient site. In 115, Antioch was the third largest city in the Roman world, with an estimated population of about half a million people—only Alexandria and Rome were bigger. The quake was felt all over the Near East and generated a tsunami that reached Judea, but it hit Antioch hardest of all. The earthquake began there with a bellowing roar. The ground shook, trees and buildings went up in the air and came crashing down, raising an almost impenetrable cloud of dust. With an estimated magnitude of a ferocious 7.3 or 7.5 the quake destroyed much of the town and caused a loss of life made worse by the influx of soldiers and civilians. They thronged what had become in effect a temporary capital because the emperor was there. Trajan was wintering in Antioch between military campaigns.

The quake killed one of the consuls, who was also in Antioch. Trajan was luckier—he managed to escape from a damaged building by climbing out a window, suffering only minor injuries. He proceeded to live outdoors in the city's hippodrome for the next few days while the aftershocks continued to rumble. For a man who compared himself to Hercules and Jupiter it was a humiliating turn of events. To soften the blow Trajan let it be known that a being of superhuman stature had led him to safety. Still, it was a far cry from the official art that showed Jupiter lending his thunderbolt to Trajan as his divinely chosen deputy on earth.

The Antioch earthquake was more than a geological event. It symbolized an interrelated series of military, political, and cultural shocks, and arguably intensified them. Jews and Christians believed that cataclysmic natural events announced the "end of days." To them, the earthquake might have seemed like what climate change seems to some today: a sign of the apocalypse. To add to it, there was a war going on, and a big war, Rome's invasion of Parthia. It was the greatest military adventure of the most warlike emperor that Rome had ever known: Trajan.

Not just Jews and Christians but pagan Romans as well had long predicted that the destiny of Rome and its subjects would play out in the East. Was Trajan's invasion of Parthia the sign of the end-times? So it might have seemed to those who began another war in the wings, a war between the Jews and Rome that threatened to divert Rome from Parthia.

That second war is known as the Diaspora Revolt. More accurately, it should be called the Diaspora Revolts, because it was a series of uprisings that stretched from today's Benghazi to Baghdad. There was violent fighting in Cyrenaica, Egypt, Cyprus, and Mesopotamia as well as lesser disturbances in Judea.

The Diaspora Revolt demonstrates the enduring military traditions of the Jewish people, even without a state of their own. It points to the abiding desire to rebuild the Temple and Jerusalem and to restore what the rebels thought of as the Land of Israel. It shows the continuing appeal of a messiah for many Jews. Messianism is emotional, but the Diaspora Revolt also features strategic acumen on the ice-cold level of Richelieu or Bismarck.

And behind the revolt looms the image of the king of Parthia. In the previous century Parthia and Judea had flirted with each other more than

TRAJAN, PARTHIA, AND THE DIASPORA REVOLT

once: in Agrippa I's meeting in 43 of Near Eastern client kings who might be friendly with Parthia, and in the support for the Great Revolt in 66 to 70 by the royalty of Adiabene, who were Parthian vassals. But not since Pacorus put a pro-Parthian ruler on the throne of Judea in 40 BCE had the fates of Parthia and Roman Jews been so closely linked as they were in the events of 116 to 117. With Jewish help, the king of Parthia drove the Roman invader out. The outcome was so favorable to Parthia that a historian can't help but wonder if the Parthians set the Diaspora Revolt in motion.

As one historian has pointed out, the summer of 116 is the only time in ancient history when Jews in different parts of the Diaspora revolted at about the same time.[1] No other rebellion in the early Roman Empire took place on this scale, nor did any other rebellion in that era occur both within the empire and outside its borders. Nor was the threat small. By threatening to seize control of the harbor of Alexandria, the rebels could have cut the grain supply between Egypt and Italy, a lifeline as vital to the Romans as today's oil route from the Middle East. And the timing of the revolt is salient: it broke out while the emperor and his legions were engaged in the most ambitious military operation in 150 years, the invasion and conquest of a substantial part of Rome's only remaining imperial rival. From the geostrategic point of view, the new revolt challenged Rome even more than the Great Revolt had. In short, the Diaspora Revolt offered a major threat to the Roman Empire.[2]

Despite all that, the Diaspora Revolt is the least well-known of the three Jewish rebellions against Rome, and for an understandable reason. It had no Josephus to immortalize it. He died around the year 100. The revolt's leaders are little more than names to us, unlike Josephus or Eleazar son of Yair in the Great Revolt or Bar Kokhba, the rebel of 132 to 136 who is one of the legends of Jewish history. The documentation of the Diaspora Revolt is poor, especially from the Jewish side. Most of what we know comes from pagan or Christian sources, and they are often fragmentary or summaries of earlier work. There is some archaeological evidence, but not much. It takes historical detective work of the first order to put the pieces together. Fortunately, previous scholars have done so, to great effect. Although it requires a considerable amount of speculation and surmise, a portrait of the Diaspora Revolt can be sketched. Rome's invasion of Parthia is the place to begin.

Trajan's Parthian War

Trajan symbolized the vast majesty of the Roman Empire. Born in Hispania around 53 and raised in Italy, he made his name as a soldier in Germania, ascended to the throne in Rome in 98, gave the capital city the grandest of all its imperial forums, made his signature domestic initiative a welfare program for poor children in Italy, and conducted a successful war of conquest in Dacia in 101 to 102 and again in 105 to 106. But he found his real destiny in the Near East, where he launched Rome's most ambitious war against Parthia since Antony's ill-fated expedition 150 years earlier. This was the war that Trajan was born for. This was the war his father had bequeathed him, a man who had reached his career height as a soldier and statesman in Judea, Syria, and Asia Minor. And it was a war in which Trajan would run into determined opposition not only from the Parthians but from the Jews.

Trajan seems to have recognized the danger of arousing Jewish hostility in Rome's eastern provinces at a time when he needed peace on the home front. That might explain why he ruled harshly in 113 and 115 against prominent Alexandrian Greeks who had instigated anti-Jewish riots in their city. But he was prepared to go only so far in his generosity.[3]

Trajan renewed the hated two-drachma tax that every Jew in the empire, no matter how pro-Roman, had to pay annually to the treasury of the chief god of Rome, Jupiter Capitolinus—Jupiter of the Capitoline Hill, Rome's storied citadel. His predecessor, Nerva, had lessened the impact of the tax, probably by reducing the categories of Jews who had to pay it. Not so Trajan, who restored the full force of the impost. Perhaps he wanted to remind Jews of Rome's authority, or perhaps he just needed the money: war is expensive.

In his forties, when he became emperor, Trajan was in the prime of life. He was strong physically and mentally, and he was full of energy and plans.

TRAJAN, PARTHIA, AND THE DIASPORA REVOLT

His portrait busts, of which many survive, have the determined look of an aging athlete. His hair is carefully arranged in a style reminiscent of Augustus. His features are regular and could be called classical except for thin, tightly compressed lips. A modern detractor said that Trajan looked stupid and was believed honest. Some of the statues do look dull, but the man depicted in Trajan's coin portraits appears no less shrewd than other emperors.[4]

Trajan had a passion for soldiering. He loved the military life—what one contemporary called "the camps, bugles and trumpets, sweat and dust and heat of the sun."[5] Trajan spent almost half his reign away from Rome on campaign. He was the greatest conqueror to rule Rome since the days of Julius Caesar. Rome acquired Britannia under Claudius and reconquered Judea under Vespasian and Titus, which they marketed as a new conquest. But no one since Mark Antony had invaded Parthia.

Around the same time as it was conquering Dacia, in 106, Rome annexed what it called Arabia (roughly, modern Jordan, the Sinai Peninsula, and the northwestern Arabian peninsula). With the addition of these two new provinces the Roman Empire reached its maximum geographical expansion. But Trajan wanted more.

Perhaps because he identified with Alexander the Great, perhaps because he lusted to fulfill the unfinished business of Caesar and Mark Antony, perhaps because he saw no greater potential rival on the horizon, Trajan made war on Parthia. The pretext was a disagreement over Armenia, long a buffer state between the two empires. Rome claimed a veto power over Armenia, but the Parthians chose Armenia's most recent king. Even so, when Rome insisted and the Parthians backed off, Trajan refused to take yes for an answer. He wanted his war and the real reason was glory.

Trajan's timing was key. With Parthia divided between two claimants to the throne it would be hard to rally the country. Hence, Trajan invaded. He brought with him a potentially useful traitor, a son of the Parthian king, who had been raised in exile in Rome. Trajan headed east in 114 and made Antioch his base. From there, he and the army proceeded to take control of Armenia. The Romans killed the king and declared Armenia to be a Roman province.

The next year, 115, Trajan and his forces conquered northern Mesopotamia, which was also declared a Roman province. But the regular Parthian army was nowhere to be found. One might say that the hardest opposition that Trajan faced was the earthquake in Antioch in December 115, when Trajan barely escaped with his life.

Then, in 116, the Romans drove southward. They conquered Adiabene, captured the Parthian capital city of Ctesiphon, in central Mesopotamia, and accepted the submission of the rich trading state of Characene at the head of the Persian Gulf. One of Trajan's legates (commanders) in Mesopotamia, incidentally, was a certain Julius Alexander, who was perhaps the son or grandson of Tiberius Julius Alexander. The legate also probably served as consul in 117 and as member of an important group of Roman priests in 118.[6] He was certainly not a practicing Jew, which is a commentary on the legacy of Tiberius Julius Alexander, if the man in question was indeed his descendant.

When he reached the Persian Gulf, Trajan looked wistfully eastward toward India and Alexander the Great's farthest conquests. Trajan was forced to admit that, as a man of about sixty-three, he was too old to emulate his hero, who invaded India when he was thirty. Trajan said: "I should certainly have crossed over to the Indi, too, if I were still young."[7] But he wrote the Senate that he had advanced farther than Alexander. They in turn declared him Parthicus, to honor his conquest of Parthian territory, and said that he could celebrate a triumph for as many nations as he pleased, since he had written to them about more triumphs than they could follow.

But nemesis awaited. As in a more recent invasion of Iraq, the Roman expedition was a great victory—until it wasn't. Parthia's way of war, as Rome learned, was not to defend every inch of territory. Rather, the Parthians embraced the doctrine of strategic retreat followed by counterattacking. The sources aren't good enough to make clear whether what happened next represented a coordinated initiative or a series of spontaneous moves against a hated invader. But moves there were, and on several different fronts. Revolts broke out in Mesopotamia and Armenia and the insurgents killed Roman garrison troops.

A regular Parthian army finally arrived in Mesopotamia and Armenia and took on the Romans. The war went back and forth, with a mixed series of successes and failures on both sides. The Parthians defeated and killed a Roman commander; the Romans captured and sacked important Parthian cities. For Parthia, the low point came when Trajan appointed a new king of Parthia: namely, the Parthian prince he had brought from Rome—a puppet king who bowed in obeisance to the emperor. The Romans regained control of most of Mesopotamia, but lost Adiabene and Armenia. The key to reconquering those two areas was the rich northern Mesopotamian trading city of Hatra. The Roman army laid siege to Hatra in 117, an operation led by Trajan himself at great personal risk, but to no avail. The siege failed: the low point of the war for Rome.

The insurgents who revolted against Rome have not left any manifestos behind, but a series of motives are imaginable. Few people appreciate an invading army; Roman legions were not famous for leniency. In one city, for example, they burned down a temple. After centuries under Parthian rule, many of the inhabitants of the newly occupied territories had long-standing business and political ties with the Parthian overlords, ties that were now cut. And then there was money. Rome imposed new taxes and threatened to muscle in on the lucrative trade with the East that passed through Mesopotamia. There were plenty of reasons to rebel.[8]

Trajan wanted to resume the offensive, but he faced stiff opposition.

The Fighting Jews of Mesopotamia

Mesopotamia had a mixed and multiethnic population. The rebels included Greeks and Arabs as well as Aramaeans, Babylonians, Syrians, and Jews.[9] Jews generally had good relations with their Parthian rulers. Jews could hardly have thought well of Rome, not after the destruction of the Temple and Jerusalem. Nor could they have wanted the humiliating Jewish tax imposed upon them. In short, Mesopotamian Jews had good reason to revolt against the Roman invaders.

Jewish participation in the insurgency is stated most clearly in Christian sources, although admittedly some of them are late and contradictory. Eusebius of Caesarea (ca. 260–339), a Christian historian, writes that when the Jews of Mesopotamia rebelled—or were merely suspected of being about to rebel—Trajan sent Lysias Quietus "to extirpate them from the province." Quietus marched against them, writes Eusebius, and slew "countless thousands."[10] Other sources clarify that the general's name was Lusius. Other, later Christian sources follow Eusebius and echo the claim of a slaughter by Quietus; one says that he lured the Jews into a trap. Eusebius notes that, as a reward for his work in Mesopotamia, Quietus was named the procurator of Judea.[11] That appointment was surely a chilling event for the Jews there.

Cassius Dio, an earlier, pagan source, also says that Quietus put down a Jewish revolt, but his account of this period is abbreviated and confused, because it survives only in an eleventh-century Byzantine abridgment. At one point Dio says that Trajan sent Quietus to subdue the Jewish rebels in Egypt, Cyrene, and Cyprus. At another point he says that Quietus suppressed rebels in Mesopotamian cities. He doesn't mention Jews in this context, but other sources indicate that a substantial Jewish population lived in the very cities that Dio names.[12]

Another contemporary source may well refer to Rome's harsh suppression of Jewish rebels in Mesopotamia. Arrian (b. ca. 85–90), a Greek-speaking soldier-politician-historian who was close to the Roman emperor Hadrian, wrote a now-lost history of Trajan's Parthian War. One of the few preserved lines states:

> Trajan was determined above all, if it were possible, to destroy the nation utterly, but if not, at least to crush it and stop its presumptuous wickedness.

As one scholar has argued at length, there is good reason to think that the nation in question was the Jews.[13]

For all their flaws, the sources indicate that Jewish rebels in Mesopotamia played a leading role in the Parthian revolt against Rome. They might have fought alongside Gentile neighbors, but Eusebius says that Trajan specifically targeted Jews and ordered that they be driven out of the province. Given the military tradition of Jews in Babylonia (southern Mesopotamia), it is not surprising that Jewish rebel soldiers in 116 were taken seriously by Rome.

An Iranian Proxy War?

The chronology of the revolts is a problem. It used to be thought that they began in 115, but a reevaluation of the evidence makes a start date of late spring/summer 116 more likely. The sources suggest that the Romans suppressed the revolt in Egypt by summer 117. In short, the revolt probably lasted about a year, from late spring/summer 116 to summer 117.[14]

The coincidence of dates—or, to be more precise, the possible coincidence of dates—of the outbreak of uprisings in Egypt and Mesopotamia raises the question of coordination. It is hard not to suspect that at least some of the rebels in different countries coordinated their activities. This seems especially likely in the three former Ptolemaic provinces—Cyprus, Cyrenaica, and Egypt—where the several Jewish communities enjoyed historic ties. The revolts took place while the Roman army was engaged in a war of conquest against Parthia. The time was propitious for rebelling against the Roman emperor.

The biggest question is Parthia's involvement. It was certainly convenient for the Parthian king to see rebellions break out in the Roman rear as well as in Mesopotamia, which was Parthian territory. Scholars have speculated about the possibility that Parthians incited or at least encouraged the revolts. Jewish communities had reasons of their own to consider rebelling, as discussed, but there were surely those who argued in favor of the status quo, as there were in other, better-documented Jewish uprisings against Rome. Support from abroad might have tipped the balance in favor of revolt. Did the Parthians help unleash a Jewish proxy war against Rome?

Parthia was no stranger to getting others to fight its battles. It had a long experience of encouraging Armenia to fight Rome. If the Parthians consulted the history of an earlier Iranian dynasty, the Achaemenid Persians (ca. 550–330 BCE), they would have found many examples of proxy wars. The Achaemenids were masters of balancing rival Greek states against each other to wear them out and to keep them from uniting and attacking the Persian territory. The Achaemenids followed this policy during the Peloponnesian War in the fifth century BCE and during the various wars among the Greek city-states that ensued in the next century. The Achaemenid king sent agents, who handed out subsidies to Greek politicians. The money was to be used either for buying arms or it was an outright bribe, depending on the individual case. Later, when Alexander the Great began his invasion of Persian territory in Asia Minor, Persia launched a naval campaign in the Aegean to stir up a Greek revolt in Alexander's rear. Only the untimely death of Persia's admiral ended the initiative.[15]

Parthia had a motive for raising a revolt in Rome's rear. Parthia lacked a navy in the Aegean, and so couldn't follow anywhere near as aggressive a policy as its predecessors had. But it could certainly have pursued diplomacy and dispensed bribes.

Parthia was hardly cut off from the Roman world. The border between the two empires was not closed. Parthian hostages lived in Rome. A Parthian ambassador met Trajan in Athens in 113 to try to talk the emperor out of invading. Parthian Jews traveled between Mesopotamia and Judea on business and rabbinical missions, and they could have continued onward to Egypt, Cyrenaica, or Cyprus. While traveling they could have acted as diplomats for the Parthian king and encouraged potential Jewish rebels against Rome.

Nor were the Parthians indifferent to Rome's enemies. During his wars with Trajan, the king of Dacia sent a captured slave, probably a Greek, to the Parthian king. The slave served the Parthian ruler for many years and eventually acquired a ring with the king's image engraved on it. A military relationship between Parthia and Dacia might also have existed, as suggested by the Parthian-style armored heavy cavalrymen depicted in the scenes from the Dacian Wars on Trajan's column.[16]

In short, it is possible that the Parthians encouraged Jewish revolt in the Roman Empire, even if speculation is the best that the historian can do. The evidence doesn't permit certainty.

Cyrenaica, Egypt, and Cyprus

At around the same time that the uprising against Rome began in Mesopotamia a violent Jewish revolt raged in Cyrenaica, Egypt, and Cyprus. The rebels may have included the descendants, whether physical or spiritual, of Sicarii refugees who fled Judea for Egypt and Cyrenaica after the failure of the Great Revolt in 70. Like the Sicarii before them, the rebels of 116 were moved by a combination of religious motivation and strategic thinking. They sought to avenge humiliations and punishments at the hands of Gentiles, whether Roman overlords or Greek or native neighbors—all three countries had significant Greek populations. The rebels of 116 had no patience for those Jews, often in the elite, who still believed in collaboration with Rome.

Although neither the rebels nor the Romans have left a record of what the strategy of the revolt was, historians have stitched together, from the scattered sources, a plausible account.[17] The rebels wanted to hurt the Roman Empire at its heart by cutting off the grain supply from Egypt that did so much to feed Italy. Cyrenaica was another important source of grain and weakly defended, too, which may be why the rebels probably struck first there before marching to Egypt. The rebels surely noticed that Rome was in the process of conquering Parthian Mesopotamia and Armenia. Whether they acted independently or in collaboration with Jewish or Parthian representatives from the East, they wanted to strike while Rome had shipped off some of its soldiers to fight the Parthians. Although they might have cared more about affairs at home and in Judea than in Mesopotamia, they could not have wanted to see Trajan's Parthian invasion succeed and bring the Jews of Mesopotamia under hated Roman rule. At home, the rebels wanted to destroy the shrines of pagans, whom they considered to be idol worshippers.

Most important of all, they wanted to restore the Jewish people to its homeland in the Land of Israel, as they might have thought of it. This meant leaving exile and migrating to Judea. To Diaspora Jews, a return to the Land of Israel represented freedom; it represented liberation and redemption. Philo, the Jewish philosopher of Alexandria, wrote several generations earlier of a return of the exiles to the Promised Land:

> For even though they dwell in the uttermost parts of the earth, in slavery to those who led them away captive, one signal, as it were, one day will bring liberty to all.[18]

"Liberty" and "redemption" were the watchwords of the Great Revolt. It is likely that these terms were also in the minds of the rebels of 116.

The rebels had a knowledge of geostrategy, but they also had expectations of the apocalypse. The apocalypse was rarely far from Jewish thinking in this era. The coming of the messiah, the breaking of the heathens, and the restoration of Israel were key themes of apocalyptic writing. Another theme was the role of the East. As noted, Jewish, Christian, and, for that matter, even pagan Romans wrote that the destiny of Rome would be decided in the East. Other Jewish prophecies suggested that the messiah would come while Rome ruled over Egypt. Fighting against Rome in Egypt and Parthia alike might have seemed like a holy mission. And it seemed plausible to some that wars across much of the Jewish world marked the birth pangs of the messiah.[19]

The revolts in Cyrene and Cyprus each seem to have had a messianic leader or leaders. In Cyrenaica, his name was Lukuas. Another source disagrees and calls him Andreas. Either one of the sources is wrong, or there were two men, or one man who had two names, as was not unusual at the time. At any rate, he or they led the Jewish rebels in Cyrene. Another man, Artemion, is recorded as the leader of the Jewish revolt in Cyprus. The sources call Lukuas "their [the Jews'] king." That is reminiscent of how Josephus, writing about an earlier period, also refers to Jewish rebel leaders as "kings," which can be interpreted as meaning "messiah." Given the power of the messianic idea at this time, it is not difficult to imagine the rebel movements in Cyrene or Cyprus rallying behind messiah figures.[20]

There was no shortage of Jewish soldiers in Egypt. Jews in the Roman Empire continued to serve in military settlements along the Nile, as they had in Ptolemaic times. The Ptolemies encouraged Jews to serve as security forces, whether as soldiers or policemen. Jews had a reputation as good soldiers. They followed their own national customs and were unlikely to assimilate to native ways, which made them suitable as a force to patrol the Egyptian population. (The Ptolemies might have preferred Greeks as soldiers, but the number of Greek immigrants to Egypt was limited.) The downside for the Jews, of course, was concomitant friction with Egyptians. After Rome conquered Egypt in 30 BCE, it continued to find Jewish soldiers useful as forces to keep order. The military threat posed by the Jewish rebels in Egypt suggests that at least some of them were soldiers by profession. In addition, the sources suggest that the land of a Jewish military colony was confiscated after the revolt was put down, a hint of participation in the uprising by Jewish professional soldiers.[21]

In Cyrenaica as well, the Ptolemies planted Jewish military colonies. Although those colonies no longer seem to have been in existence at the time of the Diaspora Revolt, the population included Jewish tenant farmers descended from those Ptolemaic-era soldiers.[22] One historian suggests that some of the Cyrenaean insurgents received training in the desert regions for years, and maybe the Egyptian ones did, too.[23]

The insurgents attacked many public buildings in the region. In just the city of Cyrene the rebels damaged or destroyed law courts, archives, temples, baths, a gymnasium, a marketplace, and the road to the sea. They also attacked farms in the interior. Dio or his abridger claims that the rebels treated their opponents barbarously. Supposedly they sent some victims to the beasts in the arena and forced others to fight each other as gladiators. Worse still, they supposedly ate their victims' flesh and did macabre things with their flesh and entrails. After they were finished in the Cyrenaica, the rebels marched across the desert to Egypt, where they found many Jews willing to join them.[24]

At first the rebels from Cyrene won a battle as they marched eastward.

The location, it has been suggested, was on the coast road, perhaps near the site of the World War II battles of El-Alamein.[25] But the rebels did not repeat their success in Alexandria, where the Gentile forces recouped and engaged in a slaughter of the Jewish population. It is unclear whether Roman troops took part in the massacre or whether the perpetrators were mainly Greeks. Perhaps this is when the huge and magnificent Great Synagogue of Alexandria with its double colonnade was destroyed, an event lamented in the Talmud.[26] Jewish rebels in turn destroyed a monument to Pompey, the hated conqueror of Jerusalem and desecrator of the Temple, although an ancient source says it fell to the necessities of war and not in an act of iconoclasm.[27]

The fighting spread southward and eastward in Egypt. Outside of Alexandria it involved the Delta region, and the Nile Valley as far as about eight hundred miles south to Apollonopolis Magna, and possibly even farther southward to Nubia. Jewish forces now won a series of victories, defeating Egyptian as well as Greek militias and Roman forces in, for example, the central Nile Valley. Greek papyri mention farmland laid waste and buildings burned by the Jews. They record a regional governor arming up, and the worries of Greek women who wouldn't cut their hair and could barely eat, so concerned were they about their men off fighting.[28]

In the northeastern Delta, Jews had traditionally been and probably still were river guards, which may explain why Jewish forces nearly took control of its waterways. The Greek writer Appian of Alexandria, best known today as a historian, describes his narrow escape from the rebels on a passing warship after his guide lost his way at night, causing Appian to miss the boat that was supposed to take him to safety. That first boat later ended up in rebel hands.[29]

In the meantime, the revolt spread to Cyprus, which lies about 250 nautical miles from Alexandria. On Cyprus, Jewish rebels are said to have destroyed the city of Salamis-in-Cyprus, an important port, and killed all the Greek inhabitants, according to one source. Another source claims that the rebels killed 240,000 people, no doubt an exaggerated number, as ancient statistics often are.[30] In any case, the strategic significance of the rebellion was potentially great. From Salamis-in-Cyprus it was a short trip by sea to the port of Antioch. It was probably still recovering from the earthquake of 115, but Antioch gave access to a major paved road that led to Judea. The rebellion in Cyprus, therefore, opened another potential entryway for Jews to return to the Promised Land.

The rebels clearly had ships as well as infantry. If they had continued their success, they might have been able to march into Judea. They might even have been able to take Alexandria. The Romans, however, were determined to stop them. Perhaps Trajan's wife, Plotina, helped convince the emperor to act. At least the Talmud blames her, stating:

> His [Trajan's] wife sent a message to him, saying, "Instead of going to conquer the barbarians, come and conquer the Jews, who have rebelled against you."[31]

Plotina was very powerful, and strong women in the Roman world tended to attract criticism. Still, she may have influenced her husband. In any case, in late 116 or early 117 Trajan diverted troops from the Parthian front to Egypt. They fought under one of his best generals, Quintus Marcius Turbo. This brought muscle to the Roman response to the revolt, while depriving Trajan of important military resources in the East.

The result proved devastating to the rebels. Turbo had ships as well as land forces. He found willing helpers against the Jews in the Greek and Egyptian population. Hard fighting lay ahead, and the Romans suffered heavy losses, but they crushed the revolt in the end. The repression aimed not only at defeating the rebel forces but wiping out Jewish civilian life. Appian writes that Trajan undertook the process of "utterly destroying the Jewish people in Egypt."[32] Terms like "ethnic cleansing" and "annihilation" appear in modern scholarship to describe the bloodbath in some areas.[33] Jewish property in Egypt was confiscated. In Cyprus, Jews were forbidden to set foot on the island, on pain of death. Scholars disagree as to whether all or merely most of Jewish life in Egypt, Cyrenaica, and Cyprus was wiped out. In its heyday, Alexandria had been the largest Jewish city in the world; now, no longer. In any case, it took more than a century before significant Jewish populations returned to the former Ptolemaic lands.

Judea

The Mishnah is a collection of rabbinic traditions, of fundamental importance for Judaism, compiled around the year 200. The Mishnah refers to the Kitos War, or War of Quietus. After his successful suppression of Jewish revolt in Mesopotamia, Quietus was rewarded by Trajan with the governorship of Judea. Ancient sources and archaeological evidence both hint at unrest in Judea. The sources are vague and fragmentary. One theory is that there was a violent Jewish reaction to the paganization of Jerusalem. A contemporary inscription shows that around 117 the soldiers of the Third Legion dedicated either a statue or altar in the city to the Greco-Egyptian god Serapis. A much later Christian source claims that Trajan set up a statue of a goddess on the Temple Mount. Either action might have been enough to arouse armed Jewish resistance. There is no sign of significant advance planning and preparation, and the Jewish violence might have been little more than a riot. But that might have been enough to cause the Roman military repression that is suggested in the sources.[34]

Jewish sources refer to two martyrs who some associate with Judea. The wealthy Jewish men Pappus and Lullianus offered financial support to exiles who wanted to ascend (as the return was called) to the Holy Land, for which they set up banks from Antioch to Ptolemaïs. For this they were arrested, tortured, and executed, supposedly by Trajan, but more likely by one of his representatives, perhaps by Quietus. The sources disagree about whether Pappus and Lullianus were executed in Laodicea, the port city of Antioch, or in Lydda, a rabbinic center in Judea. Given their activity on the route from Syria, Laodicea seems more likely. In later centuries, the martyrs were commemorated in the spring on the twelfth of the month of Adar, just before Purim, a holiday that celebrates a Jewish victory over persecution.[35]

For the Jews of Cyrenaica, Egypt, and Cyprus, the Diaspora Revolt ended in disaster. Judea got away relatively unscathed, if being left to the ruthlessness of Lusius Quietus can be considered safety. Unfortunately, a bloody future lay ahead. Rome had not wiped out the Jewish desire to fight for freedom; far from it.

Hadrian

Rome's battles against a resurgent enemy in 116 and 117 did not convince Trajan to give up the war against Parthia. He was ready to resume it, but his body was not. Trajan suffered a stroke. His entourage decided to bring him back to Rome, but he died on the way, in an obscure city in what is now southern Turkey. It was August 117. The new emperor, Hadrian, reversed course and decided to pull out of Mesopotamia. He withdrew Roman forces back to the previous boundary between the two empires, the Euphrates River.

It was a bold and controversial move; so controversial that Hadrian ordered the execution of its leading opponents. They were four of Trajan's marshals, including Quietus. They were killed without a trial, which made the Senate shiver, but also made Hadrian's point. No further protests of his foreign policy are recorded.

Hadrian withdrew from Mesopotamia because he had seen enough. Parthian resistance was too great; Roman losses too heavy; military expenditures too burdensome. Hadrian had seen all that and the Diaspora Revolt.

Hadrian would devote his reign to strengthening Rome's military at home, within the borders of the empire. It was a policy of training, traveling, and building, building both infrastructure and morale. The most famous result is Hadrian's Wall in northern England, parts of which still stand.

But there was an infamous outcome as well. It was a disaster for Rome and even more for the Jewish people. It stemmed from Hadrian's desire to settle scores in the eastern part of the empire and to demonstrate to the Jews, once and for all, that Rome was the master. The result was the bloodiest revolt, at least in Judea, of all the Jews' rebellions against the Roman Empire.

Chapter Eleven

BAR KOKHBA

Sometime, someplace in the Judean Hills in the year 132 the storm broke. It had been a long time coming, but even so it shocked the Romans. It shocked them enough that it may have cost them a legion and possibly the life of the governor of the province of Judea. "May have" is necessary because the sources of evidence are scarce and because the detective work that has gone into reconstructing the war is as conjectural as it is ingenious. And yet, the story is as dramatic as any of the Jewish revolts against Rome and more decisive.

The war was the third of the three major Jewish revolts against Rome. Fifteen years had passed since the end of the Diaspora Revolt and sixty-two years since the destruction of Jerusalem. This third Jewish rebellion is known as the Bar Kokhba War, after the leading Jewish rebel. It lasted for three and a half years, during which the rebels not only created an army but administered an independent state. The revolt was centered in the traditional Jewish heartland, the region of Judah, but it spread into adjacent areas as far as the coastal plain, western Samaria and the Negev. Galilee played only a very small part, but the revolt probably spread into the province of Arabia Petraea and may have involved Arab as well as Jewish rebels against Rome.

The war was a duel between two men, Bar Kokhba and Hadrian. Bar

Kokhba took the title of *nasi*, or "prince," of Israel. Hadrian was the Emperor, Imperator Caesar. Both men were hard, violent, and driven by a vision of what each thought was right. Bar Kokhba was a warrior, Hadrian a man of peace—but peace, Roman-style, that is, a peace enforced by armies of occupation, financed by humiliating taxes and presided over by foreign deities. Bar Kokhba was a messiah, Hadrian the son of a god.

Bar Kokhba observed the commandments of Judaism; Hadrian was a pagan. Bar Kokhba honored tradition; Hadrian founded a new religious cult. Although married, Hadrian found the love of his life in a Greek teenage boy named Antinous. When Antinous drowned in the Nile in the year 130, Hadrian had him proclaimed one of Rome's many gods. Bar Kokhba worshipped the one God of Israel. Hadrian built a new city in Egypt dedicated to Antinous. Bar Kokhba dreamed of restoring the Temple in Jerusalem. Hadrian built the Pantheon in Rome, a shrine for all the gods. Bar Kokhba considered Hadrian an idolater; Hadrian considered Bar Kokhba a savage.

No war did more than the Bar Kokhba Revolt to shape the destiny of the Jewish people, and few wars are so poorly documented. The only historical narrative from antiquity is a sketchy account in Cassius Dio, less than two dozen lines long. As with his history of the Diaspora Revolt, the surviving version of his text is an eleventh-century, Byzantine abridgement. Fortunately, that brief text offers a good overview of events from the Roman point of view. Ancient Jewish sources in the Talmud and Midrash offer a mix of fact and legend. Midrash is a type of Jewish interpretation of scriptural texts, often used to support a legal ruling or to undergird a sermon. The revolt is mentioned briefly as well in a few late-antique Christian works. In contrast, there is a great deal of material evidence, and here is where the search for the past gets exciting. It's not just the light from Latin inscriptions nor the shining images and proud legends on the rebel coins. Archaeology has uncovered underground hiding places used by rebel fighters and caves that served as refuges for those fleeing the Romans. The caves have yielded household objects brought by refugees who did not survive to retrieve them. But the most sensational discovery is various letters, found in several caves, and written by Bar Kokhba himself as well as by his fellow insurgents. These documents, in Aramaic, Greek, and Hebrew, open a window into a Jewish world in crisis, a culture with one foot planted in its heroic past and another finding its way in a region of clashing cultures, a society whose single-minded war leader, Bar Kokhba, was trying to bend it to his steely will. Hadrian had no less unflinching a resolve, and he also had thirty legions.

Hadrian, Parthia, and the Jews

Hadrian began his reign in that bitterest thing for a Roman, the acknowledgment of defeat. Romans did not end wars: they won wars, but Hadrian ended Rome's war with Parthia without victory. After taking the purple he ordered an immediate withdrawal from the little territory that was left of Trajan's conquests in the Parthian Empire, and he made peace with the Parthian king. Hadrian concluded that Rome's security was best served by keeping its armies on the west bank of the Euphrates. There was no getting around Rome's massive loss of prestige from its failed invasion of Parthia, no way of denying in private that Parthia had won a great victory.

Not that Hadrian would admit the fact in public. He issued coins that identified himself as DIVI TRA(IANI) PARTH(ICI) FILIO, "Son of Divine Trajan Parthicus," with "Parthicus" connoting "Conqueror of the Parthians." The phrase not only glossed over Trajan's defeat but left out Trajan's other military titles as Conqueror of Dacia and Germania. The same title, "Son of Divine Trajan Parthicus," appears on a triumphal arch for Hadrian in Judea, probably erected in 130 by an ingratiating legion to mark the emperor's visit.[1] It also appears on an inscription on a now-missing monument in Jerusalem from the same year. It was a hollow title, of course, since the Parthians drove Trajan out, but Hadrian claimed it anyhow. Worse still, he staged a posthumous triumph for his predecessor. Never mind that Trajan was dead and his victory was dust: Hadrian put an effigy of the late emperor in a chariot that he had pulled through Rome.[2] Coins, arches, and dummies were one thing, armies another. Hadrian had no intention of sending the legions back into dubious battle on Parthian soil.

The new reality is illustrated by Hadrian's response to rumbling on the Parthian frontier early in his reign. The emperor's answer was not military but diplomatic. One ancient source reports that

> War with the Parthians was in prospect at the same time and it was checked by a personal intervention (*conloquium*) on Hadrian's part.[3]

The source for this information, the *Historia Augusta*, is quirky and not always reliable. Still, most historians accept the historicity of the event and date it to 123. Parthian dynastic matters were still an issue between the two empires. Trajan had set up a puppet king of Parthia who Hadrian relocated, probably to a Roman client kingdom in what now straddles northern Syria and southern Turkey. The legitimate Parthian king was Osroes II (also known as Chosroes, the Parthian Khosrow, r. ca. 109–129).[4] The Romans still held Osroes II's daughter, taken captive by Trajan, as well as the royal throne.

Some scholars imagine Hadrian's "personal intervention" as a conference on the Euphrates River, the frontier where Roman and Parthian officials often deliberated. It has even been suggested that Hadrian met Osroes II in person. That would have been a first. Roman emperors sent underlings to meet the Parthian king, but the emperor did not go himself, as he did not want to acknowledge the Parthian ruler as his equal. If Hadrian's meeting with the Parthian ruler did happen, it shows how strong Parthia was in 123. Nor was it the last time that Hadrian had to keep a wary eye on the Parthian frontier. In 129, he traveled east to central Asia Minor, where he inspected the armies of the frontier and met with Rome's client princes.[5] In the end, Hadrian returned the Parthian king's daughter, but only promised the throne. It was still in Roman hands under Hadrian's successor.[6]

Hadrian was prudent but not weak. He devoted a large part of his reign to traveling from legionary base to legionary base, from Britannia to Africa to the Euphrates, where he inspected the troops. Often, he went on maneuvers with them. He also beefed up Roman frontier defenses, most famously in Britannia, where he built Hadrian's Wall to mark the border with the ferocious tribes to the north. And he thought about the problem of Judea.

Hadrian had been governor of Syria in 115 to 117 during Trajan's Parthian War. He knew well that when the legions were fighting to conquer Mesopotamia, Jewish soldiers fought for Parthia against them and Jewish rebels opened a second front against Rome in the rear—in Egypt, Lybia, and Cyprus—and threatened to do the same in Judea. In short, Hadrian knew that the Jews were dangerous to Rome. The solution, he might have concluded, was to be proactive. He had a plan for Judea.

To begin with, Hadrian dismissed Lusius Quietus and replaced him with a new governor, Marcus Tittius Lustricus Bruttanius. Not that Hadrian had any objection to Quietus's brutality, which is what recommended him to Trajan as the man to keep Judea in line. What Hadrian objected to was Quietus's disloyalty, for he was Trajan's man and he likely opposed Hadrian's peace policy with Parthia. Hadrian had Quietus executed, along with three others of Trajan's marshals. It was probably now that Judea was raised to the rank of consular province, meaning that the governor had to be a former consul, as Bruttanius was. In other words, from now on only an official of the highest rank could govern Judea. The new governor of Judea brought with him a second legion for the province. There were an estimated 10,000 to 12,000 legionaries and circa 8,500 auxiliaries. It was a very large occupying force for a province that did not border on enemy territory, but history suggested that rebellious Judea needed a strong Roman military presence.[7]

Bruttanius set the second legion to work building roads. Now for the first time in Judea Rome built a network of proper, well-engineered highways. They would be useful for moving soldiers, whether toward the Euphrates frontier or within the province. One purpose of the new roads was to control movement between Galilee and the Jewish heartland in the Judean hills.

Jerusalem without Jews

Even more dramatic than building roads, Hadrian planned to rebuild the ruined Jerusalem. What was left of the city was the headquarters of the Tenth Legion. There were probably some civilians there, as was usually the case in ancient times with "destroyed" cities. A Christian source mentions seven synagogues in Jerusalem, although he might have meant churches, assuming seven isn't merely a symbolic number (i.e., seven days in a week).[8]

The city's new name was Colonia Aelia Capitolina. The new city would be anything but Jew-friendly. It would be thoroughly Roman, laid out on a grid plan, and named after both Hadrian (whose full name was Publius Aelius Hadrianus) and Jupiter (Capitolinus, after Capitoline Jupiter). Both names in fact recalled Hadrian, since the emperor prided himself on his connection to the Greek equivalent of Jupiter, the god Zeus. The new city would be a Roman *colonia*, or colony: the first, and for nearly a century the only, Roman colony to serve as a legionary headquarters. The core of its citizens probably consisted of demobilized soldiers from the Tenth Legion. That made the new colony a garrison town. The purpose of Aelia Capitolina, as one scholar puts it, was "to punish and control what they saw as a stubbornly rebellious nation" by planting "a miniature Rome" on the site of their holy city.[9]

One might argue that the purpose of Aelia Capitolina was also to send a message to Parthia. The meaning of the new Jerusalem was clear. There would be no more Jewish uprisings to help Parthia because there would be no more Jewish mother city. No longer would the tribes go up to Jerusalem; no longer would the hills enfold the Holy City. Now it belonged to the legions.

Based on coin evidence, scholars agree that the new colony was probably formally founded in the summer of 130 when Hadrian visited Judea. But archaeology shows that the main thoroughfare of the new city was begun even earlier, near the beginning of Hadrian's reign. Hence, it looks like not long after he came to the throne in 117, Hadrian had already laid plans to rebuild Jerusalem as a pagan city.[10]

Hadrian built many cities during his reign. They lent glory to his name and fostered loyalty to Rome, whose image was mirrored in new temples, forums, arches, and monumental gateways. They reminded friend and foe of Roman power. Aelia Capitolina made crystal clear to the Jews that their fondest wish would not be granted. The Temple would not be rebuilt. Dio says that Hadrian erected a Temple of Jupiter where the Jewish Temple had once stood. The Romans took over the Temple Mount as a sacred place because whatever magic their toughest foes had, the Romans wanted to have, too. It seems that the emperor was worshipped on the Temple Mount during the reign of Trajan, making it logical for Hadrian to build a pagan temple there.[11]

Perhaps some Jews supported Hadrian's building projects, or at least they swallowed hard and told him that they did. But if Hadrian thought that he could get general Jewish acceptance of his plans for Jerusalem, he couldn't have been more wrong. Hadrian was neither the first nor the last Western statesman to underestimate the degree of resistance to outside reformers in the Middle East.

Hadrian's actions were devastating to most Jews; devastating, disappointing, and insulting. History had made Jews optimistic about rebuilding the Temple. When the Neo-Babylonian empire destroyed the First Temple and sent the Jewish elite into exile in 586 BCE, the prophets predicted that God would remember His people within seventy years. Approximately seventy years after the exile, in 516 or 515 BCE, the Jewish community that had now returned to Jerusalem dedicated the Second Temple (later rebuilt on a magnificent scale by Herod). The founding of Aelia Capitolina dashed the hopes of building a Third Temple. Cassius Dio probably states Jewish reaction accurately: "the Jews deemed it intolerable that foreign races should be settled in their city and foreign religious rites planted there."[12] Or, to put it in the vernacular, Jews might have said in defiance: "This is OUR Jerusalem. You can make it a pagan city after we're all dead."

Few people like being occupied. The region of Judah had been under Roman military government for over sixty years, with the soldiers of the Tenth Legion running it directly. Even if every legionary kissed babies and extended a helping hand to the elderly, no doubt there had been ugly incidents.

A Josephus, had there been one, could have recorded them. Perhaps some remembered how Roman soldiers massacred Jews not long before in Egypt and Cyrene, Cyprus and Mesopotamia. Now, on top of all that, came Aelia Capitolina.

The sources speak of two other grievances that supposedly sparked rebellion in Judea. Hadrian is said to have reneged on a promise to rebuild the Temple. So states a rabbinical source and an early Christian text, but few scholars consider them historically reliable.[13] The *Historia Augusta* claims that Hadrian prohibited circumcision.[14] It would be understandable if he imposed this as a punishment for revolt, but less so if he decreed such an inflammatory measure in a still-peaceful province, even though many Romans looked down on circumcision as barbarous. Still, there is some evidence in a Christian source that suggests that he did just that.[15] If so, it is another example of an emperor's ignorance of or indifference to local sentiment. But the best-attested and no doubt most incendiary fuel for revolt was the paganization of Jerusalem. Enter Bar Kokhba.

Bar Kokhba

Hadrian was ubiquitous. More statues of him have survived from antiquity than of any other Roman emperor except Augustus. Bar Kokhba is a ghost, but only when it comes to his physical appearance. The ancient sources are generous when it comes to his personality.

With Bar Kokhba, the Jewish revolts against Rome finally had a hero. Josephus builds up Jewish leader after leader only to tear them down one by one. The rebel chiefs of the Diaspora Revolt are mere names. With Bar Kokhba, at last there is the real thing. He was the alpha male in the wolf pack, a charismatic warrior who got a nation to follow him into the valley of death. He called his people brothers.[16] Perhaps calling them children would have been more appropriate, as the letters found in the caves show that he ruled with a very firm hand. He was stern, imperious, and a micromanager.

He threatened to put men who didn't obey him into chains.[17] The Christian writer Eusebius of Caesarea calls him "murderous and banditlike"—shades of Josephus![18] Bar Kokhba was an excellent planner and military tactician. He claimed to be the leader of the nation. Not that he lacked detractors among his own people. The letters also show that some men disobeyed his commands, which explain his repeated threats of punishment.

Bar Kokhba joined a long line of rebels against the Roman Empire, all famous in their own countries, and most unknown in the rest of the world. They include Boudicca of Britannia, Viriathus of Lusitania, Tacfarinas of Numidia, two leaders in succession named Bato in Illyricum, Vercingetorix and Sacrovir of Gaul, Civilis of Batavia, not to mention the leaders of the two previous Jewish revolts against Rome. Of the various rebels, Arminius of Germania alone was successful, only to be killed by his own people. We might also include Mithradates, the king of Pontus, who sparked a rebellion across the Eastern Mediterranean that raged from 88 to 66 BCE, although his own country was still free. Queen Amanirenas of Kush defeated the Roman army that invaded her country (25–22 BCE). The queen's forces raided the far south of Roman Egypt in turn, enslaved the inhabitants, destroyed statues of Augustus, and buried a bust of the emperor under the threshold of a Kushite temple, so worshippers would trample it, at least symbolically. Today the bust is on display in London's British Museum. The most famous rebel against Rome was also a dramatic failure, Spartacus of Thrace, who led, in Italy, one of history's best-known slave revolts between 73 and 71 BCE.

Bar Kokhba joins their ranks. He is famous in Israel, but less familiar elsewhere. First the Zionist movement and then the state of Israel turned him into a hero. Today he is known to every Israeli schoolchild. But not every Israeli agrees about his heroism. To some, Bar Kokhba was an arrogant fool who brought on the worst massacre in Jewish history before the Holocaust. He should never have rebelled against the Romans in the first place, they maintain. Which was Bar Kokhba, hero or fool? Let the reader follow the story below and reach a judgment.

Bar Kokhba was not his original name. The texts discovered in caves in the Judean Desert call him Simon Bar Koseva, or simply Bar or Ben Koseva. "Ben" means "Son of" in Hebrew, while "Bar" means "Son of" in Aramaic, making him Simon Son of Koseva. It is unclear whether Koseva refers to his father, to his family, or to the place (perhaps in the Judean Hills) of his origin. His detractors called him Ben Koziva, "Son of a Liar."[19]

Bar Kokhba is a nom de guerre. It means "Son of a Star." The reference is to a verse in the Torah, "There shall step forth a star [*kokhav*] out of Jacob" (Numbers 24:17). The implication is that the "star" is the messiah. Whether or not his followers called him Bar Kokhba (a name attested only in Christian sources), they considered him to be the messiah. Remember that in Judaism, unlike Christianity, the messiah was purely human, without divine or supernatural characteristics.[20]

Bar Kokhba (to use the familiar name, as noted above) took the title of *nasi*, "prince," which was clearly linked with the messiah. Both the Prophet Ezekiel and the Qumran community refer to the *nasi* as a warrior and a harbinger of the End of Days. The Dead Sea Scrolls make it clear that the *nasi* will lead the final battle against the Romans, the archenemy of the Jewish people, and establish the Kingdom of God.[21]

The Talmud contains statements both about rabbis accepting Bar Kokhba as the messiah and about them rejecting him. The most famous passage concerns Rabbi Akiva, the most prominent rabbi of his generation:

> Rebbi Simon ben Yohai stated: Akiva my teacher used to preach, *there appeared a star out of Jacob* [Num. 24:17], there appeared Koziba out of Jacob. When Rebbi Akiva saw Bar Koziba he said, this is King Messiah. Rebbi Johanan ben Torta said to him, Akiva! Grass will grow from your jaws and still David's son . . . [will not have] come.[22]

Maimonides, the great medieval Jewish scholar, wrote:

> Rabbi Akiva, the greatest of the sages of the Mishnah, was a supporter of King Ben Koziva, saying of him that he was the king messiah. He

and all the contemporary sages regarded him as the king messiah, until he was killed for the sins which he had committed.[23]

Contemporary evidence suggests support for Bar Kokhba from another direction: the priests. Although the Temple was gone, the former priests and their descendants continued to have a strong identity. Bar Kokhba's coins refer to the priests and the Temple.[24] Some of the earlier coins bear the legend "Eleazar the Priest." His identity is unknown, and "Eleazar" may refer to one of Bar Kokhba's allies or to a biblical figure, the son of the first Jewish priest, Aaron.

Bar Kokhba's coins assert the identity of the Jewish people. Many of the coins depict a building that is probably the Temple, and some depict various objects that played a prominent role in the Temple such as the Showbread Table or a seven-branched palm tree, symbolizing the seven-branched candelabra. Some coins may illustrate the golden candelabra that Queen Helena of Adiabene donated and was placed above the door of the sanctuary.[25]

Coins played an important role in getting the rebels' message out. The rebels probably lacked access to adequate tools and metal of their own and so they resorted to overstriking Roman or Greek or Nabatean Arab coins. The legends of the coins recall the Great Revolt. "Year One for the Redemption of Israel," "Year Two of the Freedom of Israel," "For the Redemption of Jerusalem," and "Jerusalem" are among the legends. There is also "Simon," for Bar Kokhba, and sometimes "Simon, Prince [*Nasi*] of Israel." The legends are written in Hebrew, in archaic script, just like the legends of the coins of the Great Revolt. Hebrew was also used on legal documents from the era of Bar Kokhba. Aramaic was the common language of the Jews of Judea. Hebrew, as noted earlier, was the language of Jewish nationalism and independence.

As in the Great Revolt, so in Bar Kokhba's Revolt the notion of Israel was central. Jews still thought of their country as Israel, an older and more inclusive name than Judea. In addition to the coins, contemporary letters, which survive on papyrus documents, refer to Bar Kokhba as Prince (*Nasi*) of Israel. The letters also refer to the state that he administered as the "House of Israel."[26] Even after the revolt, the term survived. A deed written in 140 (or possibly 139) bears the date "Year 4 of the Destruction of the House of Israel."[27]

Between the emphasis on the Temple, the similarities between some of his coins and those of the Great Revolt, the use of Hebrew, and the title *nasi*, Bar Kokhba presented himself as a great figure of the Jewish past. Legends clung to him. Typical of them is one that says that he caught enemy catapult bolts on his knee and hurled them back and killed his foes.[28]

Bar Kokhba was a powerful personality, a charismatic leader, an impressive manager, and an innovative commander. The foundation of Aelia Capitolina provided a motivation for rebellion. The question remains, though: Why did Bar Kokhba and his followers think they could defeat the mighty Roman Empire? After all, both the Great Revolt and the Diaspora Revolt had brought ruin upon the Jewish people. Be that as it may, history is full of examples of people who talk themselves into believing that "this time is different." Judea had recovered from its previous defeat. A new generation had arisen, full of confidence, its hopes fueled by messianism. Bar Kokhba promised different tactics than the rebels had used in 66 to 70. Rome's utter defeat against Parthia, just fifteen years earlier, was a reminder that the empire was not invincible.

If the Jewish people had been governed by cold-blooded men and women in business suits who sat around a conference table and calculated the odds, then they might have decided not to risk war with Rome. That is the conclusion that the rabbis eventually reached. But in the early second century of our era, the Jews still adhered to a strong military culture. They saw themselves as the heirs of the Maccabees. They fought for freedom, for honor, and for what they saw as the dictates of their God. They certainly were not alone in history for risking everything for national survival. Think of a Native American rebel like Tecumseh, who went down fighting rather than surrender to the United States. Think of Churchill's response when advised in the dark days of 1940 that England had to agree to make peace with Hitler rather than risk the ravages of the Luftwaffe. He said:

Nations that go down fighting rise again, but those who surrender tamely are finished.[29]

He also said,

> if at last the long story is to end, it were better it should end, not through surrender, but only when we are rolling senseless on the ground.[30]

Bar Kokhba may well have spoken in a similar vein.

As for Parthia, the sources are silent, but they are also scanty. Did the rebels seek help from beyond the Euphrates, as they did during the Great Revolt? Maybe, just maybe, Cassius Dio hints at this in his statement about the Bar Kokhba Revolt that "the whole world, so to speak, was incited over this."[31]

Not that all of Bar Kokhba's countrymen supported him. The sketchy sources about Bar Kokhba show followers disobeying his orders or not carrying them out well. They do not reveal outright opposition to his revolt, but we can be certain that it existed, nevertheless. There never was and never will be a people that rebels with unanimity, especially not one who could see the price of failure in the ruins of their holy city. Then, too, the Roman way of governing a province always sought out local elites to do business with, and Judea was surely no different. There as elsewhere in the empire some people, especially in the upper classes, cooperated with the Romans. The name of one Jewish soldier who fought with the Romans against Bar Kokhba has survived, and there were surely others.[32]

A famous passage in the Talmud illustrates the range of sentiment that likely existed in Roman Judea.[33] Three rabbis were having a conversation. One of them praised the Romans for establishing marketplaces, opening bathhouses, and building bridges. The second rabbi sat in silence, but the third one struck back. He said that the Romans established marketplaces to put prostitutes in them; opened bathhouses to pamper themselves; and built bridges to collect tolls. The first rabbi reported the conversation to others, and word eventually got to the Romans. They rewarded the rabbi who praised them and sent the second rabbi into exile from Judea to a city in Galilee. The rabbi who attacked them was sentenced to death. The story was written down long after Bar Kokhba's era. It may be embellished or invented. It refers to the generation after the revolt, but it probably reflects more generally the range of opinion in second-century Judea. (The story may remind some readers of the "What have the Romans ever done for us?" sketch in Monty Python's film *Life of Brian*.)[34]

The Course of the Revolt

According to Dio, the rebels waited until Hadrian had finished his tour of Egypt and Syria. After adding Asia Minor to his itinerary, he landed in his favorite city, Athens. Hadrian lavished rebuilding projects on this Greek city, a much better fit than Jerusalem for the pagan philhellene that he was. It was probably in Athens in 132 that Hadrian got the news: a rebellion had broken out in Judea.

Dio writes that the rebels took the Romans by surprise. Then again, most rebellions took Rome by surprise because the Romans tended to ignore the subjects of their empire except for the local bigwigs who flattered them and did the rulers' bidding, especially by collecting taxes. Roman arrogance usually made it a shock to discover that the natives were unfriendly and that they knew how to fight, even when past experience suggested otherwise. It was even worse when they hit Rome where it hurt, and nothing hurt Romans so much as hit-and-run, guerrilla tactics. Roman history offers a long roll call of generals who knew how to line up the men and fight a set battle or lay siege to a walled city, but who walked clueless into ambushes or got caught with their armor off by raiders.

Bar Kokhba knew how to wrong-foot the enemy. One wonders how he learned the art of war. Could he perhaps have served as a Roman auxiliary or, less likely, as a legionary? Roman ranks did indeed include Jews, and Roman rebels numbered among them such ex-Roman soldiers as Spartacus and Arminius. In any case, Bar Kokhba knew the military art. Apparently, he understood that the rebels of 66 to 74 had played into Roman hands by depending on fortresses. He intended to employ irregular tactics. Cassius Dio wrote:

> To be sure, they did not dare try conclusions with the Romans in the open field, but they occupied the advantageous positions in the country and strengthened them with mines and walls, in order that they might have places of refuge whenever they should be hard pressed, and might meet together unobserved underground; and they pierced these subterranean passages from above at intervals to let in air and light.[35]

Archaeology leaves no doubt that the rebels went underground. Investigators have found hundreds of underground hideouts in what is today central Israel as well as smaller numbers in the north. Most of the hideouts are in what were Jewish villages in the first and second century. All the hideouts have similar features. They contain cisterns, reservoirs, storage rooms, olive presses, areas for livestock, and ritual baths. The only way to get from room to room is to crawl through small, narrow, and twisting tunnels. Only a few of the hideouts can be reliably dated, but the uniformity among them makes a good case to place them all in the Bar Kokhba Revolt.

Tunnels are not unfamiliar to students of modern warfare. From the Warsaw ghetto to the Vietnam War, and in North Korea, Lebanon, and Gaza, fighters have gone underground. From there they can come out and attack the enemy unexpectedly. As the Bar Kokhba tunnels show, the tactics go back a long way.

The hideouts could serve as launching pads for sudden and surprise attacks on the Romans. Ambushes and raids are classic moves in irregular warfare and they resonate in Jewish history. The Maccabees used irregular tactics in their successful bid for independence in the second century BCE. Cassius Dio also claims that the rebels supplied themselves with weapons by tricking the Romans, who compelled them to supply Roman troops. The Jews purposely made weapons of such poor quality that the Roman army—their customer—rejected them. The rebels kept the weapons and presumably repaired them.

There is no archaeological confirmation, but it's a good story and might even be true.[36]

In addition to their underground hideouts, the rebels garrisoned a number of places—no less than fifty of them, according to Dio.[37] These ranged from Herod's citadel at Herodium (near Bethlehem) to Roman guard posts that the insurgents had captured, to fortified villages, to the city of Betar (near Jerusalem).

The rebels did what they could to keep their preparations secret. But the Romans were not blind and surely noticed at least some of what was going on. Nevertheless, as Dio wrote, the Romans "at first considered it to be of no significance."[38] One imagines the usual combination of arrogance and wishful thinking on the part of an imperial power and its well-fed soldiers living in comfortable billets. If anyone sounded the alarm about a rebellion brewing, the officers probably responded: "They wouldn't dare."

Bar Kokhba's was a people's army, probably raised mainly in the rural villages of Judea.[39] His soldiers included, as one historian puts it, "the distressed, the debtors, and the discontented."[40] Country people often make up for what they lack in urbanity by physical sturdiness and inner fortitude.[41]

Bar Kokhba's army consisted largely of light-armed troops. In the dry climate of the Judean Desert some of the rebels' weapons have survived. Slings and arrows were their primary arms, along with spears and daggers, and the occasional sword has been found as well.[42] The rebels manufactured some of these weapons on their own and looted others from the Romans. Choose the right terrain and timing and light-armed soldiers can prove deadly even to the infantrymen of the legions with their shields, body armor, and helmets.

Apparently the first battles shocked the Romans. Although no details survive, we can imagine that the rebels sallied out from their hideouts, ambushed Roman troops, stripped their armor, and plundered their weapons. They could have overrun legionary and auxiliary outposts. The Romans suffered such serious defeats that they needed to bring in soldiers and commanders from other provinces. It is possible that the rebels damaged one of the two legions in Judea beyond repair. One of those legions was the Tenth Legion, whose headquarters was in Jerusalem; the other legion was stationed in Galilee, but its identity is debated. In any case, only the men of the Tenth Legion were decorated for service during the revolt. One can only wonder if the rebels put the second legion out of commission, just as the rebels of 66 had savaged Cestius's legion in an ambush in the Beth Horon pass.[43]

Before the Romans knew it, as Dio says:

> all Judea had been stirred up, and the Jews everywhere were showing signs of disturbance, were gathering together, and giving evidence of great hostility to the Romans, partly by secret and partly by overt acts.[44]

Dio claims that "many others of foreign races joined them out of a desire for profit and, the whole world, so to speak, was incited over this."[45] Just what Dio means by this last comment is unclear. "The whole world, so to speak" is surely an exaggeration, but perhaps non-Jews in the province of Judea joined the rebellion to gain plunder. A variety of non-Jews, from discontented city dwellers to rural bandits to people who were just looking for trouble might have turned on the Romans. The sources also contain hints of rebellion in the neighboring province of Roman Arabia, and perhaps Dio had that in mind. Two groups there may have joined the rebellion. Both Jews living in the region called Perea and their Nabatean Arab neighbors may have chafed under Roman rule, a generation after Rome had annexed the formerly independent area in 106.

Jewish refugees fled the troubles in Roman Arabia to Judea. Two of them are Babatha daughter of Simon and Salome Komaïse daughter of Levi, who came from a village on the southeastern coast of the Dead Sea. They were both property owners, primarily of date groves, and both women of means. They traveled to En Gedi, where they stayed until it was no longer safe. Then they fled. Improbably, their documents survived, thirty-five of Babatha, wrapped carefully in a leather pouch, and more than a dozen of Salome.

The documents open a window into a world where Jews maintained their own traditions, while making compromises with a complicated and sometimes threatening reality. We know from the documents that Babatha had to deal with the Roman authorities in Arabia, where she originally lived, to fight for her son's inheritance after the death of his father, her first husband. Babatha followed many elements of Jewish law, but also elements of Greek and Roman law. In the Judean Desert in this era, at any rate, Jewish life was not separate, nor did the rabbis exert the influence they would in later centuries.[46]

Babatha was married twice, the second time to a man from En Gedi. As it happened, he already had a wife at the time. Polygamy was legal, and both his wives eventually outlived him—and fought a court battle over his property. Babatha's husband offers an example of Roman power. He borrowed money from a Roman centurion. The Roman was stationed in En Gedi to supervise the balsam plantations, which belonged to the emperor. En Gedi was the major source of balsam in the empire. Balsam, also known as balm, was a superstar of the ancient economy. It was used to treat wounds and as an antidote to snakebites and scorpion stings. It was an ingredient in holy oil. Above all, it was highly prized for perfume. Anyhow, the officer was generous to Babatha's husband, but not too generous, as the loan was possibly made at a usurious rate of interest, a reminder of the reality of power in an occupied country.[47]

The Empire Strikes Back

No one, it seems, was more shocked by the uprising than Hadrian himself. It is possible but by no means certain that he went back to Judea to participate in the war.[48] Whether he observed the situation in person or not, Hadrian quickly saw the need for a new commander in Judea. He acted with characteristic decisiveness.

First, he sent the governor of Syria to Judea on temporary duty as legionary commander, on one theory, because Judea's governor had been killed in the fighting.[49] Likewise, it is possible that the governor of Roman Arabia was also dispatched to Judea, although his duty might rather have been putting down disorder in his own province. But Hadrian knew that Rome's greatest hope lay in the governor of a far-off province about a month and a half's travel time away. Dio writes:

And indeed then Hadrian sent his strongest generals against them [the rebels], of whom the foremost was Julius Severus, who was dispatched against the Jews from Britannia where he was governor.[50]

As governor of Britannia, Sextus Julius Severus held one of the two most important military commands in the empire; the other was Syria. Syria bordered Parthia, while Britannia bordered violent Caledonia (roughly, Scotland) and had no shortage of rebels of its own. Normally, a move to Judea would have been a demotion, but this was an emergency, and Julius Severus was the best man for the job. In fact, he probably had been appointed Britannia's governor to put down an uprising in the northern part of the province.[51] Julius Severus knew how to deal with savages, as the Romans thought of them, and he knew all there was to know about the Roman army. Born in a Roman veterans' colony in what is now Croatia, Julius Severus had an outstanding military career. A favorite of Trajan, he commanded a legion and governed two provinces in southeastern Europe before his appointment in Britannia. When he left for Judea, Julius Severus took several talented officers with him, including three future governors of Britannia. No wonder Hadrian decided to entrust the war to him.

Roman casualties in Judea were high. Fronto, a prominent Roman orator in the 160s, wrote, when looking back at an earlier time: "When Hadrian governed the empire, how very many soldiers were killed by the Jews, how very many by the Britons!"[52] Dio is blunt about the Judean war: "Many Romans died in this war," he wrote.[53] "Therefore," he continued,

> when Hadrian wrote to the Senate, he did not use the usual opening for the emperors, "If you and your children are in good health, all is well; I and the army are in good health."[54]

Perhaps Hadrian wrote to the Senate from the front in Judea.

Rome needed more men, so they brought in soldiers from other provinces. To fill the manpower gap, Hadrian drafted soldiers in Italy, an unpopular policy that emperors tried to avoid. Just how many men were sent to Judea and from how many units is debatable, given the uncertainties of the evidence, which comes from various inscriptions recording military careers. At a minimum, Rome sent in a full legion from Syria and vexillations (units, each typically of 1,000 or 2,000 men) from six other legions. Some argue that twice as many vexillations were brought in, as many as twelve or thirteen. Auxiliary troops served in Judea as well. One historian estimates a total of about 30,000 to 50,000 Roman professional soldiers.[55] It is best to err on the conservative side and choose the lower estimate. That was only half as many men as Vespasian had in the Great Revolt, but the Bar Kokhba war covered a smaller geographical area, nor did it require the siege of a fortress like Jerusalem. Julius Severus's way of war needed manpower but, even more, it required time and patience.

The rebels declared independence and made it stick. Although they did not control the bulk of the Province of Judea, they took a large part of its central region, Judah, away from the Romans and governed it for three years. They passed laws, issued coins, and, above all, fought a war. One of their strongholds, and perhaps their headquarters, was Herodium, located about seven miles east of Jerusalem. This hilltop fortress of Herod the Great, who was buried there, was eminently defensible. As mentioned, the rebels constructed underground passages to facilitate sorties and to serve as refuges, if necessary. Their economic center was probably En Gedi. Ultimately, they would retreat to the fortress of Betar, near Jerusalem. They dreamt of Jerusalem, but never captured it.[56]

Severus arrived in Judea perhaps in late 133 or 134. Dio offers a concise analysis of the general's tactics against the rebels:

Severus did not venture to attack his opponents in the open at any one point, in view of their numbers and their desperation, but by intercepting small groups, thanks to the number of his soldiers and his lieutenants, and by depriving them of food and shutting them up, he was able, rather slowly, to be sure, but with comparatively little danger, to exhaust them, to grind them down, and to beat them.[57]

A rabbinic source adds that the Romans set up three guard posts to apprehend Jews who came out of hiding late in the revolt.[58]

Severus displayed one of the qualities of a successful commander: the ability to modify orthodox military thinking. He engaged in a counterinsurgency strategy. Dio's text as it stands isn't entirely logical, but we can make sense of it along the following lines: Severus outnumbered Bar Kokhba but, given the steep and rugged Judean terrain, perfect for ambush by the knowledgeable locals, the Roman chose his battles carefully. He sent his troops on what are now called search-and-destroy missions. When possible, they killed the enemy outright. Archaeology shows that his men overran farming villages in Judea, with burn layers and hastily buried skeletons telling the tale of ruin.[59] In other cases, Severus was satisfied with shutting the rebels in their hideouts and slowly starving them, while no doubt picking off those who ventured out. Starvation was real, to judge from a story in the rabbinic sources about Jews in hiding reduced to eating corpses.[60] Severus's was a gruesome but effective strategy, although, as Dio notes, it was not a quick route to victory. No wonder the war lasted three and a half years.

Intelligence is key in the kind of campaign that Severus waged. He might have obtained information about the enemy from captured prisoners as well as from Jewish and Christian supporters of Rome. More accurately, the latter group should be called Jewish followers of Jesus Christ; scholars sometimes refer to them as Jewish Christians, but Jewish Christ followers is more accurate.[61] In Bar Kokhba's day, many Christ followers, particularly in the Roman East, still considered themselves Jewish. Jews who accepted Jesus as the Messiah argued that they, and not other Jews, were the true representatives of the people of Israel.

For Jewish Christ followers it would have been blasphemy to accept Bar Kokhba rather than Jesus as the Messiah. Hence Jewish Christ followers in Judea refused to back the rebellion and some were tortured or killed by the rebels as a result. Arguably, the Jewish Christ followers' refusal to support the revolt and Jewish rebel persecution of Jewish Christ followers widened the divide between what ultimately became two separate religions.[62]

Like many guerrillas throughout history, the rebels based their revolt among civilians. From the Viet Cong guerrilla fighters in South Vietnam

(1950s to 1975) to the Shining Path revolutionaries in 1980s and '90s Peru to Hamas more recently, a similar pattern is found. One difference is that the Bar Kokhba rebels focused their attacks on Roman soldiers and not civilians. But by living and fighting among Jewish civilians in rural villages, the rebels maximized the ability to surprise the Romans. Unfortunately, they also maximized Roman willingness to bring the war home to the civilian population of Judea. Was anyone innocent when ordinary people allowed rebels to operate in their midst? So, the Romans might have asked themselves. Rome faced few inhibitions about killing civilians, and it did so with abandon.[63]

Betar

Betar has the same resonance for the Bar Kokhba Revolt as Masada does for the Great Revolt. Although not as famous outside Israel as Masada, Betar, too, signifies Jewish resolve. It was the place where Bar Kokhba made his last stand. It is not surprising that, in modern times, Betar has become the name of several Israeli sports teams as well as of Zionist youth groups.

The ancient sources describe Betar as "a very strongly fortified small city not far from Jerusalem."[64] It was the revolt's last stronghold after the Romans had captured Herodium and En Gedi.

The road to Betar from Jerusalem winds for 5 miles (8 kilometers) through the Judean Hills along the valley of Nahal Refaim, a stream whose name refers to ghosts or giants. The rebels never got closer to the Holy City. Betar occupies a strategic point. It sits on a steep hill that overlooks not only the Nahal Refaim but also the valley of Nahal Sorek running westward to the Mediterranean coast.[65]

Archaeology demonstrates that ancient Betar lies next to the modern Palestinian Arab town of Battir, on a tel (that is, a mound built over several centuries of occupation) called Khirbet el-Yahud, "Ruin of the Jews." The excavators found fortifications, underground halls, and a few significant artifacts such as slingstones and a stone projectile. They might have found more such objects, but the site has been extensively looted for over a century. The

Right: SHAMI STATUE. This imposing bronze statue depicts a Parthian prince or nobleman. He wears the typical clothes of a high-ranking Parthian horseman, including a headband—perhaps made of metal bands—and a torque decorated with a jewel.

Below: HEROD'S PALACE. The reconstructed pillars mark the site of King Herod the Great's palace in Caesarea-by-the-Sea, the new port that he constructed on Judea's Mediterranean coast, which he named for the emperor Caesar Augustus.

3.

Above: TEMPLE OF AUGUSTUS. These enormous stones are part of the ruins of a grand temple to the emperor Augustus built by Herod the Great ca. 20 BCE. Located at the foot of Mount Hermon, the temple enjoyed a prominent position on the road to Syria.

4.

Left: TOMB OF QUEEN HELENA. The façade of this once-magnificent monument, outside the walls of first-century Jerusalem, fronted a structure originally topped by three small pyramids. Queen Helena of Adiabene and the other members of the royal family who had converted to Judaism were buried here.

5.

Above: SHEKEL OF ISRAEL. This silver coin, issued by the Jewish rebels in 66–67 CE, bears the image of a chalice and the inscriptions "Y(ear) 1 (of Independence)" and "Shekel of Israel." The reference to "Israel" rather than "Judea" as well as the use of Hebrew rather than Aramaic are signs of nationalism.

6.

Right: SIGNS OF ROMAN DESTRUCTION. These stones lie at the foot of the Western Wall, the retaining wall built to support the massive platform on which Herod constructed the Temple and its surrounding porticos. The stones were flung from above by the Romans after they destroyed the Temple complex in 70 CE.

7.

8.

9.

10.

11.

Above: VOLOGASES The silver coin depicts Vologases I (r. ca. 51–79 CE), shown in profile on the obverse and sitting on his throne with a bow on the reverse. One of Parthia's more successful rulers, Vologases took back control of Armenia from Rome, while declining to support the rebels in Judea during the Great Revolt.

Left: TRIUMPH. This gold coin depicts the emperor Vespasian on the obverse and a scene from the triumphal procession in Rome in 71 CE on the reverse to celebrate victory in Judea. The emperor stands in his chariot on the left, and on the far right walks a bound captive, possibly the Jewish prisoner Simon son of Giora, in Roman eyes the leader of the revolt.

Below: IUDAEA CAPTA. This bronze coin shows the emperor Titus on the obverse and proclaims on the reverse that "Judea has been vanquished." A Roman soldier (Titus?) stands over a seated, mourning woman, representing defeated Judea. The palm tree in the center also symbolizes Judea, which was famous for its date palms.

12.

Above: ARCH OF TITUS RELIEF. This sculpted relief was carved on an interior panel of the triumphal arch in Rome that honored the conqueror of Jerusalem. The relief shows the seven-branched candelabra, or menorah, being carried in the triumphal parade celebrated in Rome in 71 CE.

Below: COLOSSEUM. Also known as the Flavian Amphitheater, this iconic monument was built by Vespasian and Titus and opened in 81 CE. The Colosseum served as a monument to the new dynasty's victory in Judea. It was funded in part by war booty.

13.

14.

Above: MASADA. A bird's-eye view of the diamond-shaped fortress beside the Dead Sea that faced a Roman siege in 74 CE. The rebels, more than 900 in number, chose to kill one another rather than be captured and enslaved by the Romans—an event of mythic importance in Israel today.

Below: TRAJAN. This gold coin of the Roman emperor Trajan (r. 98–117) acclaims him as the conqueror of Parthia, whose defeat is celebrated on the reverse, where Parthian captives sit beside captured weapons. It was a premature claim of victory, since a rebellion cost Rome all of its Parthian conquests.

15.

16.

Left: BAR KOKHBA REBEL COIN. This silver coin, issued by Jewish rebels in 134–135, shows a façade of the Temple of Jerusalem on the obverse and the "four species"—palm branch, myrtle, willow, and citron (still used in Jewish ritual today)—on the reverse. The inscriptions in Hebrew proclaim the name "Shimon," a reference to Bar Kokhba, and call "For the Freedom of Jerusalem." Note the overstrike of an earlier Roman coin.

17.

18.

Below: HORVAT 'ETHRI. The town, whose excavated ruins are shown here, lay in the foothills of the Judean Mountains. The Romans destroyed it when it harbored rebels during the Bar Kokhba Revolt (132–136).

19.

Left: HADRIAN. This bronze statue of the emperor Hadrian (r. 117–138) was discovered in the ruins of a Roman army camp in northern Israel. It shows the emperor in a military breastplate, appropriate for the ruler whose generals put down the revolt of Bar Kokhba (132–136).

20.

Right: MEDALLION. This unique gold medallion, decorated with a menorah, was discovered along with a hoard of coins at the foot of the Temple Mount in Jerusalem. According to one theory, the hoard comes from the hopeful period after 614 when the Persians allowed the Jews to return to Jerusalem, only to be buried when the Jews were expelled again soon afterward.

tel lies on a hilltop about 500 feet (150 meters) above the Nahal Refaim and about 2,300 feet (700 meters) above sea level. It is surrounded by the valley on three sides, and the rebels dug a deep moat on the fourth side to cut the site off. A spring provides plenty of water. In short, Betar was a promising spot for the defenders. But the Romans were coming.

The Romans laid siege to Betar in their usual, methodical manner. They built five army camps and forts that commanded the neighboring hills. They surrounded Betar with a 2.5-mile-long (4-kilometer-long) siege wall. They built an assault ramp and filled in the moat. Depending on how many camps were in use at one time, somewhere between 8,000 and 12,000 Roman soldiers took part in the siege.

Eusebius offers a few, scant details:

> The siege lasted a long time before the rebels were driven to final destruction by famine and thirst. . . .[66]

Rabbinic sources say more about the suffering of the siege, if somewhat poetically and in ways that emphasize the horror. One offers the detail that sixty fighters were killed while trying to break through the siege wall. Although not one of them was ever found, their wives were permitted to remarry.[67] Rabbinic sources sometimes exaggerate. When the Romans broke through, the sources say, there was so much blood that it immersed a horse up to its nose; so much blood that it moved heavy rocks and stained the sea (about fifty miles away). Three hundred children's brains were found on one stone. A great rabbi later said that he had been a schoolchild in Betar at the time of the siege. Of a supposed 250,000 or more (!) schoolchildren there, he alone survived.[68]

Dio states succinctly the impact of Roman tactics on the rebel army:

> Very few of them in fact survived.[69]

Bar Kokhba himself was killed. No surviving sources offer a balanced view of the man who raised the banner of freedom so high or so dangerously.

Instead, there is only venom. "The instigator of their madness paid the penalty he deserved," wrote Eusebius.[70] A rabbinic text says that Bar Kokhba was killed by a snakebite—and the city fell—as divine punishment for his execution of a rabbi, whose prayers and fasting alone had preserved Betar. When Hadrian heard the news of how the rebel leader had died, he supposedly commented that God alone could have killed Bar Kokhba.[71]

Rabbinic tradition says that Betar fell on the ninth of Av (roughly, August), the same date that the First and Second Temples were destroyed.[72] Modern scholars accept the summer of 135 as the date of Betar's capture. But the revolt was not quite over.

Surviving rebel commanders and administrators and their families fled to caves, at least some of which had been prepared in advance as refuges. Over thirty such caves have been found in the Judean Desert, with a smaller number in the Judean Hills. Together they have yielded many artifacts, among them: coins, documents, pottery, jewelry, mirrors, cosmetics, sandals, and textiles (preserved in the arid climate). In some of the caves, archaeologists found bronze keys. These presumably belonged to the homes that refugees hoped in vain to return to.

One of the refugees was Babatha. Her co-wife's brother, it seems, was no less a person than Bar Kokhba's commander in En Gedi, and he brought Babatha along with other family members to a cave about 3.5 miles from town.[73] Babatha's fate is unknown, but considering that she never retrieved her valuable documents, she probably did not survive her refuge. More than twenty skeletons have been found in the cave. One of them might have been hers. They were the victims either of starvation or thirst or of Roman attack.

And the Romans did attack. Babatha's cave is located on the side of a cliff and hard to access. But a Roman siege camp has been excavated above it, large enough for an estimated eighty to one hundred soldiers. Good luck to refugees who tried to escape them. Arrowheads discovered embedded in the ceilings of some of the caves may point to Roman invaders. Elsewhere, the Romans may have lit fires below the caves to suffocate the defenders. An educated guess is that the Romans discovered half of the refuge caves and killed most of the people in them.[74] Not until 136 did the Romans succeed in repressing the remaining rebels. Even then there were still sporadic outbursts that continued after Hadrian's death in 138 and into the reign of the next emperor, Antoninus Pius.

The Wages of Defeat

To the Romans went the spoils. Even though Hadrian may never have been physically present in Judea during the revolt, the emperor received recognition for success. Hadrian took the title of imperator, "victorious general," for only the second time in his reign. He was rewarded with a monument in Rome and a triumphal arch in Aelia Capitolina. His leading generals, Julius Severus and the governors of Syria and Roman Arabia, each obtained Rome's highest military honor, triumphal insignia, the ornamenta triumphalia.

For Jews the consequences of the Bar Kokhba War were horrendous, and far worse than the results of the Great Revolt. Eusebius paints a picture of extreme repression:

> He [the Roman governor] destroyed in heaps thousands of men, women, and children, and, under the law of war, enslaved their land.[75]

Dio describes the results of the war as follows:

> Fifty of their most important outposts and nine hundred and eighty-five of their most famous villages were razed to the ground. Five hundred and eighty thousand men were slain in the various raids and battles, and the number of those that perished by famine, disease and fire was past finding out. Thus nearly the whole of Judaea was made desolate. . . .[76]

Ancient historians didn't mind a tall tale or two, and Roman generals thought nothing of inflating their body counts. Nonetheless, archaeological surveys of sites in Israel suggests that Dio's horrendous figures are roughly accurate.[77]

The picture fits the famous description of Rome's extreme pacification policy: "They make a desert and call it peace."[78] Tacitus put these words in the mouth of a Caledonian (Scottish) rebel, but many other peoples in the legions' long path of destruction could have nodded in agreement. Rome preferred, as we might say nowadays, to win the hearts and minds of the conquered nations or at least of their elites; Rome didn't pay much attention to ordinary folk. But make no mistake about it: repeat offenders would be ground into dust. So much for counterinsurgency as public diplomacy, to refer to a contemporary concept. When pushed to the wall, the Romans were ready to pile up skulls in the manner of the Assyrians.

In addition to a massive number of deaths, very many Jewish survivors were enslaved. A Christian source says that there were so many captives that the price of a slave dropped to the mere cost of a day's feed for a horse.[79]

Galilee, which played only a small part in the war, remained largely untouched. The Romans drove most Jews out of their historic homeland in the region of Judah, the central part of the province of Judea, and into Galilee, a northern region. For centuries afterward Galilee became the center of Jewish life in what had been the province. Jewish life also recovered on the edges of Judah, for example, in the city of Lydda. Lydda became a hub of Jewish life and was known for its sages. But in the heart of Judah, the region whose crown had been Jerusalem, the region that gave its name both to the country as a whole and to its people—for "Jew" is derived from the Latin *Iudaeus*, Greek *Ioudaios*, or Hebrew *Yehudi*—the heart of Judah was now largely without Jews.

Aelia Capitolina, which rose over the ruins of Jerusalem, was closed to Jews. If Christian sources are accurate, Jews were forbidden to enter the city, much less worship or live there, except for one day of the year: the ninth of the month of Av. Only on this day that marked the destruction of the Temple were Jews allowed to enter the former Jerusalem and mourn at the Western Wall.

After the revolt Hadrian changed the name of the province of Judea to Syria Palaestina, from which the name Palestine comes. Rome changed the names of other provinces, but never to punish a rebellion. This is the only known case.[80] As one scholar puts it, "Judea was air-brushed out of the map of Roman provinces."[81]

The name "Palestine" is ultimately derived from the Philistines, invaders from the Aegean and Cyprus in twelfth century BCE who intermarried with Canaanites and formed a series of kingdoms on the coast of what is now Gaza and southern Israel. Egyptians, Assyrians, and the Hebrew Bible each used a variant of "Philistine" to refer to the land of the Philistines. Palestine was not a new name, but it was not a name used by Jews, who referred to their country as Judea, the Land of Israel, or simply Israel. It was, however, a name used by Greeks. Greek authors such as Herodotus or Aristotle used the name "Palestine" to refer to Canaan more broadly. One historian suggests that it was the Greek inhabitants of Judea who lobbied Hadrian to change the name.[82] The bad blood between Greeks and Jews in the Eastern Mediterranean was well known. So was Hadrian's philhellenism. If the name change from Judea to Syria Palaestina wasn't his idea, he might well have approved it with pleasure.

Circumstantial evidence suggests that Greeks in Syria Palaestina and around the Eastern Mediterranean hailed Hadrian's victory over Bar Kokhba. Only one Greek author says so explicitly in his surviving work. Pausanias, the celebrated second century CE author of the *Guide to Greece*, wrote that Hadrian "never voluntarily entered upon a war, but he reduced the Hebrews beyond Syria, who had rebelled."[83] But a uniquely large number of Greek writers penned paeans to Hadrian, and perhaps they included praise of his great military success, the war against the Jewish rebels.[84] In the mixed Greek-Jewish cities of Tiberias and Caesarea, temples of Hadrian were erected, while Gaza, with its similar population, sponsored a Festival of Hadrian. None of these events is securely dated, but they might represent thank-you gifts to the emperor for crushing the Jewish revolt.[85] By the reign of Hadrian's successor, the city of Sepphoris was renamed Diocaesarea, Greek for "Zeus Caesar," a name honoring both the chief pagan god and the Roman emperor.

As a result of the revolt the Romans persecuted Jews, at least in Judea. Tradition attributes the persecution to Hadrian, but perhaps it was work of the provincial governor or individual Roman commanders on the ground.

Observance of the Sabbath, teaching of the Torah, and circumcision were prohibited. Sages were persecuted, among them Rabbi Akiva, Bar Kokhba's supporter. He was arrested for openly teaching the Torah, condemned, and tortured to death. Hadrianic persecution includes the tradition of the Ten Martyrs, sages who were killed for their faith by the Romans. They are recalled to this day as part of the liturgy of the annual Day of Atonement (Yom Kippur). Scholars judge at least some of the details of the persecutions to be legendary. But there were some restrictions. Fortunately for the Jews, the restrictions were lifted in the reign of Hadrian's successor, Antoninus Pius. Still, Jews remembered even part of Pius's reign as the era of "the Danger."[86]

It is no wonder that the rabbinic tradition cursed Hadrian, saying of him, "May his bones rot!" Of Bar Kokhba, the rabbis were not complimentary, but that was in retrospect. At the time, he is likely to have had support from some rabbis including prominent ones, as the sources show. But the rabbinic movement was still in its early stages in the early second century. In many ways, Jewish society was living on the capital of the previous two centuries.

It was still a society that wanted vengeance on the Romans, still a society that expected the imminent arrival of the messiah, still a society that looked to pick up the fallen sword of the Maccabees. It was not yet clear that Jews would bow to the reality of Roman rule and that, in place of a martial ethos, Judaism would turn inward into the territory of the spirit.

The prophet Jeremiah (31:15) described the voice of Rachel weeping for her children as they were sent into captivity. Writing around 400, Jerome, the Christian scholar, returned to the image of Rachel weeping, this time for enslaved Jews as they were led off from their homeland after the Bar Kokhba Revolt.[87] And tears there might have been for the failure that the revolt represented. Could the revolt ever have succeeded? Given the brutal determination of the Romans, rebellion in 132 was a roll of the dice, even after Rome's humiliating defeat against Parthia, even after years of preparation by the insurgents. In antiquity as today, some criticized Bar Kokhba as a fool who led his country to almost certain ruin. But weeping wasn't the only response. Some gritted their teeth and continued to dream of independence.

Some even dared to hope for salvation, at long last, from the far side of the Euphrates River, where there were Jewish brethren and the horsemen of the Parthian king.

The Romans believed they had stamped out the last embers of Jewish revolt. Ruin awaited rebellion: so the legions had drummed into the heads of the Jews with their "incessant revolutionary spirit," as Vespasian once called it.[88] The Jews became good Romans in the end, but only after generations of shedding their own blood and the blood of the legions. The survivors were pacified, at least for the most part. What was left was, in the main, warriors of the spirit and lions of the soul, but Judea, or rather what was now Syria Palaestina, ceased posing a major military threat to Rome.

The rabbis, who knew their countrymen best, believed that the message of Rome's invincible military needed to be repeated often—and better in words than in iron. The rabbis argued against any thought of taking up the sword again. The Jewish nation, as they saw it, would be a kingdom of the spirit. After the failure of Bar Kokhba, the rabbis would come into their own as the leaders of their people. They did everything they could to put the Jewish rebel spirit to sleep. But it woke up again.

EPILOGUE

Tradition holds that he was born around 135 on the day that Rabbi Akiva was martyred by the Romans. Rabbi Yehuda Ha-Nasi, Judah the Prince, went on to have one of the most consequential of Jewish lives. It was with Rabbi Judah, and with other rabbis like him, that the future of the Jewish people lay.

The rabbis gave Jews the tools they needed to survive as a nation. The rabbis shaped a culture whose hallmark was resilience. The irony is that the rabbis proved to be better strategists than the warriors who had led three major Jewish revolts against Rome. The rabbis understood, as the rebels did not, that armed resistance against the Roman Empire was futile. But maybe the rabbis had to live through the rebellions to reach this conclusion.

The rabbis, the priests, and, above all, the ordinary people of Israel had the courage to survive as a nation.[1] Did they do so because of men like Simon son of Giora, Eleazar son of Yair, and Bar Kokhba, or despite them? Did the revolts fire the soul of a people or did they demonstrate what not to do?

Around the year 200, Rabbi Judah and his students compiled the Mishnah, a collection of Jewish oral traditions and one of the foundations of Judaism ever since. If Orthodox Judaism today has much in common with the Judaism of the rabbis, it is in large part thanks to the Mishnah. From the Mishnah there sprang that other fundamental Jewish text, the Talmud. Or rather, Talmuds, since both a Palestinian, also known as Jerusalem (ca. 400), and Babylonian (ca. 500) version of the Talmud exist. Organized as a commentary on the Mishnah, the Talmud is a collection of legal opinions, stories, and traditions by the rabbis. It is one of the most influential of all Jewish texts, and it goes back to the work of Rabbi Judah. He was so significant that he is often referred to simply as Rabbi.

Rabbi Judah was also a political leader who marked a new era in Roman-Jewish relations. The Romans probably appointed him as the first Jewish Patriarch. The Patriarch became the chief Jewish official both in Palestine and the Diaspora.[2] Rabbi Judah was a wealthy man who came from a long line of sages, a member of the elite, precisely the kind of local intermediary that the Romans liked to do business with. He lived in Galilee, in Diocaesarea (Sepphoris), but as an administrator and judge, he had power over the Jewish communities in other parts of the country as well as influence with the Jews in the Parthian Empire. Some considered his status almost royal.[3] Clearly, the Romans trusted him a great deal.

What a change from the era of revolts between 66 and 136! How did it happen? On the one hand, a new leadership arose in Palestine that accepted the inevitability of Roman rule and that was willing to do business with Rome. In a sense, it was a return to the days of the Second Temple and the pro-Roman Jewish aristocracy. On the other hand, a new dynasty took power in Rome after a civil war. They were the Severans (r. 193–235). With roots in Africa and Syria as well as Italy, they were Rome's most diverse and inclusive dynasty, to put it into contemporary terms. They reached out to indigenous peoples around the empire, including the Jews of Palestine. Caracalla (r. 211–217) made all free people in the empire Roman citizens, a milestone in constitutional history, even if motivated by a desire to expand the tax base. Rabbi Judah had a warm relationship with one of the emperors, rabbinic sources say, probably Caracalla.

Not that either Jews or Romans trusted each other completely. The Romans continued their military occupation of the Jewish homeland, now called Palestine. The legions remained suspicious of the Jewish inhabitants. For example, when the Romans built a road in 161 to 162 across the southern Gaulanitis eastward into Syria, they bypassed the Jewish villages. It was thirty years after Bar Kokhba, and the Gaulanitis region had played little or no part in the revolt, but the Romans remained wary. A century later they built three watchtowers on the road, arguably as a security measure against the locals.[4] The Romans continued to levy the *fiscus iudaicus*, the special tax on all Jews in the empire. It existed at least as late as the mid-third century, over a hundred years after Bar Kokhba.[5]

Rabbi Judah opposed any renewal of war with the Romans. A rabbi of a later generation stated this position clearly. Rabbi Yosei, son of Rabbi Hanina (second half of the third century), said that God had administered an oath to the nations of the world not to impose a harsh yoke on Israel and an oath to Israel not to rebel against the nations.[6]

Rabbi Judah advocated spiritual resistance. The Good Lord had, for His own reasons, put Rome in charge. As a result, it was incumbent to behave properly, even humbly, toward the ruling power. For example, the story is told that the rabbi asked one of his followers to write a letter in his name to the emperor. He wrote, "From Judah the Prince to our master, Emperor Antoninus." Rabbi Judah took the letter, read it, and tore it up. "Write," he said, "'From your servant, Judah, to our master, Emperor Antoninus.'"[7] Modeling himself on the humility that Jacob displayed in front of his violent brother, Esau, the great rabbi displayed a meek and unpretentious demeanor to the autocrat of the Roman world.

For all that, Rabbi Judah believed that Roman rule was temporary and doomed to fail. He is reported to have said that Rome was destined to fall into the hands of Persia.[8] When his son said that he was impressed by Rome's legionaries at Caesarea, Rabbi Judah replied that they were less than flies; in fact, they were nothing in the eyes of the Lord.[9] The rabbi never doubted the validity of the eternal covenant between God and the Jewish people. In His own good time, God would bring the redemption and return the

Promised Land to its rightful owner. In the meantime, the Jews would have to be patient.[10] In short, Rabbi Judah waged war against the Romans by other means.

The term *nasi*, "prince," had messianic connotations. "If the Messiah is among the living in this generation, he is a person such as our holy Rabbi," said one of his students.[11] But unlike Bar Kokhba, who also called himself *nasi*, Rabbi Judah neither claimed to save the Jews from the Romans nor to usher in the redemption. After the Bar Kokhba Revolt, the Jews came around to the idea that although the messiah would surely come, he might well tarry. The apocalyptic visions of the previous centuries began to fade, to be replaced by a deep spirituality focused on the here and now.

The Jews did not give up their commitment to what they called the Land of Israel. They merely changed tactics. They would no longer make war on the Roman Empire. But there were exceptions.

It was a turbulent period for the Roman Empire. If an observer from Rabbi Judah's era was transported to 351 or 352, he or she might have reeled at the changes. Rome now faced so many security problems, east and west, that the emperor shared power either with a co-emperor or with a sub-emperor. The emperor was styled Augustus and the sub-emperor Caesar. In addition to Rome, the empire had a second capital in the east, Constantinople (modern Istanbul). Perhaps most striking, the empire was no longer pagan. Beginning with Constantine (r. 313–337), the emperors were Christian and they began a century-long process of Christianizing the entire population. The one exception was Julian (r. 361–363), a Christian emperor who reverted to paganism. Julian gave the Jews permission to rebuild the Temple in Jerusalem, an offer that some took up with enthusiasm. But the project came to naught because of Julian's untimely death at the age of thirty-two.

The Christian empire took an interest in Palestine, which they thought of as the Holy Land. The emperors built churches and monasteries there and encouraged Christian pilgrims and immigrants. Aelia Capitolina, as Jerusalem was still called, became a showplace for the faith, with the Church of the Holy Sepulcher, built on the site of the Crucifixion, its centerpiece. The city would soon become the most sacred spot in Christendom. Jews in Palestine were tolerated, but not encouraged. Relations between the two monotheistic faiths in Palestine were generally peaceful, but tensions existed and sometimes broke out into violence. Constantine and Constantine II (r. 337–361) each passed anti-Jewish legislation aimed at encouraging conversion to Christianity and limiting Jewish freedom.

For all the changes in the Roman Empire, in one way it hadn't changed at all: it was still all about war. The main enemy continued to be an Iranian dynasty, but not the Parthians. A new dynasty, the Sasanians, ousted the Parthians in 224 and created a more aggressive, more formidable military power than its predecessor. In the mid-third century the Sasanians invaded Syria and Asia Minor and defeated and captured a Roman emperor. Then, toward the end of the century, the Romans pushed the Sasanians back and forced them to agree to humiliating peace terms. But in the fourth century the Sasanians were on the march again, led by their aggressive and long-reigning King Shapur II (r. 309–379). He was destined to be one of Iran's greatest monarchs. Shapur went on the attack in 337 and defeated the Romans in battle after battle. But in the end, he gained no new territory. In 350, Shapur had to turn eastward and deal with threats from Central Asia, but the Romans expected him to return. And he did, in a new war beginning in 358. In the same decade, in the Roman West, the emperor, Constantius II (r. 337–361), had to battle a usurper from 350 to 353. These were tough times for the empire.

With storms raging around it, Jewish Palestine opened an insurgency. Sometime during the year that ran from September 351 to September 352, violence broke out again among the Jews there. The event is called the Gallus Revolt.[12] In 351, Constantius Gallus took office as the imperial Caesar, the sub-emperor, in the Roman East, based in Antioch. It fell to him to arrange for the suppression of the insurgency in Palestine. The details, unfortunately, are murky.

Jewish sources say nothing about the revolt, unlike the previous rebellions. The sources do suggest that Gallus gave the job of suppressing it to his chief general, Ursicinus. At least that's what a reader might glean from rabbinic texts, although they don't quite say that. They indicate that Ursicinus sent troops to Palestine, but perhaps only to take part in a police action or to collect taxes.[13] The closest the sources come to making those soldiers into counterinsurgents is the statement that the Roman troops hunted Jewish men in Diocaesarea; the men in turn disguised themselves with heavy bandages on their noses. (How such a disguise might work is a good question.) Far from advocating revolt, the rabbis urged the Jews to cooperate with Ursicinus's soldiers, even if it meant desecrating the Sabbath or even Passover to bake bread.[14] That's all the rabbis report. For details of the uprising, it is necessary to go to one pagan and two Christian sources.

Our best source is Sextus Aurelius Victor and his book *On the Caesars* (*De Caesaribus*), which he wrote circa 360, that is, less than a decade after the Gallus Revolt. A high-ranking official in both Rome and the provinces, Victor was well-informed. His book is short and terse. After discussing the civil war in the West, he devotes one sentence to the Gallus Revolt:

> And meanwhile, an insurrection (*seditio*) of the Jews, who had raised Patricius against all law to a kind of royal position.[15]

Victor calls the revolt *seditio*, which means "sedition," "uprising," "insurrection," "riot," or "civil discord." No less important is what he *doesn't* call it, and that is *bellum*, which means "war." The sources use *bellum* to characterize both the Great Revolt and the Bar Kokhba Revolt. The Gallus Revolt was serious, but it was not a full-blown war.

Who was Patricius? He might have been a Jew, as Patricius is attested as a Jewish name in Palestine. One Patricius was a donor to a synagogue in Gaulanitis, for example.[16] The phrase "a kind of royal position" is reminiscent of King Messiah. Does this point to the survival of messianic hopes among Jews? But if so, why do the rabbis, who strongly opposed such sentiments, not comment on the Gallus Revolt? Another suggestion is that Patricius was a Roman, and that "against all law" refers to an illegitimate claim to the purple. But in that case, why did he not gain the support of one of Palestine's legions? In either case, it is unclear why the Jews followed a leader into an uprising. Scholars have offered various suggestions, among them: bitterness at anti-Jewish laws passed by the Christian emperors, economic distress, hope that the Roman Empire was weak, hope that the Persians would come and help the rebels. Those anti-Jewish laws existed but had little bite; the economy in Palestine seems to have been prosperous; and the Persians were busy with trouble on their eastern border. Another possibility is a tax revolt, but taxes were high everywhere that Rome ruled.

Victor was a pagan. Christian sources also mention the Gallus Revolt, of which the most important is Jerome. He was writing in Constantinople circa 380, so about thirty years later. He wrote:

Gallus suppressed the Jews, who had killed soldiers by night and captured weapons for a revolt. Many thousand people were killed, even harmless children; and their cities of Diocaesarea, Tiberias and Diospolis, as well as countless villages, he gave over to the flames.[17]

Jerome indicates that the insurgents attacked at night, killed Roman soldiers, and captured their weapons. It sounds like they used guerrilla tactics that went back to the Maccabees. The Jews were as nimble warriors as ever. Jerome also states that Rome's repression was brutal, leading to thousands of deaths including children. That would have been nothing new on Rome's part. The centers of the revolt, according to Jerome, were two cities in Galilee, Diocaesarea and Tiberias, as well as a city in southern Palestine, Diospolis—"Zeus City"—as Lydda had been renamed in Greek. The Romans burned these cities as well as numerous villages.

Another Christian writer, Socrates Scholasticus, who lived in Constantinople in the fifth century, essentially restates Jerome's points. A Christian writer in the ninth century, Theophanes, adds the detail that the insurgents attacked Greeks and Samaritans. He also claims that the Roman army destroyed the entire Jewish people and annihilated Diocaesarea.[18] The last points are clear exaggeration.

Archaeology has found evidence of destruction or abandonment in cities and villages in Galilee and Gaulanitis in this period. Whether the cause was Roman brutality or some other reason or reasons is uncertain. There was a major earthquake in 363, and that may also have been a factor.

A potentially exciting archaeological discovery was announced in June 2024. The excavators found a major public building in Lod, Israel—Diospolis. Coins show that the building dates to the period of the Gallus Revolt. The ruins include inscriptions in Greek, Latin, and Hebrew, including a reference to a Jew from a priestly family. No pig bones were present, meaning that the residents may have kept kosher. The archaeologists concluded that they had found a Jewish building, perhaps a center of the rabbis who Diospolis was famous for. It may have been a synagogue, a study hall, a meeting house, or all three. The building had been destroyed down to its foundations. Underneath the floor, the excavators discovered a cache of ninety-four coins. They posit that the coins were left by a person or persons who fled the Romans and hoped to come back to retrieve their money.[19]

The coins are all Roman, not Jewish. Unlike the rebels of the Great Revolt or Bar Kokhba Revolt, the men of 351 to 352 issued no coinage. And that brings us back to the nature of the Gallus Revolt. It hasn't revealed all its mysteries and perhaps never will.

Aggrieved Jews might have joined the mysterious Patricius in stealing Roman weapons and spreading the fire of insurgency from city to village. They did damage, but not for long. This revolt was a small matter, but it left scars on the Jewish landscape and corpses in the Jewish earth. Nor should anyone doubt the continuing presence of potential rebels in the Jewish population of Palestine. The events of one last spasm of violence, nearly three centuries later, prove that.

In 614, the Persians finally came back to the Land of Israel, as the Jews continued to call Roman Palestine. More than six centuries had gone by since the last Persian invasion under Pacorus in 40 BCE. Despite all the changes since then, Jews still looked toward Persia with hope. A great rabbi of the second century is said to have taught:

> If you see a Persian horse tied to a grave in the Land of Israel, anticipate the footsteps of the Messiah.[20]

The Persian invasion of Palestine in 614 was a small campaign in a great war, what one historian calls the last great war of antiquity.[21] A combination of ambition and opportunity, of Sasanian power lust and Byzantine weakness, sparked the decades-long conflict.

In 395, the Roman Empire had been divided for good between east and west. Each part of the empire faced a continual threat of invasion. The West failed. In 476, the West finally succumbed to German conquerors. The East prevailed for another millennium, all the way to 1453, known today as the Eastern Roman or Byzantine Empire. The long struggle between Rome and Persia went back to the first century BCE. The opposing forces now were the Byzantines and the Sasanians, but the framework of the conflict remained the same. And the Jews were caught in the middle.

The Sasanian king was Khosrow II (r. 590–628), one of the great figures in Persian history. The invasion, led by one of Khosrow II's generals, entered Palestine from the north. A prominent Jew of Tiberias named Benjamin is said to have negotiated with the invaders and secured Jewish support. There was still a large Jewish community in the Persian Empire, primarily in Mesopotamia. The Sasanians were far more tolerant of Jews than were the Byzantines. Hence, it is not surprising that Jewish military aid for Persia materialized—twenty thousand men, according to Christian sources, although those sources are biased and tend to exaggeration. But we are dependent upon Christian sources for the narrative, since Jewish sources are silent on the subject. In addition to supporting the Persians, Jews attacked churches, according to Christian sources. Although the reports are probably exaggerated, there may be some truth in them, a tit for tat in the lamentable history of Christian attacks on synagogues.

At first the invaders settled in Caesarea and hoped to avoid a campaign against Aelia Capitolina. The Christian patriarch, in Aelia, agreed to cooperate but, shortly after Easter, mobs in the city killed Persian ambassadors and launched a massacre of the city's Jews. The Sasanians, therefore, decided to attack Aelia. They marched to the city and laid siege. They took Aelia after three weeks and went on a rampage. With Jewish help in pointing out the guilty, the Sasanians executed the ringleaders of the killings. They also deported the city's Christian elite, including the Christian patriarch.

During the next two years, Jewish immigrants returned to Aelia. It was the greatest period of freedom for Jews in the city since the destruction of the Temple in 70. All the same, they ran into constant opposition from the city's Christian majority, which posed a political problem for the Sasanians. The Persian Empire had not only a large Jewish minority but a large Christian one. Furthermore, the Persians now ruled over a Christian population in the Byzantine territories that they had conquered. Most Persians were Zoroastrians. They engaged in a continual balancing act among their religious minorities. The Sasanians' main goal in Jerusalem was not to help the Jews but to maintain order. Empires do not have friends; they have interests. In 616, therefore, the Sasanians expelled all Jews who had immigrated to Jerusalem in the previous two years. That, unfortunately for the Jews, was only the beginning of their disappointment.

The tide of war turned dramatically. The Byzantines beat back the Sasanians. At the height of his power, Khosrow II lost the war and then, in 628, was deposed in a coup and was finally executed. In 630, the Byzantine emperor, Heraclius (r. 610–641), entered Aelia in triumph, carrying with him a priceless relic. The Sasanians had carried off the cross on which Jesus had been crucified to Mesopotamia; Heraclius now returned it. The Byzantines' return was bad news for the Jews. At first Heraclius promised to let bygones be bygones, but he faced pressure to punish the Jews from churchmen and the mob in Aelia. The emperor condemned many Jews to death. Then he instituted a period of forced conversion, beginning with Benjamin of Tiberias, that prominent backer of the Sasanians. Benjamin accepted baptism in the house of a Christian. Heraclius forbade any Jews from living in Aelia or within a three-mile radius of it.

Harsh terms indeed, but they did not last. In a few short years, a veritable explosion came from the south: Islam. The warriors of the fiery new faith defeated both Byzantine and Persian armies. They conquered the Sasanian empire and much of the Byzantine empire. Arab Muslim warriors siezed Palestine; they took Aelia in 638. The new rulers allowed the Jews to return to the city. Jews and Christians were tolerated as "People of the Book," that is, the Bible. They lived under restrictions, penalties, and humiliations, but they were allowed to practice their faith. The same was true for the communities in Mesopotamia. For the Jews, as important as the community in Galilee was, the one in Babylon, as the Jews called southern Mesopotamia, turned out to be even more so. Babylon became a center of Jewish culture. Having survived and thrived under Parthian rule, it continued to do so under the succeeding dynasties. It was a new era, and a story for another day.

Why did the Jews rebel so often? What made them different from other peoples of the empire? Roman persecution, especially after the year 70, had a lot to do with it, of course, but so did Jewish qualities. The Jews had a proud military tradition, but so did many if not most of the peoples conquered by Rome. But they had other resources unavailable to any other of Rome's subjects. They had a legacy of messianism that provided charismatic leaders if not always wise ones. They had the Torah and the institutions that made it live. They had a network of supporters in the Roman Diaspora. More important, they had strong connections to Rome's greatest rival in Parthia. These included the Parthian king, the converted rulers of Adiabene, and, most important, the Jewish communities of Mesopotamia. These connections survived the change of dynasty from Parthian to Sasanian.

Military historians are acutely aware of Clausewitz's dictum that war is merely policy "by other means." War is useful only to the extent that it carries out a policy goal. If that goal can be achieved without the risk of war, that is even better. Although it took centuries to make the lesson stick, the Jewish people reached the conclusion that war was not the proper means to ensure national survival. Instead, the nation's leaders, in this case, its rabbis, determined that the Jewish people could survive by means of spiritual rather than material armor. It was a bold strategy, but a necessary one. And it worked. Despite many vicissitudes, despite the threats of persecution, dispersion, and assimilation, the Jewish people has survived for two thousand years since the Roman conquest of its national homeland. Jewish culture remains remarkably similar today to what it was in the Later Roman Empire.

This is a tale of empire and resistance. It is also a story of resilience, an intangible but essential factor. Resilience refers to the strength of a society's sense of its national identity and values. A resilient society has the will to withstand defeat and to recover from it. That, in turn, requires a certain culture, leadership, and set of institutions. In terms of military resistance to Rome, the Jews of ancient Israel suffered defeat after defeat, despite some short-term tactical successes, especially in guerrilla warfare. But in terms of resilience, those same Jews achieved a signal success. Ancient Jewry is one of history's great examples of how a people can lose on the battlefield and yet prevail.

But survival without an army exacts a price. Spiritual armor preserved the Jewish soul, but it left many, many Jewish bodies unprotected. There is no need to delineate the long list of massacres from antiquity to the Crusades to the pogroms to the Holocaust and beyond. Jewish history shows that the spirit is the most important thing, but it is not the only thing. To survive, a people also needs a sword. Not only that: it needs a strategy. The heroism of the rebels against Rome fired the heart even when it didn't save the state. Zionism, the very model of a national liberation movement, has finally achieved what eluded Simon son of Giora and Simon Bar Kokhba.

The leaders of the revolts against Rome are the heroes of a Jewish *Iliad*: they

EPILOGUE

are glorious failures. For Odysseus, the cunning hero who finds his way home, one must go to the rabbis. How do you put the two of them together? How do you combine weapons with wisdom? Odysseus, after all, was a warrior. For the question is not whether to wield a sword, but how to wield it strategically.

Consider a modern postscript to the dramatic events of the 600s. In 2013, a gold medallion was discovered in an excavation, near the southern wall of the Temple Mount in Jerusalem. The medallion is large and striking. It displays a menorah in the center. On one side of the menorah is a ram's horn. On the other side, there is either a Torah scroll or a bundle of palm and myrtle branches. Perhaps the medallion decorated a Torah scroll or was worn by an official on ceremonial occasions. The symbolism suggests hope for the rebuilding of the Temple and the redemption of the Jewish people.

The medallion was found with a hoard of other objects, gold and silver jewelry and thirty-six gold coins. The excavator speculated that the hoard was meant to finance the building of a new synagogue during the hopeful period beginning in 614, when the conquering Persians allowed the Jews to return to Jerusalem. A few years later, the theory goes, someone buried the objects, either when the Persians expelled Jewish newcomers from the city or when the Byzantines were about to return. The people who buried the objects probably hoped to retrieve them when the time was right. In the end, it took almost exactly 1,400 years. The medallion and the objects found with it are now on display in the Israel Museum in Jerusalem.[22]

Today, after two millennia, the Jewish people have reestablished a sovereign state in their ancestral homeland. They kept faith with the promise of Psalm 137 to remember Zion. "If I forget thee, O Jerusalem," the psalmist sings, "let my right hand forget her cunning."[23] The Jews have returned to Jerusalem. Their state prospers, but it struggles to find acceptance by its neighbors. Israel is a small state fighting for its place among much larger states and empires, east and west. Amid so many changes in history, some constants remain.

GLOSSARY OF PLACE NAMES

Adiabene: Ancient kingdom in Mesopotamia, roughly equivalent to the Kurdish region of Iraq
Acre: *See Ptolemaïs*
Anthedon: Port city, located just north of today's port of Gaza
Antipatris: Town in Judea whose ruins are located at Tel Afek, Israel
Apollonopolis Magna: or Edfu, a city in the Nile Valley, north of modern Aswan, Egypt
Arabia Petraea: Roman province comprising most of modern Jordan, most of Sinai Peninsula, and northwestern Arabian peninsula
Arbela: Capital of Adiabene, is modern Erbil, Iraq
Armenia: Ancient kingdom, comprised of roughly today's Armenia plus the easternmost provinces of Turkey
Asia: Roman province, is roughly equivalent to today's western Turkey plus the Greek and Turkish islands off its Aegean coast
Babylonia: Region in Mesopotamia, roughly equivalent to southern Iraq
Bactria: Region roughly equivalent to today's Afghanistan
Batanea: Region in Herod's kingdom, found in what is today the hill country of southern Syria, northeast of the Sea of Galilee
Batavia: Region in today's Netherlands
Berytus: Roman colony, gave its name to Beirut, Lebanon
Betar: Ancient Jewish city lying next to modern Palestinian Arab town of Battir
Carrhae: Town in Mesopotamia, today located in Harran, Turkey
Chalcis: Independent principality, later annexed by Romans, today located in south Lebanon
Cilicia: Region and later Roman province, on Turkey's Mediterranean coast

GLOSSARY OF PLACE NAMES

Cyrenaica: Region, later a Roman province, in northeastern Libya
Cyrene: City in Cyrenaica, located at modern Shahhat in northeastern Libya
Dacia: Kingdom, later province, roughly equivalent to today's Romania
Diocaesarea: *See Sepphoris*
Edessa: City in northern Mesopotamia, today Urfa, Turkey
Edom: A region south and east of the Dead Sea in today's Israel and Jordan
En Gedi: Oasis and town on west bank of the Dead Sea, today in Israel
Gaulanitis: Roughly, the Golan, today in Israel
Giscala: Gush Halav in Hebrew, town in northern Judea, today Jish, Israel
Hatra: City in northern Mesopotamia, located today southwest of Mosul, Iraq
Herodium: Fortress located near Bethlehem, today in the West Bank (Judah)
Idumea: Judean region, south of Judah, now southern Israel to the edge of the Negev Desert
Illyricum: Roman province on the east coast of the Adriatic Sea
Jabneh: City also known as Yabneh or Jamnia, today Yavne, Israel
Joppa: Jaffa, Israel
Jotapata: City also known as Iotapata, the modern Yodfat (or Yodefat), Israel
Kush: Ancient kingdom comprising Upper (southern) Nubia
Lusitania: Roman province roughly equivalent to Portugal
Lydda: City later renamed Diospolis, today Lod, Israel
Machaerus: Fortress near the northern end of the Dead Sea, today in the village of Mukawir, Jordan
Mauretania: Kingdom and then Roman province, located in today's Algeria and Morocco
Mesopotamia: A region, mostly in today's Iraq but extending into parts of Syria and Turkey
Nabatea: Arab kingdom that stretched from southern Syria through Jordan to Israel's Negev Desert, Egypt's Sinai Peninsula, and part of Saudi Arabia
Nisibis: City in Mesopotamia, today Nusaybin, Turkey
Nubia: Ancient region extending roughly from the middle Nile River Valley south to modern Khartoum and from the Red Sea westward to the Libyan Desert
Numidia: Ancient kingdom in northwest Africa with a core in what is today Algeria
Pella: Town in the Perea, located at today's Taqabat Fahl in northwest Jordan
Perea: Greek for "Land Beyond," that is, beyond the River Jordan, a region of the kingdom and then province of Judea that is today in western Jordan
Petra: City in Nabatean kingdom, later Arabia Petra, today in Jordan
Picenum: Today, Le Marche region in central Italy
Ptolemaïs: Port city on Bay of Haifa, later known as Acre, today Akko, Israel

GLOSSARY OF PLACE NAMES

Puteoli: Port city, modern Pozzuoli, Italy

Rhandeia: Site of battle and treaty near Parthian-Roman frontier, today in eastern Turkey

Samaria: Region of kingdom/province of Judea, today in the northern West Bank

Sebaste: A city in Samaria, near today's Nablus, in the northern West Bank

Sepphoris: City, later renamed Diocaesarea by Romans, today's Tzipori, Israel

Spasines' Fort, or Spasinou Charax: Port city at the head of the Persian Gulf in Iraq

Thrace: Kingdom roughly equivalent to today's Bulgaria but also including parts of Greece and Turkey

Urbs Salvia: City, today Urbisaglia, Italy

Yabneh: *See Jabneh*. City also known as Jabneh or Jamnia, today Yavne, Israel

Zeugma-on-the-Euphrates: City, in ancient Syria, today in Turkey

ACKNOWLEDGMENTS

It is a pleasure to thank the many people who helped in the writing of this book. As always, any flaws in the book are my own responsibility.

Olga Litvak, Cornell University, and Jake Nabel, Penn State University, offered invaluable guidance on, respectively, Jewish and Parthian history. Maia Aron generously shared her expertise and knowledge of Israel. She read drafts of the manuscript and offered detailed, discerning, and wise comments, as did Adrienne Mayor, Stanford University; Marcia Mogelonsky; and John Osborn. Simcha Gross, University of Pennsylvania, was kind enough to share drafts of his article on Jewish interconnectivity.

In Israel, several academic colleagues proved generous with their time and expertise. I would like to thank Paula Fredriksen, Hebrew University of Jerusalem; Gil Gambash, University of Haifa; Ariadne Konstantinou, Bar-Ilan University; Jonathan Price, Tel-Aviv University; Daniel R. Schwartz, Hebrew University of Jerusalem; and from Shalem College, Daniel Gordis, Efraim Inbar, Leon Kass, Eran Lerman, and Russell Roberts. I would also like to thank Amos Otza-El of the *Jerusalem Post*. Mordechai Aviam, Kinneret College of the Sea of Galilee, guided me around the site of ancient Jotapata

ACKNOWLEDGMENTS

(Yodfat, Israel), which he excavated. He also generously offered advice on various archaeological and historical matters.

Rabbi Eli Silberstein generously shared his expertise in Jewish texts, as did Rabbi Zalman Levin. Reverend David Kaden, PhD, offered scholarly advice on early Christianity and its Jewish context.

In Israel, several guides provided excellent guidance to ancient sites and museums. I thank Ian Brown, Ze'ev Friedman, Alon Orion, Shlomi Peled, Ovadia Sofer. I would also like to thank Noa Weiss.

In addition, I am grateful to David Berkey, General Shlomi Binder (IDF), Darrell Birton, Dave Blome, Nikki Bonanni, Philippe Boström, Stanley Burstein, Lawrence "Doc" Cohen, Tristan Daedalus, David Dusenbury, Jason Feulner, Giovanni Giorgini, Shawn Alexander Goldsmith, Serhan Güngör, David Guaspari, Chris Harper, John Hyland, Alison Law, Gordon McCormick, Adam Mogelonsky, LeAnn Mae Racoma, Andrew Roberts, Jean-Pierre Stroweis and the late Isabelle Stroweis, and Konstantinos Zachos.

A special thank you to my longtime friend and mentor, Arthur J. Kover (who won't agree with everything I say).

I owe a debt of thanks to two great academic institutions that supported my research. At Cornell University, I am grateful for the help and encouragement of many colleagues, faculty, staff, and students, particularly in the Departments of Classics and History, and to the John M. Olin Library for its superb bibliographical resources and reference librarians. Among those Cornellians are Carol Anne Adams, Omobolanle Joseph Akinniyi, Michael Fontaine, Maria Cristina Garcia, Rick Geddes, Matthew Guillot, Isabel Hull, Sandra Greene, Tamara Loos, Sturt Manning, Michelle Nair, Mary Beth Norton, Catheryn Obern, Jon Parmenter, Eric Rebillard, Rich Robinson, Daniel Schwarz, and Michael Williamson.

The Hoover Institution of Stanford University named me Corliss Page Dean Senior Fellow. Hoover offers a remarkable intellectual environment for the study of history and of military affairs. Senior Fellow Victor Davis Hanson, whom I am privileged to call a friend, is a great leader of Hoover's Military History in Contemporary Conflict Working Group. I would like to thank

ACKNOWLEDGMENTS

him as well as the Tad and Dianne Taube Director & Senior Fellow on Public Policy Condoleezza Rice and Senior Fellows Steven J. Davis, Niall Ferguson, Stephen Kotkin, and Josiah Ober. I would also like to thank Rebekah Mercer and the Mercer Foundation for their generous support.

I have been fortunate to work for years with two superb editors at Simon & Schuster, Bob Bender and Johanna Li. Their imprint is on every page. Marketing Director Stephen Bedford is astute and innovative. Phil Metcalf and Rob Sternitzky provided very careful copyediting. I thank Editor-in-Chief Priscilla Painton, Publisher Sean Manning, and CEO Jon Karp.

My literary agent, Cathy Hemming, spun the dross of an idea into the gold of a book proposal. I am grateful for her support and advice. Thank you as well to Elizabeth Hazelton and Allison McLean of Amplify Partners.

My wife, Marcia Mogelonsky, helped me at every step of the way, from tromping around snake-ridden archaeological sites to cleaning up my cluttered prose to cutting the knot of many a logistical dilemma. I owe her more than I can say. Our children, Michael and Sylvie, offered support and encouragement. Historians study the past, but the future belongs to the young. I dedicate this book to them.

BIBLIOGRAPHY

What follows is a list of the most relevant works that I have consulted, almost all in English, for readers who would like additional information.

Ancient Sources

The following works are all available in various translations. They all appear in the Loeb Classical Library, published by Harvard University Press, which offers the Greek and Latin originals as well as translations. Most of them are available in English on the internet on such sites as LacusCurtius: Into the Roman World, http://penelope.uchicago.edu/Thayer/E/Roman/Texts/home.html; Livius: Articles on Ancient History, https://www.livius.org/; and Perseus Digital Library, www.perseus.tufts.edu. Many of these works are available in readable and accurate translations published by, for example, Oxford or Penguin. An important collection of sources, in both the original languages and English translation, is Menahem Stern, ed. *Greek and Latin Authors on Jews and Judaism* (Jerusalem: Israel Academy of Sciences and Humanities, 1974).

The main ancient works referred to in this book are:

Cassius Dio, *History of Rome*.
Epiphanius, *On Weights and Measures*.
Eusebius, *Chronicle*; *Ecclesiastical History*.
Herodian, *History of the Empire from the Death of Marcus*.

Historia Augusta.
Josephus, *Against Apion*; *Antiquities of the Jews*; *The Jewish War*; *Life.*
Martial, *Epigrams.*
Quintilian, *Institutes of Oratory.*
Tacitus, *Agricola*; *Annals*; *Histories.*
Thucydides, *The Peloponnesian War.*
Virgil, *Aeneid.*

Biblical texts are available in various translations and editions.

Various texts of rabbinic literature (e.g., Mishnah, Talmud, Midrash), most of them in both the original Hebrew or Aramic and in English translation, can be found online at Sefaria: A Living Library of Torah, https://www.sefaria.org/texts. The same site offers the text of the Tanakh (Hebrew Bible).

Reference

Bahat, Dan. *The Carta Jerusalem Atlas.* 3rd updated & expanded ed. Carta Jerusalem, 2011.
Cancik, Hubert, and Helmut Schneider, eds. *Brill's New Pauly: Encyclopaedia of the Ancient World*, English ed. Edited by Christine F. Salazar and David E. Orton. Brill, 2002–2010. It has an excellent online edition.
Encyclopaedia Iranica, https://www.iranicaonline.org/.
Ḥevrah la-ḥaḳirat Erets-Yiśra'el ve-'atiḳoteha. *The Documents from the Bar Kokhba Period in the Cave of Letters: Hebrew, Aramaic, and Nabatean-Aramaic Papyri.* Edited by Yigael Yadin, Hannah Cotton, and Andrew Gross. Jerusalem: Israel Exploration Society, 2002.
Horbury, William, W. D. Davies, and John Sturdy. *Cambridge History of Judaism: The Early Roman Period*, 1st ed. Cambridge University Press, 1999.
Hornblower, Simon, Anthony Spawforth, and Esther Eidinow. *The Oxford Classical Dictionary*, 4th ed. Oxford University Press, 2012.
Josephus, Flavius. *Flavius Josephus Online.* Edited by Steve Mason. Brill, n.d. https://referenceworks.brillonline.com/browse/flavius-josephus-online.
"Judaism and Rome: Re-thinking Rome's Encounter with the Roman Empire." https://www.judaism-and-rome.org/.
"Mantis. A Numismatic Technologies Integration Service." This is a database including ancient coins from an extensive collection of the American Numismatics Society. http://numismatics.org/search/.
"Online Coins of the Roman Empire (OCRE)." https://numismatics.org/ocre/.

BIBLIOGRAPHY

"Orbis: The Stanford Geospatial Network of the Ancient World." http://orbis.stanford.edu.

Skolnik, Fred, and Michael Berenbaum. *Encyclopaedia Judaica*. 2nd ed. Macmillan Reference USA in association with the Keter Pub. House, 2007.

Talbert, Richard J. A., ed. *The Barrington Atlas of the Ancient Greco-Roman World*. Princeton University Press, 2000. This book is also available as an app.

Works Cited

Abramsky, Samuel and Shimon Gibson, "Bar Kokhba," *Encyclopaedia Judaica*. 2nd ed., 3:156–162 (2007). Edited by Michael Berenbaum and Fred Skolnik. Macmillan Reference USA, 2007.

Allen, Joel. *Hostages and Hostage-Taking in the Roman Empire*. Cambridge University Press, 2006.

Amit, David. *Model of Jerusalem in the Second Temple Period*. Israel Museum, 2009.

Applebaum, Shimon. *Jews and Greeks in Ancient Cyrene*. E. J. Brill, 1979.

———. "The Social and Economic Status of the Jews in the Diaspora." In *The Jewish People in the First Century: Historical Geography, Political History, Social, Cultural and Religious Life and Institutions*, vol. 2. Edited by S. Safrai and M. Stern in cooperation with D. Flusser and W. C. van Unnik. Van Gorcum, 1976.

———. "The Troopers of Zamaris." *Judaea in Hellenistic and Roman Times: Historical and Archeological Essays*. E. J. Brill, 1989.

Auerbach, Jacob, Dan Bahat, and Shaked Gilboa. "Western Wall." *Encyclopaedia Judaica*. 2nd ed., vol. 21: 24–27 (2007).

Avi-Yonah, Michael. *The Holy Land: a Historical Geography from the Persian to the Arab Conquest (536 B.C. to A.D. 640)*. Carta, 2002.

———. *The Jews under Roman and Byzantine Rule: A Political History of Palestine from the Bar Kokhba War to the Arab Conquest*. Schocken Books, 1984.

Aviam, Mordechai. "The Archaeology of the Battle at Yodefat." In *Jews, Pagans and Christians in the Galilee*. Land of Galilee 1. University of Rochester Press, 2004.

———. "The Economic Impact of the First Jewish Revolt on the Galilee." In *Taxation, Economy, and Revolt in Ancient Rome, Galilee, and Egypt*. Edited by Thomas R. Blanton, Agnes Choi, and Jinyu Liu. Routledge, 2022.

———. "Yodefat-Jotapata: A Jewish Galilean Town at the End of the Second Temple Period; The Results of an Archaeological Project." In *Galilee in the Late Second Temple and Mishnaic Periods, Vol. 2: The Archaeological Record from Cities, Towns, and Villages*. Edited by David A. Fiensy and James R. Strange. Fortress, 2015.

———. "Yodefat/Jotapata: The Archaeology of the First Battle." In *The First Jew-

ish Revolt: Archaeology, History, and Ideology. Edited by Andrea M. Berlin and J. Andrew Overman. Routledge, 2002.

Avner, R., et al. "Special Announcement: A New-Old Monumental Inscription from Jerusalem Honoring Hadrian." In *New Studies in the Archaeology of Jerusalem and Its Region, Collected Papers*, vol. 8. Edited by G. D. Stiebel et al. Israel Antiquities Authority and the Hebrew University of Jerusalem, 2014.

Baltrusch, Ernst. *Herodes: König Im Heiligen Land: Eine Biographie*. C. H. Beck, 2012.

Barnes, T. D. "Trajan and the Jews." *Journal of Jewish Studies* 40, no. 2 (1989): 145–62.

Barnett, Paul W. "Under Tiberius All Was Quiet." *New Testament Studies* 21 (1975): 564–71.

Bauckham, Richard. "Jews and Jewish Christians in the Land of Israel at the Time of the Bar Kokhba War, with Special Reference to *The Apocalypse of Peter*." In *Tolerance and Intolerance in Early Judaism and Christianity*. Mazal Holocaust Collection. Edited by Graham Stanton and Guy G. Stroumsa. Cambridge University Press, 1998.

Ben-Ami, Doron, and Yana Tchekanovets. "Has the Adiabene Royal Family 'Palace' Been Found in the City of David?" In *Unearthing Jerusalem: 150 Years of Archaeological Research in the Holy City*. Edited by Katharina Galor and Gideon Avni. Eisenbrauns, 2011.

Ben Zeev, Miriam (Miriam Pucci Ben Zeev). *Diaspora Judaism in Turmoil, 116/117 CE: Ancient Sources and Modern Insights*. Peeters, 2005.

———. "Greek Attacks against Alexandrian Jews during Emperor Trajan's Reign." *Journal for the Study of Judaism in the Persian, Hellenistic, and Roman Period* 20, no. 1 (June 1989): 31–48.

———. "New Insights into the Roman Policy in Judea on the Eve of the Bar Kokhba Revolt." *Journal for the Study of Judaism* 49 (2018): 88–91.

———. "Traiano, la Mesopotamia e gli Ebrei." *Aegyptus* 59, no. 1/2 (January–December 1979): 168–89.

———. "The Uprisings in the Jewish Diaspora, 116–117," In *The Late Roman-Rabbinic Period*. Vol. 4. Edited by Steven T. Katz. Cambridge History of Judaism, 2006.

Berlin, Andrea M., and J. Andrew Overman, eds. *The First Jewish Revolt: Archaeology, History, and Ideology*. Routledge, 2002.

Berthelot, Katell. "Is God Unfair? The Fourth Book of Ezra as a Response to the Crisis of 70 C.E." In *Judaism and Crisis: Crisis as a Catalyst in Jewish Cultural History*. Edited by Armin Lange, Diethard Römheld, and Matthias Weigold. Vandenhoeck & Ruprecht, 2011.

BIBLIOGRAPHY

———. *Jews and Their Roman Rivals: Pagan Rome's Challenge to Israel.* Princeton University Press, 2021.
Bijovsky, Gabriela. "Numismatic Evidence for the Gallus Revolt: The Hoard from Lod." *Israel Exploration Journal* 57, no. 2 (2007): 187–203.
Birley, Anthony. *Hadrian: The Restless Emperor.* Routledge, 1997.
Bloom, James J. *The Jewish Revolts against Rome, A.D. 66–135: A Military Analysis.* McFarland, 2010.
Bond, Helen K. "The Coins of Pontius Pilate: Part of an Attempt to Provoke the People or to Integrate Them into the Empire?" *Journal for the Study of Judaism in the Persian, Hellenistic, and Roman Period* 27, no. 3 (1996): 241–62.
Bosworth, A. B. "Vespasian's Reorganization of the Northeast Frontier." *Antichthon* 10 (1976): 63–78.
Bowersock, Glen W. "The Tel Shalem Arch and P. Nahal Hever/Seiyal 8." In *The Bar Kokhba War Reconsidered: New Perspectives on the Second Jewish Revolt against Rome.* Edited by Peter Schäfer. Mohr Siebeck, 2003.
Bowman, Steven B., and David Flusser. *Sepher Yosippon: A Tenth-Century History of Ancient Israel.* Wayne State University Press, 2023.
Broshi, Magen. *Bread, Wine, Walls and Scrolls.* Sheffield Academic Press, 2001.
———. "Estimating the Population of Ancient Jerusalem." *Biblical Archaeology Review* 4 (1978): 10–15.
———. "The Population of Western Palestine in the Roman-Byzantine Periods." *Bulletin of the American Schools of Oriental Research* 236 (Autumn 1979): 1–10.
Byatt, A. "Josephus and Population Numbers in First Century Palestine." *Palestine Expedition Quarterly* 105 (1973): 51–60.
Campbell, Duncan B. *Siege Warfare in the Roman World: 146 BC–AD 378.* Osprey, 2005.
Cary, Earnest, trans. *Dio Cassius: Roman History.* Vol. VIII, books 61–70. Harvard University Press, 1925.
Center for Online Jewish Studies (COJS). "The Bar Kokhba Letters: Day-to-Day Conduct of the Revolt." https://cojs.org/the_bar_kokhba_letters-_day-to-day_conduct_of_the_revolt/.
Champlin, Edward. *Nero.* Belknap Press, 2003. Kindle.
Charlesworth, James H. "Christians and Jews in the First Six Centuries." In *Christianity and Rabbinic Judaism: A Parallel History of Their Origins and Early Development.* 2nd ed. Edited by Hershel Shanks. Biblical Archaeology Society, 2011.
Cohen, Shaye J. D. *From the Maccabees to the Mishnah.* 3rd ed. John Knox Press, 2014.
———. "Masada: Literary Tradition, Archaeological Remains, and the Credibility of Josephus." *Journal of Jewish Studies* 33, no. 1–2 (1982): 386–405.

BIBLIOGRAPHY

Cotton, Hannah, M. "The Date of the Fall of Masada: The Evidence of the Masada Papyri." *Zeitschrift für Papyrologie und Epigraphik* 78 (1989): 157–62.

———. "The Impact of the Roman Army in the Province of Judaea/Syria Palaestina." In *Idem, Roman Rule and Jewish Life: Collected Papers*. Edited by Ofer Pogorelsky. De Gruyter, 2022.

———. "The Languages of the Legal and Administrative Documents from the Judaean Desert." *Zeitschrift für Papyrologie und Epigraphik* 125 (1999): 219—31.

Crawford, Sidnie White. "Scribe Links Qumran and Masada." *Biblical Archaeological Review* (November–December 2012): 38–43.

Curry, Andrew. "The Road Almost Taken: An Ancient City in Germany Tells a Different Story of the Roman Conquest." *Archaeology Magazine*, March–April 2017. https://archaeology.org/issues/online/collection/germany-roman-town-waldgirmes/.

Dabrowa, Edward. "Poblicius Marcellus and the Bar Kokhba Revolt." *Rivista Storia dell'Antichità* 49 (2019): 69–84.

Davies, Gwyn. "The Masada Siege from the Roman Viewpoint." *Biblical Archaeological Review* 40, no. 4 (July–August 2014): 26–32, 70–71.

Davies, Gwyn, and Jodi Magness. "Recovering Josephus: Mason's History of the Jewish War and the Siege of Masada." *Scripta Classica Israelica* 36 (2017): 55–63.

de Lange, Nicholas. "Jewish Attitudes to the Roman Empire." In *Imperialism in the Ancient World*. Edited by P. D. A. Garnsey and C. R. Whittaker. Cambridge University Press, 1978.

Debevoise, Neilson Carel. *A Political History of Parthia*. University of Chicago Press, 1938.

della Pergola, Sergio. "Notes toward a Demographic History of the Jews." *Genealogy* 8, no. 2 (2024): 1–29.

Doležal, Stanislas. "Did Hadrian Ever Meet a Parthian King?" *AUC Philologica* 2 (2017): 111–25.

Dyson, Stephen L. "Native Revolts in the Roman Empire," *Historia* 20.2/3 (1971): 239–274.

Eck, Werner. "Hadrian, the Bar Kokhba Revolt, and the Epigraphic Transmission." In *The Bar Kokhba War Reconsidered: New Perspectives on the Second Jewish Revolt against Rome*. Edited by Peter Schäfer. Mohr Siebeck, 2003.

———. "The Bar Kokhba Revolt: The Roman Point of View." *Journal of Roman Studies* 89 (1999): 76–89.

———. "*Urbs Salvia e le sue più illustri famiglie in età romana*." In L. Bacchielli, *Studi Su Urbisaglia Romana*. Tipigraf, 1995.

Edwell, Peter M. "Rome and Parthia: Conflict and Diplomacy from Sulla to

BIBLIOGRAPHY

Caracalla." In *Idem, Rome and Persia at War: Imperial Competition and Contact, 193–363 CE*. Routledge, 2021.

Ehrlich, Uri. "Birkat Ha-Minim." *Encyclopaedia Judaica* 3: 711–12, 2007.

Eisenberg, Michael. *A Visitor's Guide to Ancient Hippos: Above the Sea of Galilee*. Millennium Ayalon, 2021.

Ellerbrock, Uwe. *The Parthians: The Forgotten Empire*. Routledge, 2021.

Eshel, Hanan. *Masada*. Carta Jerusalem, 2015.

———. "The Kittim in the *War Scroll* and in the Pesharim." In Orion Center for the Study of the Dead Sea Scrolls and Associated Literature International Symposium. *Historical Perspectives: From the Hasmoneans to Bar Kokhba in Light of the Dead Sea Scrolls: Proceedings of the Fourth International Symposium of the Orion Center for the Study of the Dead Sea Scrolls and Associated Literature, 27–31 January, 1999*. Edited by David M. Goodblatt, Avital Pinnick, and Daniel R. Schwartz. Brill, 2001.

Eshel, Hanan, and Boaz Zissu. *The Bar Kokhba Revolt: The Archaeological Evidence*. Yad Izhak Ben Zvi, 2019.

Eshel, Hanan, Esther Eshel, and Ada Yardeni. "A Document from 'Year 4 of the Destruction of the House of Israel.'" *Dead Sea Discoveries* 18, no. 1 (2011): 1–28.

Eusebius, Kirsopp Lake, J. E. L Oulton, and Hugh Jackson Lawlor. *The Ecclesiastical History*. Heinemann, 1938.

Feldman, Louis. "Financing the Colosseum." *Biblical Archaeological Review* 27, no. 4 (September–October 2001): 20–32.

Fenati, Maria Federica. *Lucio Flavio Silva Nonio Basso e La Città Di Urbisaglia*. Università degli studi di Macerata, Facoltà di lettere e filosofia, Istituto di storia antica, 1995.

Fiensy, David A. *The Archaeology of Daily Life: Ordinary Persons in Late Second Temple Israel*. Cascade Books, 2020.

Fredriksen, Paula. *When Christians Were Jews: The First Generation*. Yale University Press, 2018.

Frere, Sheppard S. "M. Maenius Agrippa, the 'Expeditio Britannica' and Maryport." *Britannia* 31 (2000): 23–28.

Fuks, A. "Aspects of the Jewish Revolt in A.D. 115–117." *Journal of Roman Studies* 51 (1961): 98–104.

Gambash, Gil. *Rome and Provincial Resistance*. Routledge, 2015.

Gamer, Robert. "Elazar ben Dinai—From Brigand to Hero." Sefaria. https://www.sefaria.org/sheets/21316.14?lang=bi.

Geiger, Joseph. "The Bar-Kokhba Revolt: The Greek Point of View." *Historia* 65 (2016): 497–519.

Geva, Hillel. "Jerusalem's Population in Antiquity: A Minimalist View." *Tel Aviv* 41, no. 2 (2014): 146.

Geza, H. "The Siege Ramp Laid by the Romans to Conquer the Northern Palace at Masada." *Eretz-Yisrael* 25 (1996): 297–306.

Grintz, Yehoshua M. "Baruch, Apocalypse of." *Encyclopedia Judaica*. Vol. 3: 184–85, 2007.

Goldfus, Haim, et al. "The Significance of Geomorphological and Soil Formation Research for Understanding the Unfinished Roman Ramp at Masada." *Catena* 146 (November 2016): 73–87.

Goldsworthy, Adrian Keith. "'Men Casually Armed against Fully Equipped Regulars': The Roman Military Response to Jewish Insurgence 63 BCE–135 CE." In *Jews and Christians in the First and Second Centuries: How to Write Their History*. Edited by Peter J. Tomson and Joshua Schwartz. Brill, 2014, 207–37.

———. *Rome and Persia: The Seven Hundred Year Rivalry*. Basic Books, 2023.

González Salinero, Raúl. *Military Service and the Integration of Jews into the Roman Empire*. Brill, 2022.

Goodblatt, David. "The Jews in the Parthian Empire: What We Don't Know." In *Judaea-Palaestina, Babylon and Rome: Jews in Antiquity*. Edited by Benjamin H. Isaac, Yuval Shahar, and Aharon Oppenheimer. Mohr Siebeck, 2012.

Goodman, Martin. "Bar-Kokhba War." In *The Bar Kokhba War Reconsidered: New Perspectives on the Second Jewish Revolt against Rome*. Edited by Peter Schäfer. Mohr Siebeck, 2003.

———. "Current Scholarship on the First Revolt." In *The First Jewish Revolt: Archaeology, History, and Ideology*. Edited by Andrea M. Berlin and J. Andrew Overman. Routledge, 2002.

———. *Herod the Great: Jewish King in a Roman World*. Yale University Press, 2024.

———. *Josephus's* The Jewish War: *A Biography*. Princeton University Press, 2019.

———. *Judaism in the Roman World: Collected Essays*. Brill, 2007.

———. *Rome and Jerusalem: The Clash of Ancient Civilizations*. Allen Lane, 2007.

———. *The Ruling Class of Judaea: The Origins of the Jewish Revolt against Rome, A.D. 66–70*. Cambridge University Press, 1989.

Gross, Simcha. "Hopeful Rebels and Anxious Romans: Jewish Interconnectivity in the Great Revolt and Beyond." *Historia* 72, no. 4 (2023): 479–513.

Hadas-Lebel, Mireille. *Hérode*. Fayard, 2017.

Harkabi, Yehoshafat. *The Bar Kokhba Syndrome: Risk and Realism in International Politics*. Edited by David A. Altshuler. Rossel Books, 1983.

Hauser, Stefan R. "Was There No Paid Standing Army?: A Fresh Look on Military and Political Institutions in the Arsacid Empire." In *Arms and Armour as Indicators*

BIBLIOGRAPHY

of Cultural Transfer: The Steppes and the Ancient World from Hellenistic Times to the Early Middle Ages. Edited by Markus Mode and Jürgen Tubach. Reichert, 2006.

Hebrew University of Jerusalem. "Ancient Golden Treasure Found at Foot of Temple Mount (Update)." Phys. Org, September 9, 2013. https://phys.org/news/2013-09-israeli-archaeologist-ancient-treasure-trove.html.

Hendin, David B. *Guide to Biblical Coins*, 6th ed. American Numismatic Society, 2021.

Hengel, Martin. *The Zealots: Investigations into the Jewish Freedom Movement in the Period from Herod I until 70 A.D.* T&T Clark, 1997.

Hezser, Catherine. *Jewish Travel in Antiquity.* Mohr Siebeck, 2011.

Horbury, William. "Beginnings of the Jewish Revolt under Trajan." In *Geschichte—Tradition—Reflexion: Festschrift für Martin Hengel zum 70. Geburstag.* Vol. 1. Edited by Peter Schäfer. J. C. Mohr, 1996.

———. *Jewish War under Trajan and Hadrian.* Cambridge University Press, 2014.

Horbury, William, W. D. Davies, and John Sturdy. *Cambridge History of Judaism: The Early Roman Period.* 1st ed. Cambridge University Press, 1999.

Howard-Johnston, James. *The Last Great War of Antiquity.* Oxford University Press, 2021.

Ilan, Tal. *Queen Berenice: A Jewish Female Icon of the First Century CE.* Studies in Theology and Religion 29. Brill, 2022.

Isaac, Benjamin. "Judea after AD 70," *Journal of Jewish Studies* 35, no. 1 (1984): 44–50.

———. "Roman Colonies in Judaea: The Foundation of Aelia Capitolina." *Talanta* 12–13 (1981): 50.

Isaac, Benjamin, and Israel Roll. *Roman Roads in Judaea.* Vol. 1. British Archaeological Reports. 1982.

Israel Museum. "A Hoard at the Foot of the Temple Mount." https://www.imj.org.il/en/collections/540582-0.

Jackson, John. *Tacitus, Annals, Books 13–16.* Harvard University Press, 1937.

Johnson, Nathan C. 2023. "Theudas (excerpt from Jewish Sign Prophets)." *Critical Dictionary of Apocalyptic and Millenarian Movements.* Edited by James Crossley and Alastair Lockhart. www.cdamm.org/articles/theudas.

Jones, Brian W. "Titus in the East, A.D. 70–71." *Rheinisches Museum für Philologie* 128, no. 3/4 (1985): 346–52.

Josephus, Flavius, et al. *Josephus.* Harvard University Press, 1976.

Josephus, Flavius, and G. A. Williamson. *The Jewish War.* Revised with a new introduction and notes by E. Mary Smallwood. Penguin, 1981.

Kennedy, David. "Parthia and Rome: Eastern Perspectives." In *The Roman Army in the East.* Edited by Idem. Journal of Roman Archaeology, 1996.

Kerkeslager, Allen. "Jews in Egypt and Cyrenaica 66-c. 235 CE." In *The Late Roman-Rabbinic Period: The Cambridge History of Judaism*. Vol. 4. Edited by Steven T. Katz. Cambridge University Press, 2006.

Kloner, Amos, Eitan Klein, and Boaz Zissu. "The Rural Hinterland (*Territorium*) of *Aelia Capitolina*. In *Roman Jerusalem: A New Old City*. Edited by Guy Stiebel and Gideon Avni. *Journal of Roman Archaeology* (2017): 131–42.

Kropp, Andreas J. M. "Crowning the Emperor: An Unorthodox Image of Claudius, Agrippa I and Herod of Chalkis." Syria 90 (2013): 377–89.

Lawler, Andrew. *Under Jerusalem: The Buried History of the World's Most Contested City*. 1st ed. Doubleday, 2021.

———. "Who Built the Tomb of the Kings?" *Biblical Archaeological Review* 47, no. 4 (Winter 2021): 30–38.

Le Bohec, Yann. "The 'Third Punic War': The Siege of Carthage (149–146 BC)." In *A Companion to the Punic Wars*. Edited by Dexter Hoyos. Blackwell, 2011.

Leslie, Donald Daniel. "Redemption." *Encyclopaedia Judaica* 17, no. 2: 151–52.

Levithan, Josh. *Roman Siege Warfare*. University of Michigan Press, 2013.

Lewis, Naphtali, Yigael Yadin, and Jonas C. Greenfield. *The Documents from the Bar Kokhba Period in the Cave of Letters*. Israel Exploration Society, Hebrew University of Jerusalem, 1989.

Livshits, V. A., and A. B. Nikitin. "Parthian and Middle Persian Documents from South Turkmenistan: A Survey." *Ancient Civilizations* 1, no. 3 (1994): 312–23.

Lukacs, John. *Five Days in London, May 1940*. Yale University Press, 1999. Kindle.

Madreiter, Irene, and Udo Hartmann. "Women at the Arsakid Court." In *The Routledge Companion to Women and Monarchy in the Ancient Mediterranean World*. Edited by Elizabeth D. Carney and Sabine Müller. Routledge Taylor & Francis Group, 2021.

Magness, Jodi. *Masada: from Jewish Revolt to Modern Myth*. Princeton University Press, 2019.

———. *Stone and Dung, Oil and Spit: Jewish Daily Life in the Time of Jesus*. William B. Eerdmans, 2011.

———. "Women at Masada." *The Shalvi/Hyman Encyclopedia of Jewish Women*. https://jwa.org/encyclopedia/article/women-at-masada#pid-13674.

Mandelbaum, Allan, trans. *The Aeneid of Virgil*. Dell, 1971.

Marciak, Michał. *Izates, Helena, and Monobazos of Adiabene: A Study on Literary Traditions and History*. Harrassowitz Verlag, 2014.

Mason, Steve. *A History of the Jewish War, AD 66–74*. Cambridge University Press, 2016.

———. "Ancient Jews or Judeans: Different Questions, Different Answers." Marginalia, June 24, 2014. https:// themarginaliareview.com/ancient-jews-judeans-different-questions-different-answers-steve-mason.

———. "Jews, Judaeans, Judaizing, Judaism: Problems of Categorization in Ancient History." *Journal for the Study of Judaism in the Persian, Hellenistic, and Roman Period* 38, no. 4/5 (2007): 457–512.

———. *Orientation to the History of Roman Judaea*. Cascade Books, 2016.

McLaren, James S. *Turbulent Times?: Josephus and Scholarship on Judaea in the First Century CE*. Sheffield Academic Press, 1998.

Meshorer, Ya'akov. *A Treasury of Jewish Coins from the Persian Period to Bar Kokhba*. Yad ben-Zvi Press, 2001.

Mildenberg, Leo. "Rebel Coinage in the Roman Empire." In *Greece and Rome in Eretz Israel: Collected Essays*. Edited by Aryeh Kasher, Gideon Fuks, and Uriel Rappaport. Yad Izhak Ben-Zvi, 1990.

Millar, Fergus. *The Roman Near East, 31 B.C.–A.D. 337*. Harvard University Press, 1993.

Mor, Menachem. "The Events of 351–352 in Palestine—The Last Revolt against Rome?" In *The Eastern Frontier of the Roman Empire: Proceedings of a Colloquium Held at Ankara in September 1988*. Edited by D. H. French and C. S. Lightfoot. B.A.R., 1989.

Nathanson, Barbara Geller. "Jews, Christians, and the Gallus Revolt in Fourth-Century Palestine." *Biblical Archaeologist* 49, no. 1 (1986): 29–36.

———. "The Fourth Century Jewish 'Revolt' during the Reign of Gallus." Thesis, Duke University, 1981.

Neusner, Jacob. *A History of the Jews in Babylonia*. Scholars Press, 1999.

Novenson, Matthew V. *The Grammar of Messianism: An Ancient Jewish Political Idiom and Its Users*. Oxford University Press, 2017.

Noy, David, and Susan Sorek. "Claudia Aster and Curtia Euodia: Two Jewish Women in Roman Italy." *Women in Judaism: A Multidisciplinary Journal* 5, no. 1 (Winter 2007): 1–13.

Olbrycht, Marek Jan. "The Arsakid Empire between the Mediterranean World and Inner Asia. Remarks on the Political Strategy of the Arsakids from Vologases I till the Accession of Vologases III (AD 50–147)." German language. In *Ancient Iran and the Mediterranean World: Proceedings of an International Conference in Honour of Professor Józef Wolski, Held at the Jagiellonian University, Cracow, in September 1996*. Edited by Józef Wolski and Edward Dąbrowa. Jagiellonian University Press, 1998.

Onn, Alexander, and Shlomit Weksler-Bdolah. "The Temple Mount at the Time of *Aelia Capitolina*: New Evidence from the 'Giant Viaduct.'" In *Roman Jerusalem: A New Old City*. Edited by Guy Stiebel and Gideon Avni. *Journal of Roman Archaeology* (2017).

Oppenheimer, Aharon. *Babylonia Judaica in the Talmudic Period*. L. Reichert, 1983.

Pausanias, W. H. S. Jones, Henry Arderne Ormerod, and R. E. Wycherley. *Description of Greece.* Harvard University Press, 1918.

Pliny, and Betty Radice. *Letters, and Panegyricus.* Harvard University Press, 1969.

Powell, Lindsay. *Bar Kokhba: The Jew Who Defied Hadrian and Challenged the Might of Rome.* Pen & Sword Military, 2021.

Price, Jonathan T. *Jerusalem under Siege: The Collapse of the Jewish State, 66–70 C.E.* Brill, 1992.

Rabinowitz, Louis Isaac, Haim Hermann Cohn, and Menachem Elon. "Suicide." In *Encyclopaedia Judaica* 19: 295–97.

Rahe, Paul A. *Sparta's Sicilian Proxy War: The Grand Strategy of Classical Sparta, 418–413 B.C.* Encounter Books, 2023.

Rajak, Tessa. "Jews." Oxford Classical Dictionary. https://doi-org.proxy.library.cornell.edu/10.1093/acrefore/9780199381135.013.3492.

———. *Josephus: The Historian and His Society.* 2nd ed. Duckworth, 2002.

———. "The Parthians in Josephus." In *Idem, The Jewish Dialogue with Greece and Rome: Studies in Cultural and Social Interaction.* Brill, 2001.

Raphael, Frederic. *A Jew among Romans: The Life and Legacy of Flavius Josephus.* Pantheon Books, 2013.

Rappaport, Uriel. "Bar Giora, Simeon." In *Encyclopaedia Judaica* 3: 150–51, 2007.

———. *John of Gischala: From the Mountains of Galilee to the Walls of Jerusalem.* 2013. An English Translation of the Hebrew Edition of 2006. https://www.academia.edu/2383453/JOHN_OF_GISCHALA_From_the_mountains_of_Galilee_to_the_Walls_of_Jerusalem_2013_An_English_translation_of_the_Hebrew_edition_of_2006&nav_from=16613259-7b5e-40aa-aa34-5ed500518f26&rw_pos=0.

Raschke, Manfred G. "New Studies in Roman Commerce with the East." In *Aufstieg Und Niedergang Der Römischen Welt: Geschichte Und Kultur Roms Im Spiegel Der Neueren Forschung* II. Vol. 9/2. Edited by Joseph Vogt, Hildegard Temporini, and Wolfgang Haase. De Gruyter, 1978.

Raviv, Dvir. "Hiding Complexes in Fortified Sites of the Bar Kokhba War." *Journal of Jewish Studies* 74, no. 2 (Autumn 2023): 273–302.

Raviv, Dvir, and Chaim Ben David. "Cassius Dio's Figures for the Demographic Consequences of the Bar Kokhba War: Exaggeration or Reliable Account?" *Journal of Roman Archaeology* 34 (2021): 585–607.

Reich, Ronny. "Baking and Cooking at Masada." *Zeitschrift des Deutschen Palästina-Vereins* 119, no. 2 (2003): 40–58.

Reinhartz, Adele. "The Vanishing Jews of Antiquity." Marginalia, June 24, 2014. https://themarginaliareview.com/vanishing-jews-antiquity-adele-reinhartz.

BIBLIOGRAPHY

Reynolds, Joyce. "Cyrenaica, I. A.D. 70–117." In *The Cambridge Ancient History*, 2nd ed.: *The High Empire, A.D. 70–192*. Cambridge University Press, 2000.

Richardson, Peter, and Amy Marie Fisher. *Herod: King of the Jews and Friend of the Romans*. 2nd ed. Taylor and Francis, 2017.

Rocca, Samuel. *Herod's Judaea: A Mediterranean State in the Classical World*. Mohr Siebeck, 2008.

———. *The Army of Herod the Great*. Osprey, 2009.

Rogers, Guy MacLean. *For the Freedom of Zion: The Great Revolt of Jews against Romans, 66–74 CE*. Yale University Press, 2021.

Roller, Duane W. *The Building Program of Herod the Great*. University of California Press, 1998.

Roth, Jonathan. "The Length of the Siege of Masada." *Scripta Classica Israelica* (1995): 87–110.

Roth, Lea. "Cestius Gallus." *Encyclopaedia Judaica* 4: 552–53.

———. "Gessius Florus." *Encyclopaedia Judaica* 7: 563–64.

Runesson, Anders. "Joshua Ezra Burns: The Christian Schism in Jewish History and Jewish Memory." *Studies in Christian-Jewish Relations* 13, no. 1 (2018): 1–5.

Russel, James R. "Cupbearer." *Encyclopaedia Iranica*, https://www.iranicaonline.org/articles/cupbearer-parthian-tkrpty-loanword-in-armenian-takarapet-cf.

Saldarini, Anthony J. "Babatha's Story: Personal Archive Offers a Glimpse of Ancient Jewish Life." *Biblical Archaeology Review* (March–April 1998): 29–33.

Sanders, E. P. *Jesus and Judaism*. Fortress Press, 1985.

Sartre, Maurice. *The Middle East under Rome*. Belknap Press, 2005.

Schama, Simon. *The Story of the Jews: Finding the Words, 1000 BC–1492 AD*. Ecco, 2013.

Schürer, Emil. *The History of the Jewish People in the Age of Jesus Christ (175 B.C.–A.D. 135)*. Edited by Géza Vermès and Fergus Millar. Clark, 1973.

Schwartz, Daniel R. *Agrippa I: The Last King of Judaea*. J. C. B. Mohr, 1990.

———. *Judeans and Jews: Four Faces of Dichotomy in Ancient Jewish History*. University of Toronto Press, 2014.

———. "On Barnabas and Bar-Kokhba." In *Studies in the Jewish Background of Christianity*. J. C. B. Mohr, 1992.

———. *Reading the First Century: On Reading Josephus and Studying Jewish History of the First Century*. Mohr Siebeck, 2013.

Schwartz, Seth. *Imperialism and Jewish Society, 200 B.C.E. to 640 C.E.* Princeton University Press, 2001.

———. *The Ancient Jews from Alexander to Muhammad*. Cambridge University Press, 2014.

BIBLIOGRAPHY

———. *Were the Jews a Mediterranean Society?: Reciprocity and Solidarity in Ancient Judaism*. Princeton University Press, 2010.

Schäfer, Peter. "Bar Kokhba and the Rabbis." In *The Bar Kokhba War Reconsidered: New Perspectives on the Second Jewish Revolt against Rome*. Mohr Siebeck, 2003.

———, ed. *The Bar Kokhba War Reconsidered: New Perspectives on the Second Jewish Revolt against Rome*. Mohr Siebeck, 2003.

Schäfer, Peter, and David Chowcat. *The History of the Jews in Antiquity: The Jews of Palestine from Alexander the Great to the Arab Conquest*. Harwood Academic, 1995.

Schalit, Abraham. *König Herodes: Der Mann Und Sein Werk*. 2nd ed. De Gruyter, 2001.

Sharon, Nadav. *Judea under Roman Domination: The First Generation of Statelessness and Its Legacy*. SBL Press, 2017.

Schlude, Jason M. *Rome, Parthia, and the Politics of Peace: The Origins of War in the Ancient Middle East*. Routledge, 2020.

Schuster, Ruth. "Archaeologists Find Evidence of the Last Jewish Revolt against Rome." *Haaretz*, June 16, 2024. https://www.haaretz.com/archaeology/2024-06-16/ty-article/archaeologists-find-evidence-of-the-last-jewish-revolt-against-rome/00000190-1ff6-df11-a3b9-bff72b6f0000.

Sebag Montefiore, Simon. *Jerusalem: The Biography*. Alfred A. Knopf, 2011.

Seneca, Lucius Annaeus, and John W. Basore. *Moral Essays*. Harvard University Press, 1928.

Shatzman, Israel. *The Armies of the Hasmonaeans and Herod: From Hellenistic to Roman Frameworks*. J. C. B. Mohr, 1991.

Simkovich, Malka Z. "Queen Helena of Adiabene and Her Sons in Midrash and History." TheTorah.com. https://www.thetorah.com/article/queen-helena-of-adiabene-and-her-sons-in-midrash-and-history.

Smallwood, E. Mary. *The Jews under Roman Rule: From Pompey to Diocletian, a Study in Political Relations*. Photochemical reprint with corrections. Brill, 1981.

Steinmeyer, Nathan. "Ancient Roman Swords Discovered Near En Gedi." *Bible History Daily*, September 8, 2023. https://www.biblicalarchaeology.org/daily/ancient-cultures/ancient-israel/ancient-roman-swords/?mqsc=E4154826&dk=ZE3390ZF0&utm_source=WhatCountsEmail&utm_medium=BHDA%20Daily%20Newsletter&utm_campaign=9_8_23_Ancient_Roman_Swords_Ein_Gedi.

———. "The Golan's Roman Road: A Roman Road and Jewish Rebellion." Biblical Archaeological Society, June 14, 2024. https://www.biblicalarchaeology.org/daily/ancient-cultures/ancient-israel/the-golans-roman-road/?mqsc=E4161986&dk=ZE4260ZF0&utm_source=WhatCountsE

BIBLIOGRAPHY

mail&utm_medium=BHDA%20Week%20in%20Review%201-90&utm_campaign=6_15_24_WIR_The_Golans_Roman_Road.

Stemberger, Günter. *Jews and Christians in the Holy Land: Palestine in the Fourth Century.* T&T Clark, 2000.

Stern, Menahem, ed. *Greek and Latin Authors on Jews and Judaism.* vol. 2: *From Tacitus to Simplicius.* Israel Academy of Sciences and Humanities, 1974.

Stern, Menahem, and Bathja Bayer. "Hasmoneans." In *Encyclopaedia Judaica*, 2nd ed., vol. 8: 446–48.

Stern, Menahem, and Jonathan Price. "Zealots and Sicarii." *Encyclopaedia Judaica* 21 (2007): 467–80.

Stiebel, Guy, and Gideon Avni, eds. *Roman Jerusalem: A New Old City. Journal of Roman Archaeology*, 2017.

Stone, Michael E. "Ezra, Apocalypse of." *Encyclopedia Judaica* 6: 654–55, 2007.

Strauss, Barry. "Jewish Roots in the Land of Israel/Palestine." *Caravan Notebook*, Hoover Institution, February 6, 2024. https://www.hoover.org/research/jewish-roots-land-israelpalestine.

———. *Ten Caesars: Roman Emperors from Augustus to Constantine.* Simon & Schuster, 2019.

———. *The Spartacus War.* Simon & Schuster, 2009.

———. *The War that Made the Roman Empire: Antony, Cleopatra, and Octavian at Actium.* Simon & Schuster, 2022.

Strothmann, Meret. "C[estius]. Cos. suff. 42 AD." In Cancik and Schneider, *Brill's New Pauly.* https://referenceworks-brill-com.proxy.library.cornell.edu/display/entries/NPOE/e230610.xml?rskey=yhNv0n&result=1.

Syme, Ronald. *Tacitus.* Clarendon Press, 1958.

Syon, Danny. "The Coins from Gamala—An Interim Report." *Israeli Numismatic Journal* 12 (1992–93): 34–55.

Tacitus. *Complete Works of Tacitus.* Edited by Alfred John Church, William Jackson Brodribb, and Sara Bryant. Perseus, reprinted 1942. http://www.perseus.tufts.edu/hopper/text?doc=Perseus%3Atext%3A1999.02.0078%3Abook%3D15%3Achapter%3D29.

Tacitus, Cornelius, Clifford H. Moore, and John Jackson. *The Histories.* W. Heinemann, 1925.

"The Expression: 'They Sacrificed to Their Standards.'" Reformed Reader Blog, November 24, 2009. https://reformedreader.wordpress.com/2009/11/24/the-expression-they-sacrificed-to-their-standards/.

"The Temple of Peace (Rome)." Judaism and Rome: Re-thinking Judaism's Encounter with the Roman Empire. https://www.judaism-and-rome.org/temple-peace-rome.

Turner, E. G. "Tiberius Julius Alexander." *Journal of Roman Studies* 44 (1954): 54–64.

Vermès, Géza. *The True Herod*. Bloomsbury, 2014.

Vogelsang-Eastwood, Gilian. "The Clothing of the 'Shami Prince.'" *Persica* 16 (2000): 31–47.

Wald, Stephen G. "Johanan Ben Zakkai," *Encyclopaedia Judaica* 11 (2007): 375–76.

———. "Judah Ha-Nasi." *Encyclopaedia Judaica* 11: 501–505.

Wandrey, Irina. "Gessius Florus." In Cancik and Schneider, *Brill's New Pauly*, https://referenceworks-brill-com.proxy.library.cornell.edu/display/entries/NPOE/e423510.xml?rskey=3DxCrX&result=1.

Weinfeld, Moshe. *Social Justice in Ancient Israel and in the Ancient Near East*. Fortress Press, 1995.

Weksler-Bdolah, Shlomit, and Alexander Onn. "Colonnaded Streets in *Aelia Capitolina*: New Evidence from the Eastern *Cardo*." In *Roman Jerusalem: A New Old City*. Edited by Stiebel and Avni. *Journal of Roman Archaeology*, 2017.

Wells, Peter S. *The Battle That Stopped Rome: Emperor Augustus, Arminius, and the Slaughter of the Legions in the Teutoburg Forest*. W. W. Norton, 2003.

Wheatcroft, Geoffrey. "Seeking Haider," *Guardian*, February 29, 2000. https://www.theguardian.com/world/2000/mar/01/austria.

Wilker, Julia. "God Is with Italy Now: Pro-Roman Jews and the Jewish Revolt." In *Jewish Identity and Politics between the Maccabees and Bar Kokhba: Groups, Normativity, and Rituals*. Edited by Benedikt Eckhardt. Brill, 2012.

Wolski, Józef. *L'Empire Des Arsacides*. In Aedibus Peeters, 1993.

Woolf, Greg. "Provincial Revolts in the Early Roman Empire." In *The Jewish Revolt against Rome: Interdisciplinary Perspectives*. Edited by Mladen Popović. Brill, 2011.

Yadin, Yigael. *Bar-Kokhba: the Rediscovery of the Legendary Hero of the Second Jewish Revolt against Rome*. Random House, 1971.

———. *Masada: Herod's Fortress and the Zealots' Last Stand*. Random House, 1966.

Zerubavel, Yael. *Recovered Roots: Collective Memory and the Making of Israeli National Tradition*. University of Chicago Press, 1995.

Zissu, Boaz. "Interbellum Judea: 70–132 CE: An Archaeological Perspective." In *Jews and Christians in the First and Second Centuries: The Interbellum 70–132 CE*. Edited by Joshua J. Schwartz and Peter J. Tomson. Brill, 2017, 19–49.

Zissu, Boaz, and Hanan Eshel. "Religious Aspects of the Bar Kokhba Revolt: The Founding of Aelia Capitolina on the Ruins of Jerusalem." In *The Religious Aspects of War in the Ancient Near East, Greece, and Rome*. Edited by Krzysztof Ulanowski. Brill, 2016.

NOTES

Prologue

1. Pliny the Elder, *Natural History*, 27.1.3.
2. See Strauss, "Jewish Roots."

Chapter One: Pompey, Pacorus, and Herod

1. Some argue that the inhabitants of Judea should be called Judeans, rather than Jews. For two opposing viewpoints on the matter by two eminent scholars, see Reinhartz, "Vanishing Jews"; Mason, "Ancient Jews or Judeans"; *Idem*, "Jews, Judaeans, Judaizing, Judaism." See also Schwartz, *Judeans and Jews*. To avoid writing Jews out of history, I follow Reinhartz and generally use the term "Jews."
2. Ezra 1:3 (King James Version).
3. On clothing customs in Second-Temple Judea, see Magness, *Stone and Dung*, 107–20.
4. On Jewish women, see Fiensy, *Archaeology*, 127–31; on men, see Magness, *Stone and Dung*, 112–17.
5. Zoroastrianism, the Iranian religion before Islam, may be said to have approached monotheism but to have been essentially dualistic. See Malandra and Choksy, "Zoroastrianism."
6. Schwartz, *Imperialism and Jewish Society*, 49.
7. Yehud was the name of the Persian administrative district roughly corresponding to the region of Judah.
8. The name "Hasmonean" may have come from an ancestor, Asamonaios, or perhaps from the village of Heshmon. Stern, *Hasmoneans*, 446.
9. Josephus, *Jewish War*, 2.120–66; Josephus, *Antiquities of the Jews*, 18.11–22.

NOTES

Antiquities of the Jews, 18.3–10, mentions a so-called Fourth Philosophy that fought for Jewish independence, but they emerged later, under the Romans.

10. Richardson, *Herod*, 215.
11. On Judah, see Goodman, *Herod the Great*, 95.
12. On Pompey's looks, see Plutarch, *Pompey*, 2; on "the teenage butcher," see Valerius, Maximus, *Memorabilia*, 6.2.8.
13. Josephus, *Jewish War*, 1.151; Josephus, *Antiquities of the Jews*, 14.71. As is usually the case with Josephus's numbers, this figure needs to be taken with a grain of salt.
14. The city was Hippos, which lies on the eastern shore of the Sea of Galilee. Eisenberg, *A Visitor's Guide to Hippos*, 61.
15. Josephus, *Antiquities of the Jews*, 14.77, trans. Josephus, Flavius, H. St. J. Thackeray, et al., *Josephus*, 6:41.
16. Josephus, *Jewish War*, 6.329.
17. The Essenes of Qumran began at that time to think of the Romans and not the Greeks as the evil Kittim. See Eshel, "Kittim," 41–44.
18. Josephus, *Jewish War*, 1:204; Josephus, *Antiquities of the Jews*, 14:159; Schalit, "Hezekiah," *Encyclopaedia Judaica*, 2nd ed., 9:90.
19. M. *Pirkei Avot*, 1.10, my translation.
20. Herodian, *History of the Empire from the Death of Marcus*, 4.10, my translation.
21. Roman relations with Parthia are a perennial topic of scholarship. They have received much attention lately. Of particular interest is the subject of possible help for rebels from beyond the Euphrates River. See, among others, Edwell, "Rome and Parthia," 25–56; Goldsworthy, *Rome and Persia*, 176–77; Gross, "Hopeful Rebels and Anxious Romans," 479–513; Olbrycht, "The Arsakid Empire," 133–47; Mason, *A History of the Jewish War*, 155–66, 459–61; Rogers, *For the Freedom of Zion*, esp. 456–59; Schlude, *Rome, Parthia, and the Politics of Peace*, 84–87, 142–44, 161–62.
22. Josephus, *Jewish War*, 1.180–81. The city was Tarichaeae, a Greek name that many scholars identify with the Hebrew-named Migdal (Magdala).
23. Josephus, *Jewish War*, 1.253, says that Shavuot was being celebrated. The holiday takes place on Sivan 6, which, according to an online calculator, took place in May 40 BCE. https://webspace.science.uu.nl/~gent0113/hebrew/hebrewyear_year.htm.
24. "Cupbearer Relief from Persepolis, Iran," Alamy, https://www.alamy.com/cupbearer-relief-from-persepolis-iran-image268827705.html?imageid=90AC246D-C10F-463A-AC77-B022DF63AE47&p=868092&pn=1&searchId=c52b73853c4bd69a1a9ad2ba9d5e8acb&searchtype=0 . On the cupbearer in Parthia, see James R.

NOTES

Russel, "Cupbearer," *Encyclopaedia Iranica*, https://www.iranicaonline.org/articles/cupbearer-parthian-tkrpty-loanword-in-armenian-takarapet-cf.

25. Pacorus is attested as a Jewish name: The name is Pacorus, son of Isa, a diminutive of Joseph, so, roughly, "Pacorus son of Yossi." Livshits and Nikitin, "Parthian and Middle Persian Documents," 318.
26. On Pacorus, see Wolski, *L'Empire Des Arsacides*, 128–40. For coin portraits of Pacorus, see "Pacorus I (ca. 39 B.C.)," Parthia, https://parthia.com/pacorus1.htm.
27. A Roman poet once described a soldier shining in his armor "just as a fiery gem shines in the golden necklace of an Arsacid [aka Parthian]," Silius Italicus, *Punica*, 8.467.
28. Josephus, *Antiquities of the Jews*, 14.403.
29. Richardson, *Herod*, 63–64.
30. The *eleutheroi hippeis*, according to Josephus, *Jewish War*, 1.255. For an example of a Parthian cupbearer supplying five hundred calvalrymen, see one Gnēl in Parthian Armenia, Russel, "Cupbearer," *Encyclopaedia Iranica*, https://www.iranicaonline.org/articles/cupbearer-parthian-tkrpty-loanword-in-armenian-takarapet-cf.
31. Here I describe the clothing of the Parthian statue known as the Shami Prince. See Vogelsang-Eastwood, "Clothing of the 'Shami Prince.'"
32. Josephus, *Antiquities of the Jews*, 14.366; Josephus, *Jewish War*, 1.270.
33. On Cleopatra and Roman politics at the time, see Strauss, *War that Made the Roman Empire*, 38–42, 254–56.
34. Plutarch, *Antony*, 29.1; Strauss, *War that Made the Roman Empire*, 146, 320 n.146.
35. Josephus, *Antiquities of the Jews*, 14.836–87.
36. Josephus, *Antiquities of the Jews*, 13.385, my translation; Josephus, *Jewish War*, 1.284.
37. Cassius Dio, *Roman History*, 41.19.
38. Josephus, *Antiquities of the Jews*, 14.439–47.
39. Josephus, *Antiquities of the Jews*, 14.490.
40. Antigonus may have been beheaded or possibly had his throat cut. The sources disagree about that and about whether Antony first had Antigonus whipped while tied to a cross. See Josephus, *Antiquities of the Jews*, 14.490, 15.8–10 (citing Strabo); Cassius Dio, *Roman History*, 49.22.
41. Josephus, *Antiquities of the Jews*, 15.284.
42. "shackles of Greece": Polybius, *Histories*, 18.11. On Herod's army and its ethnic composition, see Shatzman, *Armies of the Hasmonaeans and Herod*, 163–65, 183–86; Rocca, *Herod's Judaea*, 134–40; Idem, *Army of Herod the Great*, 9.

NOTES

43. These men, led by one Zamaris, still made up their own unit in the Roman army in 108 CE and possibly later. See Applebaum, "Zamaris," 63–65.
44. Historians have a relative wealth of evidence for Jewish life under the Sasanians, but the Jews of the Parthian period are poorly documented. Still, certain points are clear. For a very conservative summary of the evidence, see Goodblatt, "Jews in the Parthian Empire."
45. Josephus, *Antiquities of the Jews*, 18.375.
46. On Herod's building projects, see Roller, *Building Program of Herod the Great*.
47. Josephus, *Jewish War*, 1.404.
48. The city was Anthedon (just north of today's port of Gaza), which Herod renamed Agrippias or Agrippeion.
49. Josephus, *Antiquities of the Jews*, 15.268–79, 273–74, 17.255; Josephus, *Jewish War*, 2.44. On the hippodrome/amphitheater, see Richardson, *Herod*, 249–51.
50. Josephus, *Antiquities of the Jews*, 15.274–75.
51. Y. *Avodah Zarah*, 1:7.
52. Josephus, *Antiquities of the Jews*, 15.280–98.
53. Josephus, *Antiquities of the Jews*, 15.380.
54. B. *Bava Batra* 4a.
55. B. *Bava Batra* 4a.
56. "cast a fiery light": Josephus, *Jewish War*, 5.222, my translation. The Talmud says the marbles were multicolored. B. *Bava Batra* 4a.
57. Goodman, *Herod the Great*, 85–86.
58. For a portrait of Herod's Jerusalem, see Sebag Montefiore, *Jerusalem*, 169–72.
59. Augustus's right-hand man, Agrippa, for example, ordered the sacrifice of one hundred oxen when he visited Jerusalem in 15 BCE. Josephus, *Antiquities of the Jews*, 16.15.
60. Pliny the Elder, *Natural History*, 5.70.
61. The sages' names were Judas, son of Sepphoraeus and Matthias, son of Margalus. See Josephus, *Jewish War*, 1.648, and (with variant spelling) Josephus, *Antiquities of the Jews*, 17.149.
62. Josephus, *Jewish War*, 1.649, trans. Josephus, Flavius, H. St. J. Thackeray, et al., *Josephus*, modified, vol. 2: 309. For the narrative of this incident, see ibid. 1.648–55; Josephus, *Antiquities of the Jews*, 17.149–64.
63. Matthew 2:16–18 (KJV).
64. Josephus, *Antiquities of the Jews*, 18.130, 133, 136.
65. Goodman, *Herod the Great*, 89.
66. Josephus, writing a century after Herod's death, calls him Herod the Great, but the language is ambiguous, and "the Great" may simply mean "the Elder," in distinction to Herod's like-named royal descendants (some of

whom survived his murder spree). See Josephus, *Antiquities of the Jews*, 18.130, 133, 136; Goodman, *Herod the Great*, 157–58.

Chapter Two: The War for Herod's Legacy

1. *Seder Olam*; see Eshel, "Varus," 115.
2. Josephus, *Antiquities of the Jews*, 17.266; Shatzman, *Armies*, 193; Rocca, *Herod's Judaea*, 139; Rocca, *Army of Herod*, 12–13.
3. Josephus, *Antiquities of the Jews*, 17.272.
4. Josephus, *Antiquities of the Jews*, 17.285, trans. Josephus, Flavius, H. St. J. Thackeray, et al., *Josephus*, vol. 8: 505.
5. Josephus and Williamson, *The Jewish War*, 461; Fredriksen, *When Christians Were Jews*, 46.
6. See the analysis in Novenson, *Grammar of Messianism*, 140–43.
7. Josephus, *Jewish War*, 1.3; Josephus, *Antiquities of the Jews*, 1.7
8. Josephus, e.g., *Jewish War*, 2.55; *Antiquities of the Jews*, 17.272, 274, 278, 280–81.
9. For references, see Strauss, *The Spartacus War*, 193–94.
10. Martial, *Epigrams*, 11.20.
11. Later governors of Judea, down to the year 70, would be known as procurators.
12. Goodman, *Ruling Class of Judaea*, 46–49,126–29.
13. Josephus, *Jewish War*, 2.118.
14. On the Fourth Philosophy, see Josephus, *Antiquities of the Jews*, 18.3–10; Josephus, *Jewish War*, 2.118, 433, 7.253.
15. Josephus, *Antiquities of the Jews*, 18.23; trans. Josephus, Flavius, H. St. J. Thackeray, et al., *Josephus*, vol. 9: 21.
16. Josephus, *Antiquities of the Jews*, 18.9; trans. Josephus, Flavius, H. St. J. Thackeray, et al., *Josephus*, vol. 9: 9.
17. Josephus, *Antiquities of the Jews*, 18.6, my translation.
18. Josephus, *Jewish War*, 7.253; Acts 5:37 (KJV).
19. Revolt: *apostasis*; insurgency: *thorubos* (*tumultus* in Latin). Josephus, *Antiquities of the Jews*, 18.4, 10.
20. Acts 5:37 (KJV).
21. Josephus, *Jewish War*, 2.253–57, 7.254. See also Barnett, "Under Tiberius": 564 n.5.
22. Josephus, *Antiquities of the Jews*, 18.7–10.
23. Tacitus, *Histories*, 5.9.
24. Tacitus, *Annals*, 15.44.
25. In what follows, I rely on the work of several scholars, in particular, Sanders, *Jesus and Judaism*, and Fredriksen, especially, *When Christians Were Jews*.

NOTES

26. Tacitus, *Annals*, 15.44, my translation. Pilate was actually a prefect and not a procurator.
27. The main sources on Pilate are the Gospels, Josephus, Philo, Tacitus, and the archaeological and numismatic evidence mentioned below.
28. Philo, *Embassy to Gaius*, 38.301–2.
29. On the Pilate inscription, see "Inscriptions of Israel/Palestine," CAES0043, 3 September 2024. https:doi.org/10.26300/pz1d-st89.
30. See Hendin, *Guide to Biblical Coins*, 279–81; Bond, "Coins of Pontius Pilate."

Chapter Three: The Turncoat and the Convert

1. Josephus, *Antiquities of the Jews*, 20.100.
2. Born perhaps around the year 15: Tiberius became procurator in 42. The minimum-age qualification for the office is not known, but it was probably not less than the minimum age for the quaestorship, which Augustus had lowered to twenty-five.
3. Josephus, *Antiquities of the Jews*, 20.100, my translation.
4. Rajak, "Jews" (who puts "pogrom" in quotation marks).
5. "I decide who's a Jew": Karl Lueger, mayor of Vienna, 1897–1910. For the quotation, see Wheatcroft, "Seeking Haider."
6. Josephus, *Antiquities of the Jews*, 18.228; cf. Ecclesiastes 9.4 (KJV), B. *Shabbat* 30b.
7. Philo, *The Embassy to Caligula*, 202.
8. Schwartz, *Agrippa I*, 82.
9. Philo, *Embassy to Caligula*, 207.
10. Philo, *Embassy to Caligula*, 245.
11. Philo, *Embassy to Caligula*, 213–14.
12. Philo, *Embassy to Caligula*, 215–17.
13. On the Jewish readiness to go to war, see Tacitus, *Histories*, 5.9. Cf. Philo, *Embassy to Caligula*, 208, 215. See Schwartz, *Agrippa I*, 81.
14. The details are found in Philo, *Embassy to Caligula*, 188, 207–8; Josephus, *Jewish War*, 2.192–202; Josephus, *Antiquities of the Jews*, 18.261–309; Tacitus, *Histories*, 5.9.
15. Trembling behind a curtain: Suetonius, *Claudius*, 10.1–2.
16. Josephus, *Jewish War*, 2.212–213. Cf. Josephus, *Antiquities of the Jews*, 19.237–38; Cassius Dio, *Roman History*, 40.8.2.
17. Kropp, "Crowning the Emperor."
18. Persecutor: Acts 12:1–19 (KJV).
19. Josephus, *Antiquities of the Jews*, 19.338–42.

NOTES

20. Josephus, *Antiquities of the Jews*, 19.341.
21. Josephus, *Antiquities of the Jews*, 19.357. Never mind that a Jewish king allowed statues to be made!
22. Josephus, *Antiquities of the Jews*, 20.5.
23. Josephus, *Antiquities of the Jews*, 20.97–99; Acts 5.36 (KJV).
24. See Johnson, "Theudas."
25. For the details, see Josephus, *Antiquities of the Jews*, 15.403–9; 18.90–97; 20.6–14.
26. Josephus, *Jewish War*, 2.220.
27. Coin image: Sellwood type 68. "Coins Attributed to Vologases I," Parthia, https://www.parthia.com/vologases1.htm.
28. On Vologases and his policies I follow Olbrycht, "Arsakid Empire," 125–38, 151.
29. Tacitus, *Annals*, 15.28, John Jackson, trans., *Tacitus, Annals Books 13–16*, translation modified, 259.
30. Tacitus, *Annals*, 15.29, trans. Church, Brodribb, and Bryant, *Complete Works of Tacitus*, http://www.perseus.tufts.edu/hopper/text?doc=Perseus%3Atext%3A1999.02.0078%3Abook%3D15%3Achapter%3D29.
31. Pausanias, *Description of Greece*, 8.16.4.
32. Antipater of Sidon, 2nd century BCE, Anth. Pal. 9.58, s.v. "Seven Wonders of the Ancient World," *Oxford Classical Dictionary*, 5th ed.
33. Josephus, *Antiquities of the Jews*, 20.95.
34. See Lawler, "Who Built the Tomb of the Kings?"
35. On the date, see Josephus, *Antiquities of the Jews*, 20.51; Marciak, *Helena*, 241–2, 245.
36. I base this description on the silver coin of the Parthian queen Mousa, a rare visual representation of a Parthian woman. See Madreiter and Hartmann, "Women at the Arsakid Court," 239.
37. See the prudent discussion of the evidence by Applebaum, "Social and Economic Status," 723–26.
38. Raschke, "New Studies in Roman Commerce," 643.
39. Josephus, *Antiquities of the Jews*, 20.49.
40. Acts 2:9–11 (KJV).
41. B. Sukkah 51a, https://www.sefaria.org/Sukkah.51a.16?lang=bi&with=all&lang2=en.
42. B. Sukkah 51a–b, https://www.sefaria.org/Sukkah.51a.16?lang=bi&with=all&lang2=en.
43. B. Sukkah 51b, https://www.sefaria.org/Sukkah.51b.4?lang=bi&with=all&lang2=en.
44. M. Yoma 3:10.
45. Josephus, *Jewish War*, 5.252.
46. Ben-Ami and Tchekanovets, "Has the Adiabene Royal Family 'Palace' Been

Found?" 231–40. Helena's palace was located in the Ophel (Ophlas in Josephus), the area south and below the Temple Mount.
47. Archaeologists: Michael Avi-Yonah and Yoram Tsafrir. See Amit, *Model of Jerusalem*, 58–59. A total of three such structures: Josephus, *Jewish War*, 4.567, 5.252.
48. Josephus, *Antiquities of the Jews*, 20.52, my translation. A later, rabbinic source says that it was Helena's other son, Monobazos II, who later succeeded to the throne, who provided the aid. T. Peah 4:18.
49. Josephus, *Antiquities of the Jews*, 20.94.
50. Josephus, *Antiquities of the Jews*, 20.95.
51. See the discussion in Lawler, "Who Built the Tomb of the Kings?"
52. Josephus, *Antiquities of the Jews*, 20.70. The Talmud speaks of seven sons of Izates in the Land of Israel, B. Sukkah 2b. The sources say nothing about sending Izates's daughters to Jerusalem.
53. On a possible Adiabenian ambition to rule Judea, see Neusner, *History of the Jews in Babylonia*, 68–69.

Chapter Four: And the War Came

1. The account of events in Judea in this chapter relies on Josephus, *Jewish War*, 2, esp. 277–561. For Judean military matters in this chapter, I rely on the work of various scholars, particularly Mason, *History of the Jewish War, AD 66–74*, and Rogers, *For the Freedom of Zion*. See also Goldsworthy, "'Men Casually Armed'," 209, 218; Bloom, *Jewish Revolts*, 47–91.
2. Josephus, *Jewish War*, 2.509.
3. On Cestius Gallus, see Roth, "Cestius Gallus"; Strothmann, "C[estius]. Cos. suff. 42 AD." Gallus had been suffect consul in 42, an office for which the minimum age was also forty-two. Hence, he was at least sixty-six at the time of his expedition to Judea.
4. Virgil, *Aeneid*, 6.852–53, my translation.
5. Josephus, *Jewish War*, 2.409. On pro-Roman Jews, see Wilker, "God Is with Italy Now."
6. Rogers, *For the Freedom of Zion*, 145.
7. Josephus, *Jewish War*, 2.409.
8. On this point, see Dyson, "Native Revolts," 249, 269.
9. There are fine analyses of competing explanations for the outbreak of the Great Revolt in Goodman, *Ruling Class*, 1–14; Idem, "Current Scholarship"; Mason, *Jewish Revolt*, 199–280, 581–85; Rogers, *For the Freedom of Zion*, 5–11, 433–43.

NOTES

10. Goodman, *Rome and Jerusalem*, 379–402; Gambash, 182–83; and Mason, 199–280, argue that the problems of Judea were largely manageable before the Roman missteps under Nero and Florus.
11. *Contra* Mason, *Jewish Revolt*, e.g., 275–77, who argues that intercommunal conflict was the main driving factor of the war.
12. The enthusiasm of the Jewish elite for the revolt is a key argument of Goodman, *Ruling Class of Judaea*.
13. On Florus, see Roth, "Gessius Florus"; Wandrey, "Gessius Florus."
14. Josephus, *Jewish War*, 2.223–31; Josephus, *Antiquities of the Jews*, 104–17.
15. For the sources, see Gamer, "Elazar ben Dinai."
16. Josephus, *Jewish War*, 6.422.
17. Seth Schwartz, *Ancient Jews from Alexander to Muhammad*, 80.
18. Josephus, *Jewish War*, 3.3.5.
19. Josephus, *Jewish War*, 2.284–85.
20. Josephus, *Jewish War*, 295, my translation.
21. Josephus, *Antiquities of the Jews*, 20.175–76; Josephus, *Jewish War*, 2.267–68. They belonged to the unit that Claudius had first planned to send to the Black Sea as punishment for their outrageous behavior in 44, but who managed to bribe their way into staying in Judea. Their continued presence, wrote Josephus (*Antiquities of the Jews*, 19.366), enflamed tensions there.
22. Josephus, *Jewish War*, 2.307.
23. Josephus, *Jewish War*, 2.457.
24. Josephus, *Jewish War*, 2.458–60.
25. Tacitus, *Histories*, 5.10. Cf. Josephus, *Antiquities of the Jews*, 20.257.
26. Josephus, *Jewish War*, 2.293; trans. Josephus, Flavius, H. St. J. Thackeray, et al., *Josephus*, 2:437; Josephus, *Antiquities of the Jews*, 20.533.
27. Josephus, *Jewish War*, 2.499–540.
28. "Kingdom of arrogance," from the Birkat ha-Minim, part of the Amidah, a prayer recited thrice daily by Orthodox Jews. The phrase is traditionally dated to the first century CE or earlier. See Ehrlich, "Birkat Ha-Minim."
29. Josephus, *Jewish War*, 2.254–55, 525; *Antiquities of the Jews*, 20.186–87.
30. Josephus, *Antiquities of the Jews*, 20.165–66.
31. On the advantages of Masada, see Bloom, *Jewish Revolts*, 65.
32. Josephus, *Jewish War*, 4.161.
33. On the Zealots, see Hengel, *Zealots*; Stern and Price, "Zealots and Sicarii."
34. Raphael, *A Jew among Romans*, 92.
35. Josephus, *Jewish War*, 2.518, my translation.
36. Josephus, *Jewish War*, 2.510.
37. Josephus, *Jewish War*, 2.520.

38. Josephus, *Jewish War*, 1.5, my translation. In discussing Josephus and the Jews of the East, I follow Gross, "Hopeful Rebels and Anxious Romans."
39. Josephus, *Jewish War*, 2.388–91.
40. Josephus, *Jewish War*, 6.343.
41. Gross, "Hopeful Rebels and Anxious Romans," 481.
42. Chagirus the Adiabenian, son of Nabataeus, fought bravely in the defense of Jerusalem. Josephus, *Jewish War*, 5.474.
43. Josephus, *Jewish War*, 2.527.
44. See the excellent analyses of Mason, *Jewish Revolt*, 281–334, and Rogers, *For the Freedom of Zion*, 160–83.
45. Josephus, *Jewish War*, 2.546.
46. B. Sanhedrin 32b. See Isaac and Roll, *Roman Roads*, 79.
47. Josephus, *Jewish War*, 2.551–55.
48. A point made by Gambash, *Rome and Provincial Resistance*, 145–51.
49. Cassius Dio, *Roman History*, 63.3.1–7, esp. 3.2.; Edward Champlin, *Nero*, location 3050–167. I am grateful to Dave Blome, PhD, USMC, an experienced bow hunter, for providing this information.
50. Rome accepted the inevitability of rebellion: a point made by Woolf, "Provincial Revolts," 42, who compares Rome's acceptance of provincial revolts as the price of empire to the modern attitude of accepting car accidents as the price of driving.
51. Gambash, *Rome and Provincial Resistance*, 164.
52. Josephus, *Jewish War*, 3.9.
53. Gambash, *Rome and Provincial Resistance*, 144–45.
54. Tacitus, *Histories*, 2.5.
55. Suetonius, *Vespasian*, 23.3; Cassius Dio, *Roman History*, 66.14.5.
56. Bloom, *Jewish Revolts*, 76.
57. Mason, *Jewish Revolt*, 217.

Chapter Five: The War in the North

1. Josephus, *Life*, 13.
2. Time of each trip: see https://orbis.stanford.edu.
3. For the brief narrative, see Josephus, *Life*, 13–16.
4. Josephus, *Life*, 16; see Josephus, *Antiquities of the Jews*, 20.193–95.
5. Mildenberg, "Rebel Coinage." An interesting precedent: during the "Social War," the revolt of the Italian allies against Rome in 90–88 BCE, the rebels issued silver coins showing the Italian bull trampling the Roman she-wolf. See "Silver Denarius of Italia, Uncertain value, 90 BCE–88 BCE.

NOTES

1967.153.19," https://numismatics.org/collection/1967.153.19. I am grateful to Adrienne Mayor for pointing this out to me.
6. Cotton, "Languages of the Legal and Administrative Documents," 225. Cited in Schäfer, "Bar Kokhba and the Rabbis," 20.
7. Rogers, *For the Freedom of Zion*, 145–46.
8. See Weinfeld, *Social Justice*, 7–23, 241–47; Leslie, "Redemption."
9. Cotton, "Languages," 225.
10. Goodman, *Ruling Class*, 177.
11. Goodman, *Ruling Class*, 168.
12. Josephus, *Jewish War*, 5.153.
13. Josephus, *Jewish War* 3.9, trans. Mason, *Jewish War*, 326.
14. Josephus, *Jewish War*, 1.152. On the Essenes' hatred of the Romans, see Sharon, *Judea under Roman Domination*, 201–7.
15. Price, *Jerusalem Under Siege*, 51–56, 72–76. See also Goldsworthy, "'Men Casually Armed'," 209.
16. Some recent conservative estimates are 600,000 to 1 million, della Pergola, "Notes toward a Demographic History of the Jews," 2; no more than 1 million, Broshi, "Western Palestine," 7; "Bread, Wine," 102. Cf. Rogers, *For the Freedom of Zion*, p. 593, n. 28.
17. The narrative in these two paragraphs is drawn from Josephus, *Jewish War*, 2.569–646, 3.59–63; Josephus, *Life*, 8–335.
18. Josephus, *Jewish War*, 3.64–69. I follow the calculations of Rogers, *For the Freedom of Zion*, 206–8.
19. The chief general's name was Philip, son of Jacimus. See Josephus, *Jewish War*, 2.421, 2.556, 4.81; Josephus, *Antiquities of the Jews*, 17.30; *Life*, 46–47, 59–60, 179–84, 407–9.
20. This section is indebted to the work of Aviam, "Archaeology of the Battle," "Archaeology of the First Battle," "Economic Impact"; Mason, *Jewish War*, 345–48, 365–69; Rogers, *For the Freedom of Zion*, 216–37.
21. Josephus, *Jewish War*, 3.143–44.
22. Josephus, *Jewish War*, 3.193–203.
23. See, for example, "Galilee in June," Where and When, https://www.whereandwhen.net/when/middle-east/israel/galilee/june/.
24. For the excavation, see Aviam, "Archaeology of the Battle," "Archaeology of the First Battle."
25. Mason, *Jewish War*, 129.
26. The 19th of Daisios (Sivan), based on Josephus, who says that the next day was the twentieth of Daisios. Josephus, *Jewish War*, 3.282.

NOTES

27. Josephus, *Jewish War*, 3.239, trans. Josephus, Flavius, H. St. J. Thackeray, et al., *Josephus*, 2:645.
28. On Josephus's contradictory figures, which add up to a siege of thirty-eight or forty-two days, not the forty-seven days that he claims, see Mason, *History of the Jewish War*, 364n.89.
29. As cited by Smallwood, Josephus, *Jewish War*, 470.
30. Josephus, *Jewish War*, 3.354, my translation.
31. Thucydides, *Peloponnesian War*, 6.92.4, trans. C. F. Smith, Thucydides, *The History of the Peloponnesian War*, vol. 3 (Harvard University Press, 1921), 351.
32. Outstanding service: Thucydides, *Peloponnesian War*, 8.86.4.
33. On the fight at Tarichaeae, see Josephus, *Jewish War*, 3.462–542.
34. Syon, "The Coins from Gamala."
35. Josephus, *Jewish War*, 4.115.
36. See the analysis by Mason, *History of the Jewish War*, 579.

Chapter Six: Defenders of Jerusalem

1. The following discussion of John of Giscala and Simon son of Giora owes much to Stern and Price, "Zealots and Sicarii," 474–79. On John of Giscala, see Uriel Rappaport, *John of Giscala*.
2. Josephus, *Jewish War*, 2.588.
3. Josephus, *Jewish War*, 2.625.
4. Josephus, *Life*, 354.
5. Tacitus, *Histories*, 5.12, my translation.
6. M. Pirkei Avot 1.17; B. Sukkah. 53a.
7. Josephus, *Jewish War*, 4.127.
8. Josephus, *Jewish War*, 6.98.
9. See "Book Minute: Psalm 91, The Soldier's Psalm," Museum of the Bible, https://www.museumofthebible.org/book-minute/psalm-91.
10. Psalm 91:7 (KJV).
11. "*A l'exemple de Saturne, la révolution dévore ses enfants.*"—Jacques Mallet du Pan, "Considérations sur la nature de la Révolution de France et sur les causes qui en prolongent la durée," 1793.
12. Josephus, *Jewish War*, 4.161, my translation.
13. Josephus, *Jewish War*, 4.318; cf. 4.151.
14. Price, *Jerusalem under Siege*, 255–63.
15. Simon came from Gerasa, which is usually taken to be a city in Perea, but

NOTES

some think it refers to another Gerasa, a small town either in Judah or Samaria. See Rappaport, "Bar Giora."

16. Josephus, *Jewish War*, 5.309, trans. Josephus, Flavius, H. St. J. Thackeray, et al., *Josephus*, 3.99, modified.
17. Tacitus, *Histories*, 5.12.12, trans. Moore, *Histories*, 197.
18. Josephus, *Jewish War*, 5.5–12, 100–105, 252–54.
19. Josephus, *Jewish War*, 5.248–50.
20. Tacitus, *Histories*, 12.3; cf. Stern, *Greek and Latin Authors*, 2:59.
21. Mason, *Jewish Revolt*, 459.
22. B. Yoma 9b.
23. Including the new suburbs within the Third Wall, Jerusalem was about 425 acres (175 hectares) in size, that is, about 0.67 square miles or 1.7 square kilometers. Horbury, Davies, and Sturdy, *Cambridge History of Judaism: The Early Roman Period*, 3.
24. Josephus, *Jewish War*, 4.622–29.
25. (ARN1 4, 22–24, ARN2, 19; Lam. R. 1:5, no. 31; Git. 56a–b.) See Wald, "Johanan Ben Zakkai," 375–76.
26. Rather than follow my standard practice of translating "ben" as "son," I retain "ben" here, because the rabbi is commonly known as Ben Zakkai.
27. Price, *Jerusalem under Siege*, 264–70.
28. Eusebius, *Ecclesiastical History*, 3.5.
29. On Rome's advantages in sieges, see Levithan, *Roman Siege Warfare*, 20–46.
30. On the dangers of hindsight and the reasons for rebel optimism, see Goodman, *Ruling Class*, 177–83.
31. One might also mention another failed siege during a civil war, Mutina in 43 BCE, but that failed only because a relief army came to the aid of the besieged.
32. Rogers, *For the Freedom of Zion*, 521. Byatt, "Josephus and Population Numbers," 56–57, estimates 220,000 in the city and environs; Broshi, "Jerusalem," 119, estimates 80,000; Geva, "Jerusalem's Population," 146, estimates 20,000 or less. For the range of estimates, see Geva, "Jerusalem's Population," 145–46.
33. On the numbers, see the discussion in Price, *Jerusalem under Siege*, 205–9; Rogers, *For the Freedom of Zion*, 428–29, 713–20.
34. Josephus, *Jewish War*, 1.434, 2.389, 6.343.
35. As Gross argues in "Hopeful Rebels and Anxious Romans."
36. Tacitus, *Histories*, 2.81–82.
37. Josephus, *Jewish War*, 6.343; Mason, *History of the Jewish War*, 461.
38. Neusner, *History of the Jews in Babylonia*, 69–70.

NOTES

39. The classic example is Corinth's call for volunteers to help the Athenian rebel city-state of Potidaea in the run-up to the Peloponnesian War in 433 BCE, Thucydides, *Peloponnesian War*, 1.60.1.
40. Josephus, *Jewish War*, 2.389.
41. Josephus, *Jewish War*, 6.343.
42. Tacitus, *Histories*, 4.51. See Jones, "Titus in the East," 350.
43. On the unlikelihood of Parthian aid to the Jewish rebels, see Mason, *Jewish Revolt*, 155–66.
44. Cassius Dio, *Roman History*, 66.4.3.
45. Tacitus, *Histories*, 2.4.3.

Chapter Seven: Titus at Jerusalem

1. Millar, *Roman Near East*, 76.
2. Josephus, *Jewish War*, 5.43–44; Tacitus, *Histories*, 5.1.2–3; Rogers, *For the Freedom of Zion*, 429.
3. Josephus, *Jewish War*, 5.45–46, 6.237, calls Tiberius Alexander commander (*archon*, commander, or *eparkhos*, Greek for the Latin *praefectus*) of all the armies. See Turner, "Tiberius Julius Alexander," 62.
4. Josephus, *Jewish War*, 5.46.
5. Josephus, *Jewish War*, 2.487–98.
6. As Mason, *Jewish War*, 464, points out.
7. The following discussion of the siege of Jerusalem relies heavily on the scholarship of modern authors, in particular, Campbell, *Siege Warfare*; Price, *Jerusalem Under Siege*; Levithan, *Roman Siege Warfare*; Mason, *History of the Jewish War*; Rogers, *For the Freedom of Jerusalem*.
8. I follow the dating scheme of Mason, *History of the Jewish War*, 439.
9. Josephus, *Jewish War*, 5.100–105.
10. Tacitus, *Histories*, 5.13.1, my translation.
11. Tacitus, *Histories*, 5.13.1.
12. On the typical stages of Roman sieges, see Levithan, 47–79.
13. Levithan, *Roman Siege Warfare*, 152.
14. Levithan, *Roman Siege Warfare*, 152.
15. Josephus, *Jewish War*, 5.279.
16. Josephus, *Jewish War*, 5.28, 287.
17. Cassius Dio, *Roman History*, 65.5.4. On the successive waves of desertion, see Price, *Jerusalem Under Siege*, 258.
18. Josephus, *Jewish War*, 5.304–7. Cf. Cassius Dio, *Roman History*, 65.4.4.
19. Josephus, *Jewish War*, 5.353.

NOTES

20. Josephus, *Jewish War*, 5.490, trans. Josephus, Flavius, H. St. J. Thackeray, et al., *Josephus*, 3:155, modified.
21. Josephus, *Jewish War*, 5.475, trans. Josephus, Flavius, H. St. J. Thackeray, et al., *Josephus*, 3:151, modified.
22. Josephus, *Jewish War*, 5.474.
23. Cassius Dio, *Roman History*, 65.4.5, trans. Cary, *Dio Cassius*, 225.
24. The men considered that beneath their dignity: Tacitus, *Histories*, 5.11.2.
25. Josephus, *Jewish War*, 5.499.
26. Seneca, *On the Shortness of Life*, 18.5, trans. Seneca and Basore, *Moral Essays* 2:349. See also Tim Ferriss, "On the Shortness of Life: An Introduction to Seneca," https://tim.blog/2009/04/24/on-the-shortness-of-life-an-introduction-to-seneca/ .
27. Josephus, *Jewish War*, 6.13.
28. Josephus, *Jewish War*, 6.17.
29. Levithan, *Roman Sieges*, 165.
30. Cassius Dio, *Roman History*, 65.6.2.
31. Sulpicius Severus, *Chronica*, 2.30.3, 6–7; Stern, *Greek and Latin Authors*, 2:64–67.
32. Josephus, *Jewish War*, 6.236–43.
33. ferocious and greedy for booty: Tacitus, *Histories*, 5.11.2.
34. Josephus, *Jewish War*, 6.275.
35. Josephus, *Jewish War*, 6.317. Sacrificing to the standards is attested otherwise only in a possible, oblique reference in the Habakkuk Pesher, a text from Qumran. See "The Expression: 'They Sacrificed to Their Standards,'" Reformed Reader Blog.
36. Josephus, *Jewish War*, 6.5,151, 373; Josephus, Williamson, and Smallwood, *Jewish War*, 368.
37. Suetonius, *Titus*, 5.2. This seems like an odd detail, since Romans were not fond of archery.
38. Josephus, *Jewish War*, 6.276–77.
39. Pericles called Aegina "the eyesore of the Piraeus [Athens' harbor]": Plutarch, *Pericles* 8.5.
40. Gil Gambash, *Rome and Provincial Resistance*, 144–61.
41. Letter 66.13, trans., Seneca, Lucius Annaeus, and Richard M. Gummere, *Ad Lucilium Epistulae Morales*, vol. 2 (W. Heinemann, 1917), 11.
42. Josephus, *Jewish War*, 4.567, 5.252–53, 6.354.
43. Josephus, *Jewish War*, 6.356.
44. Josephus, *Jewish War*, 2.520.
45. Price, *Jerusalem under Siege*, 123.

46. Carthage: see Le Bohec, "'The Third Punic War.'"
47. Josephus, *Jewish War*, 5.257, trans. Josephus, Flavius, H. St. J. Thackeray, et al., *Josephus*, translation modified, 3:281.
48. B. Yoma 9b.
49. On roughly 15 percent, or one-seventh, of the Roman armed forces, see Millar, *Roman Near East*, 76. On the huge Roman blood sacrifice, see Goodman, *Rome and Jerusalem*, 418–19.
50. Titus: Cassius Dio, *Roman History*, 65.5.1. Josephus: Josephus, *Jewish War* 5.541–44.
51. Estimate: Rogers, *For the Freedom of Zion*, 369.
52. "folly of revolutionaries": Josephus, *Jewish War*, 7.4, my translation.

Chapter Eight: Survivors

1. Millar, *Roman Near East*, 76.
2. Auerbach, Bahat, and Gilboa, "Western Wall," 24.
3. Josephus, *Life*, 422; Josephus, *Jewish War*, 7.377; Price, *Jerusalem Under Siege*, 414.
4. B. Makkot 24b:2–4.
5. See Isaac, "Judea after AD 70," 44–50.
6. Josephus, *Jewish War*, 6.420.
7. Schwartz, *Imperialism*, 10–11, 41; della Pergola, "Notes toward a Demographic History of the Jews," 2.
8. Zissu, "Interbellum Judea," 22–25.
9. Kloner, Klein, and Zissu, "Rural Hinterland," 131–32; Isaac, "Judea after AD 70," 50.
10. Gross, "Hopeful Rebels and Anxious Romans," 489–91, 500–501.
11. Gambash, *Rome and Provincial Resistance*, 159.
12. Kerkeslager, "Jews in Egypt and Cyrenaica," 58–59.
13. As noted by Geiger, "Bar-Kokhba Revolt," 504. See also Gross, "Hopeful Rebels and Anxious Romans," 501–5.
14. Josephus, *Jewish War*, 7.117–20; Suetonius, *Titus*, 5.3.
15. Josephus, *Jewish War*, 6.356.
16. Hostages marched in Republican-era triumphs: see Allen, *Hostages and Hostage-Taking*, 97–101; in Vespasian's day as well a general still boasted: Ibid., 108–9; a coin image can be interpreted as showing Simon son of Giora marching as a captive in the triumph of 71: RIC II, Part 1 (2nd ed.) Vespasian 1127, "Online Coins of the Roman Empire," http://numismatics.org/

NOTES

ocre/id/ric.2_1(2).ves.1127. British Museum 1864, 1128.255, https://www.britishmuseum.org/collection/object/C_1864-1128-255.
17. Josephus, *Jewish War*, 7.133.
18. Juvenal, *Satires*, 1.131; Turner, "Tiberius Julius Alexander," 63.
19. Gambash, *Rome and Provincial Resistance*, 144–51.
20. Judea had been a potential ally of the Parthians. See Simcha Gross, "Hopeful Rebels and Anxious Romans," 499–500.
21. Berthelot, *Jews and Their Roman Rivals*, 430.
22. "The Arch of Titus in the Circus Maximus," Judaism and Rome, https://www.judaism-and-rome.org/arch-titus-circus-maximus.
23. For an overview of the Temple of Peace, see "The Temple of Peace (Rome)," Judaism and Rome, https://www.judaism-and-rome.org/temple-peace-rome.
24. See Feldman, "Financing the Colosseum."
25. Meshorer, *Treasury*, 185, cited in Ilan, *Queen Berenice*, 145n.24.
26. See "Dedication of the Colosseum on a Coin," Israel Museum, Jerusalem, https://www.imj.org.il/en/collections/549659-0; Hendin, *Guide to Biblical Coins*, 377–79.
27. Josephus, *Jewish War*, 1.483, 2.389; 6.343.
28. Tacitus, *Histories*, 2.81–82.
29. Cassius Dio, *Roman History*, 66.15.3; Suetonius, *Domitian*, 2.2; Bosworth, "Vespasian's Reorganisation," 68–69.
30. Aurelius Victor, *de Caesaribus*, 9.10; Pseudo-Aurelius Victor, *Epitome de Caesaribus*, 9.12; Bosworth, "Vespasian's Reorganisation," 77.
31. Ilan, *Queen Berenice*, 122.
32. Josephus, *Jewish War*, 7.23–24, 37–40. See Ilan, *Queen Berenice*, 128–29, and the works by Wilker and Vasta cited there.
33. Turner, "Tiberius Julius Alexander," 63.
34. Suetonius, *Titus*, 7.2; Quintilian, *Institutes of Oratory*, 4.1.19; Cassius Dio, *Roman History*, 66.18.1; Pseudo-Aurelius Victor, *Epitome de Caesaribus*, 10.7.
35. Suetonius, *Titus*, 7.2. The self-consciously literary Suetonius was probably invoking, with this phrase, both Virgil's Queen Dido and Catullus's Queen Berenice II of Ptolemaic Egypt. Ilan, *Queen Berenice*, 139–40.
36. Julius Alexander, Son of Tigranes VI, great-great-grandson of Herod the Great, was both king of the client kingdom of Cetis and consul. C. I. Alexander Berenicianus, arguably a descendant of Berenice and her son Berenicianus, was senator, consul, and took part in Trajan's Parthian War. His brother, Gaius Julius Agrippa, was also a Roman senator. Gaius Julius Agrippa had a son, Lucius Julius Gainius Fabius Agrippa, also known as

Lucius Julius Agrippa. He was an important official in Syria and served on several embassies to the emperor in Rome.
37. Noy and Sorek, "Claudia Aster and Curtia Euodia," 3. Proculus's name has been restored. In what follows, I have benefited greatly from the insights of this article.
38. See Stone, "Ezra, Apocalypse of"; Grintz, "Baruch, Apocalypse of"; Berthelot, "Is God Unfair?"
39. Mark 13:5–6, 21–23 (KJV).
40. Schäfer, *History of the Jews in Antiquity*, 139.

Chapter Nine: Masada

1. Josephus does not state the year in which Masada was conquered. Hints in his text have long convinced scholars to place the event in April 73. Recent reexamination of the evidence of inscriptions and papyri make April 74 more likely, but still not 100 percent certain. See Cotton, "Date of the Fall of Masada."
2. For these and other estimates of Roman and Jewish forces at Masada, see Roth, "The Length of the Siege of Masada," 91–95.
3. The bibliography about Masada is vast. I have benefited in particular from Magness, *Masada*; Yadin, *Masada*; Eshel, *Masada*; the discussions in Mason, *History of the Jewish War* and Rogers, *For the Freedom of Zion*, 398–431; as well as various scholarly articles and chapters cited below.
4. Suetonius, *Augustus*, 3.1.
5. Yitzhak Lamdan, "Masada," see "Masada," in "Encyclopedic Dictionary," Zionism and Israel, https://zionism-israel.com/dic/Massada.htm.
6. "Masada," UNESCO, https://whc.unesco.org/en/list/1040/#:~:text=Masada%20is%20a%20dramatically%20located,complex%20in%20classical%20Roman%20style.
7. Josephus's account of Herodium appears in *Jewish War*, at 7.163; of Machaerus, at 7.164–215; of Masada, at 7.252–407.
8. Josephus, *Jewish War*, 7.164.
9. Josephus, *Jewish War*, 7.215.
10. Josephus, *Jewish War*, 7.303.
11. Josephus gives measurements in furlongs and cubits. I have supplied the rough equivalents in modern measurements.
12. Josephus, *Jewish War*, 7.408, my translation.
13. On these points, see Roth, "The Length of the Siege of Masada," 95–98.
14. Magness, "Women at Masada."

15. Magness, "Women at Masada."
16. Roth, "The Length of the Siege of Masada," 87–90, 109–10.
17. Roth, "The Length of the Siege of Masada," 91–94.
18. Levithan, *Roman Siege Warfare*, 55.
19. On the ramp, I follow Davies, "Masada Siege." The 2016 study is Goldfus, Avni, Albag, and Arubas, "Significance of Geomorphological and Soil Formation Research." Mason, *History of the Jewish War*, 560–61, 572–73, follows their approach (as presented by the authors in an earlier study) and takes it even further. The rebuttal is Davies and Magness, "Recovering Josephus."
20. Geza, "Siege Ramp."
21. Rabinowitz, Cohn, and Elon, "Suicide."
22. Cohen, "Masada," 386–92.
23. Bowman and Flusser, *Sepher Yossippon*, 392.
24. As Werner Eck argues, a member of the senatorial order would not have started his career in the lowly office that marked Silva's debut in public life. He was a *triumvir capitalis*, one of the three men traditionally responsible for executions in Rome. Eck, "*Urbs Salvia*," 58.
25. Eck, "*Urbs Salvia*," 58–63.
26. On the amphitheater, see Eck, "*Urbs Salvia*," 57, 69–70; Fenati, *Lucio Flavio Silva*, 138–40.
27. Rupert Brooke, "The Soldier": "If I should die, think only this of me: / That there's some corner of a foreign field / That is forever England."
28. Josephus, *Jewish War*, 2.447.
29. Josephus, *Jewish War*, 2.443.
30. Josephus, *Jewish War*, 2.434, 442.
31. Josephus, *Jewish War*, 2.443.
32. Josephus, *Jewish War*, 7.297.
33. Josephus, *Jewish War*, 7.275. 967: 960; dead plus seven survivors, ibid., 7.398–401.
34. On this and the following paragraph, see Josephus, *Jewish War*, 4.399–407, 516.
35. Josephus, *Jewish War*, 7.255; Mason, *History of the Jewish War*, 533.
36. Mason, *History of the Jewish War*, 549. "Underground Railroad" is my term. To call Masada a "displaced persons camp" (Reich, "Baking and Cooking," 152) or a "bandit society" (Mason, *History of the Jewish War*, 565) is to underestimate its importance.
37. Josephus, *Jewish War*, 4.503–8.
38. See Crawford, "Scribe Links Qumran and Masada"; Mason, *History of the Jewish War*, 552n.97.

39. Josephus, *Jewish War*, 7.410–53.
40. Josephus, *Jewish War*, 7.334, trans. Josephus, Flavius, H. St. J. Thackeray, et al., *Josephus*, modified.
41. Josephus, *Jewish War*, 7.386, trans. Josephus, Flavius, H. St. J. Thackeray, et al., *Josephus* modified.
42. Cohen, "Masada," 395–97.
43. Roth, "The Length of the Siege of Masada," 108–9.
44. Josephus, *Jewish War*, 7.399, 405.
45. Josephus, *Jewish War*, 7.427, trans. Josephus, Flavius, H. St. J. Thackeray, et al., *Josephus* modified.
46. On the correspondence between Macedonian and Jewish months, I follow the argument of Price, *Jerusalem under Siege*, 209–11.
47. For the distance, see "The Stanford Geospatial Network Model of the Roman World," Orbis, https://orbis.stanford.edu/.
48. Josephus, *Jewish War*, 7.418.
49. Josephus, *Jewish War*, 7.419.
50. Josephus, *Jewish War*, 7.401.
51. Josephus, *Jewish War*, 7.437–38.
52. Following the calculations of "The Stanford Geospatial Network Model of the Roman World," Orbis.
53. Josephus, *Antiquities of the Jews*, 20.144.

Chapter Ten: Trajan, Parthia, and the Diaspora Revolt

1. Ben Zeev, "Uprisings in the Jewish Diaspora," 102.
2. Applebaum, *Jews and Greeks in Ancient Cyrene*, 341.
3. Ben Zeev, "Greek Attacks against Alexandrian Jews," 31–48, esp. 45, n.32.
4. Syme, *Tacitus*, 39.
5. Pliny the Younger, *Letters*, 9.2, trans. Pliny and Radice, *Letters*, 2:83.
6. Cassius Dio, *Roman History*, 68.30.2. See Turner, "Tiberius Julius Alexander," 63; Schürer, *History of the Jewish People in the Age of Jesus Christ*, 1:458, n. 9.
7. Cassius Dio, *Roman History*, 68.29.1, trans. Cary, *Dio Cassius*, 417.
8. They burned down a temple: in Dura-Europos. See Ben Zeev, *Diaspora Judaism in Turmoil*, 202, n.46.
9. I follow the arguments of Ben Zeev, *Diaspora Judaism in Turmoil*, 190–217.
10. Eusebius, *Chronicle*, 18. The *Chronicle* does not survive in its original Greek. I refer to the Latin translation by Jerome. For the English translation, see Horbury, "Beginnings," 287. In his *Ecclesiastical History* 4.2.5 Eusbeius states that Trajan merely suspected a Jewish revolt.

NOTES

11. Eusebius, *Chronicle*, 18; Eusebius, *Ecclesiastical History*, 4.2.5.
12. Cassius Dio, *Roman History* 64.30.1–2, 65.32.3. Goodblatt's skeptical reading of the evidence supports a Jewish community in Nisibis at the time and perhaps ones in Edessa and Seleucia. See Goodblatt, "Jews in the Parthian Empire," 264–78. On Seleucia, see Oppenheimer, *Babylonia Judaica*, 220–21.
13. Translated with commentary by Stern, ed., *Greek and Latin Authors on Jews and Judaism*, vol. 2, 332a, pp. 152–55.
14. On the chronology, I follow Barnes, "Trajan," 145–62; Kerkeslager, "Jews in Egypt and Cyrenaica, 59–62"; and Ben Zeev, *Diaspora Judaism in Turmoil*, 143–66. For a defense of the earlier chronology, see Horbury, "Beginnings of the Jewish Revolt," 283–304, and *Jewish War*, 166–79.
15. This was the advice that the Athenian Alcibiades gave to the Persian satrap Tissaphernes in 411 BCE during the Peloponnesian War, and which Tissaphernes tended to accept, at least according to his actions. Thucydides, *Peloponnesian War*, 8.46.1. On the Sicilian Expedition as a proxy war, see Rahe, *Sparta's Sicilian Proxy War*.
16. Pliny the Younger, *Letters to Trajan*, 10.74; the cavalrymen are labeled "Sarmatians," but Sarmatians were an eastern Iranian people who fought in the Parthian army. Debevoise, *Political History of Parthia*, 217.
17. I rely on the account of Applebaum, *Jews and Greeks in Ancient Cyrene*, 201–344, with modifications by Barnes, "Trajan," 145–62; Horbury, "Beginnings of the Jewish Revolt," 283–304, and *Jewish War*, 164–277; Reynolds, "Cyrenaica," 547–53; Kerkeslager, "Jews in Egypt and Cyrenaica," 59–62; and Ben Zeev, *Diaspora Judaism in Turmoil*.
18. Philo, *On Rewards and Punishments*, 163–64, cf. 165–69, trans. Philo, Colson, and Whitaker, *Philo*, 8:417.
19. Horbury, "Beginnings of the Jewish Revolt under Trajan," 299–301.
20. Eusebius, *Ecclesiastical History*, 4.2.4; Cassius Dio, *History of Rome*, 67.32. On Josephus, see above, pp. 38–39.
21. Gonzalez-Salinero, *Military Service*, 69–70.
22. Ben Zeev, *Diaspora Judaism in Turmoil*, 127, with references to Applebaum, *Jews and Greeks in Ancient Cyrene*, and Kerkeslager, "Jews in Egypt and Cyrenaica."
23. Applebaum, *Jews and Greeks in Ancient Cyrene*, 228–29, 337.
24. Dio or his abridger: Cassius Dio, *Roman History*, 68.32.1–2.
25. Horbury, *Jewish War under Trajan and Hadrian*, 225.
26. "It has been taught: Said R. Judah, 'Whoever has never seen the double colonnade (the basilica-synagogue) of Alexandria has never seen Israel's glory

in his entire life.'" Y. Sukkah, V 1 55a–b, translated in Ben Zeev, *Diaspora Judaism in Turmoil*, 107.
27. Appian, *Civil Wars*, 2.90.
28. Ben Zeev, *Diaspora Judaism in Turmoil*, 18–51.
29. Appian, *Liber Arabicus* F19 = *GLAJJ* II, 348, pp. 185–86, in Ben Zeev, *Diaspora Judaism in Turmoil*, 78–79; Horbury, *Jewish War*, 240–41.
30. Orosius, *Against the Pagans*, 7.12.8; Cassius Dio, *Roman History*, 68.32.2.
31. Y. Sukkah 5.1.55a–b, in Ben Zeev, *Diaspora Judaism in Turmoil*, 108. Ironically, a Greek source accused Plotina of being pro-Jewish, Horbury, *Jewish War*, 213–14.
32. Appian, *Civil Wars*, 2.90, my translation.
33. Kerkeslager, "Jews in Egypt and Cyrenaica," 61.
34. Ben Zeev, "New Insights into the Roman Policy in Judea on the Eve of the Bar Kokhba Revolt," 88–91.
35. I follow the analysis of Horbury, *Jewish War*, 264–69.

Chapter Eleven: Bar Kokhba

1. See Eck, "Bar Kokhba Revolt," "Hadrian," and Bowersock, "Tel Shalem Arch."
2. Schlude, *Rome, Parthia, and the Politics of Peace*, 172, 174; Avner, Greenwald, Ecker, Cotton, "Special Announcement: A New-Old Monumental Inscription from Jerusalem Honoring Hadrian."
3. "Hadrian," *Historia Augusta*, 12.8, 13.8. Translation: Birley, *Hadrian*, 151.
4. Or rather, the legitimate Parthian king whom Rome accepted. Another man, Vologases III (ca.105–129), ruled in part of the Parthian Empire at the same time, but it is not clear in which part. Ellerbrock, *Parthians*, 60.
5. Scholarship on the *conloquium*: Schlude, *Rome, Parthia, and the Politics of Peace*, 165; Doležal, "Did Hadrian Ever Meet a Parthian King?" 118–24.
6. "Hadrian," *Historia Augusta*, 13.8, 21.10; "Antonius Pius," 9.7.
7. The date of the stationing of the second legion in Judea is not certain. For an argument that it came with Bruttanius, see Ben Zeev, "New Insights into Roman Policy in Judea," 92. For the number of legionaries, see Eshel and Zissu, *Bar Kokhba Revolt*, 12.
8. Epiphanius, *On Weights and Measures*, 14.
9. Goodman, "Bar-Kokhba War," 28–29, cited by Ben Zeev, "New Insights into Roman Policy in Judea," 100–101.
10. Weksler-Bdolah and Onn, "Colonnaded Streets," 21–22.

NOTES

11. Onn and Weksler-Bdolah, "Temple Mount at the Time of *Aelia Capitolina*," 92–94.
12. Cassius Dio, *History of Rome*, 69.12.2, trans. Cary, *Dio Cassius*, 8:447.
13. Sources: Genesis Rabbah 64:29; Epistle of Barnabas 16:3-4. For a summary of scholarship, see Zissu and Eshel, "Religious Aspects of the Bar Kokhba Revolt," 396–99.
14. "Hadrian," *Historia Augusta*, 14.2.
15. Schwartz, "On Barnabas."
16. E.g., Letter of Shimon bar Kosiba to the People of En Gedi, Center for Online Jewish Studies (COJS), "The Bar Kokhba Letters."
17. Letter of Shimon ben [sic] Kosiba to Yeshua ben Galgoula, Center for Online Jewish Studies (COJS), "The Bar Kokhba Letters."
18. Eusebius, *Ecclesiastical History*, 4.6.2.
19. The name Bar Kokhba is too well known to replace it with "Son of Kokhba."
20. This and the following paragraph follow the arguments of Peter Schäfer, "Bar Kokhba and the Rabbis," 1–22.
21. Schäfer, "Bar Kokhba and the Rabbis," 15–18.
22. Y. Taanit 4:5, https://www.sefaria.org/Jerusalem_Talmud_Taanit.4.5.13?lang=bi, slightly revised. See also B. Sanhedrin 93b.
23. Maim.Yad, Melakhim, 11:3, translated Samuel Abramsky and Shimon Gibson, "Bar Kokhba," *Encyclopaedia Judaica* 3:58.
24. The following discussion of Bar Kokhba's coins is largely derived from Hendin, *Guide to Biblical Coins*, 325–46.
25. M. Yoma 3.10, V.Ber. 26a; Hendin, *Guide to Biblical Coins*, 338–39.
26. Various letters by Bar Kokhba, see Center for Online Jewish Studies (COJS), "The Bar Kokhba Letters."
27. Eshel, Eshel, and Yardeni, "A Document from 'Year 4 of the Destruction of the House of Israel.'"
28. Midrash Rabbah Lamentations 2:2–4.
29. "The Life of Churchill/War Leader/Convinces Cabinet to Fight on, Belgium Surrenders," International Churchill Society, https://winstonchurchill.org/the-life-of-churchill/war-leader/convinces-cabinet-to-fight-on-belgium-surrenders/.
30. Hugh Dalton, cited by Lukacs, John, *Five Days in London*, 5.
31. Cassius Dio, *Roman History*, 69.12.2, my translation.
32. Barsimso son of Callisthenis. CIL XVI 106, cited by Isaac, "Roman Colonies in Judaea," 50.
33. B. Shabbat 33b. I follow the version in sefaria.org, https://www.sefaria.org/

Shabbat.33b.5?lang=bi. The three rabbis are, in order, Judah bar Ilai, Yosei ben Chalafta, and Shimon bar Yochai.
34. Hat tip to Powell, *Bar Kokhba*, 125.
35. Cassius Dio, *Roman History*, 69.12.3, trans. Cary, *Dio Cassius*, 8:449.
36. Cassius Dio, *Roman History*, 69.12.2.
37. Cassius Dio, *Roman History*, 69.14.1.
38. Cassius Dio, *Roman History*, 69.13.1.
39. People's army, Harkabi, *Bar Kokhba Syndrome*, 32.
40. Horbury, "Beginnings of the Jewish Revolt under Trajan," 326.
41. On the rural basis of Bar Kokhba's army, see Zissu, "Interbellum Judea, 70–132 CE," 19, 47–49.
42. Steinmeyer, "Ancient Roman Swords Discovered Near En Gedi."
43. See Dabrowa, "Poblicius Marcellus," 74–76.
44. Cassius Dio, *Roman History*, 69.13.1, trans. Cary, *Dio Cassius*, 8:449.
45. Cassius Dio, *Roman History*, 69.12.2, my translation.
46. See Lewis, Yadin, and Greenfield, *Documents from the Bar Kokhba Period in the Cave of Letters*. For an overview, see Saldarini, "Babatha's Story"; Schama, *Story of the Jews*, 168–70.
47. See Lewis et al., *Documents from the Bar Kokhba Period*, 11. "Loan on Hypothec," 41–46.
48. Inscriptions refer to the campaign as the "Judean expedition" (*expeditio iudaica*, *CIL* VI 1523 = *ILS* 1092; VI 3505). Although "expedition" often refers to a campaign in which the emperor participated personally, there are exceptions: see Frere, "M. Maenius Agrippa," 25, n.12.
49. Dabrowa, "Poblicius Marcellus," 75–76.
50. Cassius Dio, *Roman History*, 69.13.2, my translation.
51. See Frere, "M. Maenius Agrippa," 23–28.
52. Fronto, *On the Parthian War*, 2—Van den Hout = F192R; Stern, *Greek and Latin Authors on Jews and Judaism*, 2:342, p. 177.
53. Cassius Dio, *Roman History*, 69.14.3, my translation.
54. Cassius Dio, *Roman History*, 69.14.3, my translation.
55. Powell, *Bar Kokhba*, 174.
56. The near-total absence of Bar Kokhba coins in Jerusalem, despite over 15,000 ancient coins found in the city, makes it clear that the rebels never took the place. See Eshel and Zissu, *Bar Kokhba Revolt*, 140–41.
57. Cassius Dio, *Roman History*, 69.13.3; Cary, *Dio Cassius*, 8:449.
58. Lamentations Rabbah i 45 on 1:16; see Horbury, *Jewish War*, 325.
59. Powell, *Bar Kokhba*, 189–91.
60. Lamentations Rabbah i 45, on 1:16; Horbury, *Jewish War*, 395.

NOTES

61. Anders Runesson, "Joshua Ezra Burns' *The Christian Schism*," 4.
62. Justin Martyr, *I Apology*, 30.6; Eusebius, *Chronicle*, "Hadrian's Year 17"; *Ecclesiastical History*, 4.8.4; Orosius, *Against the Pagans*, 7.13; Jerome, *Apology for Himself against Rufinus*, 3.31; Bauckham, "Jews and Jewish Christians," 228–29; Powell, *Bar Kokhba*, 180–81; Charlesworth, "Christians and Jews," 344–45.
63. Harkabi, *Bar Kokhba Syndrome*, 60–61.
64. Eusebius, *Ecclesiastical History*, 4.6.3, my translation.
65. For the descriptions in this and the following paragraphs, see Eshel and Zissu, *Bar Kokhba Revolt*, 118–21.
66. Eusebius, *Ecclesiastical History*, 4.6.3, trans. Eusebius, Kirsopp, et al. *Ecclesiastical History*, 113: 313.
67. T. Yebamot 14.8, cited by Eshel and Zissu, *The Bar Kokhba Revolt*, 121.
68. Rabbi Shimon Son of Gamaliel II, Y. Taanit 4.5.
69. Cassius Dio, *Roman History*, 69.13.3, trans. Cary, *Dio Cassius*, 8: 449.
70. Eusebius, *Ecclesiastical History*, 4.6.3, trans. Eusebius, Kirsopp, et al. *Ecclesiastical History*, 1:313.
71. Y. Taanit 4.5.
72. Y. Taanit 4.5.
73. His name was Jonathan Son of Beianus.
74. Eshel and Zissu, *Bar Kokhba Revolt*, 62–83.
75. Eusebius, *Ecclesiastical History*, 4.6.1, trans. Eusebius, Kirsopp, et al. *Ecclesiastical History*, 1:311. Eusebius refers to Quintus Tineius Rufus, governor of Judea, 130–133, but Eusebius was not always careful about chronology. Presumably he has in mind the results of the revolt overall.
76. Cassius Dio, *Roman History*, 69.14.1–2, trans. Cary, *Dio Cassius*, 8:449.
77. Raviv and Ben David, "Cassius Dio's Figures for the Demographic Consequences of the Bar Kokhba War"; Eshel & Zissu, *Bar Kokhba Revolt*, 152–53.
78. Tacitus, *Agricola*, 30.
79. Dindorf, ed., *Chronicon Pascale*, 1.74; Jerome, *Comm. In Zach.* iii on ii 45; cited in Horbury, *Jewish War*, 401–2, n. 481.
80. Eck, "Bar Kokhba Revolt," 88–89.
81. Cotton, "Impact of the Roman Army," 398.
82. Geiger, "Bar-Kokhba Revolt," 501–2.
83. Pausanias, *Description of Greece*, 1.5.5, trans. Pausanias, Jones, et al., *Description of Greece*, 1:27.
84. Geiger, "The Bar-Kokhba Revolt," 497–519.
85. Geiger, "The Bar-Kokhba Revolt," 503–4.
86. Horbury, *Jewish War*, 409–18.

87. Jerome, *Commentary on Jeremiah*, vi 18 on 31:15; Horbury, *Jewish War*, 402.
88. Josephus, *Jewish War*, 7.421, my translation.

Epilogue

1. Formerly in charge of the Temple, the priests and their descendants remained conscious of their heritage and continued to perform certain offices in the synagogue—as they do to this day.
2. In the mid-fourth century the Romans renamed the province of Arabia as Palaestina Salutaris, with its capital in Petra. Around 400, Syria Palaestina was divided into Palaestina Prima in the south and Palaestina Secunda in the north; Palaestina Salutaris was renamed Palaestina Tertia. For simplicity's sake, I use the name Palestine in this chapter for the former Judea.
3. Origen, *Epistle to Africanus*, 14.
4. Steinmeyer, "Golan's Roman Road." On the potential use of such roads against Parthia, see Kennedy, "Parthia and Rome," 84–85.
5. Origen, *Epistle to Africanus*, 14
6. B. Ketubot 111a; ShirhaShirim Rabah 2:7.
7. Genesis Rabbah 75.5.
8. B. Yoma 10a.
9. Midrash Tanchuma, Vayeshev 3.
10. PdRK (Pesikta de Rabbi Kahana) 130. See Wald, "Judah Ha-Nasi," 502.
11. B. Sanhedrin 98b, Sefaria translation modified, https://www.sefaria.org/Sanhedrin.98b.16?lang=bi .
12. The following discussion of the Gallus Revolt is indebted to the work of several scholars, in particular to Stemberger, *Jews and Christians*, 161–184.
13. Stemberger, *Jews and Christians*, 168.
14. For the sources and their meaning, see Mor, "Events of 351–352," 339.
15. Aurelius Victor, De Caesaribus, 42.11, trans. Stemberger, *Jews and Christians*, 172.
16. J. Naveh, *On Stone and Mosaic*, 57–58, cited in Stemberger, *Jews and Christians*, 173, n. 29.
17. Jerome, *Chronicon* 282nd Olympiad, § 5 (GCS 47, 238), trans. Stemberger, *Jews and Christians*, 162. Cf. Jerome, *Commentary on Daniel*, 11.34 (CC 75 A, 924).
18. Stemberger, *Jews and Christians*, 162–63.
19. Schuster, "Archaeologists." Note that, as of this writing, the findings have not been published nor submitted to scholarly scrutiny or debate.
20. ShirhaShirim Rabbah 8:9, https://www.sefaria.org/Shir_HaShirim_Rab

bah.8.9.3?lang=bi; Eikhah Rabbah 1:41, https://www.sefaria.org/Eikhah_Rabbah.1.41?lang=bi.
21. Howard-Johnston, *The Last Great War of Antiquity*. In what follows, I depend largely on Howard-Johnston's work.
22. "Hoard at the Foot of the Temple Mount"; "Ancient Golden Treasure Found."
23. Psalm 137:5 (KJV).

INDEX

Aaron (first Jewish priest), 255
Achaemenid (Persian) Empire, 9, 236
Actium, Battle of, 25, 28, 41
Adiabene, 289; *see also* Helena (queen of Adiabene)
    civil war leading to Great Revolt and, 134, 147–51
    Roman prisoners of, 169–71, 183, 185
    Trajan's Parthian War and, 232
Aelia Capitolina, 250–52, 270–71, 279, 284–85
Aeneid (Virgil), 84
Agrippa, Marcus Antonius, 225
Agrippa, Marcus Vipsanius, 28, 29, 31, 34, 93, 229, 316n59
Agrippa I (Herod Agrippa, Marcus Julius Agrippa, king of Judea), xv, 59–65, 67, 71, 92–94, 155
Agrippa II (Herod Agrippa II, Marcus Julius Agrippa II, king of Judea)
    Berenice as sister of, 93–94, 156, 190–93
    governed regions of, 113
    Great Revolt and role leading to events, 93–94, 98, 99, 141, 145, 146
    Helena and, 81
    as Roman ally against Jerusalem, 153–56
Akiva (rabbi), 179, 254–55, 272, 275
Alans, 148
Alcibiades of Athens, 126–27
Alexander, Gaius Julius, 190
Alexander (son of Herod the Great), 42, 43
Alexander the Alabarch, 56–57, 64
Alexander the Great, 9, 12, 52, 56, 231, 232, 236
Alexandria, Egypt, 52, 55–59, 72, 186, 240
Amanirenas (queen of Kush), 253
Ananias (merchant), 75
Ananias son of Nebedeus, 85, 94, 96
Ananus son of Ananus, 137
Andreas, 238
Annals (Tacitus), 51
Annia, 214
Anthedon, 289
Antigonus, 16, 19–21, 23–25, 315n40
Antinous, 246
Antiochus, Gaius Julius, 190
Antiochus IV (king of Commagene), 119
Antipas, 35, 36, 44, 52, 119

INDEX

Antipater, 14, 16
Antiquities of the Jews (Josephus), 116
Antoninus Pius (emperor of Rome), 269, 272
Antonius (commander), 114
Antony, Mark, 21–25, 28, 41–43, 56, 194, 206, 231
The Apocalypse of Baruch, 196
The Apocalypse of Ezra, 196
Appian of Alexandria, 240
Arabia, annexation by Rome, 231, 261, 338n2
Arabs
    of Nabatea, 25–26, 40, 119, 261, 290
    Tholomaeus's attack on, 66
Aramaic language, 39, 71, 109, 112, 129, 162, 254, 255
Archelaus, 35–38, 41–45, 51
Arch of Titus, 167, 186–87
Aristotle, 271
Armenia, 289
    Nero's humiliation in, 102–3
    strategic location of, 68–70, 72, 74
    Tiberius in, 52
    Trajan's Parthian War and, 231–33, 236, 237
    Vespasian's balance of power and, 189
    Vologases I and, 148
Arminius, 48–49, 112, 127, 134, 253, 258
Arrian, 234
Artemion, 238
Ascalon campaign, 114–15
Aster, Claudia, 194–96
Athronges, 38–39
Augustus (Octavian, emperor of Rome), xv
    on Alexandria, 56
    Armenia policy of, 68

    cult of, 27–29, 31, 253
    Herod and, 34, 36–37, 41, 43–45, 49–53, 194
    Jewish policy of, 59
    reign of, 25
    Triumph custom and, 182

Babatha daughter of Simon, 261–62, 268
Babylonia and Neo-Babylonian Empire
    Babylon and Jewish culture, 285
    Babylonia, defined, 289
    Babylonian Captivity, 96–97
    Babylonian Jewish cavalrymen, 26–27, 119, 235
    First Temple destruction, 251
    Jerusalem's proximity to Babylon, 72
    Jewish Diaspora and, 5, 8
    Parthian capital city in Babylonia, 19
bandits, Josephus on, 39, 115, 175
Bar Kokhba (Simon Bar Koseva), xvii; *see also* Bar Kokhba War
    characterization of, 245–46, 252–59
    death of, 267–68
    legacy of, 229, 253, 272
    name of, 253
Bar Kokhba War, 245–73
    Bar Kokhba's and Hadrian's characterization, contrasted, 245–46
    Bar Kokhba's characterization, 252–58
    Betar as last stand in, 266–69
    consequences to Jews, 269–73
    documentation and artifacts found, 246–47, 250, 252–53, 255–57, 264, 268, 336n56

INDEX

events of rebellion, 258–62
Hadrian's defeat in Parthian War, 247–49
paganization of Jerusalem as motive for, 250–52
Rome's military response, 262–66
as third rebellion against Romans, 245
Bassus, Sextus Lucilius, 204–5
Batavian Revolt, 146
Bato, 253
bellum (war), 280
Benjamin of Tiberias, 283, 284–85
Berenice (Julia Berenice, queen of Chalcis), xvi
Agrippa I as father of, 65
Agrippa II as brother of, 93–94, 156, 190–93
Great Revolt and preceding Judean civil war, 141
Marcus Antonius Agrippa as nephew of, 225
Tiberius Julius Alexander as former brother-in-law of, 57, 191
Titus as lover of, 154
Betar, 266–69, 289
Bible, *see* Hebrew Bible; New Testament (Christian Bible)
Book of Revelation, 197
Boudicca, 253
Britannia, 243, 249, 263–66, 269
Britannicus, 154
Brooke, Rupert, 215
Bruttanius, Marcus Tittius Lustricus, 249
Byzantine Empire, 283–85, 287

Caesarea-by-the-Sea (Caesarea Maritima), 28, 91–93, 95, 178

Caesarea Philippi (city), 128–29, 154, 190–94
Caligula (emperor of Rome), 58–64
Canaan, 271
candelabra, symbolism of, 30, 77, 187, 255
Caracalla (emperor of Rome), 16, 275
Carthage, Roman conquest of, 1, 3, 16, 143–44, 172
Cassius (Gaius Cassius Longinus), 18
Catullus, 223–24, 225
Ceagira, 163
Cenedaeus, 98, 170
Cestius Gallus
army of, 119
Battle of Beth Horon Pass and, 95, 97–101, 103–6, 113, 114, 261
as governor of Syria, 90, 320n3
Jerusalem attacked by (66 CE), 153, 170, 174
as Roman senator, 84
Simon son of Giora and, 138
Twelfth Legion's significance to Great Revolt, 83–85, 146
Chares of Gamala, 130, 131
Christianity; *see also* Jesus of Nazareth
Acts of the Apostles, 66
apocalyptic thinking and, 228
Book of Revelation, 197
Byzantine Empire and, 283–85, 287
Christianization of Roman Empire, 278–79
Essenes and, 10
Gospel of Mark, 197
Gospel of Matthew, 33
Great Revolt and consequences to, 143, 174–75
inception of, 4
on Jesus as messiah, 39, 197

INDEX

Christianity (*cont.*)
    New Testament of, 76, 86
    "People of the Book" and, 285
Churchill, Winston, 256–57
circumcision practice, 252
Civilis, 253
Claudia Aster, *see* Aster, Claudia
Claudius (emperor of Rome), 63–65, 67–70, 81, 106, 154, 231, 321n21
Cleopatra (queen of Egypt), 21–22, 25, 43, 56, 193, 206
client kings/kingdoms, defined, 189–90
coins
    Bar Kokhba War and, 246, 250, 255–56, 264, 336n56
    Claudius and, 64
    Cleopatra and, 21
    Gallus Revolt and, 282
    in Gamala, 130–31
    in Jerusalem, of rebels of 66, 109–12
    Judean, under Pilate's authority, 53
    Masada artifacts, 217
    Pacorus (crown prince) and, 19
    Parthian War and, 247
    Simon son of Gamaliel and, 139
    "Social War" (90–88 BCE) and, 322n5
    Temple Mount excavation (2013) and, 287
    Triumph over Judea depicted by, 183, 188, 328n16
    Vologases I and, 69
Colonia Aelia Capitolina, 250–52, 270–71, 279, 284–85
Colosseum, 188, 214
Commagene, 119, 153, 189–90
Constantine (emperor of Rome), 278
Constantine II (emperor of Rome), 279
Constantius II (emperor of Rome), 279

Coponius, 45
Corbulo, Gnaeus Domitius, 68, 69, 104, 154, 213
Corinth, 103, 129, 144, 172
Crassus, Marcus Licinius, 16–17
crucifixion, 40–41, 50–53, 284
Cumanus, 89
cupbearer role, 20, 315n30
Cyprus, Diaspora Revolt in, 235, 237–42, 249
Cyrenaica (Libya), 223–25, 235, 237–42, 249, 290
Cyrus the Great (Persian ruler), 8–9, 19

Dacia, Trajan's conquest of, 230, 231, 236, 290
David (king of Judah and Israel), 7
Day of Atonement (Yom Kippur), 67, 272
Dead Sea Scrolls, 10, 254
Diaspora Revolt(s), 227–43
    documentation of, 229–30, 235
    Hadrian's reign and, 234, 243
    importance of, 228–29
    Kitos War (War of Quietus), 242–43
    revolts in Cyrenaica, Egypt, and Cyprus, 235, 237–42, 249
    Trajan and Antioch earthquake, 227–28
    Trajan's Parthian War and, 230–33
    Trajan's Parthian War and Jewish opposition, 230, 233–35
    Trajan's Parthian War and Jews as possible proxies, 235–37
Dio, Cassius
    on Bar Kokhba War, 246, 251, 257–65, 267, 269
    on Diaspora Revolt, 234, 239

INDEX

on Great Revolt and preceding Judean civil war, 149–50
on Jerusalem siege, 156, 163, 166
Roman History, 156
Diocaesarea, 271, 276, 280–81, 291; see also Sepphoris (city)
Diospolis (Lod, Israel), 282
Domitian (emperor of Rome), 116, 167, 182, 184, 190, 191, 225
Drusilla, 65, 225

eagle incident, Herod the Great and, 32–33, 36
Eastern Roman Empire (Byzantine Empire), 283–85, 287
Edom, Idumeans and, 20, 290
Egypt
    Alexandria, 52, 55–59, 72, 240
    Diaspora Revolt in, 235, 237–42, 249
    Ptolemaic Egypt, 16, 56–62
    Roman rule and Judea's geographic importance, 34
    Sicarii in, 221–23
Eleazar son of Ananias, 85, 96, 106
Eleazar son of Dinai, 89
Eleazar son of Sameas, 123
Eleazar son of Simon, 101, 113, 136–40, 150, 158
Eleazar son of Yair, 201, 206, 207–8, 212, 215–20, 275
"Eleazar the Priest," 255
Emesa, 119, 153
En Gedi, 216, 261–62, 264, 268, 290
equestrians (knights), 44, 69, 88, 92
Esau (biblical figure), 277
Essenes, 10, 46, 114, 217–18, 314n17
ethnarch title, 13, 41
Eusebius of Caesarea, 234–35, 253, 267, 268, 269

Fadus, Cuspius, 65–67
Felix, Antonius, 225
Flavian dynasty, 168, 177, 185; see also Vespasian (Titus Flavius Vespasianus)
Florus, Gessius, 88, 89–95, 99, 106, 112, 174
Fourth Philosophy, 46, 110, 215
fox incident, Rabbi Akiva and, 179
freedom (liberty), Jewish context of, 111, 238
Fronto (orator), 263

Galba (emperor of Rome), 141
Galilee
    Agrippa I as ruler of, 60
    Ascalon campaign, 114–15
    Herod's death and ensuing rule of, 35, 38, 40, 44, 50–52
    Herod's ruling positions of, 15, 22
    Parthian invasion, 18
    Sepphoris (city), 38, 40, 84, 118–20, 271, 276
Galilee, Battle of, 107–32
    Gamala conquest and, 128–32
    Giscala massacre, 131–32
    Jewish rebels' goals for, 109–12
    Jewish soldiers on Roman side of, 113, 119
    Josephus and, 107–8, 113–19, 125–28
    Jotapata conquest and, 119–25
Galilee, Sea of, 129
Gallus (Flavius Constantius Gallus Caesar), xvii, 279–80, 281
Gallus Revolt, 279–82
Gamala, conquest of, 128–32
Gaulanitis, 290
    Agrippa I as ruler of, 60

INDEX

Gaulanitis (*cont.*)
    Herod's death and ensuing rule of, 35, 44
    Roman road in, 277
    Sicarii and, 95–96
Germania, 37–42, 48–50, 101, 134
Germanicus, 64, 127
Giscala, massacre in, 131–32, 290
Glaphyra (princess), 42–43
Gospel of Mark, 197
Gospel of Matthew, 33
Gospels, on timing of Jesus's birth, 45
Grapte, 170
Great Fire of 64, 89, 102
Great Revolt, 83–106
    Agrippa II's rule and, 93–94, 98, 99
    Battle of Galilee, 107–32; *see also* Galilee, Battle of
    Caesarea violence between Greeks and Jews as pretext to, 91–93
    Cestius and Battle of Beth Horon Pass, 95, 97–101, 103–6
    Cestius and Twelfth Legion's significance to, 83–85, 146
    civil war in Jerusalem and, 133–51; *see also* Great Revolt, civil war leading to
    early events leading to, 6, 47
    Florus as procurator of Judea and, 88–95, 99, 106
    Helena's legacy to, 82; *see also* Helena (queen of Adiabene)
    Jewish ethnic conflict leading to, 85–88, 95–97, 101
    Nero's role in events leading to, 88–90, 101–6
    rebels of, 3
    Sicarii's role in, 47, 87, 95–96
    survivors of, 177–200; *see also* Great Revolt aftermath
    timing of, 85–87
    Titus at Jerusalem and, 153–75; *see also* Titus (Titus Caesar Vespasianus, emperor of Rome), at Jerusalem
Great Revolt, civil war leading to, 133–51
    Ben Zakkai's mission to Vespasian and, 142–43, 198–99
    Christ followers' escape to Pella during, 143
    grain supplies destroyed, 139–40
    John of Giscala's role in, 134–36, 138–40
    Josephus on consequences of, 172–73
    lack of military power of rebels, 143–47
    Simon son of Giora as chief of rebellion, 138–41, 150
    Vespasian's inactivity and civil war among Judeans, 133–34, 141–43
    Vologases I's role in, 147–49
    Year of the Four Emperors and, 141
    Zealots' role in, 136–39, 150
Great Revolt aftermath, 177–200
    Christ followers and, 177
    Claudia Aster and, 194–96
    Jewish apocalyptic thinking and, 196–97
    Johanan ben Zakkai and rabbinic Judaism, 197–200
    Judea under Roman rule and, 177, 178–81
    Roman authority over Parthia and, 177, 189–90
    Rome's Triumph and, 13, 149, 182–88, 328n16

INDEX

Titus and Berenice during, 190–94
Great Synagogue of Alexandria, 240
Greek culture
    Diaspora Revolt and, 237
    Greek-Jewish animosity during Roman Empire, 91–93, 155, 271
    Greek language, 56, 111
    in Judea (63–4 BCE), 7, 9–11, 13, 15, 17, 22, 25–28, 34
    Judea's early Roman support against Greco-Syrians, 11–12
    Julius Caesar and, 14, 21, 22
    Olympic Games, 28, 103
    sophists and, 46
    Torah and, 57
    Vologases on Iranian culture vs., 148
Guide to Greece (Pausanias), 271

Hadrian (Publius Aelius Hadrianus, emperor of Rome), xvii
    Bar Kokhba War revolt and retaliation by, 258, 262–63, 269–72; *see also* Bar Kokhba War
    characterization of, 245–46, 252
    Diaspora Revolt and role of, 234, 243
    Hadrian's Wall, 243, 249
    paganization of Jerusalem by, 250–52
    Parthian War defeat of, 247–49
Hanina (rabbi), 277
Hannibal, 143
Hasmoneans
    background, 10–12, 313n8
    ethnic conflict in Judea and, 87
    as High Priests, 36
    Idumeans conquered by, 20
    Josephus as descendant of, 107
    name of, 313n8

Hebrew Bible; *see also individual names of biblical figures*
    on Cyrus the Great, 8
    Israel and Judea, defined in, 109
    on Masada events, 202
    "People of the Book" and, 285
    on Philistines, 271
    reading of, in synagogue, 11
    Septuagint (Greek translation), 56
    on Zion, 110
Hebrew language, 39, 80, 109–12, 130, 254–56
Helena (queen of Adiabene), xv
    Adiabene background of, 74, 80, 98, 170, 171
    conversion to Judaism by, 55, 74–76
    in Jerusalem, 72–74, 76–80
    Judea's connection to Parthian Empire as legacy of, 71–72, 80–82, 98
    Temple candelabra donated by, 255
    tomb of, 70–72, 79–80
Heraclius (Byzantine emperor), xvii, 284–85
Herodium (fortress), 204, 260, 264, 266, 290
Herodotus, 5, 271
Herod the Great, xv
    assassination plot against, 29
    Babylonian Jewish cavalrymen of, 26–27, 119, 235
    Berenice's relationship to, 57
    construction by, 27–31, 64, 202–4, 206, 209, 215, 225, 251, 260, 264, 266, 290
    eagle incident and, 32–33, 36
    Idumean heritage of, 19–20, 22, 26, 81, 107
    illness and death of, 31–33

INDEX

Herod the Great (*cont.*)
    Jerusalem siege (37 BCE), 172
    as king of Judea, under Augustus, 7, 21–23, 25
    legacy of, 33–34
    Pilate's shields in palace of, 52
    rise to power by, 19–25
    sister of, 33, 35, 42
    "the Great" designation of, 34, 316–17n66
    trial of, 15–16, 25
    wealth of, 27, 35–36
Herod the Great, war for legacy of, 35–53
    Jewish community established by, east of Galilee, 98
    rebellion of 6 CE following death of, 45–48, 67
    succession and descendants of, 35–45, 68, 93, 103, 155–56, 190, 194, 329–30n36
    Tiberius's reign and, 37, 47, 49–53
    "war of Varus" and, 37, 48–50
Hezekiah, 15, 25, 38
Historia Augusta, 248, 252
Histories (Tacitus), 156, 166
Hitler, Adolf, 256–57
Holy of Holies, 12, 14, 24, 30, 179
Hyrcanus, 12–16, 19–21

Idumea and Idumeans, 290
    civil strife with Zealots, 136–39, 158
    Herod and, 19–20, 22, 26, 81, 107
    Tholomaeus's attack on, 66
imperial Caesar (sub-emperor), 279
Iran, *see* Parthian Empire; Sasanian dynasty
Islamic Conquest (638 CE), 72, 285
Israel; *see also* Judea

Hebrew Bible definition of, 109
Land of Israel name, 228, 238, 271, 282
modern-day, 287
name of, 2–3, 109, 255, 271
Twelve Tribes of Israel, 81, 184
Itureans, 25
Izates (king of Adiabene), 72, 75–76, 79, 80, 149, 170, 171

Jabneh (city), 199, 290
Jacob (biblical figure), 277
James (apostle), 64
James (son of Judah the Galilean), 68, 215
Jeremiah (prophet), 97, 272
Jerome (Christian scholar), 272, 281
Jerusalem; *see also* Temple
    City of David and first-century layout of, 78–82
    divisions of, leading to Great Revolt, 139–40; *see also* Great Revolt, civil war leading to
    fortification Walls of, 64, 113, 140, 145
    as Jewish center of world, 186
    map, xx
    paganization of, by Hadrian, 250–52; *see also* Bar Kokhba War
    Roman destruction of, 4; *see also* Great Revolt
    Titus's destruction of city, 168–69
Jesus of Nazareth
    baptism of, 202
    birth of, 8, 23, 45
    Christ followers, 143, 177, 265
    as Christian messiah, 39, 197
    Roman crucifixion of, 50–53, 284
    tomb of, 70–71

INDEX

Jewish Diaspora; *see also* Diaspora
    Revolt(s)
    following Great Revolt, 180
    geographic area, during Roman
        Empire, 5
    Herod the Great and, 27–31
    Jews of Egypt during Roman
        Empire, 4
Jewish holidays
    Ninth of Av commemoration, 166,
        268, 270
    Passover, 51, 73, 221
    pilgrimage festivals (Sukkot,
        Shavuot, Passover), 73
    Purim, 242
    Shavuot, 20, 38, 314n23
    Sukkot, 73, 77, 110
    Yom Kippur (Day of Atonement),
        67, 272
Jewish Palestine, 275–87
    Byzantine Empire and, 283–85, 287
    Christianization of Roman Empire
        and, 278–79
    Gallus Revolt in, 279–82
    as Land of Israel, 282
    modern-day Israel and, 287
    Palestine name, defined, 2–4,
        270–71, 338n2
    Persian invasion (614) of, 282–83
    resilience of Jews throughout
        history and, 285–87
    Sasanian dynasty and, 72, 279, 283–85
Jewish texts and oral tradition; *see also*
    Hebrew Bible; Talmud; Torah
    Midrash as interpretation of, 246
    Mishnah, 242, 254, 275–76
Jewish War, *see* Great Revolt
The Jewish War (Josephus), 85, 115–17,
    125, 162, 225, 315n30

Johanan ben Torta, 254
Johanan ben Zakkai, xvi, 142–43,
    197–200
John (apostle), 64
John of Giscala, xvi, 117, 118, 131–32,
    134–36, 138–40, 158–65, 171, 182–84
John the Baptist, 202
John the Essene, 114, 218
Jonathan (weaver), 223–24
Joppa, massacre at, 84, 95, 290
Joseph of Gamala, 130, 131
Josephus (Joseph son of Mattathias,
    later T. Flavius Josephus),
    biographical information, xvi
    background of, 107, 115, 197–99
    Battle of Galilee and role of, 108,
        111, 113–32; *see also* Galilee,
        Battle of
    controversial legacy of, 13, 86–87,
        121, 125–28, 140, 145, 212
    death of, 229
    imprisonment of, 128, 142
    Jerusalem siege and role of, 156–58,
        160–65
    land owned by, 179
Josephus (Joseph son of Mattathias,
    later T. Flavius Josephus), written
    works of
    on Alexander the Alabarch, 56, 57
    Antiquities of the Jews, 116
    on bandits of Judea, 24, 39, 115, 175
    on Caligula, 61, 62
    on civil strife of Jews, 172–73
    on Claudius, 63–66
    on events leading to Great Revolt,
        85–87, 89, 95–99, 101, 104,
        134–35, 137–38, 140, 145, 149–50
    on Fourth Philosophy, 46, 110, 215
    on Helena, 71, 73, 75, 78–79

Josephus (*cont.*)
   on Herod, 16, 27, 29, 30, 32, 34, 38–39
   on Jewish enslavement, 180
   The Jewish War, 85, 115–17, 125, 162, 225, 315n30
   The Life, 116–18
   on Masada events, 201–2, 204–12, 215–21
   messiah references by, 238
   on Parthian invasion of Judea, 18
   on Pompey, 13, 14–15
   on rebellion of 6 CE, 45–48
   Rome mission of (64 CE), 107–8
   on Sicarii, 221–25
   on Tiberius Alexander, 68, 154, 155
   on Titus, 166–67, 170, 182–84, 191–93
"Josephus problem," 125–26
Joshua (biblical leader), 66
Jotapata, conquest of, 119–25, 290
Juba II (king of Mauretania), 43
Judah son of Ari, 205
Judah son of Hezekiah, 38, 39, 40, 46
Judah the Galilean, 46–47, 68, 138, 215
Judah the Prince (Yehudah ha Nasi, Rabbi Judah), xvii, 275–78
Judah (region); *see also* Judea
   Archelaus's reign in, 35
   as Bar Kokhba War location, 245
   defined, 11
   Herod's death and ensuing rule of, 35, 43, 44
Judaism; *see also* Jewish holidays; Jewish texts and oral tradition; Temple; Temple Mount
   apocalyptic thinking in, 39, 196–97, 228, 238, 254, 280
   candelabra (menorah) symbolism and, 30, 77, 187, 255, 287
   circumcision practice, 252
   clothing and religious garments, 8–9
   forced conversion, Byzantine Empire, 284–85
   on freedom and redemption, 111, 139, 238, 287
   God-fearers and, 75, 92, 108
   on God's will, 13–14, 96, 198, 277
   Hadrianic persecution of, 272
   Helena's conversion to, 55, 74–76; *see also* Helena (queen of Adiabene)
   Jews as dominant Judea population, 1, 313n1; *see also* Judea
   Judah as homeland of, 11
   Masada worship practices, 209
   monotheism of, 9
   rabbinic Judaism, 4, 10–11, 197–200, 273, 275–78
   rebellious spirit of Jews against Rome, 6, 14–15, 41, 42, 62–63, 86, 273, 285–87
   on return to Israel, 238, 242
   Twelve Tribes of Israel, 81, 184
Judas son of Sepphoraeus, 316n61
Judea; *see also* Galilee, Battle of; Great Revolt; Helena (queen of Adiabene); Jerusalem; Judea, 63 to 4 BCE; Temple; Temple Mount
   as consular province, under Hadrian, 249; *see also* Bar Kokhba War
   Diaspora Revolt and role of, 242–43
   early Roman support against Greco-Syrians, 11–12
   ethnic populations of, under Herod, 25
   Hebrew Bible definition of, 109

INDEX

inhabitants of, as Judeans vs. Jews, 313n1
insurgencies against Rome, overview, 1–6
Josephus on bandits of, 39, 115, 175
Kitos War (War of Quietus), 242–43
name of, 3, 109
procurators, defined, 317n11
rebellion of 6 CE, 45–48, 67
Roman Empire relationship, overview, 101, 104
Roman rule following Great Revolt, 177, 178–81
Tiberius Julius Alexander appointed procurator of, 67–70, 81; *see also* Tiberius Julius Alexander
Judea, 63 to 4 BCE, 7–34
  early Roman rule in Judea, 11–14
  Hasmonean dynasty during, 10–12, 20, 313n8
  Herod's rule during, 7, 15–16, 19–34; *see also* Herod the Great
  Jesus's birth during, 8, 23
  Jewish rebels during, 14–16
  Jews' return under Cyrus the Great, 8–9, 19
  Judea as client state of Rome (63 BCE), 7
  Maccabees' rebellion, 9–10
  Pacorus (crown prince of Parthia) and, 18, 19, 23, 33–34
  Parthian Empire as Rome's enemy during, 14, 16–21; *see also* Parthian Empire; Roman Empire
  Persian Empire and Jews' return to Judea, 8–9
  Pompey the Great and, 12–14, 20, 24, 25, 33

Julian (emperor of Rome), 278
Julius Alexander (possible descendant of Tiberius Julius Alexander), 232
Julius Caesar, 14, 21, 22, 52, 83–84, 231
Jupiter (Roman god), 23, 106, 181, 228, 230, 250–52
Justus of Tiberias, 116, 118

Khirbet el-Yahud ("Ruin of the Jews"), 266
Khosrow II (Sasanian king), xvii, 283, 284
Kitos War (War of Quietus), 242–43
knights (equestrians), 44, 69, 88, 92
Kushan Empire, 148

Land of Israel, 228, 238, 271, 282; *see also* Israel
language(s)
  Aramaic, 39, 71, 109, 112, 129, 162, 254, 255
  Greek, 56, 111
  Hebrew, 39, 80, 109–12, 130, 254–56
  of Josephus's written works, 39, 218
Leontopolis, Temple of, 222–23
Levites, 31
liberty (freedom), Jewish context of, 111, 238
The Life (Josephus), 116–18
Livia, 36, 53
Lucius Flavius Silva Nonius Bassus, *see* Silva
Lukuas, 238
Lullianus, 242

Maccabees, 9–10, 97, 112, 256, 259
Macedonia, Persian conquest by, 9; *see also* Greek culture
Machaerus (fortress), 204–5, 290

– 351 –

INDEX

Maimonides, 254–55
Malchus II of Nabataea, 119
Mariamme, 65
Marsus, Gaius Vibius, 64
Masada, 201–25
    archaeological evidence of, 203, 208–10
    dating of events at, 330n1
    destruction of, 105
    Eleazar son of Yair's role in, 201, 206–8, 211, 212, 215–20
    Josephus's account of, 201–2, 204–12, 215–21
    legacy of, 203–4
    mass suicide accounts about, 207–8, 210, 211–12, 218–21
    physical description of, 202–3, 205–6
    Sicarii and, 96, 138, 201, 212, 215–25
    Silva's role in, 201, 205–8, 212–15, 219–21
    as transit point, 217–18
Massacre of the Innocents, 33
Matthias son of Margalus, 316n61
Menahem, 215–16
menorah (candelabra), symbolism of, 30, 77, 187, 255, 287
Mesopotamia, 290
    Adiabene and Helena, 74, 80, 98
    Parthian Empire and, 26–27
    Trajan's Parthian War and, 233–35
messiah concept (Jewish), 39, 238, 254, 280
Midrash, 246
Mishnah, 242, 254, 275–76
Mithradates (king of Pontus), 253
Monobazos I (king of Adiabene), 74–75
Monobazos II (king of Adiabene), 75–76, 79, 98, 170, 320n47

Monobazos (probable grandson of Helena), 98, 170
Mousa (queen of Parthia), 319n36
Mutina, siege of, 325n31

Nabataeus, 163
Nabatea and Nabateans, 25–26, 40, 119, 261, 290
names and titles of people; *see also individual names of people*
    cast of characters, xv–xvii
    client kings, defined, 189–90
    consul ordinarius, 214
    equestrians (knights) and class hierarchy, 44, 69, 88, 92
    ethnarch title, 13, 41
    imperial Caesar (sub-emperor), 279
    nasi (prince), 246, 254, 256, 278
    Patriarch (Roman designation), 277
    procurators, defined, 317n11
    rabbi, defined, 10–11
    tetrarch title, 22, 41, 81
nasi (prince), 246, 254, 256, 278
Nehemiah, 19
Neo-Babylonian Empire, see Babylonia and Neo-Babylonian Empire
Nero (Nero Claudius Caesar Drusus Germanicus, emperor of Rome), xvi
    Armenia's strategic location and, 68–70, 189
    Battle of Galilee and, 112, 126, 129
    characterization of, 101–2, 169
    death of, 133, 141
    Great Revolt and role in events leading to, 88–90, 101–6
    Johanan ben Zakkai's prediction about successor to, 142–43, 198–99

INDEX

Josephus's meeting with, 13
Silva and, 213
Tiberius Alexander appointed prefect of Egypt by, 155
Nerva (emperor of Rome), 225, 230
Netiras of Ruma, 123
New Testament (Christian Bible), 76, 86
Niger of Perea, 97, 114
Ninth of Av commemoration, 166, 268, 270

Octavian, *see* Augustus
Olympic Games, 28, 103
Onias IV (High Priest), 222–23
On the Caesars (Victor), 280–81
Osroes II (Chosroes, the Parthian Khosrow), 248
Otho (emperor of Rome), 141

pacification policy (Rome), 87, 120, 187, 221, 270
Pacorus (Pakur, crown prince of Parthia), xv, 18, 19, 23–24, 33–34, 229
Pacorus the Parthian (cupbearer), 18–20, 24, 315n25
Palaestina Salutaris (Palaestina Tertia), 338n2
Palestine, *see* Jewish Palestine
Pappus, 242
Parthian Empire; *see also* Adiabene
  Adiabenian prisoners of Rome and consequences to, 169–71, 183, 185
  Armenia's strategic location to, 68–70, 72, 74
  geographic area and trade, 4–5
  Helena and Judea's connection to, 71–72, 80–82, 98

  Jews of, 26–27
  Judea and Helena's connection to, 71–72, 80–82
  map, xviii–xix
  Pacorus (crown prince) of, 18, 19, 33–34
  Rhandeia defeated by, 69
  Roman authority over, following Great Revolt, 177, 189–92
  as Rome's enemy, 14, 16–21, 314n21
  Rome's Twelfth Legion and, 83–85, 146
  rule of, during period after Herod's death, 37, 48, 52
Parthian War, 230, 233–37, 247–49
Passover, 51, 73, 221
Patriarch (Roman designation), 277
Patricius, xvii, 280–81, 282
Paul (apostle), 174
Pausanias, 71, 271
Peloponnesian War, 127, 236, 298, 333n15
"People of the Book," 285
Perea, 35, 38, 39, 44, 52, 60, 261, 290
Persian (Achaemenid) Empire, 9, 236
Persian invasion of Judea (614 CE), 282–83
Peter (apostle), 64
Petronius, Publius, 60–63
Pharisees, 10–11, 15–16, 32, 46, 64, 135
Phasael, 21
Philip of Ruma, 123
Philip (son of Herod the Great), 35, 44, 51
Philip son of Jacimus, 323n19
Philip V (king of Macedon), 143
Philistines, 271
Philo (Philo Judaeus), 52, 56–58, 60–62, 238

– 353 –

INDEX

philosophies, sects as, 46
Phinehas, 96
Pilate, Pontius, 51–53, 93, 318n27
places, glossary of, 289–91
places, maps of, xviii–xix, xx
Pliny the Elder, 31
Plotina, 241
pogroms, first recording of, 58–59
Pompey the Great (Gnaeus Pompeius Magnus, Roman general and statesman), xv
   client kings of, 189
   death of, 50
   Jerusalem and Judea conquered by, 12–14, 16, 20, 24, 25, 33, 41, 86, 172, 240
Poppaea Sabina, 108
Proculus, Tiberius Claudius, 194–96
procurators
   Claudius's appointments, 65–67, 81, 318n2
   defined, 317n11
Psalm 137, 287
Psalm 91 ("Soldier's Psalm"), 136

Quietus, Lysias (Lusius), 234, 242, 243, 249
Quintilian, 193
Quirinius, Publius Sulpicius, 45, 68
Qumran, 10, 114, 217–18, 254

rabbi, defined, 10–11
rabbinic Judaism, 4, 10–11, 197–200, 273, 275–78; *see also* Jewish texts and oral tradition
rebellion of 6 CE, 45–48, 67
redemption, Jewish context of, 111, 139, 238, 287

"Rejoicing of the Water-Drawing House," 77
Rhandeia, Parthian defeat of, 69, 291
Roman Empire; *see also* Galilee, Battle of; Great Revolt; Roman Syria; Senate (Roman)
   Agrippa I as consul to, 63–64
   Armenia's strategic location to, 68–70, 72, 74
   class hierarchy in, 44, 88, 92
   crucifixion used by, 40–41, 50–53, 284
   Eastern Roman Empire (Byzantine Empire) and, 283–85, 287
   Germania's revolt against, 37–42, 48–50, 101, 134
   Great Fire of 64, 89, 102
   Herod the Great's rule of Judea, 7, 15–16, 19–34; *see also* Herod the Great
   Josephus's mission to Rome (64 CE), 107–8
   Judea as Roman province and rebellion of 6 CE, 45–48, 67
   Judea's insurgencies against, overview, 1–6
   map, xviii–xix
   pacification policy of, 87, 120, 187, 221, 270
   Parthian Empire as enemy of, 14, 16–21, 23, 33–34, 314n21
   Pompey's Jerusalem and Judea conquest, 12–14, 16, 20, 24, 25, 33
   Rhandeia and Parthian defeat, 69
   size of, under Nero, 103–4
   Tenth Legion of, 123, 157, 178, 201–4, 225, 251, 260–61
   Tiberius Julius Alexander's loyalty to, 55, 81–82; *see also* Tiberius Julius Alexander

INDEX

Roman History (Dio), 156
Roman Syria
    Antioch, Jewish civil rights in, 192
    Antioch, Vespasian threatened by, 186
    Antioch earthquake, 227–28
    Berenice's importance in, 191, 192
    Cestius as governor of, 84, 320n3
    Hadrian as governor of, 249
    Herod's death and ensuing rule of, 37, 40, 41, 44, 45, 47, 48, 52, 53
    Jerusalem's proximity to, 72
    Maccabees and Greco-Macedonian rule of, 9–10
    Parthian invasions/conquest of, 18–21
    Roman invasions/conquest of, 12, 15, 23–24, 34
Rome (city)
    Colosseum of, 188, 214
    Transtiberim as Jewish quarter of, 198

Sabinus, 37–38, 40
Sacrovir, 253
Sadducees, 10, 46
Salome Komaïse daughter of Levi, 261
Samaria and Samaritans, 291
    Herod's death and successive rulers of, 35, 38, 40, 43, 44
    Herod's rule of, 25, 26
    as Jews' rivals, 89
    Pilate and, 53
    Samaria as Bar Kokhba War location, 245
    Samaritan worship practices, 91–92
    Sebaste (city), 27, 291
Samias, 16, 25
Sanhedrin, 15–16, 25

Sasanian dynasty, 72, 279, 283–85, 316n44
Scholasticus, Socrates, 281
Schulten, Adolf, 208
Sebaste (city), 27, 291
Segestes, 127
Senate (Roman)
    Cestius in, 84
    Claudius and, 63, 64
    Hadrian and, 243
    Herod and, 22–23
    Silva in, 212–13, 331n24
    Tiberius Alexander in, 193
    Trajan and, 232
    on Triumph following Great Revolt, 149, 182, 184
    Vespasian and, 142
Seneca the Younger, 102, 169
Sepphoris (city), 38, 40, 84, 118–20, 271, 276, 291
Septuagint (Hebrew Bible, Greek translation), 56
Severan dynasty, 276
Severus, Julius Sextus, 263–66, 269
Shapur II (Sasanian king), 279
Shavuot, 20, 38, 314n23
Shemaiah, 16
Showbread Table, 184, 255
Sicarii (Dagger Men), 47, 87, 95–96, 111, 138, 201, 212, 215–25; *see also* Masada
Silas the Babylonian, 97–98, 114
Silva, 201, 205–8, 212–15, 219–21, 331n24
Simon ben Yohai, 254
Simon of Perea, 38, 39
Simon son of Gamaliel, 135
Simon son of Giora, xvi, 98–99, 106, 138–41, 150, 158–65, 171, 182–84, 217
Simon son of Judah the Galilean, 68, 215

– 355 –

INDEX

slavery, 18, 40, 180, 194–96, 270, 272–73
"Social War" (90–88 BCE), 322n5
Sohaemus of Emesa, 119
"Soldier's Psalm" (Psalm 91), 136
Solomon (king of Israel), 7, 36
sophists, defined, 46
Sosius, Gaius, 24, 25, 156, 172
Spartacus, 202, 253, 258
Spasines' Fort, or Spasinou Charax, 291
Suetonius, 194
suicide pacts
   during Battle of Galilee, 125–26
   at Masada, 207–8, 210, 211–12, 218–21
Sukkot, 73, 77, 110
survivors of Great Revolt, *see* Great Revolt aftermath
Syria, *see* Roman Syria
Syria Palaestina, name of, 4, 270–71, 338n2; *see also* Jewish Palestine

Tacfarinas, 253
Tacitus
   Annals, 51
   on Florus, 95
   Great Revolt and preceding Judean civil war, 134, 135, 139, 140, 151
   Histories, 156, 166
   on Jerusalem siege during Great Revolt, 156, 159, 166
   on Rome's pacification policy, 270
   on Tiberius Alexander, 69, 70
   on Tiberius's reign, 50
Talmud
   on Akiva and fox incident, 179
   on Bar Kokhba, 254, 257–58
   defined, 246
   on gladiatorial games, 29

   on Great Synagogue of Alexandria, 240
   on Herod and Temple, 30
   Palestinian (Jerusalem) and Babylonian versions of, 276
   on Plotina, 241
   on Temple customs, 77
taxes
   Agrippa I on, 64
   fiscus Judaicus, 181, 276, 277
   on Parthian Jews, 27
   by Pompey, 12
   on public urinals, 105
   6 CE rebellion and, 44–48
   Temple tax, 31, 90, 106
   by Trajan, 225
Temple
   animal sacrifice, 4, 10, 30–31, 67, 85, 105–6, 165, 223
   Caligula's statue plans for, 59–63
   First Temple destruction, 251
   Herod's reconstruction of, 29–31
   Holy of Holies, 12, 14, 24, 30, 179
   Jesus on corruption of, 51
   Ninth of Av commemoration, 166, 268, 270
   Pilate's use of funds from, 53
   Pompey's conquest of, 12, 14
   priests, 9, 31, 44, 63, 67–70, 222–23, 255
   priests and modern-day descent, 199, 338n1
   "Rejoicing of the Water-Drawing House," 77
   Second Temple construction, 29–31, 251
   Second Temple destruction, 4, 105–6, 165–67, 181, 187; *see also* Great Revolt; Titus (Titus

INDEX

Caesar Vespasianus, emperor of Rome), at Jerusalem
  taxes on, 31, 90, 106
  Third Temple aspiration of Jews, 251, 278, 287
  Western Wall and significance to, 179, 270
Temple Mount
  Antonia Fortress of, 162–65
  civil strife at, 158
  description of, 30–31
  Eleazar and coup at, 85, 88
  paganization of, 242, 251–52
  Pompey's conquest of, 12–13
Temple of Apollo, 41
Temple of Capitoline Jupiter, 181, 184
Temple of Onias, 222–23
Templum Pacis (Temple of Peace), 187–88
Ten Martyrs, 272
Tenth Legion (Rome), 123, 157, 178, 201, 204, 225, 251, 260–61
tetrarch title, 22, 41, 81
Theophanes, 281
Theudas, 66, 223–24
Tholomaeus, 66
Thrace, 291
Tiberias (city), 51–52, 62, 64, 116, 118–20, 129, 135
Tiberius (emperor), 37, 47, 49–53, 59
Tiberius Julius Alexander, xv
  Berenice's relationship to, 57, 191; *see also* Berenice
  Caligula's reign before ascent of, 58–64
  Claudius and, 63–70, 81, 318n2
  descendant of, 232
  Egyptian background of, 55–58
  Great Revolt and preceding Judean civil war, 141

  Judah the Galilean's sons killed by, 215
  as Roman ally during Great Revolt, 154–56, 167
  Roman loyalty of, 55, 81–82
  Rome's Triumph over Judea and, 182–83, 185
  in Senate, 193
Tigranes, 68, 102, 103
Tiridates (king of Armenia), 69, 70, 102–3
Titus (Titus Caesar Vespasianus, emperor of Rome), xvi
  Arch of Titus, 186–87
  Battle of Galilee and, 118–20, 123, 124, 129, 131, 132
  birth year of, 213
  Cyrenaica revolt and, 224
  Great Revolt aftermath and, 177, 182–84, 186–89, 190–94
  Great Revolt and preceding Judean civil war, 142, 145–48
  Jewish gladiators and, 214
  on Jews' rebelliousness, 14–15
  Josephus on, 98
  military background of, 116
  reign of, 225
  Trajan compared to, 231
Titus (Titus Caesar Vespasianus, emperor of Rome), at Jerusalem, 153–75
  Adiabenian prisoners taken by Romans, 169–71
  Arch of Titus, 167
  consequences for Jews and Romans, 172–75
  desertion by both sides, 153, 160–61, 163, 165, 173
  Jerusalem destruction, 168–69

INDEX

Titus (*cont.*)
    Jews' infighting during battle, 158
    Jews in Titus's entourage, 153–56
    negotiation attempts, 155, 157, 159–60, 174
    siege, John's and Simon's roles during, 158–65, 171
    siege, opening phase, 156–59
    siege and Jews' lack of food supply, 164, 172
    Temple destruction, 165–67
Torah
    Agrippa I's reverence for, 64
    Bar Kokhba name and, 254
    Greek culture and, 57
    laws of, 9
    Pharisees and Oral Law on, 11
    rabbinic Judaism and importance of, 199–200
    Roman Triumph and depiction of, 184
    Samaritans and, 26
Trajan (Marcus Ulpius Traianus, emperor of Rome), xvii
    Antioch earthquake and, 227–28
    characterization of, 230–31
    death of, 243
    Diaspora Revolt in Cyrenaica, Egypt, and Cyprus, 235, 237–42, 249
    Judean opposition to, 242–43
    name and ascent of, 225
    pagan worship of, on Temple Mount, 251
    Parthian War defeat and, 247–49
    Parthian War offensive by, 231–33
    Severus and, 263
Triumph in Rome, 13, 149, 182–88, 328n16

Turbo, Quintus Marcius, 241
Twelfth Legion (Roman Empire), 83–85, 146
Twelve Tribes of Israel, 81, 184

Urbs Salvia, Silvia and, 213–15, 291
Ursicinus, 280

Varus, Publius Quinctilius, 37–42, 48–50, 86, 127
Vercingetorix, 253
Vespasian (Titus Flavius Vespasianus, emperor of Rome), xvi
    Battle of Galilee and, 116, 118–24, 126, 128–32
    characterization of, 104–5
    Cyrenaica revolt and, 224
    death of, 225
    Flavian dynasty of, 168, 177, 185
    Great Revolt, events following, 177–93, 197, 199; *see also* Great Revolt aftermath
    Great Revolt and Jerusalem conquest, 153, 154, 167, 168, 174, 264; *see also* Titus (Titus Caesar Vespasianus, emperor of Rome), at Jerusalem
    Great Revolt and preceding Judean civil war, 133–34, 141–43, 146, 149
    on Jews' "revolutionary spirit," 273
    Silva and, 213
    Temple of Onias and, 222–23
    Trajan compared to, 231
Victor, Sextus Aurelius, 280–81
Virgil, 84
Viriathus, 253
Vitellius (emperor of Rome), 141, 142, 149
Vologases I (king of Parthia), xvi, 69, 147–49, 189, 192

– 358 –

INDEX

Western Wall, 179, 270; *see also* Temple

Yadin, Yigael, 208, 211
Year of the Four Emperors, 141, 182
Yehohanan, 41
Yom Kippur (Day of Atonement), 67, 272
Yosei (rabbi), 277

Zadok, 36, 46–47
Zamaris, 316n43
Zealots
    Battle of Galilee and, 111
    civil strife with Idumeans, 136–39, 158
    civil war leading to Great Revolt, 136–38, 150
Eleazar son of Simon, 113
Great Revolt and ethnic conflict, 87, 96, 101
Judah son of Ari, 205
Masada accounts about, 208, 216
Zion, terminology for, 110
Zionism
    on Bar Kokhba, 253
    on Betar, 266
    on Masada, 203, 208
    as national liberation movement, 286
Zoroastrianism, 74–75, 284, 313n5

ILLUSTRATION CREDITS

1. Alamy
2. Barry Strauss
3. Noa Weiss
4. Barry Strauss
5. © Israel Museum, Jerusalem, by David Harris
6. Barry Strauss
7. Berlin State Museums, Coin Cabinet/Lutz-Jürgen Lübke (Lübke and Wiedemann)
8. Bibliothèque Nationale de France
9. Bibliothèque Nationale de France
10. © The Israel Museum, Jerusalem
11. © The Israel Museum, Jerusalem
12. Barry Strauss
13. Barry Strauss
14. Alamy
15. Berlin State Museums, Coin Cabinet / Lutz-Jürgen Lübke (Lübke and Wiedemann)
16. © The Israel Museum, Jerusalem
17. © The Israel Museum, Jerusalem
18. Barry Strauss
19. © The Israel Museum, Jerusalem, by Pierre-Alain Ferrazzini
20. Hanan Isachar

Also by BARRY STRAUSS

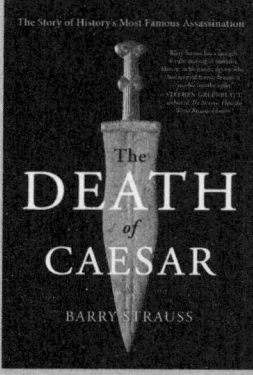

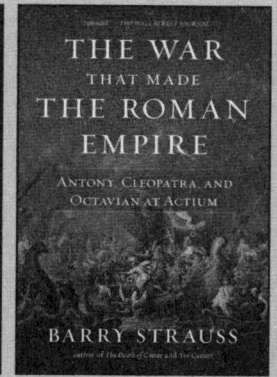

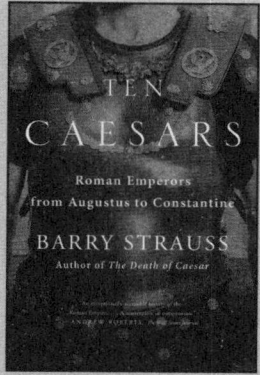

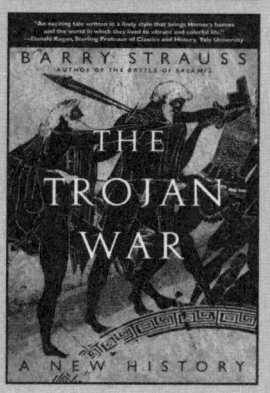

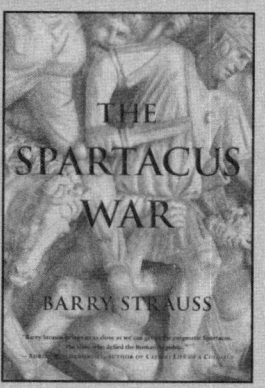

The Death of Caesar

The War That Made the Roman Empire: Antony, Cleopatra, and Octavian at Actium

Ten Caesars: Roman Emperors from Augustus to Constantine

Masters of Command: Alexander, Hannibal, Caesar, and the Genius of Leadership

The Trojan War: A New History

The Spartacus War

"Barry Strauss has a rare gift for the crafting of narrative history: in his hands, figures who had seemed forever frozen in marble breathe again."

—Stephen Greenblatt, author of *The Swerve: How the World Became Modern*

AVAILABLE WHEREVER BOOKS ARE SOLD OR ON SIMONANDSCHUSTER.COM

SIMON & SCHUSTER